T0247556

HIDE YOUR CHILDREN

HIDE YOUR CHILDREN

EXPOSING THE MARXISTS BEHIND THE ATTACK ON AMERICA'S KIDS

LIZ WHEELER

Regnery Publishing
WASHINGTON, D.C.

Regnery® is a registered trademark and its colophon is a trademark of Salem Communications Holding Corporation

Cataloging-in-Publication data on file with the Library of Congress

ISBN: 978-1-68451-391-8
eISBN: 978-1-68451-478-6

Published in the United States by
Regnery Publishing
A Division of Salem Media Group
Washington, D.C.
www.Regnery.com

Manufactured in the United States of America

10 9 8 7 6 5 4 3 2 1

Books are available in quantity for promotional or premium use. For information on discounts and terms, please visit our website: www.Regnery.com.

*To my mama, Kathy, who gave me shelter from the evil
pervading our culture before it was cool*

Contents

INTRODUCTION
The Threat We're Facing   ix

Part I

Infiltrated by Marxists   xvii

CHAPTER 1
The New Marxists   1

CHAPTER 2
A Nuclear (Family) Bomb   29

CHAPTER 3
The Race Bait   47

CHAPTER 4
Hook, Line, and Queer Theory   57

CHAPTER 5
What the Marxists Want   73

CHAPTER 6
The Biggest Corporate Groomer of All   89

CHAPTER 7
Education Subverted: Critical Pedagogy   105

CHAPTER 8
Unsocialized Homeskoolers   119

CHAPTER 9
"The Experts"   137

Part II

Charting Our Way Back   149

CHAPTER 10
What Is Liberty?   153

CHAPTER 11
Good versus Evil   169

CHAPTER 12
How We Win   181

APPENDICES ·
Resources for the Fight   199

APPENDIX I
The Declaration of Independence   201

APPENDIX II
The United States Constitution   207

APPENDIX III
Qui Pluribus   225

APPENDIX IV
Quod Apostolici Muneris   241

APPENDIX V
Quadragesimo Anno   253

APPENDIX VI
Divini Redemptoris   309

Acknowledgments   345

Notes   347

Index   393

INTRODUCTION

The Threat We're Facing

E xpect escalation.
    I write this book as both a warning and a call to action. However,
I am also energized and confident about the available road ahead,
should we choose to seek it.

We've notched some monumental victories in the past year.

Parents have exposed Critical Race Theory (CRT) in their children's classrooms. Concerned American citizens—people like you
and me—have challenged and unseated school board members who
embraced the racist ideology of CRT. We have influenced state legislators to ban the racialist ideology of CRT in many public schools.
Bottom line: *Parents won.*

Thanks to concerned citizens, state legislatures across the country
are passing laws prohibiting the bodily mutilation of children—barbaric,
irreversible, unscientific surgeries performed in the name of "gender
identity" and an evil transgender ideology.[1]

At the behest of horrified adults—both parents and non-parents—states are beginning to prohibit sexually graphic drag shows for children.[2]

Again, thanks to concerned citizens, corporate groomers like Disney have lost more than two million subscribers after parents rejected the radical gender theory that Disney inexcusably infuses into its children's programming. Disney's stocks continue to plunge.[3] Bottom line: *Children won.*

The fight on college campuses to abolish diversity, equity, and inclusion (DEI) initiatives—which is just a euphemism for racism, discrimination, and religious persecution—is picking up speed by the day.[4] Bottom line: *Students will win.*

At the same time, the U.S. Supreme Court struck down the most heinous ruling in our nation's history, casting *Roe v. Wade* to the ash heap of history.[5] Bottom line: *Life won.*

You did this.

Many of you reading this book wrote to your elected representatives demanding action. You posted on social media. You educated family members, debated friends, and organized protests and rallies, calling out the left's lies and countering the false narratives from the mainstream media. You refused to be bullied, canceled, or maligned. You poured your time, your money, your passion, and your activism behind good causes. You recognized this culture war as a battle between good and evil. You stood up for truth.

And yet, as I sit here writing, the United States of America, its history, its founding ideals, and its moral fabric are still under ideological and physical assault. The insanity aimed at our children in public schools, in science and medicine, from corporations, on social media, in government, and in entertainment is escalating. The left is waging a deliberate, relentless attack on our children.

Instead of subduing the assault, resistance from parents and concerned citizens has intensified the left's extremism and zealotry. Our resistance and our victories have increased the stakes for the left.

For nearly a century, the left has seeded Marxist ideology in our institutions, patiently waiting and working for decades to reshape our culture while complacent conservatives and parents were blithely unaware until it was too late . . . almost. Leftists enjoyed this cushion to plot, infiltrate, indoctrinate, subvert, and ultimately overthrow our cultural institutions, and then hijack and weaponize our government institutions to reengineer society according to their political goals with very little challenge . . . until now.

This is a decisive moment for the left. This is their last chance. Because of our victories, their time to impose Marxism on our nation is either now or never. They are pulling out all the stops.

Of all the creepy, intentional assaults Marxists are waging against our nation, the assault on children is by far the most evil. This is their final frontier.

The left has torched the nuclear family as outdated and oppressive, redefined marriage, substituted the relativism of "gender" in place of the reality of sex, restricted political free speech, vilified religion as a haven of bigotry, trashed our shared patriotic history, and denied that there is such a thing as objective truth. They have taught this at all levels of education—including elementary schools, high schools, and universities—across the country. They hammered it home with all the cultural power they have. They even convinced many conservatives that all this was necessary to have a truly tolerant, pluralistic, diverse, free, liberal, "progressive" society.

Now, the left is destroying children, intentionally. That's the obvious reality. As you will soon read,

- Planned Parenthood is pushing gender identity indoctrination of our children in public schools (and then supplying young people with "transgender" hormones at a profit).
- Groomer teachers are actively exposing children to Queer Theory (which advocates outright for pedophilia).
- Big Tech is aiding and abetting child abusers by banning the word "groomer" on their platforms.
- Teachers' unions are pushing Critical Race Theory on innocent children, poisoning their minds with evil ideas about racial identity, racial guilt, and racial grievance.
- School counselors are practicing the quack psychology of "social-emotional learning" (SEL) on our children to condition young minds for political indoctrination.
- Disney executives admit they intentionally add a "queerness agenda" to their children's programming.
- Harvard professors are trying to ban homeschooling (and therefore obliterate parental rights) by claiming it's a form of child abuse because it deprives children of a "public school experience."
- The Centers for Disease Control and Prevention (CDC) and pediatricians (thanks to the incredibly corrupt money behind them) dismiss reality on biology and vaccines to the detriment of our children.

Add all this and more to the decades-long assault on the nuclear family, despite the reality that children are less likely to suffer poverty or mental illness or commit crimes if they're raised by their married biological mother and father. The result of this deliberate destruction of our children will be the fall of our nation. *Which is exactly what it was intended to achieve.*

How did we get to this crisis point?

- Where the White House is advocating for hormones and "early" transgender surgeries for children in the name of "gender identity"[6]
- Where pediatricians bully parents into a schedule of seventy-plus vaccines (that we *know* are not all necessary, safe, and effective) because "the experts" say so
- Where *Antiracist Baby* is read to toddlers in day care or elsewhere to indoctrinate them in Critical Race Theory
- Where Marxism is the ultimate goal and our children are the final pawns the left must capture before our entire nation falls

Perhaps it's hard to fathom that we are fighting *actual* Marxists, just as it was difficult to believe the reality that CRT and the transgender ideology pervade our local elementary schools . . . until, thanks to "Zoom school," parents caught a glimpse of the poison being poured into the minds of our children.

Some on the right refuse to acknowledge the reality of the political enemy we are fighting within our own nation. Many prefer to believe we are simply engaged in a negotiation with a well-intentioned political opposition who agree on bedrock principles but mistakenly propose unwise policies in support of our shared American values. These voices of the right include Senator Mitt Romney, who called Joe Biden "a genuinely good man"[7] while excoriating Donald Trump as a "phony" and a "fraud,"[8] and David French, who wrote in *The Atlantic* that the left's hate speech laws targeting conservatives and Christians on college campuses had "virtuous" intentions but were problematic.[9]

This is a grave and critical mistake.

We are not negotiating with a well-intentioned political opposition with whom we share bedrock principles but who propose unwise policies to support our shared values. We are battling against Marxists who seek to destroy our country by subverting our cultural institutions from within. These Marxists are willing to wage a war on our children in order to accomplish their destruction.

If we refuse to recognize the political enemy we face, we will not fight well.

This book will illuminate the actual Marxists who underpin the deliberate assault our children. They include institutions and individuals from teachers' unions to school counselors, from Planned Parenthood and the graphic sex-education curriculum it promotes to proponents of Critical Race Theory and Queer Theory, from university academics assaulting parental rights and the nuclear family to the useful idiots at the CDC, the American Academy of Pediatrics, and corporations like Disney who have been poisoned with corporate wokeism.

Our choice is simple. We must save our children for the sake of their individual souls and because our children are the last, best hope of mankind on earth. The next generation of Americans will decide the fate of the American experiment: Will we continue to steward and protect the freest, fairest country the world has ever known? Or will we lose our nation forever?

Here is your roadmap to this book.

To find answers to the existential questions we face:

- We'll chart our way from Antonio Gramsci's plan for Marxist revolution that was designed to destroy Western civilization—by first destroying civil institutions.
- We'll expose the attacks on the nuclear family and the Marxists behind the assaults. It's an ugly story that includes Wilhelm Reich's twisted sex fetishes (including the sexualization of children), Betty Friedan's *Feminine Mystique* (and the Marxist ideology behind it), Kimberlé Crenshaw's Marxist "intersectionality" theory that aims

to destroy men, and the history of the LGBTQ+ lobby that was never about tolerance but instead about the destruction of traditional marriage.

- We'll unpack Max Horkheimer's Marxist Critical Theory that underpins Critical Race Theory and expose the modern Marxist CRT intelligentsia that includes Herbert Marcuse, Derrick Bell, Barbara Applebaum, Robin DiAngelo, and others.

- We'll expose Gayle Rubin, authoress of the disturbing founding document of Queer Theory, which lays out the ideological framework for the radical gender identity indoctrination in public schools. We'll unravel how Critical Race Theory and Queer Theory are a deliberate one-two punch intended to turn a generation of American children into unrepentant Marxist revolutionaries.

- We will expose DEI (diversity, equity, and inclusion) for the reality of what it is: a "thought reform" tactic lifted from Mao Zedong. We'll also expose the danger posed by Klaus Schwab's ESG (environmental, social, and governance) metrics and his dangerous "stakeholder capitalism" ideology.

- We will examine the phenomenon of corporate wokeism and expose the biggest corporate groomer of all: Planned Parenthood and its founder Margaret Sanger's penchant for Bolshevik-style Marxism. We'll examine Alfred Kinsey, the "Father of the Sexual Revolution," and his unspeakable sexual experiments that underpin the "comprehensive sexuality education" (CSE) that is taught by Planned Parenthood in public schools and promoted by the United Nations.

- We will examine Brazilian Marxist Paulo Freire, who is responsible for the word "woke" and likewise responsible for the neo-Marxist "social-emotional learning" (SEL) in public schools.

- We'll expose John Dewey, the "father of Progressive education in America," and his lavish praise for Soviet Russia's "Great Experiment" in public education, as well as the Harvard professor who—citing Dewey—is pushing for a ban on homeschooling.
- We'll also examine technocracy or "rule by the experts" as the stepping stone from capitalism to communism.

Frankly, the first half of this book can be heavy stuff, but once we establish the reality of the political enemy we're facing, we'll begin to chart our way back, because all hope is not lost—there *is* a path to victory, if we choose to walk it. Ultimately, we will demonstrate what Sun Tzu wrote long ago: "If you know the enemy and know yourself, you need not fear the result of a hundred battles."[10]

By the close of this book, we will know the reality of the enemy permeating our nation, understanding that if we willfully blind ourselves to the reality of the Marxist plot to destroy our nation, we will be the last generation to live in a free United States of America. If we choose to cast off our blindfolds, we will have what it takes to win this war.

Before we begin, I offer you a word of encouragement: Do not lose hope. If we are ready to fight this existential battle for our children, then all hope is not lost. We *can* save the greatest nation in the world and our children with it.

PART I

Infiltrated by Marxists

CHAPTER I

The New Marxists

In the course of researching this book, I discovered a nugget of information that tickled me pink.

I was reading Antonio Gramsci (1891–1937), a founder of the Italian Communist Party and a very bad man. Gramsci isn't as well known as the mid-twentieth-century cadre of Frankfurt School Marxists or the original German Marxists like Karl Marx or Friedrich Engels, but it could be argued that his influence has eclipsed his more notorious peers in the present day.

Gramsci was a Marxist in Fascist Italy in the 1920s and 1930s whose outspoken criticism of the Fascist dictator Benito Mussolini landed him in prison. While imprisoned, the bespectacled Gramsci transcribed his political theory into notebooks smuggled into his prison cell that were later published after his death in the aptly named *Prison Notebooks*.

Gramsci's theory of cultural hegemony is what we're currently seeing play out in our nation as the Marxists seek to subvert our cultural institutions in order to topple our government. In fact, Gramsci's pivotal contribution to Marxist ideology brought an otherwise dying twentieth-century Marxism back to life in the twenty-first century.

Marx and Engels argued that the working class—the proletariat—was economically oppressed by the ruling class, the capitalist bourgeoisie. Their *Communist Manifesto* called for the proletariat to revolt against the bourgeoisie and establish a new system of worldwide government.

In the *Communist Manifesto*, Marx and Engels wrote, "The proletariat will use its political supremacy to wrest, by degree, all capital from the bourgeoisie, to centralise all instruments of production in the hands of the State, *i.e.*, of the proletariat organised as the ruling class." They sought to affect this radical assault on capitalism and society via violent revolution. "If the proletariat . . . is compelled . . . by means of a revolution, it makes itself the ruling class, and, as such, sweeps away by force the old conditions of production, then it will . . . have swept away the conditions for the existence of class antagonisms and of classes generally. . . . In place of the old bourgeois society, with its classes and class antagonisms, we shall have an association, in which the free development of each is the condition for the free development of all."[1]

In a nutshell, Marx and Engels sought, via violent uprisings across the entire planet, to eliminate all class structures and capitalist economic systems and develop a "utopian" society, in which human freedom and political liberty would be erased in favor of collectivist communism.

However, Antonio Gramsci recognized that Karl Marx's plan for a worker-led revolution to overthrow the ruling class wasn't going to happen. The proletariat wasn't going to revolt against the bourgeoisie, no matter how abused Marx told them they were. The reason, Gramsci posited, was because the workers were too comfortable surrounded by their cultural institutions that would be upset by a Marxist revolution. Gramsci contended that as long as the proletariat adhered to the belief system and values of the ruling class (such as nuclear families, a capitalist economic system, religious belief in God, and the patriotic values that protect a nation-state from within), Marx's revolution was dead on arrival.

Gramsci was right.

Instead of a mere workers' revolt, Gramsci suggested that Marxist theory needed a new vanguard. To create a new vanguard required reeducation of the proletariat. This, Gramsci believed, would be the first step in tearing down cultural norms and subverting the cultural institutions on which the ruling class relied. Once that was achieved, the proletariat would no longer be too comfortable to stage a revolution against the capitalist ruling class.

The familiarity of Gramsci's theory of cultural hegemony is striking. What is happening within our own nation? We watch as the radical left assaults the family, our free market economy, religion and people of faith, our national sovereignty, and even our patriotic American values. This aligns perfectly with Gramsci's theories.

The ultimate goal of the Marxists is to topple democracy and capitalism and impose communism. The new Marxists understand that in order to topple capitalism and limited government, they first must destroy the cultural institutions on which people rely.

This new strategy was spawned by Antonio Gramsci.

Gramsci differentiates between political society and civil society, the former being the legal system, the state law enforcement apparatus, and the military, the latter being the family and the education system. This is essentially the distinction between what we colloquially understand as governmental institutions and cultural institutions. Gramsci encouraged a more strategic approach to Marxist revolution, where the newly reeducated vanguard attacks the cultural institutions of civil society in order to topple the people's reliance on those institutions before it overthrows the government.

Unlike Marx himself, or Herbert Marcuse—whose influence on transforming "Critical Theory" into "Critical Race Theory" will be discussed later—Gramsci's theory of cultural hegemony wasn't widely disseminated among American Marxists until his "prison notebooks" were translated into American English between 1992 and 2007, by a man named Joseph Buttigieg.

Yes, *that* Buttigieg. Joseph Buttigieg is the father of current U.S. secretary of transportation and former mayor of South Bend, Indiana, Pete Buttigieg, and his name is clearly splashed on the front of the three-volume set of Gramsci's *Prison Notebooks*.

I confess I didn't notice it the first thirty times I picked up the book. When I finally saw it, it tickled me pink.

The father of the current secretary of transportation—and former (and presumably future) candidate for president of the United States of America—was dedicated to the Marxist Antonio Gramsci, and was himself a Marxist.[2]

Why has nobody seriously questioned Pete Buttigieg about this? Mayor Pete ran for *president of the United States*, and not a single enterprising journalist asked him whether he avowed or disavowed the communist ideology of his father?

Buttigieg senior was a founding member of a Gramsci fan club called the International Gramsci Society.[3]

Pete Buttigieg named his son Joseph after his father, and we're not supposed to care whether an ideological connection exists in addition to the biological relation?

Gramsci's theory of subverting civil institutions before destroying governmental institutions in order to impose Marxism isn't abstract. Gramsci identified many pillars of culture that need to be attacked in order to tear down the norms on which the proletariat relies, but chief among them were *religion, family, education, media,* and *law.*

While Gramsci was certainly in favor of deconstructing society's capitalist elements, he was uniquely focused on identifying cultural—rather than economic or political—institutions that needed to be attacked first. According to the Acton Institute, Gramsci believed that "Socialism is precisely the religion that must overwhelm Christianity. . . . In the new order, Socialism will triumph by first capturing the culture via infiltration of schools, universities, churches, and the media by transforming the consciousness of society."[4] Moreover, according to Roger Kiska, Gramsci held that "[c]ultural hegemony is maintained by the capitalist ruling class through the institutions that make up society's superstructure. Gramscian Marxists define the superstructure as everything not directly having to do with production such as family, culture, religion, education, media, and law."[5]

Are goosebumps creeping up your arms? Does this sound familiar?

It should, because this is the incipient revolution that has been playing out within our own culture. Think back to 1962, when the Supreme Court prohibited prayer in public schools. Then fast-forward to 2020, when religious people were prohibited from attending houses of worship in the name of COVID-19 lockdowns. Christian doctors, nurses, pharmacists, bakers, florists, wedding planners, and parents now face legal persecution for conscientious objections to abortion, euthanasia, harmful vaccines, homosexual "marriage," and transgender ideology. Our education system has been infiltrated by teachers' unions propagating anti-capitalist, anti-American, anti-science, and racist ideology while undermining the rights of parents. The family unit has been the victim of constant Marxist propaganda and the sexual revolution and feminism of the 1960s and 1970s and the anti-male #MeToo movement. Media entities from Hollywood to CNN serve as propaganda outlets for deep-state operatives. The ongoing vilification of our legal system at the hands of Marxist Critical Legal Theory (and the self-avowed Marxists who run the Black Lives Matter movement[6]) has resulted in one of the most significant lapses of public confidence in our criminal justice system in our nation's history.

Many think of Marxism as primarily an economic doctrine, but from the beginning it was aimed not only against capitalists, but against religion (especially Christianity) and the family. The goal of communism was not merely economic, but a revolutionary transformation of society.

From the beginning, Marx and Engels dripped with disdain for the nuclear family. They believed the abolition of private property would lead to the inevitable demise of marriage and therefore of the family.

Marx wrote, "The bourgeois family will vanish as a matter of course when its complement vanishes, and both will vanish with the vanishing of capital."[7]

Engels's view on marriage and family reeked of even deeper disdain than Marx's cynical view that marriage was purely an economic arrangement in a capitalist society. In a chapter called "The Monogamous Family" in his book *The Origin of the Family, Private Property, and the State*, Engels contended that monogamous marriage between one man and one woman was never a mutual relationship or "reconciliation of man and woman" but was "subjugation of the one sex by the other."[8]

The two original Marxists couldn't wait to be rid of monogamous marriage, though this may have been due to personal factors in addition to political ones—Engels, for example, was very sexually promiscuous. Both Marx and Engels advocated for communal rearing of children. Again, this may have been motivated by personal reasons. Marx, after draining his parents' life savings and siphoning Engels's wealth, was forced to move his family to a poor house where several of his small children died because Marx refused to provide for them.[9] According to their own twisted political philosophy, when the bourgeoisie were overthrown by the proletariat, the nuclear family would be rendered obsolete anyway.

History has substantiated Gramsci's theory. Marxists who staged successful revolutions did so after targeting civil institutions first: religion, family, education, media, and law.

When the Bolsheviks seized power during the Russian Revolution in 1917, they first obliterated the church. In October of 1917, the Bolsheviks declared a separation of church and state. They severed the Russian church's official association with the government, expropriated the church's property, and seized control of the church's parochial schools. The Bolsheviks abolished Christianity as the state religion and instead imposed atheism as the official state-sponsored religion in Russia.[10]

"Communism," Marx had written, "begins where atheism begins."[11]

Bolshevik revolutionary leader and eventual founder of the Soviet Union Vladimir Lenin agreed: "Religion is the opium of the people—this dictum by Marx is the corner-stone of the whole Marxist outlook on religion. Marxism has always regarded all modern religions and churches, and each and every religious organisation, as instruments of bourgeois reaction that serve to defend exploitation and to befuddle the working class."[12]

The Bolsheviks wielded their hammers and sickles against people of faith, establishing a government-sponsored program to forcibly convert Christians to atheism administered by the newly installed Communists in government. The Bolsheviks praised "science" as superior to faith and weaponized the media to attack religious beliefs as superstition as part of their anti-religion propaganda campaign.[13]

Russian clergy were mercilessly persecuted. As many as two hundred thousand Russian priests were murdered by the Bolsheviks, and many of those were tortured, scalped, and crucified as part of their execution. Some clergy who weren't murdered outright were committed to "mental hospitals" where they were tortured for the "crime" of being Orthodox priests.[14]

The press was immediately quashed. In November 1917, one month after their coup, the Bolsheviks issued the "Decree on Press," which forbade the publication of any criticism of the Communist regime.[15]

Abortion and divorce became legal and prevalent in Soviet Russia, decimating the Russian family. Without the church, without a free press, without respect for marriage and family, without a private education system, the Bolsheviks cut off every avenue for the Russian people to escape communism.

Gramsci saw all this and recognized that *this*—destroying cultural staples on which people rely—is how to condition a population to accept communism when the workers won't revolt against the ruling class on their own.

I imagine before Gramsci's prison scribbling, the question must have arisen: What if that conditioning happened *before* the revolution? Would that lead to a successful Marxist revolution without a fight?

We're about to find out in America.

This is what I mean when I say the radical left's deliberate assault on children today is their final frontier.

Religion in our country has been decimated. Today, in what was once a famously church-going nation—G. K. Chesterton called America "a nation with the soul of a church"[16]—fewer than one in five young people attend church regularly after high school.[17] In 2020 "only 47 percent of U.S. adults belonged to a church, synagogue, or mosque," a dramatic decrease of more than twenty points since the turn of the twenty-first century.[18] A mere 31 percent of young people "believe in God as described in the Bible."[19]

Marxists throughout their history have always tried to infiltrate institutions and subvert them from within. The Soviets attempted to do this to the Catholic Church in Eastern Europe, and churches in America became targets as well. While mainline Protestant churches have collapsed the fastest and the farthest in percentage terms of their number of adherents, the Communists have, in the West, made a particular target of the Catholic Church because of its size and influence and because it has been, alongside the governments of the free West, the most stalwart and important anti-Communist influence in the world. No other institution offered so direct a challenge to communism on the basis of philosophy and its understanding of the nature of man and his destiny. As Pope Pius XI declared in his 1931 encyclical *Quadragesimo anno*, "[N]o one can be at the same time a good Catholic and a true socialist."[20] At the time, the pope spoke for the largest religion in the world; Catholicism remains the largest Christian denomination in the world.

The Church was, and is, a big target, and the Communists over the last hundred years have done everything they could to tarnish it, undermine it, and destroy it. Communist subversion of the Church was an international effort. The Soviet Union and its satellite Communist security services openly targeted the Church, but also operated through covert operations.[21]

Communist operations against the Church in Europe are relatively well known.

The Soviets considered the Vatican a "mortal enemy" of socialism in Europe. According to Lieutenant General Ion Mihai Pacepa, head of the Romanian secret police and the highest-ranking intelligence officer ever to defect from behind the Iron Curtain,

In February 1960, Nikita Khrushchev approved a super-secret plan for destroying the Vatican's moral authority in Western Europe. The idea was the brainchild of KGB chairman

Aleksandr Shelepin and Aleksey Kirichenko, the Soviet Politburo member responsible for international policies. Up until that time, the KGB had fought its "mortal enemy" in Eastern Europe, where the Holy See had been crudely attacked as a cesspool of espionage in the pay of American imperialism, and its representatives had been summarily jailed as spies. Now Moscow wanted the Vatican discredited by its own priests, on its home territory, as a bastion of Nazism.[22]

In 2007, Pacepa contended that there were at least thirty-nine priests in Poland "whose names have been found in Krakow secret police files, some of whom are now bishops."[23]

In other words, the Marxists sent in infiltrators—and this wasn't the first time.

Less well known, or conveniently forgotten, is how the Communist Party worked to subvert the Catholic Church in the United States by infiltrating Communists into the clergy and church hierarchy.

According to former Communist Bella Dodd, who testified to the House Un-American Activities Committee, "In the 1930s, we put eleven hundred men into the priesthood in order to destroy the Church from within. The idea was for these men to be ordained, and then climb the ladder of influence and authority as Monsignors and Bishops."[24]

Dodd converted to Catholicism in 1952, and under the spiritual direction of Bishop Fulton J. Sheen, she spent the rest of her life in penitence, working to expose the evil of which she had been a part in the Communist infiltration of the Catholic Church. Still, allegedly at the direction of Bishop Sheen, Dodd refused to reveal the names of Communist clergymen,[25] though she later stated that the Communist infiltration was so extensive that in the future, "you will not recognize the Catholic Church."[26]

In a public statement, Dodd detailed the Marxist strategy against the Church, including the plot to plant Communists among seminarians. She wrote, "In the late 1920s and 1930s, directives were sent from Moscow to all Communist Party organizations. In order to destroy the [Roman] Catholic Church from within, party members were to be planted in seminaries and within diocesan organizations . . . I, myself, put some 1,200 men in [Roman] Catholic seminaries."[27] In the most shocking revelation of all, a decade before Vatican II, Dodd said, "Right now they are in the highest places in the Church."[28]

Dodd's description was corroborated by Manning Johnson, another former official of the Communist Party in America who also spoke before the House Un-American Activities Committee in 1953, testifying about the Communist infiltration of American Catholic seminaries. Manning testified:

> Once the tactic of infiltration of religious organizations was set by the Kremlin . . . the communists discovered that the destruction of religion could proceed much faster through the infiltration of the Church by communists operating within the Church itself. The communist leadership in the United States realized that the infiltration tactic in this country would have to adapt itself to American conditions and the religious makeup peculiar to this country. In the earliest stages it was determined that with only small forces available to them, it would be necessary to concentrate communist agents in the seminaries. The practical conclusion drawn by the Red leaders was that these institutions would make it possible for a small communist minority to influence the ideology of future clergymen in the paths conducive to communist purposes. . . . The policy of infiltrating seminaries was successful beyond even our communist expectations.[29]

A contemporary of Bella Dodd, theologian and professor Alice von Hildebrand, contended that Dodd told her that "when she was an active party member, she had dealt with no fewer than four cardinals within the Vatican who were working for [the Communists]."[30]

Maybe this was what Our Lady at Fátima was talking about in 1917 when she warned the three shepherd children, Lúcia dos Santos and cousins Francisco and Jacinta Marto, that if Russia did not repent of her evil, bad things would befall mankind. Our Lady admonished the children, "If my requests are heeded, Russia will be converted, and there will be peace; if not, she will spread her errors throughout the world, causing wars and persecutions of the church. The good will be martyred, the Holy Father will have much to suffer, various nations will be annihilated."[31]

Former KGB propagandist Yuri Bezmenov, after defecting to the West in 1970, confirmed that undermining religion was a key tactic in the Marxist effort to subvert the free world. Bezmenov detailed that 85 percent of the KGB's resources were devoted to "ideological subversion," the goal of which was to "corrupt the young, get them interested in sex, take them away from religion. Make them superficial and enfeebled [. . .] destroy people's faith in their national leaders by holding the latter up for contempt, ridicule and disgrace [. . .] cause breakdown of the old moral virtues: honesty, sobriety, self-restraint, faith in the pledged word."[32]

The Soviets knew their enemy. They knew, as Pope Pius XI had declared, that "No one can be at the same time a good Catholic and a true socialist."[33] So, they tried to destroy Catholicism.

We're seeing the result of this in America today. The American Church is now a pathetic shadow of the force for moral good it once was. Lax catechesis, too much conformity with the secular world, and the sex scandals that have plagued the hierarchy of the Catholic Church—due in large part to leftist moral relativism that has seeped into seminaries—have obscured the truth from untold millions, including members of her own parishes. According to Pew Research, a mere 31 percent of Catholics believe in the Real Presence of Christ in the Eucharist,[34] the central doctrine of the Catholic faith, the "source and summit of the Christian life" per the Catechism of the Catholic Church.[35]

The Biblical admonition to serve the poor with charity has been twisted by compromised clergy into "social justice," a purely political endeavor that is a euphemism for socialism. The radical environmentalism shamefully preached from pulpits closer resembles paganism than anything found in the Bible. Shockingly, many clergy are willing stooges in their refusal to discuss the grave moral evil of abortion and homosexuality.

In many Protestant and Evangelical churches, the situation is equally as dire. Prominent mega-churches like Hillsong Church and Joel Osteen's Lakewood Church preach the heretical prosperity gospel.[36] In 2021, the Evangelical Lutheran Church in America appointed its first transgender bishop.[37] In direct contradiction to biblical teaching, the Episcopal Church endorses homosexual "marriage."[38] The Maine Council of Churches—including the Episcopal Church, United Methodist Church, Unitarian Universalist Association, United Church of Christ, Presbyterian Church (USA), Evangelical Lutheran Church in America, and Religious Society of Friends (Quakers)—argues abortion is ethical.[39]

Faithful individuals aren't faring much better. Pockets of devout Christians are considered oddballs who must make the deliberate decision to live counter culturally if they desire to follow seriously the tenets of their faith, because mainstream culture is increasingly anti-Christian. Pious Catholics, like Supreme Court Justice Amy Coney Barrett, are demonized as extremist figures from the dystopian novel *The Handmaid's Tale*. Practicing Christians, like Jack Phillips of Masterpiece Cakeshop, are subject to decades of litigation for the crime of practicing their religious beliefs in public.

The media in our country has also been compromised. The history of Hollywood's love affair with communism didn't start with Queer Theory or with actor John Cena apologizing to the Chinese Communists in Mandarin for "accidentally" calling Taiwan a country.[40] As early as the 1920s, the Communist Party of the United States—which was heavily funded by Moscow—actively sought to subvert Hollywood.[41] Communist International agent Willi Muenzenberg stated that harnessing Hollywood as a propaganda agent for communism was a priority. "One of the most pressing tasks confronting the Communist Party in the field of propaganda," Muenzenberg said, "is the conquest of this supremely important propaganda unit, until now the monopoly of the ruling class. We must wrest it from them and turn it against them."[42]

In 1935, the Communist Party USA's cultural commissar V. J. Jerome established a party branch office in Hollywood that raised money, recruited Hollywood stars and starlets to the Red cause, and perhaps most influentially, created and controlled powerful sector-specific Hollywood labor unions.[43]

According to a report from Kenneth Billingsley in *Reason* magazine, the Communist Party of the United States "not only helped organize the Screen Writers Guild, it had organized the Story Analysts Guild as well. Story analysts judge scripts and film treatments early in the decision-making process. A dismissive report often means that a studio will pass on a proposed production. The [Communist] party was thus well positioned to quash scripts and treatments with anti-Soviet content, along with stories that portrayed business and religion in a favorable light."[44]

Billingsley writes, "In *The Worker*, Dalton Trumbo [Communist Party USA member and at one time the highest-paid screenwriter in

Hollywood] openly bragged that the following works had not reached the screen: Arthur Koestler's *Darkness at Noon* and *The Yogi and the Commissar*; Victor Kravchenko's *I Chose Freedom*; and *Bernard Clare* by James T. Farrell, also author of *Studs Lonigan* and vilified by party enforcer Mike Gold as 'a vicious, voluble Trotskyite.'"[45]

Entertainment writer Mark Horowitz contends, "Hollywood liberals were hardly naive about Communists. Before the war, they had worked alongside Communist Party members in the Hollywood Anti-Nazi League, one of the largest and most successful Popular Front organizations of the period. But after the Hitler-Stalin non-aggression pact in 1939, Moscow secretly ordered Party members to cease opposition to Hitler and promote isolationist policies instead. Many of the future "Hollywood Ten," including screenwriters John Howard Lawson, Dalton Trumbo, and Lester Cole, shamelessly flip-flopped overnight and turned on their former allies, denouncing liberal colleagues as warmongers and traitors."[46]

Communist talent agents retaliated against their anti-Communist clients, refusing to shop their work and deliberately slandering Hollywood stars in an effort to ruin their careers if the anti-Communists didn't cave to Communist demands.[47]

One Hollywood actor, a former liberal named Ronald Reagan, who would become the most beloved conservative president in our nation's history, fought back against the Communists embedded in the talent guilds in Hollywood, but not before, as Kenneth Billingsley writes, "bloody warfare broke out in the streets outside every studio."[48]

The House Un-American Activities Committee and the blacklist of the Hollywood Ten followed in an effort to rout the poisonous ideology and its cupbearers from American entertainment, but the stain remains. Hollywood to this day is tainted with Marxism, Satanism, and greedy elitism, the three hallmark characteristics of a true communist.

The mainstream news media may be even worse.

The *New York Times*, *Washington Post*, CNN, MSNBC, the Associated Press, and countless other formerly reputable outlets now operate like the Soviet *Pravda*, parroting the desires of the regime, specifically the Democrat Party and the permanent government. These media organizations use "anonymous sources" within the government to "report" various leftist talking points, pretending their sources are "independent." The government also pretends the news reports are independently sourced and uses that information as justification to weaponize the federal government against their political opponents, as in the Russiagate hoax, the Ukraine "whistleblower" case, the January 6 riot at the Capitol, the FBI Mar-a-Lago raid, the inconvenient COVID-19 truthtellers, and countless other examples.

It doesn't matter how often the mainstream media's stories are refuted or exposed as propaganda or are self-evidently planted and then exploited by leftists in Washington, whether it was the ridiculous but rabid media insistence that President Donald Trump was a Russian agent or the media's attempt to shut down the apparent truth that COVID-19 leaked from a Chinese lab. The mainstream media can get caught lying, deceiving itself, mindlessly running from one false leftist meme to another, censoring the news, and it simply doesn't care, because it has power.

How did news media in our nation devolve into such pitiful lying partisans insulated from competition, real fact-checking, and honesty?

The anticlimactic short answer is that news media in the United States was never "straight news" or "just reporting"—not even in the supposed halcyon days of Edward Murrow, Walter Cronkite, and the early days of CNN. The *New York Times*, in fact, became notorious for its 1930s pro-Soviet "reporting" from correspondent Walter Duranty.[49] During the Vietnam War, the North Vietnamese Communists regarded slanted American news coverage as a strategic advantage for the Communist cause. The news media in our nation has *always* reflected the agenda of editors, reporters, news producers, anchors, and executives.

There have always been efforts by politicians to censor media content that counters their preferred position. This goes back to the founding of our nation; during the framing of our Constitution, the Federalists tried to block anti-Federalist publications.[50]

This isn't particularly surprising. News media is biased because human nature is biased. We all have opinions, values, and perspectives that shape our viewpoints and our politics. Most of us have agendas. The difference between modern-day news media and the history of U.S. news media is simple. In the past, news sources were open about their political bias. For example, during the Civil War era, many cities had an openly Republican newspaper and an openly Democrat newspaper.[51]

This changed in the late nineteenth century when, according to the Hoover Institution's Bruce Thornton, "the progressive movement promoted the notion that the proper function of the media was to instruct and shape the opinions of voters too uninformed and irrational to be trusted with making the right choice based on facts alone."

Things got worse in the late twentieth century. Prior to the late twentieth century, news reporting had been a blue-collar job. Thornton notes, "As late as the 1970s, when my wife began her career as a reporter, most of the veterans in the newsroom lacked college degrees. They had worked their way up from being a copy-kid or a writer of obituaries, earning by experience the job of reporter. Any biases tended to reflect those of class as much as of political ideology."

But then "journalism became a 'profession' certified by a university degree." Thornton writes, "Once reporters started coming out of colleges and universities, however, they were shaped by the leftist perspective of those institutions. These perspectives, once marginal in American public discourse, became increasingly prominent in the press and television news shows. Now the old progressive view that the press should not just report facts, but mold public opinion to achieve certain political ends, served an ideology fundamentally adverse to the free-market, liberal-democratic foundations of the American Republic."[52]

In the early parts of the twentieth century, as the progressive view took hold, the leftist news media began to disguise its bias with a veneer of neutrality, spawning the earliest prototype of the pathological partisans pretending to be fact-based reporters that populate our media today.

One man is largely responsible for this.

In 1934, President Franklin Delano Roosevelt established the Federal Communications Commission (FCC) via the Communications Act. The FCC was responsible for issuing (or denying) licensure to radio broadcasters. Almost immediately, the FCC was used as a tool of government control over the news media.

FDR used this federal bureaucracy to target his critics who opposed his "New Deal."

Ostensibly neutral, the first FCC Commissioner was a man named Herbert Pettey who ran the radio operations for the FDR presidential campaign.[53] Radio stations, fearful of losing their license to broadcast, quickly curtailed their criticisms of the Roosevelt administration, but not before some dissidents of the FDR administration were forced off the air.

As David Beito notes in *Reason* magazine,

> NBC . . . announced that it was limiting broadcasts "contrary to the policies of the United States government." CBS Vice President Henry A. Bellows said that "no broadcast would be permitted over the Columbia Broadcasting System that in any way was critical of any policy of the Administration." He elaborated "that the Columbia system was at the disposal

of President Roosevelt and his administration and they would permit no broadcast that did not have his approval." Local station owners and network executives alike took it for granted, as *Editor and Publisher* observed, that each station had "to dance to Government tunes because it is under Government license." Some dissident radio commentators, such as Father Charles Coughlin and Boake Carter, gained wide audiences. But radio as a whole was firmly pro-Roosevelt—and both Coughlin and Carter were eventually forced off the air for pushing the envelope too far.[54]

Roosevelt's meddling in what should be our constitutional right to a free press was further exacerbated by the Fairness Doctrine, introduced in 1949 under President Harry Truman. It required licensed broadcast entities to present both sides of pivotal issues, which sounds nice, but it was really another effort to push conservative voices off the air. President John F. Kennedy, for instance, exploited this unconstitutional rule to quash right-wing radio hosts who were criticizing him. The Kennedy administration, citing the Fairness Doctrine, had the FCC demand that right-wing radio shows give equal time to Kennedy supporters. Democrat Party operatives made a point of using the Fairness Doctrine to harass small radio stations that often carried conservative commentary. The Fairness Doctrine loomed over the news media until Ronald Reagan sent it to its grave in 1987.[55] Now unhindered by government regulation, conservative talk radio exploded in popularity, including the phenomenal success enjoyed by Rush Limbaugh, who became the king of talk radio.

That victory for freedom of the press was short-lived as independent content creators now face the Big Tech behemoth that has worked hand in glove with Democrats to censor political speech, punish conservatives, and enforce an unquestioned leftist narrative in public discussion.

Big Tech has been especially censorious in shutting down discussion about election integrity and voter fraud, in promoting the transgender ideology, and in disallowing dissent to the government-mandated COVID-19 policies that were unprecedented in their assault on our civil rights and immensely harmful to our health.

Big Tech was one of the earliest enforcers of the transgender ideology. Under the guise of leftist "inclusion," Big Tech platforms have done everything from banning "misgendering" (which means referring to a man by male pronouns if the man "identifies" as a woman) to banning "deadnaming" (which means referring to a person by the legal name given to him at birth versus his chosen transgender name). If you use the word "groomer" to describe adults grooming children into identifying as transgender, you will also be banned on Reddit and, formerly, Twitter.[56] In other words, if you speak the plain biological, scientific, incontestable truth, you will be canceled.

In the pre–Elon Musk days at Twitter, one of the most powerful Twitter accounts in the country, Libs of TikTok, was suspended multiple times for merely directing more attention to videos created and posted by leftist teachers, among others. In these videos, teachers admitted—indeed bragged—about deliberately exposing children to their own sexual fetishes and encouraging them to explore sex and "gender identity."[57] These videos were—and are—created by leftists. Libs of TikTok simply reposted them so that more people could see what these teachers are doing to our children. When Libs of TikTok exposed Children's National Hospital in Washington, D.C., for performing "gender affirming" hysterectomies on healthy girls as young as fifteen and sixteen years old, Libs of TikTok was suspended—not because it violated any law or the Twitter terms of service, but because the left's own atrocious behavior contradicted their narrative that transgenderism is good.[58]

For many, the nefarious power of Big Tech was exposed most blatantly during the COVID-19 pandemic when, under the guise of combatting "misinformation and disinformation," the social media giants censored criticism of the COVID-19 vaccines and the use of face masks (criticism that was well-founded, as it turns out). In the name of "the science," Big Tech shut off public scientific debate and even blocked the publication of real science that contradicted "the narrative."

On YouTube, for two years you weren't allowed to state that scientific studies show that cloth face masks with gaps in the sides do not prevent the transmission of respiratory viruses like COVID-19.[59] Scientists had long known that face masks make little to no difference when it comes to contracting or spreading respiratory viruses,[60] but you weren't allowed to say so on YouTube until late 2022, when apparently the public health narrative was forced to allow this confession because of overwhelming evidence, much of which already existed prior to the mask mandates. Criticizing the COVID vaccines as dangerous and ineffective remains cause for suspension.[61] Former Biden press secretary Jen Psaki even admitted that the White House gave Big Tech a list of vaccine misinformation "offenders" to censor and ban, despite most of the prohibited information being the truth.[62]

The social media censors will go after anyone who violates their ideological narrative. Even then president of the United States Donald Trump was booted off social media in the name of "protecting our democracy" for questioning the outcome of the 2020 presidential election. Conservatives who weren't banned outright from social media often face what I call algorithmic suffocation, as the social media algorithms prevent posts from conservatives from reaching the audience who follows them and the discovery algorithm directs consumers away from conservative content as a whole.

My own Facebook page has been demonetized and my videos censored on the newsfeed, causing me to lose millions of dollars and see my reach diminished to a mere fraction of the hundreds of millions of views I used to achieve organically. All the suspensions and shadow-banning flow in one direction: the censorship of conservatives who challenge leftist ideology.

But I should note, it's not *just* conservatives. Liberals who buck the leftist narrative are also punished. In cases like that of former *New York Times* journalist Alex Berenson, himself a liberal—but one who made his mark as a brave and prominent skeptic of the COVID-19 narrative—there is irrefutable proof that the federal government and Big Tech colluded in an attempt to silence him on social media. According to Berenson, Biden administration advisor Andy Slavitt directly pressured Twitter to ban Berenson, and Twitter promptly complied. Documents revealed during the "Twitter Files" saga indicate that Twitter, at the behest of former FDA commissioner and current Pfizer board member Scott Gottlieb, along with close Gottlieb confidant and Biden administration senior advisor Andy Slavitt, worked hand in glove to silence Berenson.[63]

Mark Zuckerberg, the CEO of Meta, Facebook's parent company, told Joe Rogan on an episode of the *Joe Rogan Experience* podcast that the FBI warned Facebook about "Russian disinformation" in the leadup to the 2020 presidential election. That warning led Facebook to censor the Hunter Biden laptop story, which revealed Hunter Biden's nefarious business dealings and influence peddling. The story was true, and the FBI knew it was true, but Big Tech treated it as disinformation, the mainstream media tried to ignore or discredit the story, and more than fifty former intelligence officials denounced the story as Russian disinformation. They were all willing accomplices in a politically motivated lie.[64]

In one poll conducted after the election, 17 percent of Democrats said that if they had known about Hunter Biden's conduct they might not have voted for Joe Biden.[65] In other words, collusion between government officials, Big Tech, and the news media could have changed the outcome of a presidential election.

A concurrent ideological remaking has happened in the American education system.

Seizing control of education is, of course, another goal of every Marxist revolutionary. Vladimir Lenin once proclaimed, "Give me four years to teach the children and the seed I have sown will never be uprooted."[66] And again: "Give me just one generation of youth, and I'll transform the whole world."[67]

In what will be a surprise to some readers, however, indoctrination was the purpose of compulsory public education in the United States too (just not Marxist indoctrination).

Noah Webster, "the father of American scholarship and education," and the author of many of our first textbooks, began the title page of his work *An American Selection of Lessons in Reading and Speaking* with a quote from Comte de Mirabeau which read, "Begin with the infant in his cradle: let the first word he lisps be the name of WASHINGTON."[68]

One of the first proponents of a publicly funded—but not compulsory—education system in the United States was Thomas Jefferson. Jefferson believed the object of public education was forming citizens fit for a republic. "The objects of this primary education. . . . would be," Jefferson noted,

> To give to every citizen the information he needs for the transaction of his own business;
> To enable him to calculate for himself, and to express & preserve his ideas, his contracts & accounts in writing;
> To improve by reading, his morals and faculties;
> To understand his duties to his neighbors and country, and to discharge with competence the functions confided to him by either;
> To know his rights; to exercise with order and justice those he retains; to choose with discretion the fiduciaries of

those he delegates; and to notice their conduct with diligence, with candor, and judgment;

And, in general, to observe with intelligence and faithfulness all the social relations under which he shall be placed;

To instruct the mass of our citizens in these, their rights, interests and duties, as men and citizens, being then the objects of education in the primary schools, whether private or public, in them should be taught reading, writing and numerical arithmetic, the elements of mensuration, (useful in so many callings,) and the outlines of geography and history. And this brings us to the point at which are to commence the higher branches of education, of which the Legislature require the development; those, for example, which are,

To form the statesmen, legislators and judges, on whom public prosperity and individual happiness are so much to depend;

To expound the principles and structure of government, the laws which regulate the intercourse of nations, those formed municipally for our own government, and a sound spirit of legislation, which, banishing all arbitrary & unnecessary restraint on individual action, shall leave us free to do whatever does not violate the equal rights of another;

To harmonize and promote the interests of agriculture, manufactures and commerce and by well informed views of political economy to give a free scope to the public industry;

To develop the reasoning faculties of our youth, enlarge their minds, cultivate their morals, and instill into them the precepts of virtue & order;

To enlighten them with mathematical and physical sciences, which advance the arts, and administer to the health, the subsistence, and comforts of human life;

And, generally, to form them to habits of reflection, and
correct action, rendering them examples of virtue to others,
and of happiness within themselves.

These are the objects of that higher grade of education,
the benefits and blessings of which the Legislature now propose to provide for the good and ornament of their country,
the gratification and happiness of their fellow-citizens, of the
parent especially, and his progeny, on which all his affections
are concentrated.[69]

Jefferson's ideas for public education took a turn in the early nineteenth century, when the United States welcomed a large influx of
immigrants, many of them Catholic. Politicians mandated public
schooling to drum both American and Protestant values into the
nation's youth.

As education scholar Kerry McDonald has noted, "Between 1830
and 1840 U.S. immigration quadrupled, and between 1840 and 1850,
it tripled again. Particularly troubling to lawmakers at the time was
the fact that many of these new immigrants were Irish Catholics who
threatened the dominant Anglo-Saxon Protestant cultural and religious
customs. 'Those now pouring in upon us, in masses of thousands
upon thousands, are wholly of another kind in morals and intellect,'
mourned the Massachusetts state legislature regarding the new Boston
immigrants."[70]

In response public schooling became mandatory for children in
our country, starting in Massachusetts in 1852 and rapidly spreading
to other states.

It's hard to appreciate the original intentions of public school advocates whose goal was to drum American values into our nation's children, considering that Marxists hijacked the system less than a century
after public schooling became compulsory. Neo-Marxist radicals took

the reins at teachers' colleges and filled the leadership roles in teachers' unions. What is now inculcated into the minds of America's children in public schools today is not Protestantism or Americanism, but rather atheism, Marxism, and anti-Americanism. What began as a center for American indoctrination has fallen to our domestic enemies.

Let me be very clear: I endorse the idea that our education system should be used for indoctrination. Indoctrination is morally neutral; it's what's being indoctrinated that determines its morality. One side is going to indoctrinate, it's either going to be them or us. It used to be us; we used to indoctrinate students in the history of our country and our traditions, and the result was generations of patriotic Americans. Now, our country suffers from a lack of patriotic citizens—and this is one big reason why. We don't indoctrinate children to be patriots anymore, and in the absence of our indoctrination, the left swooped in to fill that void with anti-Americanism while we sat complacent. We forgot that the *purpose* of our education system was to indoctrinate children into American values, and in the vacuum of "neutrality" that we left, the left seized our education system as indoctrination centers for Marxism instead.

And then there is the institution of law and justice, which has become so badly compromised in our nation. Real justice can be hard to find, thanks to "social justice." Leftists have relentlessly redefined the word "justice" to serve their own political agenda. They have politicized the courts and mercilessly decriminalized criminal activities from drug dealing, carjacking, and shoplifting to vandalism, rioting, arson, and looting. So-called progressive prosecutors funded by leftist billionaire George Soros refuse to prosecute even violent crimes, following the Black Lives Matter movement's quick evolution from "police reform" to "abolish the police" and "abolish prisons."[71]

The Department of Justice and the FBI have weaponized the power of the federal government against conservatives for selective investigation and prosecution—everyone from parents who oppose Critical Race Theory in public school classrooms to pro-life protesters to Second Amendment defenders to traditional Latin Mass Catholics. The FBI secretly labeled citizens who fly the Gadsden flag (also known as the "Don't Tread on Me" flag) or the Betsy Ross flag as possible "Militia Violent Extremists."[72]

In reality, evidence suggests that to paint lockdown skeptics as violent domestic extremists, high-level FBI agents fomented a kidnapping plot against Democratic governor Gretchen Whitmer of Michigan, setting up their patsies for arrest.[73]

In another case, FBI agents raided the homes of three Project Veritas journalists after the journalists purchased Ashley Biden's diary—which allegedly contained information that would damage President Biden's political career—in a clear illustration of how our institutions have been weaponized against dissent.[74]

Simple patriotic conservatives have been treated as possible criminals or even potential domestic terrorists, merely for their beliefs. Protesters who mobbed the Capitol building on January 6, 2021, have been thrown in prison, often in solitary confinement, and denied due process, in contrast to the Black Lives Matter rioters who fomented actual violent insurrections in cities across the country, causing roughly $2 billion in damages, killing nineteen people, and injuring countless others.[75] Democrats reacted with applause to these riots, and the BLM extremists have faced very few legal repercussions for their incendiary actions, despite causing multiple orders of magnitude more chaos and harm than the January 6 rioters. One could go on and on. The examples are legion.

For one particularly egregious example, the FBI raided former President Donald Trump's residence at Mar-a-Lago under the guise of an accusation of criminal mishandling of classified documents, despite the fact that there has not been even a whisper of an indictment for prominent Democratic politicians who have done the exact same thing, including President Biden and Hillary Clinton, among others. The Mar-a-Lago raid followed a highly concerning pattern of the DOJ targeting the former president with false allegations of Russian collusion based on the Steele dossier, named after former British spy Christopher Steele and commissioned and purchased by the Hillary Clinton campaign and the Democratic National Committee.[76] The now-debunked Russiagate scandal was a blatant attempt to smear then candidate Trump with false accusations of treason in order to prevent him from winning the 2016 presidential election.

At this point, four of Gramsci's five pillars of American civil society have been compromised by Marxist infiltrators and their useful idiot collaborators: the church, the media, the education system, and the law. The last remaining cultural pillar is the traditional family, and its survival as a cultural norm is hanging by a thread.

CHAPTER 2

A Nuclear (Family) Bomb

The assault on the American family has been nearly two centuries in the making.

It's fashionable now to point to the number of births to unmarried women as a way of charting the collapse of the American family. In 1960, about 5 percent of American births were to unmarried women. Since then, that number has octupled to about 40 percent.[1]

It's also true, as the Center for Children and Families notes, that, "70% percent of gang members, high school dropouts, teen suicides, teen pregnancies and teen substance abusers come from single mother homes."[2]

Inarguably, the consequence to our society of a massive increase in the percentage of births to unwed mothers has been serious.

But this is not the *reason* for the collapse of the American family; this is the *result* of a much more nefarious, intentional agenda.

Socialists, communists, and self-avowed Marxists began this assault upon the American family as early as the turn of the nineteenth century.

In 1825, for example, a wealthy Welshman named Robert Owen (1771–1858) purchased the town of Harmony, Indiana. Owen, a socialist, subsequently established the town of New Harmony, which he declared to be a commune for collectivist living. On July 4, 1826—the fiftieth anniversary of the Declaration of Independence—Owen proclaimed his own "Declaration of Mental Independence," which included this revolutionary charter: "I now declare, to you and to the world, that Man, up to this hour, has been, in all parts of the earth, a slave to a TRINITY of the most monstrous evils that could be combined to inflict mental and physical evil upon his whole race. I refer to PRIVATE, OR INDIVIDUAL PROPERTY—ABSURD AND IRRATIONAL SYSTEMS OF RELIGION—AND MARRIAGE, FOUNDED UPON INDIVIDUAL PROPERTY, COMBINED WITH SOME ONE OF THESE IRRATIONAL SYSTEMS OF RELIGION."[3]

In Owen's socialist commune, children were to be separated from their parents, raised collectively, and indoctrinated by the town administrators. But, as Dan O'Donnell of the MacIver Institute notes, Owen's communist society rapidly collapsed: "The community couldn't produce enough food to be self-sufficient, primarily because when its hardest-working members realized that they would earn the same benefits as the laziest, they stopped working. With no new houses being built for the growing community and food shortages becoming an epidemic, homelessness and famine ran rampant until eventually New Harmony's experiment with socialism ended in March, 1827."[4] The community limped on for another two years, with allowances for private property and free enterprise, but was dissolved in 1829. Owen himself abandoned his utopia before it imploded.

Undaunted by Owen's spectacular failure, others tried to establish similar collectivist communities in the United States, and also failed.

Albert Brisbane (1809–1890), a follower of the French socialist Charles Fourier, inspired and established a series of communes (sometimes called "associations" or "phalanxes") where he hoped to abolish the "selfishness" of families and private industry. Instead, Brisbane aspired to collectively parcel out child-rearing, education, and economic production and the profits arising from that production. Unsurprisingly, Brisbane's communes failed as well.

John Humphrey Noyes (1811–1886), the son of a former congressman, helped establish a bizarre commune in Oneida, New York, that mixed collectivist economics with Noyes's heretical, crackpot "Christian" theology. His followers practiced "Complex Marriage," which translated to Noyes tricking younger women into sleeping with him or with other older men. Children of this commune were raised collectively. Facing rape charges, Noyes fled the country. His commune dissolved shortly thereafter, with its consolidated businesses transitioning to the surprisingly successful enterprise of fashioning and selling silverware, ironically illustrating the superiority of capitalism as compared to communism.

Modern Marxists dismiss this tried-and-failed history of collectivism. But they learned something from it: incrementalism. Modern Marxists understand that in order to topple the traditional nuclear family, it must be destroyed one element at a time. The five basic elements of a nuclear family are man, woman, marriage, sex, and children.

Sex

As Dr. Paul Kengor notes in his book *Takedown: From Communists to Progressives, How the Left has Sabotaged Family and Marriage*, "Among certain extreme-left elements, there was a pronounced sexual radicalism. . . . One such element was the neo-Marxists of the Frankfurt

School, which had an especially strong impact on the universities, particularly in the 1960s."[5]

Kengor continues, "Georg Lukács, Herbert Marcuse, and Wilhelm Reich . . . were sexually extreme, and they peddled practices conspicuously contrary to traditional morality and marriage, to normal sexual relations, and to the nuclear family."[6]

That might be the understatement of the year.

The term "sexual revolution" was actually coined by the Marxist Wilhelm Reich (1897–1957), a perverted, sex-obsessed, mentally deranged psychoanalyst from Europe who believed that Marxist revolution would not happen until Christian sexual morality was overthrown. "A sexual revolution is in progress," Reich proclaimed, "and no power on earth will stop it."[7]

Reich contended that sexual repression was responsible for ill health, and even for fascism. Reich claimed that "there is only one thing wrong with neurotic patients: *the lack of full and repeated sexual satisfaction*."[8] Reich also blamed capitalism for mental illnesses, neuroses, and emotional instability.

Ironically, Reich later invented and profited off a device called an "orgone energy accumulator"—a sort of closet that one entered and sat in—that was somehow supposed to harness orgasmic and organic energy in order to cure a variety of mental and physical illnesses. This absurd device became so popular in the United States in the 1940s and 1950s that Albert Einstein analyzed it and subsequently refuted Reich's invention as being without any scientific basis. The U.S. government later convicted Reich of fraud and sent him to prison where he died.[9]

Reich argued that sexual promiscuity and immorality weren't *that*, but were actually political activism that would free repressed people from patriarchal capitalist oppressors. Reich advocated for free love, which he defined as sexual activity free from guilt. He claimed this would only be possible in a Marxist society.

In 1939, Reich fled Europe in favor of a teaching position at The New School in New York. Just three years prior to his immigration, in his book *Die Sexualität im Kulturkampf*—which was later translated into English under the title *The Sexual Revolution*—Reich condemned marriage, the family, and Western civilization's opposition to "infant sexuality." Reich contended that children quickly develop active sexuality, and if children's sexuality is repressed, it leads to mental illness. Unsurprisingly, Reich dismissed biblical morality and natural law as an artificial social structure. Children's sexual activity, Reich said, should be normalized.[10] His cure for society's ills was the sexualization of children, promiscuity, and Marxism.

Culturally, Wilhelm Reich's perverted, promiscuous, and increasingly popular Marxist ideology helped lay the groundwork for the sexual revolution in the United States. Reich was no seer; he anticipated such a revolution because *he* helped instigate it.

The sexual revolution warped American attitudes towards sex and promiscuity; and the deliberate destruction of traditional sexual norms inflicted terrible damage on the American family and society as a whole.

Women

In 1963, Betty Friedan published a book titled *The Feminine Mystique*. It sold more than three million copies in its first three years in print.[11]

Friedan declared, "Fulfillment as a woman had only one definition for American women after 1949—the housewife-mother."[12]

Friedan's goal with the book: destroy the housewife-mother.

Friedan decried marriage and motherhood—things women naturally want and enjoy—as stifling, limiting institutions of oppression forced upon women that ultimately render them unhappy. Yet data from subsequent decades would prove this was the opposite of the truth;

women's levels of happiness have dropped precipitously since the 1970s, when feminism took hold.[13]

In her book, Friedan portrayed herself as the average American housewife who, naively, didn't initially recognize she was oppressed by men and marriage. Friedan claimed that the idea—the reality—that women are happiest and best fulfilled as wives and mothers is a myth, and she called this myth the "feminine mystique." Friedan contended that the feminine mystique is a lie indoctrinated into women by a patriarchal society. According to Friedan, she was trapped by this mystique from the time she graduated from college until she wrote her book.

In the pages of *The Feminine Mystique*, Friedan describes her own experience living the supposed quintessential American dream as a housewife and mother in a suburban home, supported by a successful husband. While that might sound idyllic to many, Friedan described her life as a "comfortable concentration camp."[14]

Ironically, Friedan's ex-husband pointed out that Friedan "was in the world during the whole marriage" and "seldom was a wife and a mother." Moreover, despite Betty's complaints in her book about housework, she employed a full-time maid.[15]

Friedan's portrayal of herself as the typical American housewife was a lie. She was nothing of the kind.

Daniel Horowitz, a professor of American Studies and History at Smith College, explains, "If Rosa Parks refused to take a seat at the back of a segregated bus not simply because her feet hurt, then Friedan did not write *The Feminine Mystique* simply because she was an unhappy housewife."[16]

Betty Friedan was steeped in Marxist ideology.

Friedan's maiden name was Bettye Goldstein. Long before *The Feminine Mystique* sent generations of American women spiraling away from marriage and family, Bettye Goldstein spent decades committed to Marxist political causes.

Professor Horowitz notes, Friedan "acknowledged that before her marriage and for several years after she had participated in radical activities and worked for union publications. She and the friends with whom she lived before marrying considered themselves 'the vanguard of the working-class revolution,' participating in 'Marxist discussion groups,' going to political rallies, and having 'only contempt for dreary bourgeois capitalists like our fathers.'"[17]

Friedan claimed to be "just" an unhappy housewife. Actually, she was a Marxist.

Horowitz writes, "Off and on from October 1943 until July 1946 [Friedan] was a staff writer for the Federated Press, a left-wing news service that provided stories for newspapers, especially union ones, across the nation." Horowitz continues, "For about six years beginning in July, 1946, precisely at the moment when the wartime Popular Front came under intense attack, Friedan was a reporter for the union's paper UE News." Horowitz contends, "Popular Front ideology shaped the way Friedan viewed American society and politics."[18]

According to Horowitz, "Something else enriched Friedan's perspective in the years after she stopped working for the UE. Shortly after its 1953 publication in English, Friedan appreciatively read Simone de Beauvoir's The Second Sex. Yet when she mentioned this later, she did not point to the book's Marxism or to the author's politics. Instead in The Feminine Mystique, she hailed its 'insights into French women' and in 1975 she stated that from it she learned 'my own existentialism.'"[19]

Friedan sanitized her history of Marxist political activism from the account of her life in The Feminine Mystique. But Horowitz writes, "Still, not very hidden in her book was a simplified, Marxist view of ideological domination. In the pivotal chapter of her second and more radical narrative, titled 'The Sexual Sell,' the task she set for herself was to explain the 'powerful forces' served by the feminine mystique. What, she asked, undermined the force of feminism and fueled the retreat of women into the privatism of the suburban home? In seeking an answer, Friedan articulated arguments congruent with what she learned from [leftist economics professor Dorothy W.] Douglas and as a labor journalist."[20]

Horowitz concludes, "*The Feminine Mystique* played a critical role in reshaping the ideology and social composition of the American left. Along with others, such as Herbert Marcuse, Friedan was exploring how to ground a cultural and social critique by rethinking the contributions of Freud and Marx. What Marcuse did in *Eros and Civilization: A Philosophical Inquiry into Freud* (1955), Friedan did almost a decade later: respond to the cold war by attempting to minimize her debt to Marx even as she relied on him."[21]

In her 1976 book *It Changed My Life*, Friedan wrote, "In a certain sense, it was almost accidental—coincidental—that I wrote *The Feminine Mystique*, and in another sense my whole life had prepared me to write that book; all the pieces of my own life came together for the first time in the writing of it."[22] What she didn't acknowledge, except obliquely, was that her views were grounded in Marxism.

Friedan's book galvanized a new radical feminist movement that inflicted incalculable damage upon the American family, as women were led to believe that marriage and children were limiting and oppressive, and that it was men who imposed this oppression. To achieve their full potential, women instead were told to abandon their role as wife and mother, pursue careers, and find value in a paycheck.

Betty Friedan's books and feminist activism were an integral part of the sexual revolution of the 1960s and 1970s, and little has been more damaging to women and the institution of the family than Friedan and her work.

Men

Masculinity is under attack in the United States. When the second gentleman of the United States, Doug Emhoff, husband of Vice President

Kamala Harris, appears on national television to condemn toughness as "toxic masculinity" and claim real men don't exhibit such traits, we had best realize that things are spinning wildly out of control.[23]

"I always think of [testosterone] as a toxin," says famed movie director James Cameron, "that you have to slowly work out of your system."[24]

According to a documentary by Jennifer Siebel Newsom—wife of California's Democratic governor Gavin Newsom—one of the most destructive phrases a young boy can hear while growing up is to "be a man."[25]

That entire concept of masculinity is under direct and sustained assault in our country. Pornography has perverted masculinity and sexual desire against women. Video games have hijacked the natural male instinct to protect and create and twisted it into an addictive, harmful, pseudo-violent pastime. The #MeToo movement has neutered chivalry and demonized the innate manliness of the male sex. Pornography has degraded masculinity and perverted it, so that men become passive voyeurs of the abuse of women.

Our country's institutions are biased against men.

Education systems are rigged for men to fail. Compared to their female counterparts, men receive lower grades, lose the majority of scholarships and academic prizes, and are less likely to attend college at all. If they do attend college, men are still less likely to earn bachelor's or advanced degrees than women.[26] Today, partly as a consequence of this, "single, childless women in their 20s now earn 8 percent more on average than their male counterparts in metropolitan areas."[27]

The suicide rate for men in our country is nothing short of a national tragedy.[28] So is the rate of substance abuse and opioid overdoses among young men.[29] Overall, men live shorter lives than women by a significant margin. Men are expected to live seventy-six years compared to women's expected eighty-one years.[30]

Feminist Christina Hoff Sommers contends that most people are familiar with the feminist trope claiming men enjoy "male privilege." Yes, most CEOs are men, Sommers says, but the individuals doing the dirtiest, most dangerous work in our country are also men. That's why 92 percent of workplace accident fatalities in the United States affect men. About 85 percent of active duty military are men, too.[31]

Sommers notes how dangerously our society is structured for men. Men are more likely to be victims of violent crime: 78 percent of murder victims are men. Likewise, 78 percent of suicides are men, 60 percent of homeless people are men, and 93 percent of federal inmates are men too, according to Sommers, and it's not only because men commit more crimes. Sommers ran a statistical analysis comparing men who committed crimes to women who committed the same crimes with the same criminal history and found that, when all else was equal, men were given harsher sentences and longer prison times than women.[32]

Over the course of the past decade, we've seen a spate of mass shootings committed by deranged, mentally ill, and sociopathic young men. These men have been failed by their institutions, whether it be their families, schools, churches, communities, or a combination of all of them. Left completely adrift, with no support system to fall back upon, these men are unsurprisingly vulnerable to the influence of evil. These abandoned, broken, lonely, and mentally ill young men turn instead to violent video games, pornography, drugs and alcohol, and often dark corners of the internet that exacerbate their problems.

Masculinity under attack. Our nation is suffering from a self-inflicted crisis of young men. Marxists understand that masculinity is a problem, something that needs to be undermined. Destroy men, destroy their role as a protector—a defender of a wife, children, society—and you can then overthrow that society.

In 1989, an "antiracist" feminist law professor named Kimberlé Crenshaw coined the term intersectionality.[33]

Kimberlé Crenshaw is a Marxist.

Crenshaw contended that intersectionality is a new way of looking at oppression by considering how the overlapping social identities of an oppressed person are greater than their linear sum. She claimed this was new thinking—but it's no such thing.

Debuting her new theory of intersectionality in an essay published through the University of Chicago, Crenshaw posited, "Because the intersectional experience is greater than the sum of racism and sexism, any analysis that does not take intersectionality into account cannot sufficiently address the particular manner in which Black women are subordinated. Thus, for feminist theory and antiracist policy discourse to embrace the experiences and concerns of Black women, the entire framework that has been used as a basis for translating 'women's experience' or 'the Black experience' into concrete policy demands must be rethought and recast."[34]

Crenshaw invented the word "intersectionality," but her proposal is hardly original. It's simply an echo of Marx and Engels.

The most basic description of Marxist theory is that everyone is either an oppressor or the oppressed. Marx and Engels claimed it was the bourgeoisie oppressing the proletariat; Crenshaw's theory of intersectionality simply takes that premise and twists it to include sex and race, helping move economic Marxism towards cultural Marxism.

Kimberlé Crenshaw also coined the phrase "Critical Race Theory" (CRT), which is the intellectual grandchild of the Frankfurt School's Marxist Critical Theory.[35] At its core, CRT is racialized Marxism. Crenshaw herself admitted this during a 2019 panel discussion, describing herself and her contemporaries: "We discovered ourselves to be critical theorists who did race. . . ."[36]

Through the lens of Crenshaw's intersectionality theory, oppression can be accumulated based on overlapping social identities—such as being female, a person of color, or transgender, for example, or a combination of minority characteristics—which renders those who are "guilty" of one type of oppression guilty of all types of oppression, as defined by Crenshaw.

Who, then, are the guilty? Men. Particularly, "cisgender," heterosexual, white Christian American men.

Since it was such men who built this nation, it is convenient for the Marxists—whose goal is the destruction of our nation—to declare that the United States Constitution, American history and tradition and society are illegitimate and oppressive, because the Founders granted "privilege" only to white, heterosexual Christian men, and that this "white privilege" has been handed down to white, heterosexual Christian men today in a society of systemic racism, sexism, and "cisgenderism."

To wit, we see revisionist history like this in many forms, such as the *New York Times'* 1619 Project (which views all American history through the prism of slavery and racism), Howard Zinn's *A People's History of the United States* (a standard textbook, unfortunately, that takes a Marxist view of American history), and DEI (diversity, equity, and inclusion) initiatives (which are discrimination, socialism, and religious persecution in the name of righting past wrongs).

This may seem—it should seem—hateful and ludicrous on its face. It is even more so when you consider that not a single white Christian man living in America today has ever had anything to do with slavery (which was abolished in 1865). Segregation lost all legal sanction with the 1964 Civil Rights Act. This is history, and throughout our nation's history, many of these "evil," white Christian men have been the most ardent champions of equality for racial minorities and for women.

These troublesome facts don't matter to Marxists like Kimberlé Crenshaw. According to cultural Marxists, modern men are evil because they share immutable characteristics with men in our nation's history who did bad things. Worse, modern men are irredeemable because it doesn't matter what men feel, how they act, or whether they treat others with dignity and respect. "Male privilege" and "white privilege" are something they inevitably assume as their birthright. According to Marxist intersectionality theory, modern men are the ineluctable beneficiaries of hundreds of years of systemic racial and sexual discrimination in our nation; they are an oppressive class. When the Marxist view is assumed to be true, it is little wonder that white men are disdained, manliness is scorned, and the institutions in our nation are rigged against men. The assault on modern men is the result of Marxist intersectionality, which assumes that discrimination against white, heterosexual Christian males and destruction of masculinity is justice.

Marriage

Where does that leave marriage? Man, with his masculinity, and woman, with her femininity, are essential, complementary, basic elements of a marriage. So is sex. All three have been compromised by Marxism.

The original Marxists disdained marriage and eagerly awaited the inevitable demise of monogamous marriage in a post-capitalism communist utopia.

The later sexual revolution encouraged promiscuity and perverted sexual behavior. This was promoted and normalized by influential Marxists like Wilhelm Reich and others who aimed to destroy the sanctity of the marital union.

Feminist Betty Friedan belittled a woman's role as wife and mother in the home, denigrated marriage as a tool of male oppression, and persuaded an unfortunate number of women to either divorce their husbands or avoid marriage altogether.

The vilification of men on the basis of sex and race has turned many men away from their natural, wholesome instincts to protect and provide for their wives, children, and families and instead towards despair, the faux competitive outlet of computer games, and the sterility of pornography.

One often-overlooked factor in the decline of marriage is no-fault divorce. California became the first state to legalize no-fault divorce in 1969, in a bill signed by then governor Ronald Reagan (who, according to W. Bradford Wilcox, "later admitted [it] was one of the biggest political mistakes of his life").[37]

The modern concept of no-fault divorce was pioneered by the Soviets during the Russian Revolution. Shortly after the Bolsheviks took power, responsibility for marriage and divorce was transferred from churches to the government, and marriages could be dissolved for any reason. According to legal scholar Donald Bolas, "One spouse simply filled out the paperwork at city hall and the other party was then notified by mail that they were no longer married." Marriage became no more than a casual, breakable relationship with no permanence, no covenant before God, and no establishment of a family. Bolas noted that some people in Bolshevik Russia were married twenty times.[38]

The effect in the United States, however benevolent the intentions of Governor Reagan, was similarly devastating. Once no-fault divorce became permissible in court, the divorce rate quickly doubled in the United States.[39] Now, thousands of marriages are broken by divorce in the United States every day.[40]

How can marriage *be* marriage if it can be broken as easily as sending a postcard? How can marriage be marriage if politicians arbitrarily redefine the word to include same-sex couples?

Long before homosexual "marriage" became law in the United States, the LGBT lobby (it didn't have a QIA+ back then) built its culture on the backs of Marxist theory.

Marxists didn't always embrace homosexuality. Marx himself snickered about homosexual sex behind the backs of his contemporaries who engaged in such behavior. The Soviets in Russia initially legalized homosexual sodomy following the Bolshevik takeover, then banned it, then allowed it again.[41] As Kengor notes in his book *Takedown*, support for "gay marriage" itself was nearly unheard of for close to a century after the publication of *The Communist Manifesto*, even among sexually deviant Marxists.[42]

Nonetheless, the modern LGBTQIA+ lobby exists because mid-twentieth-century homosexual activists structured their activism after the Marxist pattern.

History professor Jim Downs, author of *Stand by Me: The Forgotten History of Gay Liberation*, points to the Stonewall riots as the precipitating moment that this evolution into political Marxism began for the homosexual lobby in the United States.[43] In 1969, police officers raided a homosexual bar in New York City, resulting in violent clashes between police and patrons that became known as the Stonewall riots and are usually considered the beginning of the homosexual rights movement in American politics. In her infamous appearance on *RuPaul's Drag Race*, Congresswoman Alexandria Ocasio-Cortez not only said transvestite strippers should be "teaching" kids, but praised the drag queen at Stonewall who threw the first brick at police.[44]

Professor Downs argues that the Stonewall riots weren't the *political* force they're often considered to be, but rather were the beginning of a *philosophical* redefinition of gay oppression by homosexual activists, as they began incorporating Marxist theory into their political agenda.

Downs contends, "LGBT activists were looking for a structural understanding of oppression, for core insights about how society works, not just reforms to existing laws."[45]

Downs postulates that homosexual activists turned to socialism and Marxism as their answer. He writes,

[T]he political fervour of Stonewall launched LGBT people on a much deeper, more difficult journey. They began to rethink the very meaning of political power, ideology, and the role of the government. Instead of turning toward the state for recognition, they often turned away from it. They began to transform themselves, intellectually and politically, in ways that revolutionised how they understood oppression and the meaning of governmental and economic power. Throughout the 1970s, LGBT people theorised about the benefits of socialism in books and pamphlets and critiqued capitalism in the growing newspaper and print culture. In doing so, they also began to redefine their identity and to rewrite their history.[46]

Ultimately, the homosexual rights movement built its political apparatus on socialist and Marxist theory (despite Downs noting that the activists responsible for this are underappreciated figures in modern gay culture). Mid-twentieth-century gay activists simply redefined their homosexual preference and the societal response to it not as an issue of morality or sexual or psychological deviancy, but through the lens of an oppressed class.

Adopting Marxist theory wasn't hard to do. Friedrich Engels wrote in *The Origin of the Family, Private Property and the State* that the traditional nuclear family consisting of a married man and woman was unnatural. He argued that traditional marriage was the product of a capitalist society. He claimed marriage was a tool of bourgeois oppression and posited that the only solution was socialism, which would lead to the destruction of the nuclear family.[47]

Almost 150 years before homosexual "marriage" became legal in the United States, Friedrich Engels gave homosexual activists everything they needed to harness Marxism to their own advantage.

According to Downs, in the 1970s a group of academically minded homosexual men met every Saturday evening for dinner to "read Engels and Karl Marx, and discuss the implications for gay liberation."[48]

One of these men was Jonathan Ned Katz, who eventually wrote *Gay American History*. He said that by studying Marx, "I was experiencing a change in my self-conception and conceptions of gays in a very short time."[49]

Downs relates the transformation: "Growing up, [Katz] and the other members had all been taught that homosexuality was a sickness that could be treated by psychologists. Now they were beginning to realise that was not the case. *Oh my God*, Katz remembered thinking, *was I stupid to fall for that idea that I was sick?* Sitting on secondhand furniture in a crowded apartment, members of the reading group came to understand that they were not sick, but oppressed, a concept uncovered by reading Engels and Marx. To make that distinction was 'mind-blowing,' Katz recalled. 'I would get dizzy and have to lie down.'"[50]

When the United States Supreme Court declared that marriage in the United States must be redefined to include same-sex couples, it did so on the basis of an unconstitutional jurisprudence called "substantive due process," which the court used to create a "right" not found in the Constitution. That is bad enough.

But the consequences of the act itself are explicitly Marxist. George Orwell called the practice of redefining words "Newspeak," and saw it as part of the totalitarianism of Marxism. In his classic novel *Nineteen Eighty-Four*, Orwell wrote,

> Don't you see that the whole aim of Newspeak is to narrow the range of thought? In the end we shall make thought-crime literally impossible, because there will be no words in which to express it. Every concept that can ever be needed will be

expressed by exactly *one* word, with its meaning rigidly
defined and all its subsidiary meanings rubbed out and
forgotten. . . . But the process will still be continuing long
after you and I are dead. Every year fewer and fewer words,
and the range of consciousness always a little smaller. Even
now, of course, there's no reason or excuse for committing thought-crime. It's merely a question of self-discipline,
reality-control. But in the end there won't be any need even
for that. . . . Has it ever occurred to you, Winston, that by
the year 2050, at the very latest, not a single human being
will be alive who could understand such a conversation as
we are having now?[51]

If leftists are allowed to redefine words, they become the arbiters
of truth. Arbiters of truth can change "truth" at any time, for any reason, to serve any agenda. Redefining the objective truth of marriage—
which is, in fact, the union of one man and one woman—to include
homosexual "marriage" destroys the notion of marriage altogether.

The left has utterly redefined what we think of men, women, marriage, and sex, four of the five basic elements of the nuclear family. That
leaves children. Children are the final frontier. If children are destroyed,
what stands between America and Marxism?

CHAPTER 3

The Race Bait

My friend Andrew Klavan once contended that Critical Race Theory is "strikingly similar" to pornography.

Pornography, Klavan said, is "just shapes and pictures in your mind—I know there are real women on one end of the pornographer's business—but when it comes to the audience, it's just a shape, it's just a picture."

Men who watch pornography, Klavan says, "become impotent because the woman will not act like the woman in that picture." Men who consume pornography "cannot make that leap from the shape of a woman to an actual real woman."

As a result, they often become pornography addicts, indulging more and more in pornography to satiate their sexual desires that now cannot be fulfilled by real sex, rendering them exponentially "more alienated from reality."[1]

Likewise, Critical Race Theory teaches that white people are inherently racist and black people are inherently oppressed based solely on the color of their skin. Like pornography, CRT is a delusional fantasy with no basis in reality, and those who indulge in the poisonous ideology of CRT become addicted and subsequently disassociated from reality.

Klavan contends that radical leftists persist in promoting Critical Race Theory because their ideas don't work in real life, which is analogous to—as Klavan insightfully adds—"[t]he same way people double down on porn because the porn disables them from acting in real life."[2] CRT-addicted leftists need to redouble their efforts to prove how anti-racist they are, because their leftist policies, particularly their governance of inner cities, have been a disaster for black Americans. But leftists can always explain away their failures, and double down on their harmful policies, by invoking Critical Race Theory. This is evident when it comes to so-called "equity" policies, Klavan says.[3]

Equity isn't equality before the law, or equality of opportunity, or the equality of every human in the eyes of God. It is the reverse of that. Equity is a euphemism for racial discrimination against the oppressive "white people" in the name of Critical Race Theory. "Equity sees people, just like porn does, as objects," says Klavan.[4]

Just as pornography turns women into objects to be abused for sexual gratification, Critical Race Theory turns people into objects to be used to achieve political agendas based on the color of their skin.

In July 2021, I asked Dr. Marc Lamont Hill on his then primetime TV show *Black News Tonight*, "Do you believe that all white people are inherently racist?"

Dr. Hill responded, "Yes, I do. I do believe that all white people are, at some level, at the unconscious level, connected to racism."[5]

While debating the essence of CRT, Hill disputed that a racist book called *Not My Idea: A Book about Whiteness* embodied the principles

of Critical Race Theory. The book—which was being read to kindergar-
teners in Evanston, Illinois—literally portrays white people as the Devil.
Satan's primary role in the book is to tempt children with "whiteness."
It's nasty, horrifying stuff.[6]

Hill conceded that it was inappropriate to teach this to children.
He claimed, however, that conservatives vilified Critical Race Theory
and labeled every leftist idea as Critical Race Theory. Then, he said,
whenever Republicans don't like something, they can yell "CRT!" and
voters will condemn it.[7] But that, as we know, is ridiculous. We criticize
CRT because it is a dangerous, hateful ideology.

Hill was unperturbed by his own racist answer to my question
about whether all white people are racist. Judging an entire group of
people based on their skin color is clearly racism. I have no idea if Marc
Lamont Hill is personally a racist, but Critical Race Theory, racialized
Marxism, is exactly what most parents don't want taught in their children's classrooms. That is why parents fight back against books like
Not My Idea: A Book about Whiteness.

The proposition that all white people are racist or "connected to
racism" is a core tenet of Critical Race Theory. Barbara Applebaum,
a CRT "scholar" and author of *Being White, Being Good*, writes that
"all white people are racist or complicit by virtue of benefiting from
privileges that are not something they can voluntarily renounce."[8]
Indeed, according to Applebaum, "white complicity" means that "all
whites, by virtue of systemic white privilege that is inseparable from
white ways of being, are implicated in the production and reproduction
of systemic racial injustice."[9]

Another leading proponent of Critical Race Theory, who helped
launch CRT into popular American culture with the publication of her
wildly bestselling book *White Fragility*, is Robin DiAngelo. DiAngelo
says, "White identity is inherently racist; white people do not exist
outside the system of white supremacy."[10] DiAngelo, incidentally, is a

white woman who now profits by giving lectures to other white people about why white people are bad. She is able to enrich herself thanks to capitalism, which neo-Marxist theories like Critical Race Theory condemn as evil.[11]

It's important to note the difference between teaching students the academic theory of Critical Race Theory abstractly, like "This is Critical Race Theory and this is what it teaches" versus teaching the tenets of Critical Race Theory, like "All white people are racist" as if the latter is objective truth. The former is a concept, the latter is an application to reality.

Curricula that include sources like *A Book about Whiteness* contain the tenets of Critical Race Theory. Whether it's white complicity, white privilege, white fragility, DEI (diversity, equity, inclusion), or intersectionality, the tenets of Critical Race Theory are taught in our children's classrooms. Our sons and daughters are told this poisonous ideology is true.

It is not true. It is Marxist revisionist history that intends to poison our children to the point that they reject everything America has stood for, its history, its Constitution, its principles.

This effort goes back a long way, and much of it started in Germany. The Institute for Social Research in Frankfurt, Germany, was a buzzing hive of Marxists in the 1920s. Founded by Marxist academic Félix Weil and funded by his wealthy father, it was created to be a breeding ground for Marxist ideology in academia. In fact, Weil and his cohorts originally planned to name the school *Institut für Marxismus* (Institute for Marxism), but fearing backlash from the public, they decided to conceal their Marxist ideology with a more neutral-sounding name.[12]

The Frankfurt School, as it became known, became a petri dish of modern Marxism. The "orthodox" Marxists recruited by the Frankfurt School's first director Carl Grünberg were quickly surpassed by the institute's most influential director, Max Horkheimer.

Horkheimer was thoroughly evil. He was a committed Marxist who praised the Bolsheviks and excused their brutality during the Russian Revolution, writing, "He who has eyes for the meaningless injustice of the imperialist world, which in no way is to be explained by technical impotence, will regard the events in Russia as the progressive, painful attempt to overcome this injustice."[12]

At the hands of the Bolshevik vanguard, priests were scalped, tortured, and crucified. Citizens were violently separated from their property. Any dissent to Communist ideology was punished by law. The free press was eradicated, and any literature the Communist authorities disapproved of was banned.[13] That doesn't sound like "overcoming injustice" to me.

Horkheimer was disappointed that no such revolution had succeeded in Germany.

At the Frankfurt School, Horkheimer groomed a new generation of cultural Marxists like Theodor Adorno, Herbert Marcuse, and Erich Fromm, all of whom Horkheimer would later import to American universities. In 1937, Max Horkheimer penned a manifesto titled "Traditional and Critical Theory." In it, Horkheimer contended that there is no such thing as objective truth. Instead, Horkheimer claimed, everything is simply a competing political narrative and the winner of that competition is the arbiter of "truth."

This might ring a bell today when the left tells us that there is no objective truth—that "your truth" can be different from "my truth."

Horkheimer observed that traditional theory attempts to understand and describe the world. Critical Theory, however, was meant to change the world. This idea is straight from Karl Marx, who wrote in his short work *Theses on Feuerbach*, "The philosophers have only interpreted the world, in various ways; the point, however, is to change it." These words were so central to Marx's ideology that they were inscribed on his tomb.[14]

The cultural institutions and societal norms on which civilization is built, Horkheimer said, can be destroyed through "relentless criticism." Thus, Critical Theory. According to Horkheimer, relentless criticism of cultural institutions, viewing every issue through the Marxist prism of "oppressed versus oppressors," would allow a new vanguard to destroy the social structures and beliefs that serve as an impediment to Marxist revolution.[15]

We recall from chapter 1 that Antonio Gramsci wrote that the proletariat will not revolt against the bourgeoisie as long as the proletariat relies on the cultural institutions and social norms of the bourgeoisie. Gramsci contended that this begets a need for the proletariat to be reeducated to form a new vanguard, which requires the destruction of societal norms. Such cultural institutions, as Horkheimer and Gramsci both fervently believed, must be torn down. Horkheimer offered the tools to do it.

Two years before Max Horkheimer published "Traditional and Critical Theory," he imported his cast of mad Marxists to the United States. With the rise of Adolf Hitler and the Third Reich, the Frankfurt School (many of whose members were secular Jews) fled from Germany to Switzerland, and eventually to the United States. They found a home at Columbia University Teachers College, and the Frankfurt School's ideas and theories soon began to spread through academic circles, primarily through radical college professors teaching at American universities.

Horkheimer eventually returned to Germany after World War II, but he left behind his assistant, Herbert Marcuse (1898–1979).[16]

It was Marcuse who helped morph Critical Theory into the tenets of Critical Race Theory in the United States by casting American racial minorities as the new "workers" whose consciousness of oppression could be raised or entirely invented. After convincing minorities of their oppressed status through reeducation, they would be ready, able, and motivated to overthrow the social and cultural norms of Western civilization.

In the words of Marcuse, "[U]nderneath the conservative popular base [of American society] is the substratum of the outcasts and outsiders, the exploited and persecuted of other races and other colors." According to Marcuse, these people would need ideological leadership. But Marcuse contended that "their opposition is revolutionary even if their consciousness is not."[17]

Since a worker-led revolution wasn't happening, the Marxists needed another "oppressed" class to serve their purpose. That purpose was to tear down Western institutions and stage a Marxist revolution. Marcuse proposed using racial minorities and feminists and anti–Vietnam War protesters as the new Marxist vanguard. Even if an insufficient number of workers felt oppressed by capitalists, who better to serve as the new revolutionary vanguard than a demographic of people whose ancestors had suffered oppression based on skin color? Who better to paint as continuing victims of the belief systems of the "oppressors" and therefore to claim the only path to liberation was the destruction of the institutions themselves?

Max Horkheimer gave us Critical Theory. Herbert Marcuse adapted it for Critical Race Theory. Both are revolutionary Marxist ideology. But there was yet another academic iteration between Critical Theory and Critical Race Theory: Critical Legal Studies.

According to Cornell University, "Critical legal studies (CLS) is a theory which states that the law is necessarily intertwined with social issues, particularly stating that the law has inherent social biases. Proponents of CLS believe that the law supports the interests of those who create the law. As such, CLS states that the law supports a power dynamic which favors the historically privileged and disadvantages the historically underprivileged. CLS finds that the wealthy and the powerful use the law as an instrument for oppression in order to maintain their place in hierarchy." Moreover, "Many in the CLS movement want to overturn the hierarchical structures of modern society and they focus on the law as a tool in achieving this goal."[18]

Harvard Law professor Derrick Bell (1930–2011), known as the godfather of Critical Race Theory, contended that Critical Race Theory and Critical Legal Studies were perfectly aligned; drawing from the words of Angela Harris, both theories were committed to dismantling all aspects of Western society via relentless criticism and pressure.[19]

Bell wrote, "As I see it, critical race theory recognizes that revolutionizing a culture begins with the radical assessment of it." Bell also believed that the idea of natural rights, as codified by the Constitution, was flawed because the "concept of rights is indeterminate, vague and disutile."[20]

One law student who admired Derrick Bell and spoke in praise of him was a future president of the United States, Barack Obama.[21]

Another CRT founder, Richard Delgado, wrote in his massively popular book *Critical Race Theory: An Introduction* that "critical race theory builds on the insights of two previous movements, critical legal studies and radical feminism. . . ."[22] And, of course, Marxism. Delgado described himself at a conference—and others including Kimberlé Crenshaw and Derrick Bell—as "a bunch of Marxists."[23]

It was Crenshaw who coined the term Critical Race Theory after it gradually evolved from Critical Theory and Critical Legal Studies. Crenshaw said that she and her colleagues "discovered ourselves to be critical theorists who did race. . . ."[24]

The Marxist lineage of Critical Race Theory is clear. First, Critical Theory posits there is no such thing as objective reality, only competing political narratives and "lived experiences." Therefore, cultural norms and institutions can be overthrown through relentless criticism of the prevailing narrative of "truth."

In tandem, Critical Legal Studies posits there can be no neutrality in law, and therefore all law serves the interests of the oppressors and marginalizes the oppressed. The answer to this, according to CLS, is to harness the law as a tool to tear down the societal norms imposed by the oppressor.

To cap it off, Critical Race Theory defines everyone by skin color, dividing black people from white people, with the latter being the oppressors and the former being the oppressed, weaponizing race to create a new vanguard to tear down Western civilization.

Critical Race Theory is taught as truth not only in colleges and universities across the country, but in public schools all the way down to the primary grades. Our children are literally being taught Marxist ideology, developed from the Frankfurt School, that is intended to overthrow the United States of American from within. The Marxists are using our children to do it. As if that's not alarming enough, Critical Race Theory would be nothing without another Critical Theory: Queer Theory.

CHAPTER 4

Hook, Line, and Queer Theory

R eading the founding document of Queer Theory was one of the
most disturbing things I've ever done. I was reading Gayle Rubin's
pivotal essay "Thinking Sex" in order to understand the agenda behind
transgender ideology and why it is being pushed on children in our
public schools.

Gayle Rubin is—and I will be blunt—a big, fat woman with a short,
gray, butch haircut. She wears small, oval glasses and appears to wear
no makeup. At first glance, you might mistake Rubin for a man given
the baggy, masculine clothes and necktie she often wears.

More important, Gayle Rubin is a deeply disturbed individual.

Rubin is a neo-Marxist college professor who identifies as a cultural
anthropologist, but a more accurate description of her work would state
that Rubin is an activist for radical gender theory, and an unadulter-
ated pervert and sexual deviant. Rubin is a founder of Queer Theory.
Rubin is also a lesbian who founded several leather BDSM (Bondage,

Discipline, Dominance, and Submission/Sadomasochism) clubs for lesbians in San Francisco in the late 1970s and 1980s.[1] Rubin currently serves on the Board of Governors for the Leather Hall of Fame.[2] (One cringes to wonder what qualifies a person to be inducted into that hall of fame.)

Is your stomach turning?

Gayle Rubin shouldn't be allowed within a ten-mile radius of our children for reasons we'll detail momentarily, and yet, Rubin's Queer Theory is increasingly being used to indoctrinate our children in school.

What, exactly, are groomer teachers, comprehensive sex educators, and Planned Parenthood agents telling classrooms of children about sex and gender in the name of Queer Theory?

Girls are taught that if they feel like a boy, they can be one. Boys are told if they desire to be a girl, they can be.

Children are taught they are not created male and female, that there is no sex binary; instead, they exist on a "gender spectrum."

Children are taught that "gender" is different from sex, that gender is unrelated to biology and only reflective of "identity."

Finally, children are taught that no sexual activity is immoral or wrong, as long as it is consensual.

This is not merely a random assortment of destructive nonsense.

These are the principles of Queer Theory.

Just as Critical Race Theory is the ideological underpinning of the notion that "white people are inherently racist," Queer Theory is the ideological underpinning of the "gender identity" propaganda being indoctrinated into children in school.

In "Thinking Sex," an essay that is widely acknowledged to be the founding document of Queer Theory, authoress Gayle Rubin argues against the idea that "gender" is the same as sex and that sex is biologically ordained. Rubin calls the view she opposes "sex essentialism."[3]

Another phrase for "sex essentialism" would be scientific fact.

Instead of sex essentialism, which Rubin asserts is an oppressive imposition of the patriarchy and Western Christian culture, she argues for gender "identities" without essence—across a wide and fluid gender spectrum unrelated to biological sex. This is the basis of gender identity.

Rubin says that "gender" is merely a social construct, and therefore mutable, as changeable as we desire.

Finally, Rubin encourages transgression, which is a fancy way of claiming that no sexual behavior is immoral as long as it is consensual.[4]

This area of Queer Theory is deeply disturbing, especially in its consequences for children, as we'll soon see.

Queer Theory is an offshoot of Marxist Critical Theory, and like Critical Race Theory, is a rejection of objective reality. Queer Theorists reject the reality that there are two sexes, male and female. In Marxist fashion the "oppressed" are recast as those with "non-binary gender identities," while the "oppressors" are the heterosexual, "cisgender" Christian patriarchs. The Marxist strategy is to relentlessly criticize the reality of sex, traditional notions of "gender," and Christian sexual morality. The goal is to overthrow the cultural institution of the family and impose Marxism. According to Queer Theory, the destruction of children's sexual innocence and sexual identity is a key tool to achieve the ultimate goal of a Marxist society.

That's why Rubin argues, "Sex is always political."[5]

Children are the primary targets of this sexual-political assault, which is why Rubin advocates for the sexualization of children, writing that the "notion that sex *per se* is harmful to the young has been chiselled into extensive social and legal structures designed to insulate minors from sexual knowledge and experience."[6]

Experience? What kind of sexual experience for minors does Rubin support?

Read on, if you have the stomach for it. Rubin details exactly what she means when she defends child pornography.

Rubin is a strong advocate for child pornography, expressing shock that it's illegal to possess images depicting the sexual abuse and torture of children. She claims, "Although the Supreme Court has also ruled that it is a constitutional right to possess obscene material for private use, some child pornography laws prohibit even the private possession of any sexual material involving minors."[7]

Rubin says flatly, "The laws produced by the child porn panic are ill-conceived and misdirected. They represent far-reaching alterations in the regulation of sexual behaviour and abrogate important sexual civil liberties. But hardly anyone noticed as they swept through Congress and state legislatures. With the exception of the North American Man/Boy Love Association and American Civil Liberties Union, no one raised a peep of protest."[8]

Civil liberties? In no sane world does a pedophile have a human right to sexually abuse children. That, by the way, is the dedicated mission of the North American Man/Boy Love Association (NAMBLA) that Rubin mentions, an organization that lobbies for pederasty and pedophilia. According to the organization's own website, "NAMBLA's goal is to end the extreme oppression of men and boys in mutually consensual relationships by: building understanding and support for such relationships; educating the general public on the benevolent nature of man/boy love; cooperating with lesbian, gay, feminist, and other liberation movements; supporting the liberation of persons of all ages from sexual prejudice and oppression. Participation, only in the above context, is open to everyone sympathetic to man/boy love and personal freedom."[9]

As it turns out, Gayle Rubin advocates for the same. Rubin sympathizes with pedophiles: "It is harder for most people to sympathize with actual boy-lovers. Like communists and homosexuals in the 1950s, boylovers are so stigmatized that it is difficult to find defenders for their civil liberties, let alone for their erotic orientation."

"Consequently," Rubin says, "the police have feasted on them. Local police, the FBI, and watchdog postal inspectors have joined to build a huge apparatus whose sole aim is to wipe out the community of men who love underaged youth. In twenty years or so, when some of the smoke has cleared, it will be much easier to show that these men have been the victims of a savage and undeserved witch hunt. A lot of people will be embarrassed by their collaboration with this persecution, but it will be too late to do much good for those men who have spent their lives in prison."[10]

Men who love underage boys? Erotic orientation? Undeserved lives in prison?

Are you sick to your stomach?

I have never read anything more disgusting and disturbing in my life.

Rubin conveniently forgets the countless children who are sexually abused, assaulted, tortured, and murdered by the pedophiles she paints as victims. She ignores the *real* victims—the children—because to Rubin, sex is always political.

Children are taught the principles of Queer Theory in their public school classrooms, but like Critical Race Theory, these theories are not presented in an abstract academic manner. Instead, children are told that the principles of Queer Theory are *reality*.

Boys are taught they can be girls; girls are taught they can be boys.

The consequences of this are manifold. When children are told their identity is disassociated from their sexual essence, it brainwashes children into thinking they don't know who they are. This is incredibly destructive.

Children are born with an innate sense of identity based on sex. *I am a boy. I will grow up into a man. I will be a husband and a father. I will protect and provide for my family. I am a girl. I will grow into a woman. I will be a wife, a mother.* This is part of our essence as human beings. It's not something we choose. It's something we *are*.

When teachers instruct children to believe that their "gender identity" isn't correlated to their sex, but rather based entirely on whim or delusion, this deconstructs the paradigm on which children's entire worldview is built; it deconstructs their essence as human beings; it deconstructs who they *are*. This too is intentional. It is the deliberate creation of identity crises in our young people.

If I'm not a boy, then who am I? If I'm not a girl, then who am I?

Queer Theory emerged in our culture on the heels of Critical Race Theory, both aimed primarily at children in their formative years. This is not a coincidence.

Queer Theory contends that sex is political, without biological essence, and that gender is a sociopolitical construct. Therefore, if gender is a social construct, then gender is malleable. It naturally follows that political actors will indoctrinate children to construct sex and gender in a way that serves a political agenda. There's another, more accurate word for this type of insidious sexual indoctrination: grooming.

The conventional definition of grooming is conditioning a child for sexual abuse, or the process by which an adult conditions a child to accept sexual abuse. The conventional definition is why the left protests the usage of this word, as it applies to teachers indoctrinating children with Queer Theory. The left claims that groomer teachers are not pedophiles and do not personally sexually abuse children in their classroom. While that may be true, what they do is just as evil, as the founder of Queer Theory—which is taught in school—advocates for pedophiles, child pornography, and the sexualization of children.

Groomer teachers expose children to transgender ideology, often encouraging children to be transgender or "non-binary," which leads to "gender affirming" health care. "Gender affirming" health care for children entails mutilating a child's body, his or her sexuality and fertility. I want to make this point very clear: mutilating a child's body with "puberty blocking" pharmaceuticals or cross-sex hormones, committing irreversible surgical damage to children by removing healthy organs with medically unnecessary mastectomies and hysterectomies on girls and castration of boys, and intentionally destroying their sexuality and fully functional fertility—is abuse. It's sexual abuse. It's medical abuse of nightmarish proportions, and it is being promoted in our public school classrooms to our children.

Adults who expose children to this notion of gender identity—who praise it, encourage it, and facilitate it—are grooming vulnerable children to accept sexual abuse to their bodies.

Tragically, these grooming tactics are working.

A recent Gallup survey found that 20.8 percent of Generation Z self-identify as LGBTQ, compared to just 10.5 percent of Millennials, 4.2 percent of Generation X, 2.6 percent of Baby Boomers, and less than 1 percent of those who are older.[11]

Now, why is this?

Is it because our culture has grown more "tolerant," and now more people feel it's okay to acknowledge their "gender identity?"

It's hard to reconcile that proposition with the narrative coming from the same leftists claiming that the United States is a hostile and dangerous place to be a "queer-identifying" person. Which is it?

A more likely explanation would identify this sudden phenomenon of one in five Gen Z-ers identifying as "queer" as the direct result of *something*. That something is grooming, which manifests in several forms.

Journalist Abigail Shrier reports on the social-contagion effect of the transgender ideology, especially among young girls, where "pockets" of rapid-onset gender dysphoria crop up among social cliques.[12]

Transgender psychologist Erica Anderson blames the medical community. According to the *Los Angeles Times*, Anderson believes that "some clinicians are failing to subject minors to rigorous mental health evaluations before recommending hormones or surgeries" and blames social media for the "popularity of alternative identities."[13]

Social contagion, peer pressure, social media influencers, and a corrupt medical industry looking to make dollars off "gender-affirming care" all play a role in grooming children into delusional gender identities. But those are downstream effects of the indoctrination children face in public school where they are taught that the tenets of Queer Theory are *reality*, that the so-called victims of "cis-hetero-patriarchal oppression" must be liberated and celebrated, and that the biology of sex and Christian sexual morality are oppressive structures that must be overthrown.

The percentage of Generation Z who identify as LGBTQIA+ defies incremental cultural evolution anyway. The dramatic increase in the number of young people who are identifying as LGBTQ—particularly as "transgender" and "non-binary"—is a direct result of classroom grooming.

The Montgomery County Public School District is the largest in Maryland. In 2022 the school district accidentally reported a 582 percent increase in the number of students who identified as "gender nonconforming."[14] I say "accidentally reported" because this number was never intended to be seen by parents or taxpayers. The number had been shared with a gay club called the "Pride ALLiance," but an overly enthusiastic teacher named Elicia Eberhart-Bliss tweeted photos from the event including the screen of a PowerPoint slide showing the exploding number of students identifying as "gender nonconforming" since 2019.[15]

How did the school know which students identify as "gender nonconforming"?

According to Chrissy Clark at the Daily Caller, Montgomery County Public Schools "gathered this data from forms school counselors fill out when students approach them to talk about gender identity issues."[16]

The documents show that school staff aren't taking a neutral position on "gender identity" when talking to students either.

According to the Montgomery County Public Schools Guidelines for Student Gender Identity, "All students have a right to privacy. This includes the right to keep private one's transgender status or gender nonconforming presentation at school."[17] In addition, "Transgender and gender nonconforming students have the right to discuss and demonstrate their gender identity and expression openly and decide when, with whom, and how much to share private information. The fact that students choose to disclose their status to staff members or other students does not authorize school staff members to disclose students' status to others, including parents/guardians and other school staff members."[18]

Additionally, the district instructs teachers and staff to reject the "gender binary" and "affirm" gender-fluid, nonconforming, and non-binary "self-identifications." The school district propagates Queer Theory phrases like "sex assigned at birth" and requires the use of "preferred" pronouns. The district mandates that males who identify as female be allowed in women's locker rooms and bathrooms and be allowed to play on women's sports teams. The official policy of the Montgomery County Public School District provides the following directive for teachers and staff: "Complaints alleging discrimination or harassment directed at a student based on a student's actual or perceived gender identity or expression should be handled in the same manner as other discrimination or harassment complaints."[19] So, would female students who express discomfort sharing a bathroom with a male who identifies as a female be punished by staff for discrimination and harassment?

In economics there is a saying that if you subsidize something, you'll get more of it. The Montgomery County Public School District is subsidizing, supporting, and enforcing the spread of Queer Theory to its students. Is it any wonder the school district accidentally reported a 582 percent increase in children identifying as gender nonconforming?[20]

In short, grooming by authority figures in public schools across the country is incredibly effective.

Its extraordinary efficacy is why the left pretends that classroom instruction about sexual orientation and gender identity doesn't happen in school, because they don't want you to know; they just want to force you to live with the results, levy zero complaints, and content yourself with a Bud Light plastered with the image of Dylan Mulvaney while ignoring your child's sexual journey into madness.

It's not just the innumerable instances of blue-haired teachers on TikTok claiming they are gender-queer witches or bragging about teaching kindergarteners how to be gender-fluid, or the kindergarten teacher on MSNBC admitting he shares pictures of his gay lover in his classroom to elicit questions from children about his sexual preferences.[21] Unfortunately, Queer Theory has also infiltrated our legal system.

Some states actually mandate classroom instruction about gender identity and sexual orientation. The Maryland State Department of Education, for instance, instructs teachers to teach kindergarteners about gender identity so that children "recognize a range of ways people identify and express their gender."[22] This mass indoctrination is institutional. For instance, the LGBTQ+ Caucus of the National Education Association, the nation's largest teacher's union, promoted a badge teachers can wear that features a QR code for students to scan that populates a website on the child's smartphone showing kids how to engage in queer sex.[23]

What's happening to our children is horrendous and disturbing, but as Dr. James Lindsay points out, the destruction of childhood innocence is a central part of the Marxist strategy to subvert the family.

Lindsay writes, "The [neo-Marxist] belief is that the innocence we encourage in children is part of the systems of power (specifically generated through performativity) that enforce heteronormativity and cisnormativity and thus lead to dysphoria or oppression of gay and potentially trans kids."[24]

What does this mean? According to Queer Theory, LGBTQ people are reduced to permanently marginalized status regardless of whether they enjoy equal rights under the law because the "bourgeois" nuclear family—which according to Marxist theory is a product of capitalism—protects the innocence of children as a way of conserving the power of the ruling class.

According to Queer Theory, the only way to rectify this alleged power imbalance would be to destroy the systems of power, namely, capitalism and the nuclear family, which ostensibly enforce said marginalization.

To accomplish this, Marxists believe that children must be alienated from their parents and from the cultural norms of bourgeois society. Childhood innocence must be destroyed. Children must be reduced to "marginalized" neo-Marxist queer identities who are then permanently turned against their parents and secured as Marxist revolutionaries who want to overthrow the "oppression" of Western civilization.

Proponents of Queer Theory like Professor Hannah Dyer, an associate professor of Child and Youth Studies at Brock University in Canada, openly advocate for the sexualization of children. Dyer rejects the "gender binary" and urges children to experiment sexually. In one of her more recent academic papers, Dyer argued, "Applying queer methods of analysis to studies of childhood can help to queer the rhetoric of innocence that constrains all children and help to refuse attempts to calculate the child's future before it has the opportunity to explore desire."[25]

The goal of Queer Theory also hinges on a precarious reality. If equality under the law is achieved for LGBTQ individuals, then those individuals will not feel marginalized—angry, vulnerable, fearful, or desperate enough to be exploited for political purposes. LGBTQ individuals, if they are relatively satisfied with their social status, would be unlikely to wage war against the cultural institutions the Marxists seek to destroy. Yet, Queer Theorists are seeking to *weaponize* queer people as a "marginalized" vanguard to wage a Marxist revolution against their "oppressors." Committed Queer Theorists can't want equality for LGBTQ people. Queer Theorists *need* LGBTQ people to feel permanently oppressed.

Because to them, sex is a political weapon.

This is not a new tactic. Grooming children in order to alienate them from their parents and their family values has long been a hallmark of Marxist strategy. Hungarian Marxist György Lukács, for instance, used the "queering" of children to alienate them from their families.

In his book *Georg Lukács' Marxism: Alienation, Dialectics, Revolution; A Study in Utopia and Ideology,* Professor Victor Zitta noted that while Lukács administered educational affairs for the short-lived Hungarian Soviet Republic in 1919, he imposed a perverse sexual education program. Zitta noted, "Special lectures were organised in schools and literature printed and distributed to 'instruct' children about free love, about the nature of sexual intercourse, about the archaic nature of the bourgeois family codes, about the outdatedness of monogamy, and the irrelevance of religion, which deprives man of all pleasure. Children, urged thus to reject and deride paternal authority and the authority of the Church, and to ignore precepts of morality, easily and spontaneously turned into delinquents with whom only the police could cope."[26]

Does that sound like educational curricula designed to foster equality under the law for LGBTQ identifying people? Obviously not. Likewise, children in the United States today are indoctrinated with the principles of Queer Theory not to advance equality or tolerance, but rather to groom them into accepting a "marginalized" neo-Marxist identity.

You might say that Critical Race Theory and Queer Theory pack a one-two punch.

Critical Race Theory tells children they are bad based on their race. According to CRT, white children are racist because they are white, notwithstanding their thoughts, feelings, beliefs, or actions. CRT posits that white children benefit from "white privilege" and the "institutions of white supremacy," and there is no way for children to redeem themselves and their identity from such "systems of racism." CRT tells white children they are irredeemably evil; and from whom did they inherent this evil identity? From their parents. Therefore, their parents made them bad.

Imagine the self-loathing children must feel after Critical Race Theory imposes this evil, irredeemable identity on their innocent, impressionable minds and bodies. Imagine the loathing children must feel towards their *parents*.

This is an assault on children's identity as human beings.

Queer Theory offers an antidote. Thanks to Queer Theory, even "racist" white children can pick a *different* identity, a *marginalized* identity that supersedes their "whiteness" and allows them to reject their parents who made them "evil." Instead, children can turn themselves into fashionable, accepted victims by choosing a "queer" identity. According to Queer Theory, you can molt your parents' bad legacy of oppression and transform yourself into the oppressed. According to Queer Theory, your sexual and gender identity is without essence, therefore you can be whatever you feel. According to Queer Theory, you can define yourself by embracing a non-binary or transgender identity. In the process, these children are alienated from their parents and trained to think of themselves as "the oppressed" and then insulated by leftists who praise, accept, and reward neo-Marxist identity. Thus these children are secured as leftist, Marxist revolutionaries.

Critical Race Theory without Queer Theory wouldn't do the trick. Queer Theory without Critical Race Theory would sow chaos but fall short of outright revolution. Together, however, they are nearly impregnable. CRT lands the first blow to children's identities, and Queer Theory picks up their pieces, offering confused children a new identity, as Marxists . . . even if it means mutilating their own bodies and destroying the country in which they have been raised.

What we're seeing is Maoism all over again, a cultural revolution much like that instigated in China by Communist dictator Mao Zedong. Dr. James Lindsay noted on my podcast, *The Liz Wheeler Show*, "that what Mao did to create his Revolutionary Guard, out of mostly kids and students, was that he created ten different identity categories: five of them he made bad and five of them he made good. The 'bad' ones were the black identities for fascism, and the 'good' ones were the red identities for Communism. The black identities . . . were rich farmer, landlord, counter-revolutionary, bad influence . . . and then right-winger. . . . The five red categories were, for the hammer you have the laborers, for the sickle you have the peasants, and then you have revolutionaries, revolutionary cadre members, and revolutionary martyrs."[27]

Lindsay notes how Mao used good-versus-bad identities to secure young people as Communist revolutionaries in Red China:

> What Mao did was, if you, say as an adult or a parent, had one of the black identities, then your children by proxy got a black identity too. If you had a red one, so did your

children, probably, depending on how they behaved. If you as a child were labeled the black identity, they treated you worse. They treated you differently. They gave special stuff to the red-identity students as they created a pressure to move out of the black identities into the red identities. You might maybe denounce your parents; you might rat your parents out. You might go engage in revolutionary activism. You might go desecrate a temple. You might go destroy a statue or something like this, and then you can be in the revolutionary category within the red identities. So he made bad-identity categories, treated kids badly if they were in the bad-identity categories, and then created a set of solutions to adapt to that pressure, that struggle session–style pressure, by giving people an out, which was, "Become a revolutionary for our cause" (or I guess a peasant or a laborer—but not as a child) "and then you can be free of this stigma that we've attached to you and your identity."[28]

Does this sound familiar?

This is what we're watching play out in the United States. Instead of "black" and "red" Maoist identities, modern American Marxists demonize straight, white Christian identities and elevate LGBTQIA+ and BIPOC (black, indigenous, people of color) identities as desirable. They embed a structure in our school systems that rewards the "red" LGBTQIA+ and BIPOC identities and punishes the "black" straight, white Christian identities. In government, academia, and corporate America, this reward/punishment system includes diversity, equity, and inclusion (DEI) initiatives. It also includes environmental, social, and corporate governance (ESG) initiatives, which we'll discuss in the next chapter.

Candace Owens reported in her documentary *The Greatest Lie Ever Sold* that Black Lives Matter—an organization built on the principles of Critical Race Theory, and whose founders admit to being "trained Marxists"[29]—transferred money donated to BLM to multiple transgender/gender identity/LGBTQ+ groups.[30] That's no coincidence. Critical Race Theory needs Queer Theory to achieve the ultimate agenda of the modern Marxists: radical alienation of children from their parents, the subversion of the family, the denial of objective reality, the imposition of an authoritarian arbiter of "truth," and the mental, spiritual, bodily, and ideological transformation of an entire generation of young children into fervent Marxist revolutionaries.

This leaves one question hanging over this chapter. Who are the Marxists waging sustained assault on our children?

Behind the Critical Race Theorists and Queer Theorists lie even more powerful entities. They are the ones who want to transform the world. We'll turn to them next.

CHAPTER 5

What the Marxists Want

K laus Schwab is the founder and executive chairman of the World Economic Forum—and he's a creep.

Schwab is a balding, dour-looking octogenarian, though he could pass for fifteen years younger than he is. He speaks in heavily accented English and rarely betrays emotion on his mostly expressionless face. Schwab's idea of casual attire is a shiny, chin-high tunic fit for a Bond villain.

More important, Klaus Schwab's ideology is imperialist and evil. He has a plan for the world called "the Great Reset," which is an umbrella term to describe his vast plot to transform the Western world into a neo-Marxist hellhole. Schwab plans to "reset" global capitalism and replace it with something like the Chinese Communist Party state-managed economic model, but on a global scale. Schwab's goal is to take away control of the world's economy from people and countries and put a global bureaucratic elite in charge instead.[1]

Schwab is not particularly forthcoming about his formative years, nor about his family. Perhaps it's no wonder. In the 1930s, Schwab's father, Eugen Wilhelm Schwab moved the family out of Switzerland into Germany's Third Reich (where Klaus was subsequently born). Eugen became director of Escher Wyss AG. The company, falsely billed as a neutral Swiss engineering company, was actually an integral part of the Nazi war effort during World War II, supplying flamethrowers, turbines, and research, including related to the development of atomic weapons. Escher Wyss AG reportedly used prisoners of war from nearby Nazi camps as slave laborers.[2]

Was Klaus Schwab's father a Nazi? Eugen Wilhelm Klaus was a member of National Socialist organizations.[3] The elder Schwab was certainly complicit in the Nazi war effort, but was acquitted in post-war denazification investigations of having any close association with Hitler or any prominence within the National Socialist Party.[4]

It is interesting, however, that Klaus Schwab keeps a bust of Vladimir Lenin displayed prominently behind his office desk.[5]

One wonders why the news outlets that fawn over him and the billionaires, celebrities, and multinational corporate executives who jet into Schwab's annual World Economic Forum (WEF) gathering in Davos every winter are apparently incurious about Klaus Schwab's background and whether his ideology was informed by his father's work for the Nazi regime or by the Bolshevik Revolution led by Vladimir Lenin? Isn't this something we should know before Schwab's Great Reset takes control of our businesses, economies, and lives?

This seems important, particularly given Schwab's affinity for the Chinese Communist Party's style of enforcing communism on the Chinese people.

Let's establish an important point first.

What *is* the Great Reset?

To be sure, the Great Reset doesn't advertise itself as socialism, Marxism, communism, or fascism. To do so would result in a public relations nightmare.

Instead, Schwab calls his agenda "stakeholder capitalism," but that's misleading. Schwab's version of "capitalism" is a very different one from a traditional free market economy.[6] This should come as no surprise. Marxists intentionally redefine words to suit their political needs, and Schwab's redefinition of capitalism is no different.

In fact, Schwab specifically targets free market capitalism as the first stage of global transformation. Schwab writes, "Every country, from the United States to China, must participate, and every industry, from oil and gas to tech, must be transformed. In short, we need a 'Great Reset' of capitalism." Moreover, Schwab says that "the world must act jointly and swiftly to revamp all aspects of our societies and economies, from education to social contracts and working conditions."[7]

How does Schwab plan to execute this ideological reconfiguration of the world? According to Schwab, his Great Reset agenda would first steer the market towards "fairer outcomes." To this end, Schwab wants governments to improve coordination in tax, regulatory, and fiscal policy to "create the conditions for a 'stakeholder economy.'" Moreover, Schwab says, "governments should implement long-overdue reforms that promote more equitable outcomes." These reforms "include changes to wealth taxes, the withdrawal of fossil-fuel subsidies, and new rules governing intellectual property, trade, and competition."[8]

The second component of Schwab's plan controls investments based upon adherence to environmental, social, and governance (ESG) scoring systems.

The third component harnesses recent technological innovations to "support the public good," curiously coincidental with the COVID-19 "crisis,"[9] the threat of which Schwab and his peers at the very least greatly exaggerated and exploited to serve their political agenda.

When Schwab says the world needs a Great Reset of capitalism, he really means it—though such a reset would also entail massive social reengineering.

The only resemblance between Schwab's "stakeholder capitalism" and free market capitalism is, under Schwab's vision for the world, government doesn't directly own the means of production and distribution. But that is where any resemblance ends between Schwab's "stakeholder capitalism" and American free market capitalism. In the American free market economy—also known as shareholder capitalism—businesses pursue profit for the benefit of their investors, or shareholders. A profitable business benefits its customers, employees, and shareholders. Every interaction in a free market economy is a contract of mutual benefit; one entity brings goods and services to the marketplace for sale, and another entity purchases those goods and services, which results in a mutually beneficial transaction. Only when free markets are perverted by unjust government regulations, monopolies, or criminal behavior and fraud does the market become a shark tank where the brutal eat while the weak are eaten.

The *free* exchange of goods and services, to the mutual benefit of both seller and buyer, incentivizes high-quality products and services, increases competition, and thus supply, and results in fair pricing, created value, and prosperity.

That is shareholder capitalism.

Klaus Schwab wants to get rid of it.

Instead, Schwab wants a world economy controlled by a global elite that requires businesses to make decisions based on the interests of "stakeholders" versus the interests of the business itself and its shareholders.

What are stakeholders?

Stakeholders is an ambiguous word, as Schwab and his globalist cabal almost certainly intended it to be. Stakeholders can mean anything

Schwab wants it to mean—not only the workers and customers of a business but the impact of the "environment" and "sustainability" on the globe, the "community" at large, social causes like "diversity, equity, and inclusion," and political activism, perhaps subsidizing the abortion lobby or anything else the left wants.

In short, stakeholder capitalism is another way to say, "an economy controlled by the global elite" where the elite will both profit financially and use the economy to force their far-left political ideology on the world. The global elite will define who the "stakeholders" are (and change that at will), and businesses will be forced to consider the political causes of "stakeholders" in their operations. Therefore, the world's economy itself becomes a tool of political control for the global elite. Elitist control is at the heart of Klaus Schwab's Great Reset.

Stakeholder capitalism, according to Schwab, is not direct government ownership of the means of production and distribution, as socialism is. Likewise, stakeholder capitalism doesn't seek collective ownership of industry, as communism does. Rather, stakeholder capitalism is a tool for the global elite to seize control of economic institutions.[10]

This is where Schwab's "stakeholder capitalism" most resembles Communist China's economy. Technically, businesses are privately owned in Communist China, but the Chinese Communist Party is the ultimate stakeholder lurking behind all companies and exerting control at will. Remember Jack Ma? Formerly the richest man in China and the owner of Alibaba, a recognizable figure the world over.[11] Following Ma's criticism of a decision made by the Chinese Communist Party (CCP), he disappeared,[12] except for a handful of reports that claim sightings of Ma enjoying his "now-private life."[13]

While the Chinese Communist Party might not technically own the means of production and distribution in China's marketplace, no Chinese business owner can afford to deviate from the political agenda of the CCP, which *controls* the economy to serve its political agenda.

Aside from the brute force available to any totalitarian regime, the Chinese Communist Party relies on a "social credit score" system that rates Chinese citizens and businesses based on their behavior and adherence to "Chinese morals" as dictated by the CCP.[14]

If a Chinese citizen criticizes the Chinese Communist Party or posts negative comments about the Chinese government on social media, that person will be downgraded according to the CCP's social credit scoring system.

The penalties for "bad" behavior range from prohibitions on buying airline tickets, purchasing a house, sending your children to a private school, securing a loan, or working certain jobs to having a slow internet connection or being denied a right to travel outside the country.[15]

If you jaywalk across the street, your social credit score is downgraded. (If a child under the age of fourteen jaywalks, his or her guardian is required to undergo reeducation courses to prevent a permanent bad mark on the child's social credit score.)

The Chinese Communist Party uses the social credit score system for everything from cleaning up after your dog to cheating at an online video game (yes, they keep tabs), punishing what the Party disapproves of and rewarding what it considers good behavior.[16]

If adult children don't regularly visit their elderly parents, they will face penalties on their social credit score.[17] If you eat on the public transit system, or play music too loudly, you will receive bad marks on your social credit score.[18] If dog owners neglect to leash their dogs in public areas, they face social credit score penalties.[19] If you make a reservation at a restaurant and don't show up, or don't pay your cell phone bill on time, your social credit score is docked.[20]

Conversely, if you donate blood, you earn social credit on the scoring system.[21]

The rewards on the social credit score system include discounts on energy bills, tax breaks, lower interest rates at banks, free admission to gyms, and priority status as hospitals (yes, in government-controlled health care, they play political favorites).[22]

To conceptualize the breadth of control the Chinese Communist Party leverages against Chinese citizens using the social credit score system, which began national trials in 2014, the National Development and Reform Commission of China reported that up to June 2019, the Chinese Communist Party had denied 26.82 million airline tickets to people who were deemed "untrustworthy" because of their social credit score.[23]

Given how leftists behaved during the COVID-19 pandemic, you can see how they would love a social credit system in the United States. It would be just another way to control you so you don't dissent from the left's neo-Marxist ideology.

It's also interesting that in China just over 10 percent of the enforcement actions related to the social credit score system are levied against individuals. The vast majority of these actions, nearly 75 percent, were aimed at businesses between 2014 and 2020.[24]

Under the Chinese Communist Party corporate social credit score system, a business with a good social credit score is rewarded with lower tax rates and more investment opportunities. Businesses with bad social credit scores are penalized with higher tax rates and unfavorable conditions for obtaining new loans and are not allowed to work on government-funded projects.[25]

The purpose of the corporate social credit score system in Communist China is to force businesses to adhere to Communist ideology by threatening their ability to exist in the marketplace, primarily by controlling capital. Rather than outright ownership of property, the Chinese

Communist Party uses control as their lever, controlling the economy (and the people by extension via the marketplace).

The corporate social credit score system of the Chinese Communist Party is the prototype for Klaus Schwab's ESG (environmental, social, and governance) scores, which Schwab has universalized to score businesses on how well they participate in "stakeholder" capitalism.

ESG scores are the central enforcement mechanism of the Great Reset, similar to the Chinese social credit score system. However, in the United States, ESG scores aren't arbitrated by public authorities—though regulatory authorities have been increasingly active in helping push ESG along without getting directly involved. Instead, it is globalist international organizations, central banks, private financial behemoths, insurance conglomerates, and asset management titans that control which companies (or entire industries) are deemed worthy of receiving loans, investment, or insurance policies.[26]

Heartland Institute research fellow Jack McPherrin recently published a comprehensive policy paper that provides a sweeping overview of ESG, including proposing specific policy solutions to halt ESG in its tracks.[27]

Though ESG has many complex elements, the way it operates and mechanizes the elites' control over society is relatively simple. Similar to China's model, ESG is a social credit scoring system for businesses and soon, individuals. ESG metrics are now the primary evaluator determining whether entities—which can include businesses, sovereign countries, states, and even individuals—are deemed worthy of participation in the market via investment, loans, insurance policies, or basic access to financial services. Even if a company is immensely profitable, satisfies consumer demand, and provides value to customers through the quality of its goods and services (which is the whole point of a business), it could be frozen out of the woke financial system if it does not commit to the Marxist goals surrounding "climate change" mitigation and "social justice"—which are measured by ESG metrics.[28]

The ESG framework developed by the World Economic Forum—a framework the WEF hopes to become a universal ESG score evaluator in the coming years—is one of the most widely used. The WEF's system includes a total of fifty-five metrics organized around the pillars of "governance," "planet," "people," and "prosperity," nearly all of which are geared towards achieving Marxist goals. Some examples of these metrics include: "Impact of GHG (greenhouse gas) emissions;" "Social value generated;" "Economic, environmental, and social topics in capital allocation framework;" "Diversity and inclusion;" and "Governance body composition."[29]

But what *is* "Governance body composition?" According to the WEF, this metric measures "Composition of the highest governance body and its committees by: competencies relating to economic, environmental and social topics; executive or non-executive; independence; tenure on the governance body; number of each individual's other significant positions and commitments, and the nature of the commitments; gender; membership of under-represented social groups; stakeholder representation."[30] Clearly, that's discriminatory against people unfavored by the ESG administrators.

As McPherrin correctly states, "For instance, if certain corporate boardrooms consist of qualified and capable individuals who have been subjectively determined to belong to an 'undesirable' social group, the company could be downgraded in its ESG score because of its 'non-diverse' composition based on skin color, gender, or a yet-to-be-determined new factor. This reduces the person to an input unit in a technocratic fascist nightmare without any regard to thought, action, character, integrity, or any other traditionally valued traits of an individual in a functioning society."[31]

The same goes for regular company employees, by the way. If a company's "chief diversity officer" determines there are "too many" Asians and "not enough" Hispanics on the payroll, you can bet there will be significant personnel changes made in order to avoid a "hit" to the company's ESG score. Beyond the economic problems ESG creates (which are significant),[32] it completely eviscerates the idea of merit-based individual advancement in business and in society, undermining individualism in favor of a collectivist neo-Marxist model in which elites subjectively engineer society according to their whims.

Furthermore, the WEF's "Economic, environmental and social topics in capital allocation framework" metric is equally concerning. According to the WEF, this measures how "the highest governance body considers economic, environmental and social issues when overseeing major capital allocation decisions, such as expenditures, acquisitions and divestments."[33] So, basically, a company is judged upon whether it donated or supported certain "desirable" organizations as subjectively determined by our elitist overlords. If a company donates to Black Lives Matter or Planned Parenthood, it gets an ESG score bump. If not, or if a company donates to a religious charity, that ESG score theoretically suffers.

The bottom line is that most ESG metrics coerce businesses and individuals into complying with the neo-Marxist political agenda. Ultimately, if Klaus Schwab and his peers get their way, ESG scoring will lead to global elites picking and choosing who can participate in the marketplace, based on their fealty to far-left, Marxist political agendas.

Some states, led by West Virginia, at the behest of their state treasurer Riley Moore, are pushing back.[34] Any banking institution investing on behalf of a state is investing with taxpayer money; and some state legislatures are working to ensure that such taxpayer money is invested solely on its likely return on investment, not on ESG political goals. Moore took the lead, sending letters to half a dozen banking institutions under contract with the state of West Virginia, and terminated the state's contracts with five of them that would not guarantee their fiduciary duty to the state and its taxpayers.[35]

Every red state should follow Moore's lead, banning from state contracts companies that use ESG metrics. The danger of ESG is real to taxpayers, companies, banks, and consumers.

America's sixteenth-largest bank, Silicon Valley Bank (SVB), failed largely due to woke ESG policies (in addition to poor—or nonexistent—risk management practices, plus the federal government's COVID-19 Paycheck Protection Program loans that exacerbated SVB's poor banking practices). SVB committed more than $70 million to organizations related to the Black Lives Matter movement, while SVB had no head of risk management from April 2022 to January 2023.[36] SVB's 2022 ESG report lists such "woke" initiatives as $5 billion in "sustainable finance and carbon neutral operations to support a healthier planet" and, of course, a "diversity, equity, and inclusion" agenda.[37]

Conservatives like to chant the mantra "Go woke, go broke," and SVB's collapse is a spectacular example. It was the second-biggest bank failure in American history.[38]

Tragically, the American people will pay for these catastrophic ESG policies that led to the collapse of SVB. The FDIC, which has promised to bail out depositors at Silicon Valley Bank, is a government-backed trust composed of the largest banking institutions in the United States. These big banks will be on the hook for the billions of dollars SVB lost, and assuredly those big banks won't want to spend their own money bailing out another bank. They will pass on that cost to you, the consumer, in the form of increased administrative fees for bank account maintenance, credit cards, checks, and so on.

Still more tragically, the collapse of Silicon Valley Bank has put other regional banks in a tenuous position, and consumers will respond to this uncertainty by switching to the bigger banking institutions to keep their money safe, the same big banking institutions that, incidentally, have fully bought into ESG scores.

ESG is not a futuristic pipe dream of Klaus Schwab. ESG is already here. According to the World Economic Forum, "Since January 2021, over 160 companies have shown their support for Stakeholder Capitalism Metrics. Firms that have adopted this approach include Accenture, Bank of America, Cargolux, DP World, Eni, Fidelity International, Fubon Financial Holding, HSBC Holdings, IBM, Mastercard, Nestlé, PayPal, Royal DSM, Salesforce, Schneider Electric, Siemens, Total, UBS, Unilever, Yara International and Zurich Insurance Group, among others."[39]

ESG ratings are often the reason why woke corporations make insane business decisions. When Disney inserts a "queerness agenda" into its children's programming,[40] when Target sells "chest binders" to young women wanting to disguise their breasts and pretend they have male bodies,[41] they are not doing it because of customer demand and they are not doing it solely because they have gone "woke." They are doing it because the financial system—the big banks like Bank of America and investment firms like BlackRock—rewards them for going woke, even when customers don't. They are going woke in pursuit of ESG scores.

After the Supreme Court overturned *Roe v. Wade* and allowed states to set their own laws regarding abortion, many large corporations announced they would pay for their employees to travel to obtain abortions. These corporations included Bank of America, Citigroup, Comcast, CVS, Dick's Sporting Goods, Goldman Sachs, Hewlett Packard, JPMorgan Chase, Kroger, Lyft, Mastercard, Meta, PayPal, Procter & Gamble, Salesforce, Starbucks, Tesla, Uber, Walt Disney, Yelp, and Zillow—all of which, coincidentally, have web pages dedicated to their ESG scores and plans for increasing those scores.[42]

Additionally, Bumble, Condé Nast, Estée Lauder, IKEA, and Microsoft have pages dedicated to "sustainability," "climate change," and "diversity, equity, and inclusion," which are elements of ESG.[43]

In the United States, ESG has spread like wildfire. McPherrin, after analyzing a recently published ESG report developed by KPMG, shares that "a survey conducted by KPMG in 2020—which sampled the top 100 companies by revenue in 52 countries—found that 98 percent of American companies disclosed ESG scores, with 82 percent including sustainability-related information in their annual reports. As one KPMG partner involved in the survey remarked, 'Investors and regulators are increasingly demanding information on the non-financial performance of all investments. . . . For companies, the stakes are real. ESG reporting can impact access to capital and the ability to attract new investors.'"[44]

The European Union is equally, if not more, committed to institutionalizing ESG in its regulatory framework. In fact, it has recently proposed two new stringent ESG laws that would have far-reaching impacts outside of the European Union, including on U.S. companies. One of the laws has already passed, and the other will pass in short order. McPherrin notes that "if fully implemented, [these two laws will] have dramatic effects on the global economy and the United States. Any American company that is deemed to be insufficiently committed to diversity in corporate boardrooms or mitigating climate change, would be either sanctioned or frozen out of the value chain. As of now, there is no way to stop this."[45]

Klaus Schwab isn't the only powerful person preaching ESG. On stage at the Clinton Global Initiative annual meeting in September 2022, former president Bill Clinton moderated a panel on ESG that included the CEO of Unilever, the CEO of Blackrock, and an ESG specialist from the United Nations. Clinton's position was clear: ESG must be made universal.[46]

This is the consensus of the international elite, and few push the full institutionalization of ESG and stakeholder capitalism across the globe harder than Klaus Schwab, who has both called for a global transformation of capitalism using ESG and created a universal ESG system to control the global economy.[47]

ESG is already here. While it's not mandatory in the United States (yet), the vast majority of big businesses have "voluntarily" opted in. It's now nearly impossible to walk into your workplace, a university campus, the emergency room, or even onto an airplane without facing the *S* in ESG: diversity, equity and inclusion.

Despite what the words imply, "diversity, equity and inclusion" do not represent equality under the law or tolerance of different viewpoints, such as religious beliefs or lifestyle choices. Instead, each word has been twisted and rendered unrecognizable from its true meaning. Diversity now means racism (against white people). Equity means equal outcome (which is discrimination). Inclusion means religious persecution (of Christians).

The "diversity" promoted by DEI amounts to racial tokenism and worse, which is why a black man was fired from a "Belonging, Equity, and Inclusion committee" after he said the equity committee was "a fraud and an affront to the families of this city."[48] If an individual with the subjectively desired immutable characteristic dissents from the prevailing leftist ideology—if he doesn't think the way the left decides a black person should think—he is rejected. That is racism.

In the name of "health equity," white people in the Midwest faced racial discrimination during the COVID-19 pandemic because a health care group rationed monoclonal antibodies based on a "risk scoring calculator" that weighted race more heavily than age, weight, or preexisting conditions.[49] Equity, according to DEI, is "equal outcome" that effectively requires discrimination, often based on inherent characteristics like race or sex. At its core, equity is authoritarianism. To enforce an equal outcome, someone must pick winners and losers. The arbiters of outcome are de facto authoritarians.

As Erick Erickson so aptly wrote about the left's twisted definition of inclusion, "You will be made to care,"[50] just as Jack Phillips, the cake baker, was targeted by law enforcement for declining to design a custom cake for a "gay wedding," and women's concerns are ignored when "transgender" persons are allowed into their bathrooms and locker rooms and "transgender" athletes are allowed to compete in women's sports. "Inclusion" entails punishing religious people who dissent from neo-Marxist ideology.

The DEI structure is a funnel for Marxist indoctrination. As Dr. James Lindsay notes, DEI training and the "struggle sessions" that Mao Zedong imposed on the Chinese people—which were basically "thought reform" workshops to reeducate citizens who dissented from the Communist narrative—are the same thing.[51]

ESG embeds DEI in our institutions, because DEI *is* the *S* in environmental, social, and governance metrics.

This is why public outcry against DEI in our schools, workplaces, and corporations falls on deaf ears. Most of these institutions aren't serving their shareholders or consumers anymore. They are serving their own ESG score.

Environmental, social, and governance scores are a mechanism to enforce twenty-first-century Marxism. "Stakeholder capitalism" is not capitalism at all. It's a tool wielded by the elite to use the economy to control people and therefore politics, to coerce individuals and businesses to radically transform the world around us into a Marxist society.

Klaus and his global elite are using corporations trapped in the ESG system to capture our children.

One corporation is guiltier than almost any other.

CHAPTER 6

The Biggest Corporate Groomer of All

Margaret Sanger, founder of Planned Parenthood, was a racist and a eugenicist. Sanger founded Planned Parenthood originally as the American Birth Control League, and her goal was forcing contraception on people she didn't *want* to reproduce, people Sanger considered less worthy because of their social class, education level, mental acuity, or the color of their skin.[1] Sanger even proposed the idea of a federal "bureau of application for the unborn," which would require married couples to obtain government approval if they wanted a baby. Under Sanger's proposal, government bureaucrats would have been able to bar a married couple from procreation.[2]

Sanger inherited her eugenicist ideology from her father, Michael Higgins, who was obsessed with a practice called phrenology. The quack science of phrenology purported to study the shape of people's heads and facial features to determine their innate character.[3] Needless to say, phrenology has since been rejected by academia for failing to replicate its "findings."

But Margaret Sanger liked it. Sanger wrote of her father, "Father believed implicitly that the head was the sculptured expression of the soul. Straight or slanting eyes, a ridge between them, a turned-up nose, full lips, bulges in front of or behind the ears—all these traits had definite meaning for him. A research worker had to be inquisitive, a seeker with more than normal curiosity-bumps; a musician had to have order and time over the eyebrows; a pugilist [boxer] could not be made but had to have the proper protuberances around the ears."[4]

Sanger was heavily influenced by her father's pseudoscience; she wrote, "I could not help picking up his principles and some of his ardor, though I have never been able to analyze character so well."[5]

Sanger's transition from phrenology to eugenics happened next.

In 1922 Sanger wrote, "Eugenics seems to me to be valuable in its critical and diagnostic aspects, in emphasizing the danger of irresponsible and uncontrolled fertility of the 'unfit' and the feeble-minded establishing a progressive unbalance in human society and lowering the birth-rate among the 'fit.'"[6]

In a piece published by the *New York Times* in 1923, Sanger equated eugenics to birth control. Sanger wrote, "Birth control is not contraception indiscriminately and thoughtlessly practiced. It means the release and cultivation of the better racial elements in our society, and the gradual suppression, elimination, and eventual extirpation of defective stocks—those human weeds which threaten the blooming of the finest flowers of American civilization."[7]

When Sanger later wrote about how she coined the term "birth control," she admitted her racist agenda. "We tried population control, *race control*, and birth rate control," she said. "Then someone suggested 'Drop the rate.' Birth control was the answer; we knew we had it" [emphasis mine].[8]

And thus, the American Birth Control League was born.

Sanger founded the American Birth Control League with rabid racists, anti-Semites, and eugenicists, including Georges Vacher de Lapouge, a French eugenicist, atheist, and socialist whose Aryan supremacy ideology was later embraced by the Nazis; Johann Ferch, an anti-Semite birth control advocate from Austria; socialist Heywood Broun; and Clarence C. Little, president of the American Eugenics Society. Little would become the first president of the American Birth Control League.[9]

Margaret Sanger's racist, eugenicist ideology remains in practice by Planned Parenthood today. More than 350,000 unborn babies are killed by abortions every year at Planned Parenthood,[10] while Sanger's eugenics remain on full display—Planned Parenthood places 79 percent of its surgical abortion clinics within walking distance of black or Hispanic neighborhoods, thereby facilitating Sanger's "race control."[11] Moreover, Planned Parenthood even accepts donations specifically earmarked for the abortion of black babies.[12] About 94 percent of Planned Parenthood's services to pregnant women involve abortion.[13]

Planned Parenthood reaps billions of dollars from its abortion business. According to its 2020–2021 annual report, Planned Parenthood's affiliates held $2.1 billion in assets. Planned Parenthood and its affiliates received $633.4 million in government funding, and total revenue for the fiscal year came in at $1.7 billion.[14]

The other major part of Planned Parenthood's business also butchers human bodies for financial and ideological profit. Planned Parenthood is one of the largest distributors of transgender hormone therapy to young people.[15] Why would Planned Parenthood do this? The answer is because it is consistent with the Marxist view of the world we have been outlining throughout this book; and Planned Parenthood's founder, Margaret Sanger, was steeped in Bolshevik ideology.

Sanger never claimed to be a Marxist, but she was dazzled by the socialist Soviet Union. "Russia today is the country of the liberated woman," Sanger wrote after her trip to Joseph Stalin's Soviet Union in 1934. "The attitude of Soviet Russia towards its women . . . would delight the heart of the staunchest feminist."[16]

Stalin's totalitarian regime and genocidal policies apparently made little dent in her enthusiasm, and her pilgrimage to the socialist Soviet Union was led by a man named Sherwood Eddy, a socialist who admired Marx and communism.

Fraternization with communists became the norm for Sanger. By 1934 Sanger was neglecting her children and regularly unfaithful to her husband, taking a string of bedfellows. Sanger's son Grant bluntly confirmed this. "Mother was seldom around," he said. "She just left us with anybody handy, and ran off we didn't know where."[17]

Sanger described her first extramarital affair in 1913 as having "really set me free."[18] Among her many subsequent lovers was writer H. G. Wells, who lavished praise on Joseph Stalin and Vladimir Lenin, writing about Stalin, "I've never met a man more candid, fair, and honest." Lenin, Wells wrote, had almost convinced him to embrace Leninism. Lenin was, according to Wells, "an amazing little man."[19] H. G. Wells acknowledged the brutalities of the Bolsheviks, but excused them by arguing it was the only way to quell the chaos in Russia. Wells believed the Communist Party was the only right choice for Russia.[20]

Sanger was clearly knee deep in Marxist ideology; whether she fully embraced it herself is immaterial. The Marxists loved birth control and abortifacients because they enabled disordered sexual behavior without the consequences of pregnancy and parenthood, while simultaneously destroying femininity, masculinity, gender roles, relationships, marriage, children, and ultimately the nuclear family unit. Margaret Sanger's agenda aligned perfectly with the goals of Marxists in America.

Today, Marxists are targeting America's children like never before. They've hijacked institutions like the public school system and corporations—like Disney—to groom children with Critical Race Theory and Queer Theory. When it comes to grooming children with Queer Theory, the Planned Parenthood Margaret Sanger built is perhaps the guiltiest party.

On March 28, 2022, Republican governor Ron DeSantis of Florida signed the Parental Rights in Education bill into law.[21] The mainstream media went apoplectic over the bill, misleadingly dubbing the legislation the "Don't Say Gay" bill, which was a deliberate misrepresentation of the law.[22]

The Parental Rights in Education law does two things. It prohibits classroom instruction or discussion about sexual orientation and "gender identity" in early elementary school (kindergarten through third grade) and prohibits school districts, counselors, administrators, staff, or teachers from withholding information from parents about their children "transitioning" at school. That's it. The law is about seven pages long.[23] I invite doubters to read it in its entirety.

Contrary to the media outrage, most people support this law. According to a Public Opinion Strategies poll in April 2022, 61 percent of Americans support the law while only 26 percent oppose it. As for Democrats, 55 percent support the bill, while only 29 percent oppose it.[24]

The phrase "don't say gay" is nowhere to be found within the text of the law. The phrase is a marketing gimmick intended to get normal people to say, "Wait a minute, that's not right to ban people from saying 'gay'!" It's meant as a distraction from the actual content of the law. The phrase "don't say gay" didn't happen organically. It didn't happen by chance. It wasn't a random tweet with a catchy phrase that went viral. No, the phrase "don't say gay" comes from an organization that needs children to be groomed in public schools in order to profit from them, financially and ideologically. That organization is Planned Parenthood.

Several years ago, Planned Parenthood debuted this phrase to describe a similar bill in Missouri. According to the Planned Parenthood blog (all traces of which have since been removed, though resurrected via the Wayback Machine), "During the 2020 legislative session, Missouri introduced a 'Don't Say Gay Bill' (HB 1565 and SB 786) that takes this a step further. It requires schools to notify the parents before a teacher can mention someone's gender and/or sexual identity, and to notify them before they can talk about different genders, identities, and sexual orientation."[25]

Planned Parenthood strongly opposed this legislative effort in Missouri. Why? Because Planned Parenthood, per their website, "is the single largest provider of sex education in the United States, reaching 1.2 million people with education and outreach each year."[26]

Indeed, "Planned Parenthood sex educators teach across the lifespan—including students in elementary, middle, and high school as well as young adults, parents, and older adults. They cover topics like communication skills, decision making, birth control, how to prevent sexually transmitted infections (STIs), healthy relationships, consent, body image, anatomy, and puberty."[27]

Nearly every Planned Parenthood affiliate website now has a page dedicated to "gender affirming care," which is a euphemism for the transgender hormone therapy-to-surgery pipeline, from which Planned Parenthood profits as a distributor of transgender hormones to young men and women. Planned Parenthood's central website contains a page titled "Transgender Hormone Therapy" found within its "Get Care" menu item. The page reads in part, "Our health centers provide gender-affirming hormone therapy for transgender and non-binary patients. . . . We offer services to transgender women, transgender men, and nonbinary people. Services include: Estrogen and anti-androgen hormone therapy[;] Testosterone hormone therapy[;] [and] Puberty blockers."[28] Most Planned Parenthood affiliates at the state and local levels offer the same services.

At Planned Parenthood, you simply call and ask for transgender hormones via the phone . . . and you get them. That's it. No rigorous mental health examination. For the most part, all you have to do is pass the minimal Planned Parenthood protocols.

A Planned Parenthood website states, "To schedule an appointment, you can contact us by phone at 800-258-4448 (press 2 after dialing to schedule or press 3 to speak with a counselor) or through our online patient portal. We currently offer these appointments virtually through telehealth as well as in person at one of our health centers."[29]

In the Q&A section, Planned Parenthood answers the question, "What can I expect from my first appointment?"

The answer: "At this appointment, we will discuss your goals for treatment, go through the Informed Consent forms, review your medical history, and answer any questions you have about medication options. Depending on your medical history, we will either prescribe the hormones to you at your first visit or ask you to get some lab work done at a local diagnostic center. Once we receive lab results (usually within a week of your lab work appointment), we will review them and then prescribe hormones for you to pick up at your nearest pharmacy."[30]

We will either prescribe the hormones to you at your first visit or . . . once we receive lab results (usually within a week of your lab work appointment) we will review them and then prescribe hormones for you.

Does that make your stomach turn?

By Planned Parenthood's own admission, it's a virtual guarantee that anyone who calls with a self-diagnosed gender disorder—including young people who may be driven as much by social pressure or by preexisting mental health issues as by true gender dysphoria—is given dangerous pharmaceuticals intended to mutilate their bodies in the name of the transgender ideology.

Planned Parenthood is part of a transgender pipeline that starts in kindergarten classrooms grooming children for the next steps: puberty-blocking drugs like Lupron, cross-sex hormone therapy, double mastectomies, hysterectomies, and phalloplasties on healthy young girls, and vaginoplasties for young men. To put it plainly, we're talking about castrating young men and sterilizing young women, brutally cutting away their healthy and organic sex organs in favor of transplants.

Planned Parenthood is a chief operator of this pipeline, pouring the poison of Queer Theory into the minds of impressionable children, fighting against state laws that prohibit classroom discussion of "gender identity" in primary grades, encouraging promiscuous sexual behavior in middle and high school that often leads to abortion (which profits Planned Parenthood), and selling transgender hormone therapy to young people they have already pumped full of transgender ideology.

Planned Parenthood needs to ideologically groom children in order to profit. So they do, running the biggest sex-ed operation in the nation, promoting Queer Theory, grooming children, and then collecting cash when the groomed children call Planned Parenthood clinics for transgender hormones.

The tagline on Planned Parenthood's website claims, "Planned Parenthood Stands for Care. Your health is our highest priority and we believe your body is your own."[31]

Of course that's not true. Your health is not Planned Parenthood's priority. In no way is it healthy to steal children's innocence by bombarding them with sex education, let alone the perverse "gender identity" propaganda Planned Parenthood teaches to children. It is not healthy—mentally, physically, psychologically, or spiritually—for anyone to be promiscuous. Abortion is not healthy—certainly not for the baby, and not for the mother who is marked by its effects, physically and psychologically, for life.[32] "Affirming" people in their "gender dysphoria"—a serious mental health disorder—rather than trying to alleviate it is not healthy. Transgender surgeries and chemical treatments are not healthy—they are the opposite of healthy as they remove perfectly healthy organs in disfiguring surgeries.

The "gender affirming care" model is often justified by the argument that if we *don't* socially, chemically, and surgically "transition" them, then these gender-dysphoric young people will commit suicide.

This narrative was built from an article published in *Psychology Today* by a doctor named Jack Turban who claimed to have conducted a meta-analysis of sixteen different studies that tracked cross-sex hormones and their impact on the mental health status of gender-disordered youth.[33] Turban wanted to claim that cross-sex hormones helped prevent suicide. Turban's article has been cited innumerable times, but Manhattan Institute fellow Leor Sapir argues that Turban's claims are disingenuous at best, and most likely outright lies.[34]

Sapir published a detailed rebuttal on the Substack page of biologist Dr. Colin Wright, Reality's Last Stand, and then appeared on my show detailing Turban's errors—which Sapir believes to be deliberate.[35] Sapir demonstrated that many of the studies Turban used actually show the opposite of what Turban claimed, or were rendered useless due to confirmation bias, replication problems, and questionable funding from the pharmaceutical industry.

For instance, in the two notorious studies conducted by Dutch researchers that have been used as the primary basis for the "gender affirming" model, the cohort of young people given transgender hormones was selected specifically because they were also receiving mental health care and had strong family support systems.[36] Those confounding factors render the Dutch studies useless. In the United States, rigorous background selection, mental health care, and family support are shunted aside rather than required before young people are given transgender hormone therapies. Moreover, it was impossible to tell from the Dutch study if the reported improvements in mental health came from receiving mental health care or receiving hormone treatment. Turban ignored this issue while making sweeping statements about how "science" showed that hormone treatments improved the mental health of gender-disordered young people.[37] Since then, the Dutch studies have been exposed as fatally compromised anyway, because they were funded by pharmaceutical giant Ferring Pharmaceuticals, which happens to sell the puberty-blocking drug Triptorelin.[38]

By contrast, a well-sourced analysis from the Heritage Foundation found that when young people have easy access to transgender hormones, their suicide rate dramatically increases by 14 percent, which is the opposite of what the left claims will happen.[39]

Some countries in Europe, including the United Kingdom, Sweden, and Finland, are waking up to the incredible harm of the Queer Theory agenda and have severely limited the prescription of puberty-blocking pharmaceuticals and cross-sex hormones and discarded the "gender affirming" model of care as pseudoscience.[40]

Marxists need tools to destroy society. Margaret Sanger built them the perfect institutional tool to inflict Queer Theory on our country's youth; Planned Parenthood is the most powerful corporate groomer for Queer Theory in our nation.

Margaret Sanger is not the only villain guilty of grooming our young people and serving the Marxist agenda in the process. The abhorrent Alfred Kinsey has caused equal damage. The *New York Times* called Alfred Kinsey "the father of the sexual revolution,"[41] but he is more accurately described as a deranged pervert who sought to normalize his own evil sexual fetishes.

Alfred Kinsey was a "sexologist" who became famous for his "Kinsey Reports," which were two books called *Sexual Behavior in the Human Male* and *Sexual Behavior in the Human Female*, published in 1948 and 1953 respectively.[42] The "Kinsey Reports" are credited with changing America's views on sex and what was sexually normal, permissible, and healthy.

Kinsey contended that people's sexual orientation wasn't binary—homosexual or heterosexual—but rather rested on a seven-point sliding scale where zero was exclusively heterosexual and six was exclusively homosexual.[43]

Kinsey claimed that "37% of males and 13% of females had at least some overt homosexual experience to orgasm." Moreover, "10% of males were more or less exclusively homosexual and 8% of males were exclusively homosexual for at least three years between the ages of 16 and 55."[44] The data he used to bolster such claims were later revealed to be faulty, as the subjects he interviewed were prison inmates and sex offenders;[45] the real figure, today, shows 1.4 percent of American men identify as gay, 1.0 percent of American women identify as lesbian, and 4.2 percent identify as bisexual.[46] Though these numbers are in flux, and rising rapidly among younger generations under constant assault by groomers who are LGBTQ propagandists, Kinsey's data are off by more than 600 percent, likely due to his selection bias and his own perversions.

Kinsey regarded himself as bisexual, and his marriage to his wife was a charade, as they considered their marriage to be an "open" arrangement where both were permitted to have sex with other people.[47] Alfred Kinsey often had sex with young men who were his students.[48]

Many of Kinsey's experiments were disguises to satisfy his perverted sexual appetite. In fact, Kinsey directed his researchers to experiment in sexually deviant behavior, as he did, to better understand their subjects; Kinsey often filmed their sexual activities in his attic.[49]

Most disturbing was Kinsey's taste for homosexual sadomasochism and his argument that children had sexual appetites from birth. Kinsey even stated in his reports, "All orgasms are 'outlets' and equal between husband and wife, boy and dog, man and boy, girl, or baby? For there is no abnormality and no normality."[50] He asserted, based on "experiments" he recorded, that babies as young as two months old had orgasms. Kinsey presented this evidence positively, suggesting that sexual behavior in children was normal.[51]

In *Sexual Behavior of the Human Female*, Kinsey wrote, "It is difficult to understand why a child, except for its cultural conditioning, should be disturbed at having its genitalia touched, or disturbed at seeing the genitalia of other persons, or disturbed at even more specific sexual contacts. . . . [A]dult contacts . . . are not likely to do the child any appreciable harm if the child's parents do not become disturbed."[52]

It disturbs me even to type the words.

What Kinsey presented as "normal" was horrendous abuse inflicted by a pedophile and recorded in the pedophile's journal, which Alfred Kinsey copied. Kinsey did not report these heinous crimes to the police.[53] Instead, he argued that children are a valid "sexual outlet" for use by adults in pursuit of orgasm.[54]

Are you shaking with rage?

Gayle Rubin, in her essay "Thinking Sex," widely acknowledged to be the founding document of Queer Theory, positively cites Alfred Kinsey's work as groundbreaking in the exploration of sexual deviations.[55]

It's important to note that Alfred Kinsey founded the Institute for Sex Research in 1947 at Indiana University, and was credited as the first sexologist to study sex from a "scientific" perspective;[56] in reality Kinsey's work was built on deliberately falsified or dubious data that Kinsey refused to make public in order to "protect" the "confidentiality" of his sources.[57]

A half century after Kinsey's death, Kinsey's Institute for Sex Research exists today as the Kinsey Institute for Research in Sex, Gender, and Reproduction.[58] The Kinsey Institute continues to push for "sexual freedom," a euphemism for Kinsey's original agenda of destroying the social-sexual mores of our society. To that end, the Kinsey Institute promotes the idea that children have a "right" to sexual knowledge, an idea that provides the basis for the "comprehensive sexuality education" curricula that is now widely disseminated through international organizations like UNESCO and the World Health Organization,[59] in addition to Planned Parenthood.

Included in comprehensive sexuality education curriculum are the following tenets, among others:

- Children are sexual from birth.
- Children have a right to sexual activity.
- Children's rights to sexual activity and exploration of sexual identity (and privacy surrounding both) supersede parental rights. This includes a supposed right to have an abortion without parental knowledge.
- Children should masturbate regularly.
- Traditional values related to sex, sexuality, sexual identity, chastity, and monogamy are oppressive.
- Children have a right to comprehensive sexuality education regardless of parental consent.[60]

The United Nations bears much responsibility for driving the global comprehensive sexuality education agenda. One influential group that holds consultative status at the United Nations Economic and Social Council (ECOSOC) is an organization called the Sexuality Information and Education Council of the United States (SIECUS), which helps ECOSOC come up with alleged global norms for sexual education for the United Nations to promote.[61]

Mary Calderone, a former medical director from Planned Parenthood, launched SIECUS with money given to her by Hugh

Hefner, founder of *Playboy* magazine.[62] Calderone shared many of Kinsey's views, teaching that "from the day (children) are born, they are sexual beings." Calderone also stated, referencing Kinsey's disturbing pedophilic experiments, that "professionals who study children have affirmed the strong sexuality of the newborn."[63] According to Calderone, "Children are sexual and think sexual thoughts and do sexual things. . . ."[64]

Former Kinsey Institute director and frequent Kinsey co-author Wardell Pomeroy was on the first panel of board members at SIECUS. According to *Time* magazine, Pomeroy said, "It is time to admit that incest need not be a perversion or a symptom of mental illness. . . . Incest between . . . children and adults . . . can sometimes be beneficial."[65]

That might seem like a heinous, and criminal, attitude, but SIECUS nevertheless was a partner with the United Nations Educational, Scientific and Cultural Organization (UNESCO) in authoring UNESCO's International Guidelines on Sexuality Education, published in 2009. As you might expect, the guidelines are rife with gender identity ideology, abortion activism, and "children's right" to sexual knowledge propaganda, all while paying little respect to parental rights, the true meaning of marriage, or properly ordered sexual activity.[66]

The ties between the Kinsey Institute, SIECUS, and Planned Parenthood—all three of which hold consultative status at the United Nations—are nothing less than incestuous, evil, and indicative of the maximum effort to sexualize, indoctrinate, and transform our nation's children without any say from their parents.

Planned Parenthood is the biggest corporate groomer in the United States. It brainwashes children with "comprehensive sexuality education"—a composite of Rubin's Queer Theory and Kinsey's sexual deviance—and then reaps the profits from selling transgender hormone therapy to children once indoctrination is complete.

The mode of indoctrination occurring in our nation's public schools, however, would not be so effective without the influence of two individuals: Brazilian Marxist Paulo Freire—who also happens to be responsible for the term "woke"—and Randi Weingarten, the czar of the American Federation of Teachers.

CHAPTER 7

Education Subverted: Critical Pedagogy

A Brazilian Marxist named Paulo Freire (1921–1997), who famously said that there is "no such thing as a *neutral* educational process,"[1] is responsible for the word "woke."

Paulo Freire is not as well known as Vladimir Lenin or Mao Zedong, both of whom successfully weaponized their education systems to serve as indoctrination centers for Communist ideology, but Freire's plan for *how* to structure a Marxist takeover of education—in a non-Marxist country—is playing out in every government school in America, from radical universities all the way down to kindergarten classrooms.

Yet, most parents have never even heard of Freire, though most have become well acquainted with the wokeism he spawned.

Throughout the 1950s and 1960s, Freire conducted experiments on Brazilian peasants. Freire believed that these peasants—the Marxist proletariat—needed to be emancipated from their bourgeois rulers.

If given the right tools, Freire believed the peasants would overthrow their "oppressors." To that end, Freire staged forty-five-day educational workshops to give the peasants the "tools" they needed to vote for far-left radical political candidates. Freire called this exercise "education."[2]

In his book *Pedagogy of the Oppressed*, Freire argued that in order to liberate the poor, traditional theory—the reality that there is objective truth—must be discarded and replaced with a "critical perception of the world."[3]

You may recognize Freire's idea; it's the same argument made by Max Horkheimer of the Frankfurt School in his 1937 manifesto "Traditional and Critical Theory." Horkheimer claimed objective truth doesn't exist. According to Horkheimer, "truth" is nothing but the prevailing political narrative; he suggested that through relentless criticism, prevailing narratives could be destroyed and replaced with Marxist ideology. Freire built on Horkheimer's ideology, arguing that "oppression" was propagated by the education system. Children, Freire argued, are held hostage by the elite, because teachers "teach knowledge." Freire argued, like Horkheimer before him, that "knowledge" is nothing but the prevailing narrative that serves the ruling elite. Therefore, when teachers "teach knowledge," it's a tool of oppression wielded by the elite to indoctrinate children with elitist politics.[4]

Freire demanded "emancipation" from the oppression of "knowledge."

To that end Freire vilified what he called the "banking method" of education in which students were regarded as piggy banks into which teachers deposit facts and knowledge. The banking method is also known as "traditional pedagogy." Freire decried traditional pedagogy because he claimed it was unfair that "the scope of action allowed to the students extends only as far as receiving, filing, and storing the deposits."[5]

In Freire's mind teachers are oppressors because the power balance entirely favors the teacher. For instance, in his seminal work, Freire explained that "the teacher talks and the students listen—meekly," and when "the teacher chooses and enforces his choice . . . the students comply," and when "the teacher disciplines . . . the students are disciplined," and when "the teacher chooses the program content . . . the students (who were not consulted) adapt to it."[6]

Freire argued that, in a non-oppressive education system, the teacher must be a co-learner with the student, and the student must also teach the teacher. Otherwise, the teacher will hold all the power of "knowledge," leaving the student powerless.

Freire's pedagogy raises a fairly obvious question. How does a teacher become a co-learner and a student become a co-creator of knowledge if the student is ignorant of math, science, history, and other vital fields of study? A kindergartener can't teach calculus if he doesn't know it yet, right? What would the teacher learn in such a scenario? Indeed, under this scenario, of what value is school at all? Freire contended that students' lived experiences were worth more than teachers' academic knowledge of reality.

You might recognize this concept in our culture today as "*your truth*" or "*my truth*" versus "*the* truth."

Freire's goal, like that of Marx before him, was revolution. Freire wanted to use the education system to groom children into Marxist revolutionaries. To this end Freire developed a "pedagogy of the oppressed," which "must be forged *with*, not *for*, the oppressed (whether individuals or peoples) in the incessant struggle to regain their humanity. This pedagogy makes oppression and its causes objects of reflection by the oppressed, and from that reflection will come their necessary engagement in the struggle for their liberation. And in the struggle this pedagogy will be made and remade."[7] Instead of facts and knowledge, students should be conditioned for "critical consciousness," prepared for "emancipation" from oppression, and readied for radical political action and eventually revolution.

When we use the word "woke" in modern America, what we're actually referring to is Freire's "critical consciousness." Freire wanted to reeducate children to view the world through the lens of Critical Theory, destroy objective reality, replace truth with relativism, divide society into an oppressor class versus an oppressed class, and agitate for Marxist revolution. Freire wanted to "awaken" children's "critical consciousness" to see the world through a Marxist filter.[8] American citizens who today accept "wokeness" are in fact accepting Freire's Marxist worldview.

Freire's Marxism isn't hidden. His citations in *Pedagogy of the Oppressed* refer to Karl Marx, Mao Zedong, Vladimir Lenin, Herbert Marcuse, György Lukács, Fidel Castro, and Che Guevara.[9] These are not the sort of brutes who should influence American educational institutions. Yet, education professor Henry Giroux caught onto Freire's ideas and propagated them to the best of his ability. He popularized Freire's writings in the United States and coined the term "critical pedagogy."[10] Freire and Giroux, along with Dr. Peter McLaren, formed the "Big Three" in the Critical Pedagogy movement. Together, they emphasize the Marxist dialectic of oppressor versus oppressed inherent in Critical Pedagogy, as well as Critical Pedagogy's war against reality and objective truth. McLaren stated that "knowledge should be analyzed on the basis of whether it is oppressive or exploitative, and not on the basis of whether it is 'true.'"[11]

In our children's classrooms today, this poisonous ideology is called "teaching for social justice." "Social justice" and "social-emotional learning" (SEL) are two ways Critical Pedagogy has become widely disseminated in public schools.

In a paper titled "Critical Pedagogy: Teaching for Social Justice," researcher and data scientist Perpetual Baffour writes, "While the education problem in urban communities is a blend of social, cultural, and political factors, transforming pedagogical practices can present viable solutions to the disparities facing inner-city schools. Rather than devalue students' racial and cultural experiences, teachers can activate students' critical consciousness and integrate their cultural backgrounds into the content of their learning experiences."[12]

"Transforming pedagogical practices." "Activate students' critical consciousness." It's Freire's forty-five-day reading-to-radical boot camp, this time for our sons and daughters in public schools.

Baffour then explains, "This paper fundamentally argues that urban public school teachers can become social agents."[13] Or anti-American social revolutionaries, as it were.

One of the biggest reasons our colleges, high schools, and even grade schools have turned "woke" is because we let "critical pedagogy" run rampant. "Teaching for social justice" is incredibly widespread in our public school system, but not as universal as "social-emotional learning." Indeed, social-emotional learning has become a way to sneak Critical Pedagogy, Critical Race Theory, and Queer Theory into education under the guise of teaching morality to students.

The most powerful lobbying arm for embedding SEL in the public school system is a group called the Collaborative for Academic, Social, and Emotional Learning (CASEL). It aims to make SEL "an integral part of education and human development."[14]

SEL is not a topic or a subject matter. It is not a module or theory. SEL is disguised as "values" education, but really it is a technique to brainwash children ideologically. In many public schools, SEL is embedded into everything: curricula, teaching, sports. Children are even taught to export SEL "competencies"—such as self-awareness, social awareness, responsible decision-making, and self-management—into their home life.

Since 2020, CASEL has begun pushing "Transformative SEL." As American Enterprise Institute research fellow Max Eden noted in his testimony to the United States House of Representatives Committee on Appropriations Subcommittee on Labor, Health and Human Services, Education, and Related Agencies in 2022, "In 'Transformative SEL,' 'self-awareness' encompasses 'identity,' with 'identity' defined now through the lens of 'intersectionality.' 'Self-management' encompasses 'agency,' with 'agency' defined through 'resistance' and 'transformative/justice-oriented' citizenship. 'Transformative SEL' also embraces 'culturally relevant/responsive' pedagogy. This approach was pioneered by Gloria Ladson-Billings, the professor who brought Critical Race Theory to K–12 education."[15]

Eden continued, "In its 'Roadmap to Re-Opening,' CASEL defines 'self-awareness' as 'examining our implicit biases,' and defines 'self-management' as 'practicing anti-racism.'"[16]

Eden also noted that: "SEL in practice effectively asks teachers to act as therapists. Without much legitimate training, teachers are encouraged to uncover and address 'trauma,' to otherwise probe into students' psyches, and to promote a holistic schema through which children comprehend their family and friend relationships. . . . Suffice for now to say that there is a reason why medical ethics prohibits the practice of therapy by unlicensed and untrained individuals."[17]

In fact, SEL is so similar to quack psychology practiced by unlicensed teachers that the state of North Carolina passed legislation giving teachers and school staff preemptive immunity from medical malpractice lawsuits if they use SEL in their classrooms and schools.[18] Dr. James Lindsay at New Discourses defines "Transformative SEL" as "wholly (neo)-Marxist."[19]

Lindsay notes that Transformative SEL's "primary agenda is, in fact, to use the five competency areas to raise and foster a critical consciousness through social and emotional education. This fact is unsurprising to all who understand that 'transformative' is a term employed by all of the Dialectical Left, most notably including Marxists, to describe their goal of making the world and man into something suitable for Communism." Lindsay continues,

> Transformative SEL "social awareness" lessons are unabashedly rooted in neo-Marxist social Theories like Critical Race Theory, Gender Theory, Queer Theory, Postcolonial Theory, Fat Studies, and Disability Studies, and "Trans SEL" in that regard is a vehicle and coordinating hub for programming (literally, as in thought reform or brainwashing) into the perspectives of these Critical Theories. The goal of Transformative SEL is to program children to see their world through the lenses provided by those Critical Theories and train them to be "change agents" (that is, activists) on their behalf. Systemic Transformative SEL, which is what CASEL currently promotes, is designed to rearrange the entire school-related life of every child so that it reinforces this programming in a fully immersive way.[20]

Those who practice social-emotional learning in schools claim they are teaching at-risk children right from wrong, but SEL is not rooted in objective reality or natural law. It's rooted in Critical Pedagogy.

Social-emotional learning stems from the work of a Yale psychologist named James Comer, who in the late 1960s began investigating the educational challenges faced by black students from the inner cities. Comer was attempting to discover what impeded their learning. He sought answers not just within the classroom, but in factors like unstable or difficult home lives, crime-ridden streets, and emotional baggage that accompanies both. Dr. Comer developed what he called the "whole child" approach; teaching, he decided, isn't just about imparting knowledge and facts, but about forming the whole child.[21]

Comer's work made him famous, and in the 1990s a new age group called the Fetzer Institute picked up Comer's "whole child" approach and harnessed it to social-emotional learning, thanks largely to a professor of education named Linda Darling-Hammond, whom Dr. James Lindsay calls "the effective mother of SEL."[22] In turn, members of the Fetzer Institute launched the Collaborative for Academic, Social, and Emotional Learning (CASEL) which, Lindsay notes, "began to experiment with infusing (Critical) education theory (that is, Critical Pedagogy) into whole-child education."[23]

The "mother" of SEL, Linda Darling-Hammond, is a power player in the American education bureaucracy. According to her think tank, the Learning Policy Institute, "In 2006, Darling-Hammond was named one of the nation's ten most influential people affecting educational policy."[24] But Darling-Hammond prefers the education system of the Communist Chinese. Darling-Hammond calls the Chinese Communist education system "magical," and she praises the way teachers in China are placed on a higher pedestal than parents.[25]

"Teachers in China are revered as elders, role models, and those whom parents entrust to shape the future of their children," she writes. "In the Tao traditions of ritual, the phrase 'heaven-earth-sovereign-parent-teacher' is repeated and becomes ingrained in how people see themselves holistically governed and supported."[26]

Darling-Hammond praises how much money Communist China spends on education, apparently unconcerned that the point of such education is to produce more Chinese Communists.[27] Her writing reeks of Freire's "pedagogy of the oppressed" as she gushes about the Chinese Communists. She writes, "In the 1990's, Shanghai was the first province to implement a national curriculum that broadened beyond traditional subject areas and included change toward more active kinds of pedagogy. . . ."[28]

"I have no doubt," Linda Darling-Hammond writes of SEL, "that the survival of the human race depends at least as much on the cultivation of social & emotional intelligence as it does on the development of technical knowledge & skills."[29]

Darling-Hammond makes no secret that she's an ideological follower of Freire, citing him in multiple works including in the foreword to the 2015 *Handbook of Social and Emotional Learning: Research and Practice.*[30]

Linda Darling-Hammond is extremely influential in shaping the American education system. Darling-Hammond served as education advisor to Barack Obama's 2008 presidential campaign. President Obama later considered her as a candidate to be United States Secretary of Education, though she lost that spot to Arne Duncan.[31] In November 2020, Darling-Hammond served as leader of Joe Biden's presidential transition agency review team focusing on the Department of Education.[32] And according to the James G. Martin Center for Academic Renewal, Darling-Hammond is one of the most assigned authors in the education departments at leading universities.[33] She is currently president of the California State Board of Education, appointed by California governor Gavin Newsom.[34] Linda Darling-Hammond is also a board member emeritus on the Board of Directors of CASEL.[35] CASEL seeks to make social-emotional learning ubiquitous in public schools. It is yet another way to embed Freire's Marxist ideology into the American education system.

One of the biggest promoters of SEL in children's classrooms today is Randi Weingarten, president of the American Federation of Teachers (AFT), the nation's second-largest teachers' union.

Teachers' unions are an incredibly powerful political lobby, doling out money to Democrat politicians, levying control over curricula taught to children, and influencing local school board elections. Under

Weingarten's helm, AFT has spent an average of $44 million per year on leftist candidates and causes.[36]

Weingarten is a middle-aged lesbian "married" to a lesbian rabbi famous for her LGBTQ+ activism. Weingarten is a known insider in the Clinton orbit and a veritable kingmaker in Democrat politics. Weingarten openly pushes neo-Marxist agendas in schools. For instance, Weingarten once claimed, "Let's be clear: critical race theory is not taught in elementary schools or high schools." But, of course, it is. Weingarten simply accuses conservative critics of "bullying teachers and trying to stop us from teaching students *accurate* history" [emphasis mine].[37] Weingarten then pledged legal defense for any teachers accused of teaching Critical Race Theory in states where it's prohibited.[38]

Perhaps it is not surprising that under Weingarten's leadership the American Federation of Teachers works with a non-profit called First Book that disseminates books grounded in Queer Theory to small children.[39] First Book promotes the following books for young children:

- *The Pronoun Book*, which teaches children neo-Marxist pronouns, including *ze* and *zir*.[40]
- *Who is RuPaul?*, which introduces hypersexualized caricatures of trans strippers to small children.[41]
- *Flamer*, which discusses penis size and displays illustrations of naked adolescent boys.[42]
- *Fred Gets Dressed*, which features a naked child fourteen times and culminates in the main character cross-dressing himself and cross-dressing both his parents.[43]
- *Aristotle and Dante*, which portrays two young boys lusting over each other and fantasizing about removing each other's underwear and being naked together.[44]

- *It Feels Good to Be Yourself*, which introduces children to "non-binary" characters and "gender identity," telling kids that at birth parents and doctors guess what "gender" a baby is, but are not always correct.[45]
- *I Am Jazz*, about Jazz Jennings, a young boy whose parents facilitated a surgical transition because Jazz "feels" like a girl.[46]
- *Calvin*, about a child who comes out as transgender.[47]

Understandably, given her agenda, Weingarten is adamantly opposed to parents being involved in their children's education, particularly parents who don't want their children indoctrinated with Critical Race Theory and Queer Theory. Weingarten applauded an article critical of parental rights that stated, "Parents claim they have the right to shape their kids' school curriculum. They don't."[48] Weingarten said, "Great piece on parents' rights and #publicschools."[49]

Randi Weingarten is also an outspoken advocate for social-emotional learning in schools.

"#SEL is a critical part of every child's growth," Weingarten argues.[50] She says, "#AFTunion educators know social-emotional learning is more important than ever. . . ."[51] Weingarten publicly called for more taxpayer funding for SEL, writing, "Educators and school staff need the social-emotional training and resources to support their students."[52] She says, "We need to create more social & emotional learning and wrap services around schools. . . ."[53] The American Federation of Teachers under Weingarten's helm celebrated the 2020 "teacher of the year" because the teacher promoted the "importance of social emotional learning."[54]

Weingarten publicly lavishes praise on visible SEL in schools, tweeting, "I loved learning about the extensive SEL programs this school has to ensure students are able to thrive in and out of the classroom,"[55] and sharing photos with the caption "I was blown away by the wellness center. This is part of what meeting students [sic] social and emotional needs looks like."[56]

Weingarten highlights teachers who are implementing SEL tactics on small children as young as preschool age, tweeting, "Shout out to #NTOY20 finalist @TabathaRosproy, a preschool teacher in KS, who intentionally uses #SEL methods to empower students to use their voice for conflict resolution, critical thinking, self-regulation and connecting with others."[57]

In the AFT publication, Weingarten even highlights "Transformative SEL," which, Lindsay notes, is "wholly neo-Marxist."[58]

Randi Weingarten is a wholehearted enthusiast for indoctrinating children with Marxist propaganda.

An important ally of Weingarten is Emily Drabinski. Another middle-aged lesbian, Drabinski now sits as the president of the American Library Association and is an open, self-proclaimed Marxist.[59] In fact, after her election victory, Drabinski tweeted (in a now deleted tweet), "I just cannot believe that a Marxist lesbian who believes that collective power is possible to build and can be wielded for a better world is the president-elect of @ALALibrary. I am so excited for what we will do together. Solidarity! And my mom is SO PROUD I love you mom."[60]

Weingarten was an enthusiastic supporter of Drabinski's campaign, saying, "In the face of increasing challenges to school library books and teachers' curricula, we need a strong American Library Association defending free inquiry in our shared pursuit of the public good." "Emily Drabinski knows how to organize and mobilize on behalf of library workers and our communities."[61]

By "free inquiry," of course, the Marxists mean filling library shelves with Marxist books, or books that undermine Christianity or capitalism.

It should come as no surprise that children's libraries around the country now feature books like *Gender Queer*, which is aimed at children and contains homosexual pornographic images,[62] and *Antiracist Baby* by Ibram X. Kendi, which teaches that toddlers are racist if they have white skin and oppressed if they have black skin.[63] These same libraries are sponsoring "drag queen story hours," which, as the name suggests, involves grown men dressed in sexualized costumes and heavy makeup pretending to be women while discussing their "queer identity" with children as young as preschoolers.[64] As we discussed in chapter 4, part of the Marxist cultural revolution requires the "queering" of kids. Emily Drabinski is playing her role in making this happen, and so is Randi Weingarten.

There is "no such thing as a *neutral* educational process," Paulo Freire declared,[65] and people like Randi Weingarten, Linda Darling-Hammond, Peter McLaren, social-emotional learning lobbyists (like CASEL), woke teachers, and the left-wing education elite are making sure Freire's Marxist fever dream comes true in American classrooms by propagating hateful, exploitative, and abusive ideologies onto our children.

For Marxists, though, there remains one giant threat to their school monopoly: homeschooling.

CHAPTER 8

Unsocialized Homeskoolers

In early 2020 Harvard professor Elizabeth Bartholet published an eighty-page article in the *Arizona Law Review* called "Homeschooling: Parent Rights Absolutism vs. Child Rights to Education & Protection." In the article, Bartholet calls for a "presumptive ban on homeschooling." Parents, she says, have no right to instill their values in their own children. She writes, "Many homeschool because they want to isolate their children from ideas and values central to our democracy, determined to keep their children from exposure to views that might enable autonomous choice about their future lives."[1]

You can imagine what "views" she thinks children should be exposed to, what views she believes "are central to democracy." Unsurprisingly, her views encompass the entire Marxist Critical Pedagogy agenda shoved down the throats of our children in public schools. Bartholet's use of the word "democracy" is critical to her vilification of homeschooling. She does not mean democracy in the orthodox definition of the word.

Bartholet opposes the right of Christian parents to instill Christian values and a Christian worldview in their children, because Christianity, she contends, is at odds with the "democracy" of the "majority culture." Bartholet writes, "A very large proportion of homeschooling parents are ideologically committed to isolating their children from the majority culture and indoctrinating them in views and values that are in serious conflict with that culture. Some believe that women should be subservient to men; others believe that race stamps some people as inferior to others. Many don't believe in the scientific method, looking to the Bible instead as their source for understanding the world."[2]

We hear this endlessly from the left and from leftist anti-homeschooling activists. Christianity, they argue, is bigotry. But it is not Christianity that teaches racism; that would be Critical Race Theory. It is not Christianity that argues against science; that would be Queer Theory. It is not Christianity that is opposed to our constitutional form of Republican government: that would be Marxism.

But Bartholet believes she knows better than parents, especially Christian parents, regarding how to teach values to children, and as such, parents should be deprived of that privilege. Bartholet writes, "The legal claim made in defense of the current homeschooling regime is based on a dangerous idea about parent rights—that those with enormous physical and other power over infants and children should be subject to virtually no check on that power. That parents should have monopoly control over children's lives, development, and experience. That parents who are committed to beliefs and values counter to those of the larger society are entitled to bring their children up in isolation, so as to help ensure that they will replicate the parents' views and lifestyle choices."[3]

If you think that statement has a powerful totalitarian undercurrent, you'd be right. Bartholet argues that parents' rights over how their children are educated are "inconsistent with our legal and cultural history. From early on, our law recognized that the state has a role to play in child-rearing and that parents have responsibilities and not just rights."[4]

At best Bartholet's statements are misleading. More realistically, they are closer to absolute falsehood. Bartholet ignores the history of court rulings in our country on this subject that acknowledge with certainty that parents have the right to make educational choices including religious instruction for their children.[5]

Bartholet also claims (falsely) that homeschooled children suffer poor academic outcomes compared to their public school counterparts. According to a variety of academic measures, homeschooled students achieve significantly higher academic success than do public school students.

A 2010 study conducted by the National Home Education Research Institute (NHERI) analyzed data from fifteen independent testing services of 11,739 homeschooled students from all fifty states tracking the academic achievement of students based on a series of standardized tests. NHERI found that homeschooled students performed, on average, in the 86th percentile while public school students scored on average in the 50th percentile.[6]

Similarly, on the Classical Learning Test, homeschooled students outperformed public school students, as well as private school and charter school students. Houston Christian University professor Lisa Treleavan found that, on average, homeschooled students scored 78 points, private school students scored 75 points, charter school students scored 73 points, and public school students scored 66 points.[7]

There are many such examples, but the anti-homeschoolers prefer cherry-picking skewed data to attack homeschooling. For instance, one recent study found that, on a percentage basis, fewer homeschooled students than public school students attend college.[8] The study, however, reveals no information about academic excellence. It doesn't control for homeschooled students who are academically qualified for college but choose not to attend, perhaps for entrepreneurial reasons or ideological ones. A true comparison would examine the percentage of homeschooled students accepted into college after applying versus the percentage of public school students accepted into college after applying. A still more interesting study would have charted how successful both cohorts of students were in their lives and careers five years after graduating from high school. This study did none of that.

A better study of the academic success of homeschooled students at the university level was conducted by Michael F. Cogan from the University of Saint Thomas in Minnesota. Cogan found that homeschooled students have a higher rate of college graduation after four years than their public school counterparts, graduating at a 66.7 percent rate compared to a graduation rate of only 58.6 percent for public school students.[9]

But concern about academic success isn't the real reason Elizabeth Bartholet hates homeschooling.

From the beginning of 2020 until the end, driven largely by school lockdowns, mandatory masking of children in the classroom, and what parents witnessed through "Zoom school," the number of homeschoolers in the United States effectively doubled, from 5.4 percent of households to 11.1 percent of households, at one point topping out at 18–19 percent.[10]

The anti-homeschoolers freaked out. Harvard Law School planned an anti-homeschooling conference for June 2020.[11] In advance of the conference, *Harvard Magazine* writer Erin O'Donnell summarized Elizabeth Bartholet's eighty-page anti-homeschooling treatise in what turned into a viral article titled "The Risks of Homeschooling."[12]

The purpose of Harvard's anti-homeschooling conference was radical. The organizers sought an outright legal ban on homeschooling in the United States. This was the description of their conference: "We will convene leaders in education and child welfare policy, legislators and legislative staff, academics and policy advocates, to discuss child rights in connection with homeschooling in the United States. The focus will be on problems of educational deprivation and child maltreatment that too often occur under the guise of homeschooling, in a legal environment of minimal or no oversight. Experts will lead conversations about the available empirical evidence, the current regulatory environment, proposals for legal reform, and strategies for effecting such reform," The description also noted, "This event is private and by invitation-only."[13] Guess who wasn't invited? If you guessed parents and homeschoolers, you are correct. Bartholet and her conference co-organizer James Dwyer reserved the privilege of attendance for "the experts." The two primary points of focus—at least, this was their claim—were *educational deprivation and child maltreatment.*

Harvard Magazine—at the top of the aforementioned glowing write-up about Bartholet's anti-homeschool crusade—produced a graphic depicting a sad, red-haired homeschooled child imprisoned in a house built of books with bars on the windows. Outside the bars, other children (presumably educated at public schools) ran about happily, playing sports and dancing in the yard.

Big letters splashed along the spines of the books making up the frame of the homeschool-prison-house spelled: BIBLE, READING, WRITING . . . and ARITHMATIC. Yes, spelled like *that.* (Any homeschooled preschooler worth her salt knows arithmetic is spelled "**A R**at **I**n **T**om's **H**ouse **M**ay **E**at **T**om's **I**ce **C**ream.")[14]

Full disclosure: I was homeschooled, so I would know. And anyone who has experienced or knows anything about homeschooling is aware that it is public school children who spend their days in what's often close to an institutional prison, while homeschool kids are free. Moreover, homeschooled kids focus on actual core academic subjects such as spelling and math, rather than on Queer Theory and Critical Race Theory.

The hilarious misspelling of arithmetic wasn't intentional irony either, according to available evidence. After homeschool supporters endlessly mocked *Harvard Magazine* for the error, the publication stealthily updated its article with a new graphic in which arithmetic was spelled correctly.[15] No correction was issued acknowledging the error.

One of Bartholet's most inflammatory claims is that homeschooled students suffer child abuse at a higher rate than public school students. But again, that's a false—and heinous—accusation according to the best data available.

In a study titled "Child Abuse of Public School, Private School, and Homeschool Students: Evidence, Philosophy, and Reason," Dr. Brian Ray analyzes data that "[s]hows that an estimated 10% (or more) of public and private schoolchildren experience sexual maltreatment at the hands of school personnel, and in addition some schoolchildren are abused by their parents. The limited evidence available shows that homeschooled children are abused at a lower rate than are those in the general public, and no evidence shows that the home educated are at any higher risk of abuse."[16]

Bartholet dismisses this study in favor of sensationalism by touting a tragic crime from California committed by a man and woman who abused their thirteen children while pretending to homeschool them. Both parents were eventually convicted of fourteen felonies and sentenced to life in prison.[17] Though absolutely tragic and heartbreaking, this was an anomaly.

But again, Bartholet's real concern is not about child abuse, or academic achievement. It is about systemic control of our children's minds through America's educational institutions.

The best way to explain Bartholet's true agenda is to note her repeated disgust at the idea of parental rights. In the *Harvard Magazine* piece, Bartholet is quoted as saying, "The issue is, do we think that parents should have 24/7, essentially authoritarian control over their children from ages zero to 18? I think that's dangerous." "I think it's always dangerous to put powerful people in charge of the powerless, and to give the powerful ones total authority."[18]

This view is an echo of the virulent anti-parent attitude of Bartholet's conference co-cost, College of William and Mary professor James Dwyer, who contends, "The reason parent-child relationships exist is because the State confers legal parenthood. . . ."[19] That's a phrase a Marxist would love, but perhaps Dwyer needs to be reminded that the reason a parent-child relationship exists is because parents have children. When we talk about neo-Marxists who want to abolish parental rights, abolish the nuclear family, and abolish our God-given natural rights, Dwyer is the perfect example. He rejects "the Laws of Nature and of Nature's God," in favor of the communist position that children are the property of the state.

Bartholet specifically thanks James Dwyer for his help in drafting her *Arizona Law Review* article and cites his work dozens of times through her eighty-page piece.

Bartholet, building on Dwyer, contends that parental rights, broadly interpreted, are "inconsistent with our legal and cultural history."[20] This is completely false. We could go back into American history and America's traditional understanding of natural rights and laws to disprove Bartholet, but we don't even have to do that. Modern American law, from the twentieth century alone, proves that parental rights are—and always have been—intrinsically woven into the legal fabric of our nation. I will cite just a few examples.

In *Pierce v. Society of Sisters* (1925), the United States Supreme Court ruled in favor of parental rights and against a 1922 Oregon state law that required all parents to send their children to public schools under penalty of fines or imprisonment. The court ruled that "the fundamental theory of liberty upon which all governments in this Union rest *excludes any general power of the state* to standardize its children by forcing them to accept instruction from public teachers only" [emphasis mine].[21] Furthermore, the court, in reaffirming that parents had an inherent right to send their children to private or religious schools, stated that the "child is not the mere creature of the State; those who nurture him and direct his destiny have the right, coupled with the high duty, to recognize and prepare him for additional obligations."[22]

In *Wisconsin v. Yoder* (1972), the United States Supreme Court ruled against a state law requiring school attendance until the age of sixteen, and in favor of the religious liberty of parents (in this case Amish parents) to withdraw their children from school and rear and educate them according to their faith. The court ruled that the state, while having a legitimate interest in children's education, "is not totally free from a balancing process when it impinges on fundamental rights and interests, such as those specifically protected by the Free Exercise Clause of the First Amendment, and the traditional interest of parents with respect to the religious upbringing of their children."[23] The court recognized again that parents are the primary authority in the upbringing of their children and that this "is now established beyond debate as an enduring American tradition."[24]

In *Parham v. J.R.* (1979), the United States Supreme Court affirmed the assumption in American law "that natural bonds of affection lead parents to act in the best interests of their children."[25] In other words, parents enjoy the benefit of the doubt when it comes to the choices they make for their children. The court ruled, "The statist notion that governmental power should supersede parental authority in all cases because some parents abuse and neglect children is repugnant to American tradition."[26]

Professor Bartholet, however, not only despises parental rights, she also holds the First Amendment in contempt, because—in addition to the anti-Christian bigotry she's espoused—Bartholet recognizes that the Constitution's guarantee to the free exercise of religion is itself a protection of parental rights. At the close of her eighty-page anti-homeschooling treatise, Bartholet argues that U.S. constitutional law should be changed because the homeschool "movement relies on adult freedom of religion rights to oppose regulation affecting religious homeschoolers. But such rights should not trump child rights to exposure to alternative views, enabling them to exercise meaningful future choice about their religion."[27]

We are now reaching the crux of Professor Bartholet's anti-homeschooling crusade. "This homeschooling regime poses real dangers to children and to society," Bartholet claims. When parents homeschool their children, Bartholet contends, "Society loses out. . . ." Moreover, homeschooling "presents both academic concerns and democratic concerns."[28] But how could that be? As we've seen, homeschooled students perform better academically than public school students. As for democratic concerns, isn't the free exercise of religion and parents' rights an exercise of our legitimate constitutional freedoms? Clearly, the answer is yes, but that's not the point. The point is that Bartholet wants all children indoctrinated in neo-Marxist ideology in public schools, especially if their parents oppose it.

Appropriate education, Bartholet claims, "makes children aware of important cultural values and provides skills enabling children to participate productively in their communities and the larger society through various forms of civic engagement. Even homeschooling parents capable of satisfying the academic function of education are not likely to be capable of satisfying the democratic function."[29] I wonder what that "democratic function" might be.

So, to review, we've established that Bartholet's effort to ban home-schooling on academic grounds is unfounded. Homeschooled students outperform public school students academically by every measure. We've also noted that Bartholet's anti-homeschooling crusade is not about child maltreatment, because we know that public school children are more likely to be abused than homeschooled children. Moreover, we noted Bartholet's animus towards parents and her disgust with the First Amendment right to free exercise of religion.

Here's where Bartholet's camouflage begins to fall away, revealing that her hostility to homeschooling is nothing more than her desire to indoctrinate all children, without parental consent, in neo-Marxist ideology through the public school system. "'[P]reparation for citizen-ship,'" she writes, "including exposure to the values of tolerance and deliberative democracy, has been seen as a primary goal of public educa-tion from its origins. Based on both child rights and state rights, Rob Reich concludes that 'at a bare minimum one function of any school environment must be to expose children to and engage students with values and beliefs other than those of their parents.'"[30]

Bartholet says children who attend public school "grow up exposed to community values, social values, democratic values, ideas about nondiscrimination and tolerance of other people's viewpoints."[31]

Bartholet suggests that homeschooling "not only violates children's right to a 'meaningful education' and their right to be protected from potential child abuse, but may keep them from contributing positively to a democratic society."[32]

Democracy is widely understood to mean government of the people, by the people, and for the people, based on inherent individual rights unalienable by a government granted only limited powers. A hallmark of democracy is tolerating differing viewpoints, allowing dissent, debating competing ideas, equality before the law, and the protection of civil rights for everyone within the democratic state.

This includes those with minority opinions or beliefs, not just for the majoritarian faction.

That, however, is *not* what Bartholet means when she says the word democracy. Bartholet is parroting John Dewey, an atheistic socialist who conceptualized and then propagandized for the Marxist education system in the Soviet Union.

John Dewey is billed in history books as one of the most influential "educational reformers" of the twentieth century. A more apt description of Dewey would describe him as one of the most destructive forces behind the modern-day American education system.

There's a reason the left hails Dewey as the "father of Progressive education." Dewey's ideology is what we're seeing fail our children in the public education system right now.

In fact Hank Edmondson, a professor at Georgia College, wrote in his book *John Dewey and the Decline of American Education* that the reason American public education is "unsound" is "largely attributable to the influence of John Dewey."[33]

Years before Paulo Freire argued that "knowledge" is an oppressive system in which teachers hold power over students, before Freire suggested that teachers stop teaching objective reality and instead learn from the "lived experiences" of students, Dewey rejected the idea of teachers imparting knowledge to students. This was not real learning, he said. Instead, Dewey suggested that school should be a "social" rather than an academic institution, a force of socialization intended to serve "democratic institutions." In his seminal treatise *Democracy and Education*, Dewey wrote that "we may produce in schools a projection in type of the society we should like to realize, and by forming minds in accord with it gradually modify the larger and more recalcitrant features of adult society."[34]

This might sound familiar. This is what we see happening in our public school system today. Public schools aren't schools anymore, they're indoctrination centers. Math isn't math, it's *woke* math where grading is considered racist. Science isn't science, it's climate change alarmism, comprehensive sexuality education, and the transgender ideology of Queer Theory. History isn't history, it's been supplanted by the revisionist political narratives of Howard Zinn (who, by the way, was a fan of Paulo Freire) and the factually inaccurate 1619 Project from the *New York Times.* English Grammar and Writing have been replaced by the notion that Grammar is an oppressive system based in white supremacy. Reading has been utterly infiltrated with Queer Theory and Critical Race Theory, while "diversity, equity, and inclusion" rule the Literature choices. You can hardly walk into a public elementary school classroom without seeing the Black Lives Matter flag, the "Gay Pride" flag, and a poster announcing it's a "pronoun friendly" zone. Students are taught the Founding Fathers were racist, that capitalism is oppressive, and that the United States is built upon stolen land and grounded in slavery and is therefore irredeemably evil.

Our public schools have been transformed into the "social" indoctrination centers Dewey envisioned, where schools are producing "the society we should like to realize."

Public schools will inevitably indoctrinate children. *That's their purpose*—and that's fine and normal. As we noted before, indoctrination is a morally neutral concept. The important question is to *what end* are children being indoctrinated? The old idea was to make American students patriotic, upright citizens, with solid academic skills and sound Christian morals. But what society, through the formation of children's minds, did Dewey want to realize?

Dewey himself was not an outright Marxist, but he was a propagandist for the Russian Revolution and Bolshevik Marxism.

Dewey lavished praise on the Bolshevik school system in Communist Russia, the same system that was violently wrested from private and religious institutions and expropriated by the atheist, Communist state apparatus. Dewey called that "educational transformation."[35] In fact Dewey argued that *real* education could only take place in a collectivist society, writing, "The Russian educational situation is enough to convert one to the idea that only in a society based upon the cooperative principle can the ideals of educational reformers be adequately carried into operation."[36]

Dewey gushed about Soviet schools, and in turn, the Bolsheviks admitted John Dewey's "tremendous influence" on their school system, gobbling up John Dewey's books as quickly as they could translate them into Russian. As Dr. Paul Kengor notes in his book *Dupes*, the Bolsheviks copied Dewey's radical idea for school transformation more than Americans did at the time.[37] Really, when Dewey gushed about Soviet schools, he was gushing about his own educational theories being put into practice.

In 1928, Dewey accepted an invitation for a month-long jaunt around the Soviet Union (under the watchful eyes of his Soviet tour guides and handlers). On his return Dewey published a series of essays, later collected into a book titled *Impressions of Soviet Russia and the Revolutionary World*, in which he called Russia's Communist revolution a "success."[38] Dewey brushed aside the fact that the Communists had imprisoned, tortured, executed, and intentionally starved millions of people, writing that this was a "phase" and not true communism. "My conviction is unshaken that this phase of affairs [in the Soviet Union] is secondary in importance to something else that can only be termed a revolution. That the existing state of affairs is not Communism but a transition to it; that in the dialectic of history the function of Bolshevism is to annul itself; that the dictatorship of the proletariat is but an aspect of class-war, the antithesis to the thesis of the dictatorship of bourgeois capitalism existing in other countries; that it is destined to disappear in a new synthesis."[39]

Dewey admitted his excuses for Bolshevik violence "are things the Communists themselves tell us. The present state . . . is necessarily a

state of transition to the exact goal prescribed by the Marxian philosophy of history."[40] He chided opponents of the Soviet Union for
focusing on communism and instructed people to start appreciating
the revolution instead. "I have heard altogether too much about
Communism . . . and altogether too little about the Revolution."[41]

Dewey said he believed what he read about the millions of people
suffering oppression under the Bolsheviks, but he quickly dismissed
that "belief" in favor of what he saw with his Communist tour guides:
that "life for the masses goes on with regularity, safety and decorum."[42]
One can only imagine the Bolsheviks' delight to read Dewey's glowing
Communist apologetics, which is certainly why they invited Dewey to
visit and see his own education policies in action.

What Communist education was doing for Soviet Russia, Dewey
believed "progressive" education must do for American democracy,
which needed to be transformed by an educational revolution. Politics
alone was too slow and arduous of a process, Dewey argued, whereas
"socializing" children in public schools would take but one generation
to alter the moral fabric of America, and reconfigure American society
to be ready for an economic transformation as well.

Society ultimately becomes what students are taught. Therefore,
students are not individual learners but rather a thread in the fabric of
society at large. That was Dewey's belief—and we need to understand
that belief when anti-homeschoolers say that homeschooled students
aren't properly socialized.

Generally, this is understood to mean, "Are homeschooled kids socially
backward?" or "Do homeschooled kids lack proper social skills?" The
answer to that would be no; homeschooled students are not socially back-
wards. In fact, there is plenty of research to show that homeschooled
children are more socially competent than their public school counterparts.

As Lee Stough has written in his study of children in West Virginia,
"the necessary skills, knowledge, and attitudes needed to function in

society are also being acquired by home educated children at a rate similar to that of conventionally schooled children."[43] In fact, according to studies assembled by Stough, "In comparisons with national norms the homeschool group is typically above average" when it comes to self-esteem, and "homeschooled students were much less likely to exhibit behavior problems. . . ."[44] Moreover, Andrews University's John Wesley Taylor wrote, "Insofar as self-concept is a reflector of socialization, it would appear that few home-schooling children are socially deprived. Critics of the home school should not urge self-concept and socialization rationales. These factors apparently favor home schoolers over the conventionally schooled population."[45] According to J. Gary Knowles, who studied the outcome of homeschooled students in adult life, "I have found no evidence that these adults were even moderately disadvantaged. . . . Two-thirds of them were married, the norm for adults their age, and none were unemployed or on any form of welfare assistance. More than three quarters felt that being taught at home had actually helped them to interact with people from different levels of society."[46]

But this is not what Dewey means when he talks of "socialization." For Dewey, socialization meant harnessing the public school system to produce a political result. In Dewey's words, as noted before, the goal is to "produce in schools a projection in type of the society we should like to realize, and by forming minds in accord with it gradually modify the larger and more recalcitrant features of adult society."[47] In case you were wondering what those "recalcitrant features of adult society" were, it would be all the things that Dewey and the new Marxists most disdain about homeschoolers: that they might be religiously observant; that they might be wedded to traditional morals and ethics; that they might be individualists who resist collectivism (like that preached by Queer Theory and Critical Race Theory); and that they might be more interested in upholding traditional academic standards and patriotic values than in committing themselves to Marxism.

This is why, when Dewey uses the word "democracy," he does not mean a government of the people, by the people, and for the people. Dewey wrote that "democracy is more than a form of government; it is primarily a mode of associated living, of conjoint communicated experience."[48] Democracy, Dewey said, is composed of social relationships among people and institutions, both cultural and governmental. "[M]en are not isolated non-social atoms," Dewey wrote, "but are men only when in intrinsic relations," and therefore a majority rule governmental system can only truly represent the interests of society "so far as they have become organically related to one another, or are possessed of unity of purpose and interest."[49]

In other words, democracy is collectivism, according to Dewey. It's not, of course, but Dewey redefined the word as Marxists often do. Dewey wanted the public school system to "socialize" children to be ideologically identical. Dewey, after all, was a socialist with Communist sympathies; he wasn't a member of the Communist Party, but he was a member of the Socialist Party.[50]

He eventually broke with Stalin's Russia, but the damage Dewey inflicted on the American education system was already done.

Dewey, who staunchly believed Bolshevik Russia's education system to be a "democratic" institution,[51] remains one of the most influential figures on American public education. Dewey's books, including *Democracy and Education*, remain staples at teachers' colleges. At Columbia Teachers College, where it first gained popularity, *Democracy and Education* was considered the teachers' "bible."[52]

Harvard professor Elizabeth Bartholet embraces Dewey's work in her crusade against homeschooling. "Homeschooling," Bartholet argues, "presents both academic concerns and democratic concerns."[53] "This homeschooling regime poses real dangers to children and to society," Bartholet claims.[54] "Many homeschool because they want to isolate their children from ideas and values central to our democracy," Bartholet contends, "determined to keep their children from exposure to views that might enable autonomous choice about their future lives."[55]

Dewey demonstrated with crystal clarity what he meant by the phrase "democratic" institutions and what Bartholet means by "democracy." Dewey used the same words to describe the Communist educational structure in Bolshevik Russia. Elizabeth Bartholet repeatedly cites Dewey in her work about the socialization of homeschooled students and their participation in "democracy." For instance,

- "John Scott Gray, *Dewey and the American Movement to Homeschooling*, 46 EDUC. 3–13, 441, 442 (2018) (religious homeschool education may prevent fostering a 'permeating social spirit,' sense of collective responsibility and 'effective moral training.')"[56]
- "*See* JOHN DEWEY, DEMOCRACY AND EDUCATION 99–100 (1916) ('[I]solation makes for rigidity . . . for static and selfish ideals within the group. That savage tribes regard aliens and enemies as synonymous is not accidental.')"[57]

The crux of Bartholet's crusade against homeschooling—that homeschooled students are abused because they are deprived of a public school experience that is ostensibly the only way to prepare them for society—is built on John Dewey's ideology. Bartholet, like Dewey before her, believes public schools should indoctrinate children into a collectivist ideology and thus reshape American society. Homeschooling certainly represents an existential threat to that Marxist agenda.

Notably, Elizabeth Bartholet invited only "experts" to her anti-homeschooling conference (which incidentally was later canceled due to COVID-19 lockdowns). The invite list was not a coincidence.

The Marxist left believes it knows best: about politics, about morals, and about what your children should learn. They will continue to target homeschooling in the name of "the experts" who know better. That ideology—"rule by the experts" is also known as technocracy, and it's the subject of our next chapter.

CHAPTER 9

"The Experts"

D r. Anthony Fauci, then director of the National Institute of Allergy and Infectious Diseases at the National Institutes of Health, proclaimed on *Face the Nation* in November 2021: "So it's easy to criticize, but they're really criticizing science because I represent science. That's dangerous. To me, that's more dangerous than the slings and the arrows that get thrown at me. I'm not going to be around here forever, but science is going to be here forever. And if you damage science, you are doing something very detrimental to society long after I leave. And that's what I worry about."[1] Despite Fauci's best efforts to paint himself as a staunch defender of the sanctity of objective scientific inquiry, his words are transparent; what he really meant was that no one is allowed to challenge his political dictates. If we do, we will be branded as science-deniers and suffer the consequences, whether they be social, professional, or political. He couched this notion within a logical fallacy, the "appeal to authority" fallacy, and the public mocked him for it.

Actually, no one did more to expose the corruption that exists in the field of science and public health than Fauci. Not only was Fauci wrong, but he also blatantly lied about the efficacy of face masks, lockdown measures, social distancing, and ultimately his pet mRNA vaccine.

If we define "science" as the pursuit of truth in the natural world, supported by the rigorous testing of falsifiable hypotheses, then no, Fauci does not represent science. In that scenario Fauci might be more accurately characterized as the villain of science, the Anti-Science. If, however, we are talking about the bureaucratic *institutions* of science—medical schools, credentialing and governing boards like the American Medical Association and the American Academy of Pediatrics, Big Pharma, the Centers for Disease Control and Prevention, the Food and Drug Administration, the National Institutes of Health, and government-funded labs at universities across the country—then yes, indeed, Dr. Fauci does represent "science." Dr. Fauci is, in fact, the perfect poster octogenarian for the profiteering and corruption of *institutions* that claim to be scientific institutions.

Dr. Anthony Stephen Fauci is a technocrat. His betrayal of *real* science is a sickening example of the way technocracy has infiltrated the institutions we trust most in our nation, our medical system in particular. Dr. Fauci spent his career sitting at the nucleus of the administrative state, which wields its power over our lives in the name of technocracy.

Technocracy, to define it simply, is rule by the experts. Instead of democratically elected representatives deliberating in a majority-rule body like the United States Congress and casting votes on pieces of potential legislation, a technocracy is staffed by "experts" in various fields who dictate public policy according to "science."

Technocracy, as an idea, goes back at least to the ancient Greeks, but it is most often associated with a French socialist named Henri de Saint-Simon (1760–1825). Saint-Simon believed that government ought to be composed of "scientific experts" (and, oddly, some artists) and formed into a governing council. This would work beautifully, Saint-Simon argued, because technology and science are apolitical, therefore partisanship and competing political agendas would be eliminated from government. Even religion, Saint-Simon argued, should be rejected and clergy demoted and replaced by men of science. Science, Saint-Simon believed, would serve as the great unifier of all peoples. This would be accomplished, according to Saint-Simon, by the transition of capitalism to state ownership of industry plus control of both industry and society by a governing body of "scientific experts." Henri de Saint-Simon became known as a "utopian socialist" for his unrealistic ideas; nonetheless, Saint-Simon's ideas significantly influenced Karl Marx and a man named Thorstein Veblen, whom we will encounter shortly.[2]

Another proponent of technocracy was Alexander Bogdanov (1873–1928), a Russian scientist and physician who was also a Marxist, a founding member of the Bolshevik movement, and a critic of Vladimir Lenin. In addition, Bogdanov was a popular writer of science fiction, and his novel *Engineer Menni* depicts a civilization on Mars that was transitioning from capitalism to communism with the help of—perhaps you guessed from the title—an engineer named Menni.[3] Engineer Menni, in Bogdanov's story, was responsible for constructing canals on Mars to better connect and organize civilization. The governing body of Mars, after the transition away from capitalism, was composed of "scientific experts" who made all the political decisions. When the Martians considered colonizing Earth, the debate was not among "the people" or politicians, but between an astronautical engineer, a mathematician, and a physician who formed a panel of "scientific experts."

Bogdanov's *Engineer Menni* is a story of technocracy, an illustration of Bogdanov's belief that workers —the proletariat—lack the knowledge to run a communist society, which would necessitate rule by techno-crats, who often happen to be communist ideologues. Technocracy, according to Bogdanov, is a bridge from capitalism to communism.[4]

The word "technocracy" was perhaps first coined in the United States by engineer William Henry Smyth, who defined it as "the rule of the people made effective through the agency of their servants, the scientists and engineers."[5]

There is some debate over whether Smyth himself coined the word, or whether it had been used already to describe "rule by the scientific experts." But in any case "technocracy" soon became a social-political movement.

In the United States, it was led by self-taught engineer Howard Scott, who had acquired his engineering skills at construction sites and was later revealed as a fraud, claiming education and accomplishments he did not have. In 1919 Scott founded the Technical Alliance, a group of anti-capitalists who wanted society to be organized and ruled by technical experts. The goal of the Technical Alliance was to document the waste of capitalism—time, resources, and money—and propose technocracy (and social engineering) as a more efficient solution. Less than two years after the Technical Alliance was founded, however, it shuttered, a failure.[6]

In 1932, Scott resurrected his idea at Columbia University with the "Committee on Technocracy," which lasted only until January 1933. Scott then launched another attempt to popularize technocracy; this time he called it Technocracy Inc.[7]

Technocracy Inc. described its ideology as follows, "Technocracy is the science of social engineering, the scientific operation of the entire social mechanism to produce and distribute goods and services to the entire population of this continent. For the first time in human history it will be done as a scientific, technical, engineering problem. There will be no place for Politics or Politicians, Finance or Financiers, Rackets or Racketeers."[8] Though it still technically exists, Technocracy Inc. was plagued by dissension, disputes over the accuracy of its data, and criticism from business leaders, professional engineers, and others, and saw its popularity fade rapidly after the Second World War.

At the time, technocracy was banned in Canada. The head of the Regina branch of Technocracy Inc. in Canada, Joshua Haldeman, was arrested for being a member of an illegal organization. Haldeman was Elon Musk's grandfather.[9]

One of the prominent founding members of Howard Scott's original Technocracy Alliance was Thorstein Veblen (1857–1929), a socialist who rose to prominence during the administration of President Woodrow Wilson. In 1919, with John Dewey and others, Veblen helped found the New School for Social Research after being forced to resign from the University of Chicago for committing adultery.[10] In 1921 Veblen penned *Engineers and the Price System,* which proposed a "Soviet of Technicians" to govern society.[11] Veblen's technocratic socialist ideology was influenced by Henri de Saint-Simon, Dewey, and Charles Fourier, the socialist-collectivist who inspired Albert Brisbane to establish collectivist communities in the United States.

Given that the technocratic ruling class was inspired by communist, socialist, Marxist ideas, it was, and is, hard to believe that these governing "experts" would also be non-partisan and apolitical.

Some say that the technocracy movement faded in the 1930s because President Franklin Delano Roosevelt's New Deal made it irrelevant, but, in fact, technocracy was simply renamed. Technocracy exists today in our country. Today we know it as the administrative state.

The administrative state is the permanent bureaucracy of Washington, D.C., or what you and I might call "the deep state" or "the swamp." The administrative state is composed of government employees and appointed officials in agencies, regulatory bodies, and cabinet departments within the executive branch of the federal government. These bureaucrats are not elected and have no accountability to voters. Most of them are nearly impossible to fire, and yet the administrative state boasts the incredible power to impose rules and regulations that control nearly every aspect of our lives. These agency rules and regulations are legally binding. How did this happen?

Simply put, Congress, in a blatant dereliction of its constitutional duty to provide a necessary check on executive power, delegated much of its authority to the executive branch. When Congress passes legislation, and the president signs it, the new law is sent to the agencies of the executive branch for a process called "rulemaking." Rulemaking happens because congressional legislators rarely provide clear explanations of the policies they pretend to legislate. Instead, they use sweeping, vague language that allows them to avoid accountability for anything in a bill that might be considered unpopular by their constituents, and therefore threaten a congressman's hold on power. Because the law requires clarification, the executive branch agencies create "rules" to interpret the law so it can be implemented. In other words, the legislative branch of the U.S. federal government has effectively surrendered its legislative authority to unelected bureaucrats who exploit the broad mandates in poorly crafted legislation to fit their own political agenda. This is the administrative state, composed of unelected, unaccountable bureaucrats who rule our lives. It's the most powerful institution in our nation; it is, effectively, "rule by the experts." It's technocracy.

The administrative state, however, is not part of the United States Constitution. The Framers did not intend for Congress to give away their legislative power to executive agencies. As every American citizen used to know, each of the three branches of the federal government—legislative, executive, and judicial—was meant to check and balance the power of the other. Moreover, the power of all three

branches was limited. The federal government had only powers specifically delegated to it by the Constitution. All unspecified powers were
reserved to the states and their people.

For instance, the Ninth Amendment states, "The enumeration in the Constitution, of certain rights, shall not be construed
to deny or disparage others retained by the people."[12] The Tenth
Amendment adds, "The powers not delegated to the United States
by the Constitution, nor prohibited by it to the states, are reserved
to the states respectively, or to the people." Moreover, federal legislative power is reserved for Congress. Article I, Section 1 of the U.S.
Constitution reads, "All legislative Powers herein granted shall be
vested in a Congress of the United States, which shall consist of a
Senate and House of Representatives."[13]

For much of our nation's history, this is how our federal government operated. If the legislature attempted to "delegate" its legislative
duty to the executive branch, this was considered an obvious violation
of the separation of powers doctrine, and the judicial branch rightly
prohibited it. The separation of powers is critical to preventing the government from arbitrarily ruling over the people with no accountability
and violating people's rights in the process. This is why the Framers
of our Constitution deliberately constructed the three branches of the
federal government with separate powers, and limited those powers,
to protect people's individual rights and the rights of the states against
the federal government.

Yet, our modern legislative branch defies the Constitution by giving
away its legislative power to the executive branch. The modern executive branch happily expropriates powers *not* enumerated to it. The
modern judicial branch only checks to see that the legislature has
formally delegated its authority to the executive branch, and then will-
ingly defers to the executive branch agencies as "the experts" instead
of enforcing the United States Constitution.

It is a vicious cycle that only continues to worsen. When did our federal government get so off track? How did this happen? The short answer is "progressives" did this. More specifically, President Woodrow Wilson started it. Wilson rejected the Founding Fathers' idea that the purpose of government is to protect the inherent rights of the people. According to Wilson, the Constitution was outdated and needed to be improved. He advocated for what people today refer to as a "living constitution." Wilson himself wrote in 1912 that "[l]iving political constitutions must be Darwinian in structure and practice."[14] In other words, they must *evolve*, progressing past our constitutionally enshrined limited government.

Wilson naively envisioned a politically neutral class of government bureaucrats who would operate the government administratively in good faith without being influenced by partisan politics. Hilarious idea, isn't it? Wilson evidently believed that mankind's lust for power had been cured, and therefore, a government staffed with ostensibly neutral and unaccountable bureaucrats would make rules only in good faith without allowing partisan politics to sway them.

In the early days of his presidency, Wilson lamented that "[t]he Constitution was founded on the law of gravitation. The government was to exist and move by virtue of the efficacy of 'checks and balances.' The trouble with the theory is that government is not a machine, but a living thing. No living thing can have its organs offset against each other, as checks, and live."[15]

Wilson's philosophy mirrored that of Frank Goodnow (1859–1939), a highly influential political figure who became president of Johns Hopkins University and the first president of the American Political Science Association. An "expert" in administrative law, Goodnow—like Wilson—rejected the Founding Fathers' idea that the purpose of government is to protect the natural rights of citizens. The Founders' ideas "of social compact and natural right," he wrote, were "worse than useless," because they "retard" the "development" of government to meet new, modern demands.[16] Both Goodnow and Wilson believed that the Constitution was outdated and its current form should be discarded, and that government needed to be larger and more powerful to "take care" of people as the "times demand." You can hear the echoes of Wilson and Goodnow in every modern Democrat who wants to enlarge the scope of the federal government, wants more power for the administrative state, and thinks individual rights are of no consequence to the greater good. It was the argument behind every COVID-19-related restriction on liberty. It is the argument behind every attempt to gut the Second Amendment. It is the argument behind every assertion by education technocrats that homeschooled kids need to be subjected to—"socialized" to—Queer Theory and Critical Race Theory for the sake of "democracy."

During his presidency Woodrow Wilson wasn't successful in creating the administrative state he and Goodnow envisioned, but his radical ideas helped pave the way for the administrative state we have today. Had the Supreme Court continued to apply the "nondelegation" principle of constitutional law, prohibiting the legislature from delegating its legislative authority to executive agencies, none of this would have happened.

But in the 1930s, according to the Library of Congress, "A decline of judicial reliance on the nondelegation doctrine soon followed in the years after the Court issued its decisions in *Panama Refining* and *Schechter*. This shift in the Court's approach to the nondelegation doctrine coincided with a broader 'constitutional revolution' at the Supreme Court that largely affirmed the Federal Government's broad powers to guide the nation's social and economic development."[17] To the surprise of no one, President Franklin D. Roosevelt took advantage of this situation and rapidly expanded the power, reach, and authority of the executive branch.

Franklin D. Roosevelt's New Deal created a new bureaucracy in the executive branch that included legislative and judicial powers as part of the "rulemaking" process, a critical violation of the separation of powers doctrine in our federal government. Now, unelected bureaucrats make rules that we are beholden to follow because the agency "experts" know best.

Technocracy, in practice, is on full display in the administrative state. For instance, during judicial reviews of agency actions, or during so-called "notice and comment periods," executive agency rule-makers often justify their rules and regulations on the basis of "science" or on technical grounds. In other words, if administrative agencies argue that their rules are "science based," they are usually allowed to create binding rules over us while circumventing the legislative process.

This begets an enormous problem inherent to technocracy: "science" and "technology" are not the only variables in the equation when creating public policy. Another, of course, is the Constitution. Still another is moral judgment. The premise of democracy, of self-governance, is that people have a right to influence the policies that will have an impact on their lives. If the moral judgment of the people through their elected officials is delegated to the administrative state, then it will be the moral judgment of the unelected bureaucrats that drive our policies. And yet, there is no such thing as a "neutral" administrative class. Instead, the administrative state simply shirks responsibility for its moral judgments while technocrats impose their version of morals on us via "rule by science" or "rule by the experts."

Technocracy is embedded not only in the powerful administrative state of the federal government, but also in institutions like teachers' unions that determine much of what our children are taught in public schools. The largest teachers' union in the nation, the National Education Association, tweeted, "Educators love their students and know better than anyone what they need to learn and to thrive."[18]

Who knows best about your children? Not the children's parents; that's a job for *the experts.*

In 2021, during a gubernatorial debate with Republican candidate Glenn Youngkin, Democratic candidate and former Virginia governor Terry McAuliffe admitted he intended to exclude parents from their children's education in favor of what *the experts* think. McAuliffe said, "I'm not going to let parents come into schools and actually take books out and make their own decisions. I don't think parents should be telling schools what they should teach."[19]

Who should be in charge of a government-run, mandatory public school system that will shape the next generation of Americas? *The experts.* And not just any experts.

The experts we're supposed to listen to are those who peddle the racism of Critical Race Theory and want to sexualize our children with Queer Theory and comprehensive sexuality education. They're the experts who want to ban homeschooling and prevent religious parents from instilling their values in their children. They're the experts, like those at Planned Parenthood, who know better than parents when their child seeks an abortion or life-altering pharmaceuticals to "change genders."

The experience of our government's response to the COVID-19 pandemic—where government bureaucrats trampled on our civil rights, locked down our society, masked our children and deprived them of playgrounds, stifled free and open scientific discussion of data, unjustly scapegoated "the unvaccinated," forced vaccines on employees under penalty of being fired, and outlawed gatherings unless they were organized for neo-Marxist political purposes—served as an eye-opening moment for the public. Suddenly, the scope of technocracy in our country and the politicization of "the experts" was laid bare. Far from being a politically neutral class making science-based judgments unencumbered by partisan ideology, the technocrat experts of the administrative state proved themselves to be woke, neo-Marxist radicals.

This is true in many institutions outside government too, where "experts" pretending to be neutral administrators of science are instead propagating corruption or outright Marxism. For instance, "the experts" at the American Academy of Pediatrics push "gender identity" propaganda in the name of science while disregarding parental judgment (and science) on co-sleeping, sleep training, and breastfeeding.[20] Similarly, "the experts" at the Centers for Disease Control dictate a vaccine schedule for children that now includes over seventy shots—that are not all safe, effective, or necessary—and many of these injections are mandatory for children to attend public school.[21] Both the American Academy of Pediatrics and the Centers for Disease Control are thoroughly corrupted by financial interests and ideological agendas, yet portray themselves as neutral "experts." This is technocracy.

Technocracy is seeping into law as well. In Connecticut, a new bill would allow children as young as twelve years old to undergo vaccination procedures against the wishes of their parents if *the experts* decide it will benefit the child.[22] Likewise in Virginia a new bill would allow a child to "transition genders" against the wishes of his or her parents if *the experts* claim the child is capable of consent.[23]

Technocracy is not neutral. It is not apolitical. Technocratic rule by "the experts" *always* includes politically partisan moral judgment hidden under "the science." It is merely another means by which neo-Marxists impose their will, subvert our republican form of government, deny our rights as voters, citizens, and parents, in order to achieve the ultimate purpose Alexander Bogdanov envisioned: the total transformation of our society from free market capitalism to the totalitarianism of communism.

PART II

Charting Our Way Back

Now that I've thoroughly depressed and frightened you about the state of our nation and the targets placed on the bodies and minds of our children, let's regroup.

This is not hopeless. We haven't lost the culture war. There *is* a way forward.

Our solution begins by acknowledging one simple, objective truth:

If we refuse to acknowledge the reality of the political enemy we're facing, we won't fight well against it, and therefore, we won't win.

This has been the Achilles' heel of Republican politicians since the last great fighter, Ronald Reagan, fully recognized the threat behind the spread of Communism in our nation and around the globe and routed it. Subsequent generations of Republicans, enjoying the freedom and prosperity Reagan created, and naive about the slow march of Communism through our civil and political institutions, grew soft and bleary-eyed. We are now paying the price.

The good news is: **If we *do* acknowledge the reality of the political enemy we're facing, we *can* fight well and we *can* win.**

I want to win, and I know you do too. I love the United States of America. She has given me the freedom to live virtuously and provided an opportunity for me, my family, and my loved ones to thrive. The time for milquetoast politicians has passed. We must now recapture our institutions and restore the American dream for ourselves and our posterity.

"Freedom is never more than one generation away from extinction," Ronald Reagan reminded us in a 1961 speech. "We didn't pass it on to our children in the bloodstream. The only way they can inherit the freedom we have known is if we fight for it, protect it, defend it, and then hand it to them with the well-taught lessons of how they in their lifetime must do the same. And if you and I don't do this, then you and I may well spend our sunset years telling our children and our children's children what it once was like in America when men were free."[1]

Reagan's words remain true, but the Marxists will never allow us to restore the glorious, prosperous days of a free United States if we neglect to defeat the evil communist ideology before it consumes our nation entirely. The culture wars are our generation's grand fight for freedom. I'm ready, and I know you are too. The previous nine chapters of this book invigorated my spirit because we have learned the secret weapon for victory: we are now armed with the knowledge of exactly who we're fighting; we understand how they subverted our institutions; and we recognize the ideology they've weaponized against our children. It's only when our side fails to acknowledge those three elements—the enemy we're fighting, his tactics, and his ideological motivations—that we flounder politically.

Today, we can confidently declare: we see the reality looming before us.

We're experiencing a great awakening in our country. Tens of millions of Americans are now clear-eyed about the threats we face and courageous enough to fight back and win.

My hope is that each one of you reading this book is hungry to take up this fight, eager to face reality, and has the resolve to save our nation, no matter the trials and tribulations you might endure on the way.

In order to accomplish victory, however, we must embrace our constitutional, moral, spiritual, and legal heritage based upon *ordered liberty*.

CHAPTER 10

What Is Liberty?

Thomas Jefferson, the principal author of one of the greatest documents ever written—the American Declaration of Independence—once said, "Bacon, Locke and Newton . . . I consider them as the three greatest men that have ever lived, without any exception."[1]

Jefferson even commissioned a painting of Francis Bacon, John Locke, and Isaac Newton—all intertwined on one canvas in a rather strange shrine to the three men—because, Jefferson claimed, "as having laid the foundations of those superstructures which have been raised in the Physical & Moral sciences, I would wish to form them into a knot on the same canvas, that they may not be confounded at all with the herd of other great men."[2]

The Declaration of Independence, one of the most brilliant and inspired political documents ever written, was heavily influenced by John Locke's political philosophy. In his most famous work, "The

Second Treatise of Government," Locke argued that men are endowed with natural rights, including the rights to "life, liberty, and estate."[3] If those rights are violated, with no political recourse open to restore them, then revolution is justified. Locke wrote, "But if a long train of abuses, prevarications and artifices, all tending the same way, make the design visible to the people, and they cannot but feel what they lie under, and see whither they are going; it is not to be wondered, that they should then rouze themselves, and endeavour to put the rule into such hands which may secure to them the ends for which government was at first erected. . . ."[4]

This became the philosophical backbone for our Declaration of Independence, where Thomas Jefferson wrote:

> We hold these truths to be self-evident, that all men are created equal, that they are endowed by their Creator with certain unalienable Rights, that among these are Life, Liberty and the pursuit of Happiness.—That to secure these rights, Governments are instituted among Men, deriving their just powers from the consent of the governed,—That whenever any Form of Government becomes destructive of these ends, it is the Right of the People to alter or to abolish it, and to institute new Government, laying its foundation on such principles and organizing its powers in such form, as to them shall seem most likely to effect their Safety and Happiness. Prudence, indeed, will dictate that Governments long established should not be changed for light and transient causes; and accordingly all experience hath shewn, that mankind are more disposed to suffer, while evils are sufferable, than to right themselves by abolishing the forms to which they are accustomed. But when a long train of abuses and usurpations, pursuing invariably the same Object evinces a design

to reduce them under absolute Despotism, it is their right, it
is their duty, to throw off such Government, and to provide
new Guards for their future security.[5]

The words thrill me. Jefferson once claimed he wrote the Declaration without notes, simply allowing the American spirit to flow through
his quill pen onto parchment. Jefferson described the Declaration as
"an expression of the American mind."[6] But it was also an expression
of Jefferson's admiration for John Locke, and Locke's belief in the pri-
macy of individual rights. Locke wrote in his "Second Treatise on
Government," "The *natural liberty* of man is to be free from any superior power on earth, and not to be under the will or legislative authority
of man, but to have only the law of nature for his rule."[7]

Men, in the state of nature, Locke argued, enjoyed absolute liberty;
and government should as closely as possible guard man's natural state
of liberty. "To understand political power right," Locke contended,
"and derive it from its original, we must consider, what state all men
are naturally in, and that is, a state of *perfect freedom* to order their
actions, and dispose of their possessions and persons, as they think
fit, within the bounds of the law of nature, without asking leave, or
depending upon the will of any other man."[8]

It was from Locke that Jefferson devised his ideas of how government power should be strictly limited, divided, decentralized, and subject
to checks and balances, or even overthrown. Central to Locke's and
Jefferson's political philosophy was that government has no authority to
violate man's natural rights, rights endowed by Nature and God.[9] In the
Declaration of Independence, Jefferson argues, along Lockean lines, that
the British government violated the natural rights of the American colonists and that the colonists had been left with no recourse but revolution.[10]

Today, it's become fashionable in modern American politics for
Republicans to embrace a Lockean definition of liberty: the freedom

to do whatever one pleases, without government interference, as long as it doesn't violate another person's natural rights to life, liberty, and the pursuit of happiness. This philosophy today is called libertarianism.

Libertarians center their philosophy around absolute individual freedom, or as close to absolute liberty as a society can achieve, particularly in areas of moral judgment; for instance, drug use, pornography, prostitution, and other moral hazards. The Libertarian Party of the United States proposes, "Essentially, we believe all Americans should be free to live their lives and pursue their interests as they see fit as long as they do no harm to another."[11]

I type this description of libertarianism without the animosity some conservatives express towards the libertarian wing of the Republican Party. I wish I could be a libertarian. It sounds great. In fact, like most conservatives, a younger version of me embraced a more libertarian view on government. I adored John Locke, like Jefferson did. If I had owned a house in my twenties, I would have stuck a *Get Off My Lawn* sign in the front yard, right next to my *Hey Government, It's None of Your Business* sign. I still have great admiration for Locke, but I am not a Lockean libertarian anymore. I can't be.

Libertarianism doesn't work, for a very simple reason: it has the wrong definition of liberty.

What *is* liberty?

Ponder that for a moment.

My mind floods with competing interests.

Is liberty the freedom to do *anything*? If so, then is the absolute liberty that Locke describes anarchy? But if anarchy results in the strong dominating the weak, and the weak therefore suffering the violation of their natural rights, can anarchy be liberty? Wouldn't anarchy be the antithesis of liberty? If so, how can absolute liberty be liberty at all? Perhaps absolute liberty is actually tyranny.

Or, maybe liberty is as *close* to absolute freedom as society can achieve while protecting the natural rights of others. But in that case, wouldn't society be chaos? Doesn't society need some kind of order to thrive? Aren't legalized narcotics, pornography, and prostitution, for instance, moral hazards that, in the end, endanger a free citizenry?

Perhaps liberty is never absolute. Perhaps *true* liberty is not maximum individual freedom, but rather an ordered society in which people enjoy the freedom to make virtuous choices. In that case, is true liberty ordered liberty? If so, ordered on *what*?

What *is* liberty?

John Locke (1632–1704) and his fellow British philosopher Edmund Burke (1729–1797) wrestled with the same questions, as did our Founding Fathers and the Framers of our Constitution when they were forming our system of government.

Edmund Burke profoundly disagreed with John Locke on the definition of true liberty. Burke was an Irishman who served as a member of the British Parliament during the American Revolution. If Antonio Gramsci is the oft underestimated mastermind behind the Marxist assault on America's civil institutions, then Edmund Burke is the oft overlooked philosophical giant who provides us with a bulwark against a Gramsci-style assault. According to Burke, the definition of liberty is not the ability to do as one pleases. That is not liberty, according to Burke, but rather license, and there is no value in that. In 1774 Burke declared, "The *distinguishing* part of our constitution is its liberty. To preserve that liberty inviolate, is the *peculiar* duty and *proper* trust of a member of the house of commons. But the liberty, the *only* liberty I mean, is a liberty connected with *order*, and that not only exists *with* order and virtue, but can not exist at all *without* them. It inheres in good and steady government, as in *its substance and vital principle*."[12]

The words today sound almost radical, even to Republicans, too many of whom profess an amoral libertarianism where liberty is used as license to act on morally nebulous instincts with little regard to the effects on society. Burke contended that liberty is not an end in itself but a means to something greater. In a letter Burke wrote in 1789, he defined liberty as justice:

> Permit me then to continue our conversation, and to tell you what the freedom is that I love, and that to which I think all men entitled. This is the more necessary, because, of all the loose terms in the world, liberty is the most indefinite. It is not solitary, unconnected, individual, selfish liberty, as if every man was to regulate the whole of his conduct by his own will. The liberty I mean is social freedom. It is that state of things in which liberty is secured by the equality of restraint. A constitution of things in which the liberty of no one man, and no body of men, and no number of men, can find means to trespass on the liberty of any person, or any description of persons, in the society. This kind of liberty is, indeed, but another name for justice; ascertained by wise laws, and secured by well-constructed institutions.[13]

True freedom, Burke proposed, is the ability to do right, to act with justice. According to Burke, that requires a social order; liberty cannot exist as an abstract principle without devouring itself in anarchy. Liberty can survive only in a society that sees it as serving justice.

If you were to ask why conservatives have lost again and again in the culture wars, it is because we've allowed the left to convince people that: Black Lives Matter is racial justice; Queer Theory is justice for the marginalized; redistribution of wealth is economic justice; socialism in the name of climate change is environmental justice; and abortion is reproductive justice. The list goes on.

This is what Burke meant when he warned that liberty must be anchored in a Christian conception of justice and morality, and defended by established, trusted institutions. Otherwise, so-called liberty will be misused in the name of false justice. Burke saw this most dramatically in the French Revolution. The French Revolution claimed to be a revolution in the name of liberty, but it was a liberty divorced from Christianity and true justice.

This is where the religiously lukewarm become squeamish, because it's easier to define liberty as absolute liberty and easier to define justice as the restoration of a state of absolute liberty based only on natural rights.

Burke recognized that true justice is from God. "All human laws," Burke wrote, "are, properly speaking, only declaratory; they may alter the mode and application, but have no power over the substance of original justice."[14] Liberty without order—and by order, Burke meant virtue anchored by trusted institutions—will not beget a flourishing society. Liberty unfettered from virtue, Burke wrote, "is the greatest of all possible evils; for it is folly, vice, and madness, without tuition or restraint."[15] When conservatives speak of moral or regulated liberty, or distinguish between liberty and license, they are drawing on Burke's example.

Burke contended that true liberty is only possible within the bounds of a greater moral authority, the moral order begot by God. When we mistake liberty for license, it begets chaos, and when we remove God as the author of true justice, people lose their virtue and ultimately their liberty.

The free market, the right to private property, freedom of speech—those rights are not ends but the means to true liberty. They order society to secure true liberty, a concept that is not man-made but rather reflects the just law of God. For instance, the right to moral and religious instruction requires that institutions like the family and the church and faith-based schools are secure in their right to property, speech, and worship. Freedom is the bulwark that secures us in our pursuit of something greater; when liberty is perverted by license, the result is the crumbling of society. We require an ordered society in order to thrive.

While Locke's idea of liberty is simpler, Burke's is more complicated and rightly so. Locke forgets that people are not wild beasts roaming the plains—to which absolute freedom is still not absolute since wild beasts are governed by instinct and not free will. The free will unique to man can become tyranny in itself; Burke recognized that a society in which right and wrong are not clearly defined, recognized, and ordered will result in a people who are so corrupted by vice that they are blinded to the true purpose of liberty.

Does that sound familiar?

Unfortunately, in modern American society, we have embraced the Lockean, libertarian definition of liberty, and the result has been the proliferation of prostitution and pornography (including child pornography), the legalization of harmful drugs, the decriminalization of infidelity, the normalization of premarital (and extramarital) sexual relations, the embrace of homosexuality and transsexualism, the ease of no-fault divorce, the harm of contraception and abortion—all examples not of liberty but of abject immorality. Yet they are excused by many libertarians and libertarian-leaning conservatives as "liberty," because liberty, in their view, has no other moral end than itself.

Are we supposed to believe that the corruption, harm, and commodification of humanity that results from licentiousness is *good* because absolute liberty is a morally upright end unto itself? That doesn't make sense. I reject that notion. The chaos spawned by a society embracing "absolute liberty" ultimately serves as the bridge to a Marxist society, where atomized individuals will turn to government to take care of them, as families fade away, personal responsibility evaporates, vice and virtue are redefined (or even reversed), and justice and morality are defined not by God but by the Marxist catechism.

Libertarianism doesn't work. It is a utopian fantasy based on imaginary individuals and an imaginary social contract. In practice it is a precursor to the moral and political anarchy that is the antithesis of liberty. The best that can be said for it is that it enshrines a positive good—liberty—but without recognizing both the moral virtue and necessity of cultivating that moral virtue through cultural order required to sustain ordered liberty.

And so the debate raged among the Framers of our Constitution. Which definition of liberty would best serve the United States of America: Lockean libertarianism or Burkean conservatism and order? To our great fortune, the conservatives won. As political philosopher Yoram Hazony writes in his book *Conservatism: A Rediscovery,*

> The tension between these conservative and liberal camps finds expression in America's founding documents: The Declaration of Independence, drafted by Jefferson in 1776, is famous for promoting the Lockean doctrine of universal rights as "self-evident" before the light of reason; whereas the Constitution of 1787, drafted at a convention dominated by the conservative party, ended a decade of shocking disorder by restoring the familiar forms of the national English constitution. In accepting it, the Americans gave a strong president, serving as the chief executive, roughly the powers of the British monarch, and balanced these powers in the English fashion by means of a bicameral legislature with the power of taxation and legislation. Even the American Bill of Rights of 1789 is modeled upon the Petition of Right and the English Bill of Rights, largely elaborating the rights of Englishmen that had been described by Coke and Selden and

their followers. Notably, these later documents breathe not a word about universal reason or universal rights.[16]

Yoram Hazony once quipped on an episode of my show that "[Gertrude] Himmelfarb . . . the great conservative historian, she once told me and some friends . . . that the real sign of God's providence during the American Revolution was that at the time when it came time to write the Constitution, both Jefferson and Paine were in France, taking care of that revolution, and so the conservatives were able to write this wonderful constitution that America has."[17]

The United States Constitution ultimately embraced ordered liberty, a social liberty, in the style of Edmund Burke, as the foundation of our self-governance. James Madison, the "father of our Constitution," echoed Burke in *The Federalist* No. 51, writing, "Justice is the end of government. It is the end of civil society."[18] As John Adams famously said in 1798, "Our Constitution was made only for a moral and religious People. It is wholly inadequate to the government of any other."[19] America, he said, would remain free and prosperous only so long as it remained virtuous and pious: "We have no Government armed with Power capable of contending with human Passions unbridled by morality and Religion. Avarice, Ambition, Revenge, or Galantry, would break the strongest Cords of our Constitution as a Whale goes through a Net."[20] Morality, virtue, and religion are not add-ons to republican government, they are requirements for it to succeed; and when the founders spoke of "religion," they spoke of Christianity.

There is little doubt that the Framers of our Constitution understood and supported the Burkean philosophy they codified into the highest law of our land. President George Washington, "the father of his country" and the first President of the United States under the newly ratified Constitution, warned in his first State of the Union address in 1790 of the necessity "to discriminate the spirit of liberty from that of licentiousness, cherishing the first, avoiding the last, and uniting a speedy, but temperate vigilance against encroachments, with an inviolable respect to the laws."[21]

Many modern Republicans, however, have fallen prey to the latter, accepting and even endorsing licentiousness on alleged libertarian grounds, which has led some prominent so-called conservatives like David French (formerly of *National Review*, now of the *New York Times*) to argue that "drag queen story hours"—where male transvestite strippers read gender ideology and perform sexually suggestive shows for toddlers and preschoolers in public libraries—are simply "one of the blessings of liberty."[22]

Does that make you sick to your stomach? It should. *That* is licentiousness begot of libertarianism. Allowing grown men to sexualize toddlers is evil. There is no inherent morality in the liberty to do that.

But leftists have spent half a century exploiting libertarianism, the misapplication of liberty. Too many Republicans naively bought the lie that we cannot insert our common sense, decency, and conscience into law, and that "tolerance" for things like drag queen story hour, same-sex marriage, and legalized marijuana is a higher morality than legislating against them.

That is nonsense. Of course we can, and we should, legislate against bad things, evil things, wrong things. It is a moral and political imperative. If we *don't* and instead allow licentiousness to reign, we are empowering Marxists and dooming our Republic. All laws enforce some form of morality: it's either ours or theirs. We have history, law, and morality on our side. Our Constitution was built on Burke's idea that true liberty orders society towards justice as defined by God's original justice. Our previous lawmakers were not wrong when they crafted laws with this intent. That is how society is preserved for its greater purpose.

If you are wondering why it feels as if we are living in a chaotic era, it's because we are. Without a grounding in God's law—natural law—even words lose all meaning. But words must have meaning, particularly when the words underpin society's deliberation of what is acceptable or not, and what ought to be within the bounds of law or not. To order society, we have to start *somewhere*. We must anchor our definitions of words to *something*. Otherwise we will live in utter chaos. We are swirling in such chaos in the United States right now. What do our words *mean*?

What is a man?

What is a woman?

What is abuse?

What is harm?

What is racism?

What is reality?

What is morality?

What is right?

What is wrong?

What is fair?

What is *justice*?

If we don't answer these questions, the Marxists will answer them for us. If we don't ground the definition of justice in God's original justice, we get thugs looting a GameStop in the name of "racial justice." We get socialist redistribution of wealth in the name of "social justice." We get young boys and girls suffering surgical mutilation to their bodies in the name of "LGBTQ justice." We get unborn babies aborted in the womb in the name of "reproductive justice." And we get ESG metrics designed to socially engineer our lives in the name of "environmental justice."

None of that is justice.

The reason we are dizzy and unable to restore equilibrium in our nation is because conservatives ignorant of the Burkean foundation of our nation gullibly agreed to "withdraw" morality from our governing.

They did so in the name of Lockean "tolerance." It turns out, however, that Lockean "tolerance" was a Trojan horse for Marxism disguised as libertarianism.

Those such as Phyllis Schlafly, who warned us that conservatives were being duped, were scorned, mocked, and labeled "the religious right." (And who wanted to be associated with *that*?) To this day, the vast majority of conservatives and Republicans remain tight-lipped on the subject of gay marriage. And isn't it telling that it was ultimately outraged parents who led the charge against Critical Race Theory and now Queer Theory, rather than the representatives we have elected to ostensibly defend us from such insidious designs?

The left understood—before conservatives realized they'd been duped—that there is no such thing as the absence of morality in government. There is either true morality or false morality. When Republicans naively "withdrew" morality from our political platform, the left immediately swooped in and codified their version of morality into law and practice. The result was pro-life crisis pregnancy centers facing legal mandates to advertise free government-sponsored abortions;[23] nurses who "misgender" geriatric patients potentially facing jail time for it;[24] teachers who decline who use neo-pronouns for their students forced out of their job;[25] and Catholic group homes for sexually trafficked women at risk of losing their state certification if they refused entry to biological men who "identify" as women.[26] That is not an absence of morality. That's the left's religion—Marxism—codified into law.

All societies must answer the question of how to define morality, because that is the foundation of how we define justice. If we forget our origin and our ultimate destination, and therefore our purpose on Earth; if we allow our political enemies to redefine morality and justice to suit their Marxist agenda, our society will flounder into unspeakable chaos and spiritual darkness.

You simply cannot have a vacuum of values in a nation. Something will fill it. In the name of libertarianism, Republicans retreated, saying, "You can't legislate morality," leaving the Marxists to fill the vacuum with laws codifying their own false morality. The results have been predictably disastrous, and any time Republicans have made a peep about morality, the left has bullied them into silence by crowing about the "separation of church and state."

Few Republicans even know what "separation of church and state" really means though, or realize that it's not found in any of our nation's founding documents. Instead, it is a line that President Thomas Jefferson wrote in a letter to the Danbury Baptists in 1802. In that letter Jefferson wrote, "Believing with you that religion is a matter which lies solely between Man & his God, that he owes account to none other for his faith or his worship, that the legitimate powers of government reach actions only, & not opinions, I contemplate with sovereign reverence that act of the whole American people which declared that their legislature should 'make no law respecting an establishment of religion, or prohibiting the free exercise thereof,' thus building a wall of separation between Church & State."[27]

Jefferson defined separation of church and state as the First Amendment's guarantee that the United States would "make no law respecting an establishment of religion or prohibiting the free exercise thereof." (That did not, as a matter of history, prohibit states from having official state religions, and most of them did.) Nowhere did Thomas Jefferson, the devoted Lockean, suggest that the Constitution was intended to prohibit Judeo-Christian morality as the basis of ordered liberty. In that, he and Edmund Burke would have been in agreement.

My hope is that this chapter helps establishment Republicans understand that our government is built on properly ordered liberty.

Burkean conservatism is our heritage. We must acknowledge that morality—natural law—exists. Without it, chaos will reign.

Our Constitution begins with the preamble: "We the People of the United States, in Order to form a more perfect Union, establish Justice, insure domestic Tranquility, provide for the common defense, promote the general Welfare, and secure the Blessings of Liberty to ourselves and our Posterity, do ordain and establish this Constitution for the United States of America."[28] Without a common recognition of Burke's "original justice," political factions will war over the definition of "right" and "wrong" and "justice" and "common good." This is what we're seeing in our country today, and it doesn't end well. The Framers of our Constitution had no intention for libertarianism to place "absolute liberty" as the highest end to attain. Liberty, after all, is but a means to something greater: justice. It's time to reclaim liberty—ordered liberty—so our society can flourish. And to do that we need to understand natural law and Burke's author of "original justice."

CHAPTER 11

Good *versus* Evil

T he evil we must combat," Pope Pius XI wrote in 1937 in his encyclical *Divini Redemptoris*, "is at its origin primarily an evil of the
spiritual order. From this polluted source the monstrous emanations of
the communistic system flow with satanic logic."[1]

Some on the political right refuse to acknowledge the reality of the
political enemy we are facing within our own nation. I'm not talking
only about denying the threat of Marxism. I'm talking about a more
serious failure to recognize the supernatural reality of the Marxist
enemy we face.

Many Republicans and conservatives prefer to believe we are simply
engaged in a negotiation with a well-intentioned political opponent who
agrees on bedrock principles but mistakenly proposes unwise policies.
These voices of the right include Republican Senator Mitt Romney, who
called Joe Biden "a genuinely good man"[2] while excoriating Donald
Trump as a "phony" and a "fraud,"[3] and David French, who wrote

in *The Atlantic* that the left's hate speech laws targeting conservatives and Christians on college campuses had "virtuous" intentions but were "problematic."[4]

This is a grave and critical mistake.

We are not negotiating with well-intentioned political opponents who agree with us on bedrock principles and share our values. Rather, we are battling against Marxists who seek to destroy our country, Marxists who are subverting our cultural institutions and waging a heinous war on our children in order to accomplish their destruction.

If we refuse to acknowledge the Marxist threat to our nation, we will lose the political battle.

But we also must acknowledge that this battle we fight against Marxism is not *just a political* battle. What rages around and among us is a much larger battle; a battle between good and evil. It really is that big. This is a spiritual battle of the highest order, which can be a frightening realization. It's a realization that certainly leaves me feeling small, insignificant, and, I confess, bereft of the ability to fight back on my own.

While we laymen and laywomen have our essential roles in this battle, we need help. Given the forces arrayed against us, we cannot win on our own. In the end we cannot win this battle unless we fight it with the assistance and the leadership of the Church. When I say "the Church," I say that advisedly. I want all people of goodwill to join us in the battle, but it's also a fact that there is only one institutional church big enough—with 1.378 billion members[5]—powerful enough, and with deep enough reservoirs of philosophical and theological wisdom to win this battle: and that is "the Church," the Catholic Church, the universal Christian church (which is what "catholic" means).

The Catholic Church, the largest and most influential of all Christian denominations, recognized the Satanic elements of communism from the beginning, and recognized the spiritual battle at hand with a sharpness and clarity begot of holy minds dedicated to defense of the faith and protection of Truth.

More than a year before Karl Marx and Friedrich Engels published *The Communist Manifesto*, Pope Pius IX penned an encyclical called *Qui Pluribus* (*On Faith and Religion*).

In the 1846 encyclical, Pope Pius IX condemned "the unspeakable doctrine of Communism" as "most opposed to the very natural law." Pius IX warned, "For if this doctrine were accepted, the complete destruction of everyone's laws, government, property, and even human society itself would follow."[6]

Pius IX warned that communism embodies "the most dark designs of men in the clothing of sheep, while inwardly ravening wolves."[7] He noted that communists "humbly recommend themselves by means of a feigned and deceitful appearance of a purer piety, a stricter virtue and discipline; after taking their captives gently, they mildly bind them, and then kill them in secret."[8]

The goal of the communist ideology, Pope Pius IX wrote, was to "make men fly in terror from all practice of religion, and they cut down and dismember the sheep of the Lord." The communists accomplish their indoctrination by "widespread disgusting infection from books and pamphlets which teach the lessons of sinning. These works, well-written and filled with deceit and cunning, are scattered at immense cost through every region for the destruction of the Christian people. They spread pestilential doctrines everywhere and deprave the minds especially of the imprudent, occasioning great losses for religion."[9]

Pope Pius IX penned this prescient and chillingly accurate condemnation of communism more than half a century before the Bolshevik Revolution, which spawned arguably the most powerful and murderous Communist regime in history: the Union of Soviet Socialist Republics. Yet to read it today, one gets a profound understanding of how Marxism has crept into modern America, particularly into our children's classrooms, libraries, school counselor's offices, corporations, social media applications, and movies and television shows.

The purpose of Pope Pius IX's encyclical was to rally Christians worldwide against the looming evils of global communism. Just over thirty years later, on December 28, 1878, Pope Leo XIII penned an encyclical letter to the Church called *Quod Apostolici Muneris* (*On Socialism*), condemning "the deadly plague that is creeping into the very fibres of human society and leading it on to the verge of destruction. . . ." Leo XIII deplored "that sect of men who, under various and almost barbarous names, are called socialists, communists, or nihilists, and who, spread over all the world, and bound together by the closest ties in a wicked confederacy, no longer seek the shelter of secret meetings, but, openly and boldly marching forth in the light of day, strive to bring to a head what they have long been planning—the overthrow of all civil society whatsoever."[10]

The Church admonished the faithful to recognize not just the material threat, but the supernatural reality of the political enemy we face. The Church condemned communism as "evil of the spiritual order."[11] "From this polluted source," Pope Pius XI exhorted in 1937 in his encyclical *Divini Redemptoris*, "the monstrous emanations of the communistic system flow with satanic logic."[12]

"The Communism of today," Pius XI warned, "more emphatically than similar movements in the past, conceals in itself a false messianic idea. A pseudo-ideal of justice, of equality and fraternity in labor impregnates all its doctrine and activity with a deceptive mysticism, which communicates a zealous and contagious enthusiasm to the multitudes entrapped by delusive promises."

Pius XI wrote, "For the first time in history we are witnessing a struggle, cold-blooded in purpose and mapped out to the least detail, between man and 'all that is called God.' Communism is by its nature anti-religious. It considers religion as 'the opiate of the people' because the principles of religion which speak of a life beyond the grave dissuade the proletariat from the dream of a Soviet paradise which is of this world."

Communism, the pope argued, was contrary to just government because it violated natural law and man's God-given rights. "The enslavement of man despoiled of his rights, the denial of the transcendental origin of the State and its authority, the horrible abuse of public power in the service of a collectivistic terrorism, are the very contrary of all that corresponds with natural ethics and the will of the Creator."

Pius XI pointed out, "Both man and civil society derive their origin from the Creator, Who has mutually ordained them one to the other. Hence neither can be exempted from their correlative obligations, nor deny or diminish each other's rights. The Creator Himself has regulated this mutual relationship in its fundamental lines, and it is by an unjust usurpation that Communism arrogates to itself the right to enforce, in place of the divine law based on the immutable principles of truth and charity, a partisan political program which derives from the arbitrary human will and is replete with hate."

Communism, Pius XI states, "strives to entice the multitudes by trickery of various forms, hiding its real designs behind ideas that in themselves are good and attractive." The Communists advance their revolution through subterfuge. "Under various names which do not suggest Communism, they establish organizations and periodicals with the sole purpose of carrying their ideas into quarters otherwise inaccessible. They try perfidiously to worm their way even into professedly Catholic and religious organizations. Again, without receding an inch from their subversive principles, they invite Catholics to collaborate with them in the realm of so-called humanitarianism and charity; and at times even make proposals that are in perfect harmony with the Christian spirit and the doctrine of the Church." Pius XI cautions, "See to it, Venerable Brethren, that the Faithful do not allow themselves to be deceived!"[13]

Pius XI says clearly, "Communism is intrinsically wrong, and no one who would save Christian civilization may collaborate with it in any undertaking whatsoever. Those who permit themselves to be deceived into lending their aid towards the triumph of Communism in their own country, will be the first to fall victims of their error. And the greater the antiquity and grandeur of the Christian civilization in the regions where Communism successfully penetrates, so much more devastating will be the hatred displayed by the godless."

The battle against communism, Pope Pius XI concludes, is a "battle joined by the powers of darkness against the very idea of Divinity," and the propaganda effort by Communists is "so truly diabolical that the world has perhaps never witnessed its like before. . . . shrewdly adapted to the varying conditions of diverse peoples. It has at its disposal great financial resources, gigantic organizations, international congresses, and countless trained workers. It makes use of pamphlets and reviews, of cinema, theater and radio, of schools and even universities. Little by little it penetrates into all classes of the people and even reaches the better-minded groups of the community, with the result that few are aware of the poison which increasingly pervades their minds and hearts."[14]

Are you speechless? Do the words strike a chord in your soul?

We are witnessing, in the Marxist takeover of our institutions, what the popes saw in communism from the beginning. The Marxists today have taken advantage of people of goodwill who succumb to words like "tolerance" and "love" and "justice," not realizing those words are being perverted. We face an enemy that has immense financial and political resources at its disposal. We face a revolutionary movement that is, ultimately, as with Critical Race Theory, replete with hate; and, as with Queer Theory, based on evil—there is no other way to describe what they are perpetuating upon our children. This is not normal politics. It's not about taxes and regulations, commerce, treaties, and alliances. We are facing, as the popes knew, a profound spiritual evil.

I'm sorry to say the security of anchoring our identities in political policy preferences, such as conservative versus liberal or Republican versus Democrat, is dust in the wind. Part of me wishes we could do that: play politics and religion separately. But we can't. A narrow identity rooted in political parties alone doesn't match the reality of the spiritual as well as material war we are fighting: a supernatural battle of good versus evil. It's for this reason that the Catholic Church must be the tip of the spear against Marxism and global communism—as it was before the Bolshevik Revolution and as it was during the Cold War. Our politics must be crafted with this in mind. We are in both a spiritual and a material war. The ultimate answer, the ultimate rebuff, to communism, is God.

Now, I know that it's become fashionable in the modern Republican Party to sidestep religion entirely. I understand this, although I don't agree, because when you come down to it, as Russell Kirk said, "Political problems, at bottom, are religious and moral problems."[15]

But Republicans who want to sidestep religion generally come in three types.

The first type is probably the most numerous. They are simply not faithful anymore—that is, they've fallen away from the faith not so much from conviction, but from lack of practice. Maybe they're lapsed Catholics. Maybe they left the dying Protestant denominations, or became too busy for the exciting Evangelical mega-churches. Regardless, they are poorly catechized, can't explain religious doctrine, and so they fall prey to the false narrative from the left that any inclusion of Judeo-Christian morality in our nation is a violation of "the separation of church and state."

The second type isn't as passive. They actively disregard Christian morals because Christian morals are inconvenient to their lifestyle. Christian morals, after all, lead us away from drunkenness, licentiousness, sexual immorality, divorce, selfishness, greed, pride, resentment, and gossip. Why infuse morals into law that will hinder pursuit of gratification, no matter how amoral? These people are Republicans only because the Republican Party interferes with their pursuit of gratification *less* than the scolding, woke, high-tax, high-regulation Democrat Party.

The third type may be devout Christians themselves (I'm thinking of several prominent Republican politicians) but they have subscribed to the Lockean idea that absolute liberty is a moral end in itself and that government has no just authority in governing beyond the limited protection of natural rights. These Republicans are de facto libertarians.

The paths offered by these three types of Republicans offer no way to victory. All inevitably lead us on a path toward Marxism. So, I am eager to inform my fellow Republicans that disregarding religion in politics is pure delusion. We cannot do that if we are to keep our Republic. If we are to have a just nation, it must be based on just laws, and just laws reflect God's original justice.

I say this not as a Bible-thumper (although perhaps I am). But our laws—our just laws—have always been rooted in biblical truth since the days of the American colonies. For instance, it's illegal to murder a person; we don't allow that in our civil society. Why? Because we universally acknowledge, as a society, that human beings are created in *Imago Dei*, the image and likeness of God. This is what makes humans different from dogs or cats or gorillas. The United States from its inception was built on a foundation of natural law that presupposes that all humans are made in the image and likeness of our Creator.

That is why the Declaration of Independence refers to the "Laws of Nature and of Nature's God" and why it declares that "all men are created equal, that they are endowed by their Creator with certain unalienable Rights" and that it is to "secure these rights" that "Governments are instituted among Men. . . ."[16] This recognition of natural law, this recognition of Christian truth, is written into the very fabric of the foundation of our country and its law. Recognizing this is not Bible-thumping, it is not inserting religion where it doesn't belong, it is not merely a preference of the so-called "religious right." It is the reality of American history, and it is a political, philosophical, and theological truth.

In the book of Genesis we read, "Then God said, 'Let us make man in our image, after our likeness'" (Genesis 1:26 ESV).

The Church explains that the "human person participates in the light and power of the divine Spirit. By his reason, he is capable of understanding the order of things established by the Creator. By free will, he is capable of directing himself toward his true good. He finds his perfection 'in seeking and loving what is true and good.'" Moreover, "By virtue of his soul and his spiritual powers of intellect and will, man is endowed with freedom, an 'outstanding manifestation of the divine image.'"[17]

Francis Crick was a scientist and an atheist. He described mankind, our reason and free will, as an illusion, because "'You,' your joys and your sorrows, your memories and your ambitions, your sense of personal identity and free will, are in fact no more than the behavior of a vast assembly of nerve cells and their associated molecules."[18]

Personally, I find that impossible to believe. Most of us should find that impossible to believe. If Crick's supposition is true, then men are not endowed by their Creator with unalienable rights, because there is no such thing as natural rights, let alone a Creator. Atheists who try to erect "secular" guardrails on society have no basis to guarantee our rights, freedoms, and liberties. The best they can do is hand government over to technocrats—who, as we know firsthand, do not just govern by "science" but are perverted by partisan political agendas. The result is inevitably chaos and political anarchy; Big Government, Big Tech, Big Pharma, Big Media, and Big Education colluding in their combined agendas. The ultimate end is communism.

Again, I am compassionate towards conservatives and Republicans who writhe in discomfort at the idea of marrying religious truth to politics. It's a tough thing I'm asking of you, I know. But there is no other way. It's impossible to properly define liberty, justice, and good government without submitting to the reality that our Constitution is built on natural law. If conservatives want to keep our Republic, they need to accept this fundamental reality.

The universal Church defines natural law as follows: "The natural law expresses the original moral sense which enables man to discern by reason the good and the evil, the truth and the lie: 'The natural law is written and engraved in the soul of each and every man, because it is human reason ordaining him to do good and forbidding him to sin. . . . But this command of human reason would not have the force of law if it were not the voice and interpreter of a higher reason to which our spirit and our freedom must be submitted.'"[19] Natural law, which is the divine deposit of morals intrinsic to human nature, is the necessary starting point for "positive laws"—which are man-made laws, such as the work of legislatures and courts—if these man-made laws are to represent true justice.

Natural law, according to Dr. Robert Barker, professor emeritus of law at Duquesne University, "is knowable by human reason."[20] Saint Thomas Aquinas agreed, saying that mankind's ability to reason is a spark of the divine; it's what allows him to be governed by natural law. Of natural law, Aquinas stated in his *Summa Theologica*, "It is therefore evident that the natural law is nothing else than the rational creature's participation of the eternal law."[21] Consequently, according to Aquinas, "every human law has just so much of the nature of law, as it is derived from the law of nature. But if in any point it deflects from the law of nature, it is no longer a law but a perversion of law."[22]

Saint Augustine's views on natural law were simpler than those of Aquinas. Augustine held that the natural law, as one scholar noted, "is a 'notion' of the eternal law 'impressed' on human beings, and thus an aspect of the innate image of God."[23] Natural law exists whether we choose to acknowledge it or not. Natural law underpins the dignity of every human being.

The Church explains, "The natural law, present in the heart of each man and established by reason, is universal in its precepts and its authority extends to all men. It expresses the dignity of the person and determines the basis for his fundamental rights and duties. . . ."[24]

Moreover, the natural law is eternal, immutable, "permanent throughout the variations of history; it subsists under the flux of ideas and customs and supports their progress. The rules that express it remain substantially valid. Even when it is rejected in its very principles, it cannot be destroyed or removed from the heart of man."[25]

Conversely, Marxism is an attack on natural law. As noted earlier, Pope Pius IX wrote in *Qui pluribus* that "the unspeakable doctrine of Communism, as it is called, a doctrine most opposed to the very natural law," would result in "the complete destruction of everyone's laws, government, property, and even of human society itself."[26]

You can build a government, even in good faith, around secular "ethics"; you can even call those secular ethics "human rights," but it won't work to protect against Marxism. Marxism seeks "the complete destruction of everyone's laws, government, property, and even human society itself" and that very much includes the government and society of the United States. The only effective bulwark against it is a society rooted politically, legally, institutionally, and spiritually in natural law.

The United States Constitution is built on English common law, and English common law is built on natural law. Political scientist Joseph

Hamburger noted, "The civil rights of Englishmen, while established in custom and discovered by examining precedents, are in fact 'derivative rights,' taken from that eternal higher law which defines the true rights of all men."[27] According to Hamburger, Edmund Burke called natural law a "higher law" than man's and noted that the British Constitution was derived from natural law.[28] "All human laws," Burke wrote, "are, properly speaking, only declaratory; they may alter the mode and application, but have no power over the substance of original justice."[29] And justice, contends Burke, is the definition of true liberty. Liberty, he says, "is, indeed, but another name for justice; ascertained by wise laws, and secured by well-constructed institutions."[30] James Madison, the primary author of our Constitution, concurred in *The Federalist* No. 51, "Justice is the end of government. It is the end of civil society. It ever has been and ever will be pursued until it be obtained, or until liberty be lost in the pursuit."[31]

To win this war we're in, we must regain this understanding of natural law. We must commit ourselves, our culture, and our laws to justice, and to the Author of original justice. If you have looked at the pictures of children mutilated in transgender surgeries, or at the grotesque faces of transvestites twerking at drag queen story hour, and said, "This is Satanic," that's because it is. Our political battles are no longer the normal squabbles over taxation and regulation, or intense debates over war and peace. Instead, they are spiritual battles about the nature of reality, the nature of truth, and the nature of justice. Unless we as conservatives are willing to meet that challenge the only way it can be met—with a recourse to God and the natural law—we will not win.

CHAPTER 12

How We Win

This book was not a jolly scamper through a meadow filled with rainbows and butterflies; I'm aware of that. At some points it's been shocking and horrifying. At other times perhaps infuriating, frustrating, even depressing, but never, I trust, hopeless. My goal in writing this book was to achieve a clear-eyed understanding of what's happening in our nation, to make order out of the chaos raging around us, and hopefully to point us towards the path to victory. I'd like to think we achieved that. If you felt a shift in your perception of the political battles in our nation, I'm glad. If you can now confidently say that you recognize the Marxist reality of the political and spiritual enemy we face, I'm satisfied. If you're ready to challenge the vicious communist enemy that's infiltrated our nation and is targeting our children, and you're ready to do so by reasserting the natural law that underpins our constitutional order, then I'll consider my hundreds of hours of writing and thousands of pages of research well worth the laborious pain.

We started this book with the sobering statement that of all the creepy, intentional assaults Marxists are waging against our nation, the assault on children is by far the most evil. The left is destroying children, intentionally, targeting our sons and daughters for radical indoctrination to transform them into a Marxist vanguard that will tear down our country—its traditional values, cultural institutions, and Constitution grounded in natural rights—and replace it with a communist state. The result of the deliberate destruction of our children will be the fall of our nation—which is exactly what it was intended to do.

We opened the first chapter with Antonio Gramsci and his theory of cultural hegemony. Gramsci contended that in order to launch·a Marxist revolution and destroy Western civilization, you must first subvert and destroy the civil (cultural) institutions of bourgeois society, after which Marxists would be well-positioned to topple governmental institutions. Gramsci named five pillars of civil society that must be destroyed: religion, family, education, media, and law. It's no coincidence that we are seeing this in our nation today. Gramsci's cultural hegemony is the capture of our institutions that has degraded our colleges and universities, corrupted the public school system in the United States, compromised our media organizations, targeted our churches and synagogues and people of faith, stigmatized and delegitimized the rule of law, and most important, and finally, set its sights on the nuclear family and children.

We then exposed the Marxist attacks on the five elements of the traditional nuclear family: man, woman, marriage, sex, and children, as well as the Marxists behind the assaults. We charted our way from Wilhelm Reich's twisted Marxist theories on sex (that included the sexualization of children) to Betty Friedan's Marxism-influenced *Feminine Mystique*, which launched modern feminism and destroyed generations of women, to Kimberlé Crenshaw's "intersectionality" theory, which has men (particularly white men) in its crosshairs, to the LGBTQ+

agenda that has never cared about tolerance, liberty, or equality under the law but only about the destruction of traditional marriage, the grooming of children, and the abolition of Christian morality.

We detailed the strategy to subvert the West mapped out in Max Horkheimer's Critical Theory at the Frankfurt School, and its ideological grandchild Critical Race Theory. We exposed the Critical Race Theory intelligentsia, including Barbara Applebaum, Robin DiAngelo, Herbert Marcuse, Derrick Bell, Richard Delgado, and others. We also explained how Marxist Critical Theory morphed first into Critical Legal Studies and then developed into the insidious Critical Race Theory we see in classrooms and workplaces today.

We exposed Gayle Rubin, authoress of the founding document of Queer Theory, which lays out the ideological framework for the radical gender identity indoctrination in public schools, including the sexualization of children and propagation of child pornography and pedophilia. We established Rubin's Queer Theory as the underpinning of the transgender agenda. We unraveled exactly how Critical Race Theory and Queer Theory are a deliberate one-two punch intended to destroy the identities of children and rebuild American kids into unrepentant Marxist revolutionaries.

We looked at Klaus Schwab and his World Economic Forum as a driving force behind the ideological popularity of global Marxism today. We examined Schwab's affinity for the Chinese Communist Party's social credit score system and the ESG (environmental, social, and governance) metrics that ideologically mirror the Chinese Communist system. We examined the DEI (diversity, equity, and inclusion) initiatives buried inside ESG (DEI is the S in ESG). We exposed DEI for the reality of what it is: a thought-reform tactic in the Mao Zedong tradition.

We examined the phenomenon of corporate wokeism, which is another term for corporate grooming, and exposed the biggest corporate groomer of all: Planned Parenthood. We exposed Planned Parenthood founder Margaret Sanger's penchant for Bolshevik-style Marxism. We also exposed "the father of the sexual revolution," Alfred Kinsey, and his perverted sexual fetishes that he managed to "normalize" in mainstream culture and that exist today in "comprehensive sexuality education" in public schools (taught by Planned Parenthood and promoted by the United Nations).

We examined the man responsible for the word "woke," Brazilian Marxist Paulo Freire, who pioneered "critical consciousness" in schools by redefining "knowledge" as a tool of oppression and preparing a new pedagogy—"critical pedagogy"—to weaponize schools as Marxist indoctrination centers. We traced Critical Pedagogy to American schools, hidden in "social-emotional learning" (SEL). We examined how teachers' union boss Randi Weingarten promotes SEL and "teaching for social justice" in our children's classrooms, as well as promoting books for children that are rife with Critical Race Theory and Queer Theory.

We then unmasked John Dewey, "the father of Progressive education in America," and his lavish praise of Soviet Russia's "Great Experiment" in public education as a method to indoctrinate youth. We identified Dewey's abuse of the word "democracy" and exposed Harvard professor Elizabeth Bartholet, who is pushing for a ban on homeschooling and positively cites Dewey's Marxist education philosophies in her political activism.

We exposed "technocracy" or "rule by the experts" as a stepping stone from capitalism to communism, and examined how deeply embedded technocracy is in the administrative state.

For the first nine chapters, we soberly established that our nation's children and our cultural institutions are under attack by Marxists whose ultimate goal is to destroy the United States of America. Then, we began to chart our way back—because all hope is not yet lost.

We examined the path to secure true liberty that was paved for us by the Framers of our Constitution, which requires us to reject Lockean libertarianism and instead embrace ordered liberty in the style of Edmund Burke, which Burke defines as justice grounded in "original justice." From a practical standpoint, we examined how conservatives who neglected to govern in the Burkean tradition fell prey to the false idea of LGBTQ+ tolerance, homosexual "marriage," and the false premise of separation of church and state in the name of "absolute liberty." We examined how conservatives surrendering morality in law allowed the left to codify into law its own twisted, false morality instead. Finally, we established what secularists have denied for millennia: there is no sanity outside the Church. We established there can be no liberty and no justice without first acknowledging natural law and the Author of natural law, and that in order to defeat the communist enemy we must understand it as not just a political enemy, but a spiritual one.

We covered a lot of ground in this book, and I'm proud to be standing beside you fighting this fight. We *can* win. I'm committed to victory, and I know you are too. Now, we have one more thing to do before we close this book.

What I am about to propose might sound intimidating for a president let alone private citizens. I know it is. The reality is we can do much in our personal and family lives to impact culture, and we should. But the larger reality is we won't win this war against a Marxist enemy without fully utilizing the power of government to stop it. Not everything offered in this chapter is something you can accomplish individually, or within your household. Some of these prescriptions are complex, intricate actions our elected government officials must take. We play a role in that. We elect them. We must direct them. They work for us. It's our responsibility to hold them accountable. If this part of the book is intimidating, it should be. That's a reflection of how deeply and thoroughly compromised our institutions are by Marxist ideology. But the rest of this chapter should encourage you as well. We aren't at the end of our rope. We have recourse. We have many things left to do to stop the political enemy we face. In fact it should instill confidence within us that we can still use our system of government and its still-standing institutional framework to fight back against this evil. We must do this before those ever-weakening institutions irrevocably collapse. To this end I've prepared a list of twelve things we must do to eradicate Marxism from our institutions, protect our children from this insidious ideology, and ultimately restore our nation.

#1. Fight the Cultural Battles over Social Issues

In order to thwart the cultural hegemony Antonio Gramsci designed, it's imperative to fight the uncomfortable battles over social and cultural issues. I write this with the Grammy Awards playing in the background. Singer Sam Smith is dressed as Satan performing an unholy act surrounded by demons. British boy-band megastar Harry Styles is bleary-eyed and clad in a woman's scoop-neck jumpsuit. Entertainment commentators are gushing over rapper Lizzo's ensemble, which resembles a gigantic fluffy red bedspread draped over her head. She looks like a humongous Furby. (But if we notice she's gigantically fat, we're fatphobic; if we accurately describe her as "obese" it's a slur as bad as the n-word).[1] The whole chaotic cesspool is sponsored by Pfizer. (Not a joke, it really is.)[2]

We are not winning the culture war if *this* is our culture. It can be uncomfortable to talk about sex, abortion, birth control, relationships, marriage, family, racial ideology, gender identity ideology, and religion, but if we don't, demons will teach our children to worship Satan in the name of LGBTQ+ identity . . . literally.

We must encourage and incentivize strong nuclear families consisting of a married mother and father. A strong nuclear family is the best bulwark against evil corrupting our children. If we don't teach our children about God's design for masculinity, femininity, marriage, sex, family, good and evil, someone else will. Children are inundated with Critical Race Theory and radical gender ideology from the moment they recognize objects. Even if you wisely refuse your young child a smartphone or internet access and limit their television viewing to *The Andy Griffith Show*, every *other* child they know is on TikTok, which means your son or daughter will be exposed to the filth that pervades our culture, directly or indirectly. Our children's minds are the battlefield, and the best bulwark against evil is a strong nuclear family.

Moreover, government must recognize its inherent self-interest in protecting marriage between one man and one woman and reject legalized "gay marriage." A nuclear family composed of a married male and female couple is the best institution to form functional, well-rounded, self-sufficient, contributing members of society. Children raised in such an environment are less likely to fall to government welfare, drugs, poverty, and crime.[3] To have a future, our nation needs well-adjusted children schooled in patriotism and Christian virtue in traditional families of one man and woman joined in holy matrimony. If we allow politicians to redefine words like "marriage" to suit their political agendas by including same-sex relationships, we are no longer a nation of objectively just laws, but a nation where politicians become the arbiters of "truth." That is the road to tyranny, and we must reject it.

#2. Ban Critical Race Theory from Government, Schools, and Private Companies That Do Business with the Government

Critical Race Theory is a Marxist ideology bent on subjectively classifying certain races and ethnicities as superior or inferior. Teaching

Critical Race Theory, or its principles, must be wholly prohibited in our public schools, and those prohibitions must be strictly enforced. Critical Race Theory is not always taught overtly; oftentimes it's disguised in terms like *white privilege, white guilt, white fragility, systemic white supremacy, systemic oppression, racial justice, implicit bias*, and more. The whole of Critical Race Theory should be banned from classrooms, curricula, and school administrations. Otherwise, our schools will remain indoctrination centers where our children are brainwashed with Marxism.

Moreover, states ought to mandate that schoolchildren are taught the reality of communism and Marxism. Florida did this,[4] and it's imperative that more states across the country follow Florida's lead. We must counter Marxist brainwashing with historically accurate and morally sound education about the evils of communism.

We must never allow Marxist ideology in our government either, at the federal, state, or local levels. Federal agencies and the military must be severely penalized if they propagate Marxist ideology. Likewise, private companies should be prohibited from winning government contracts and denied any federal or state funding if they embrace Marxism or practice any Marxist principles, like *intersectionality, white privilege*, and all the rest. This includes colleges and universities if they accept federal student loans or federal research grants.

#3. Ban Queer Theory from Schools and Government

We must enact legislation prohibiting teachers, school administrators, and school counselors from talking with students about sex, sexual orientation, sexual identity, gender identity, or any element of Queer Theory, including neo-pronouns, transgenderism, and the gender "spectrum." We must prohibit comprehensive sexuality education from public schools. We must insist on parents' right to know what their children are doing in school, and prohibit school staff from hiding from parents when a child is using neo-pronouns or a different name or engaging in gender ideology or Queer Theory.

We must ban "drag queen story hours" too. Do you really want your tax dollars funding public libraries that parade drag queens in front of children as young as two years old, especially when one considers that some of these drag queens have been revealed as sex offenders?[5] We must prohibit Queer Theory from touching taxpayer-funded institutions. We must also ban drag shows for kids. We already prohibit many harmful activities for children: we don't allow children in strip clubs; we don't allow children to purchase cigarettes; we don't allow children to walk on the floor of a casino or hang out in bars. Prohibiting establishments from allowing children to attend drag shows needs to be added to that list. The goal of Queer Theory *is* the sexualization of children. We must stop it. Ending "drag queen story hours" is an obvious beginning.

Moreover, we must put anyone who sexually abuses children in prison for life, including anyone who produces, distributes, or consumes child sexual abuse material (child pornography). The possession and consumption of child sexual abuse material is not a victimless crime. Queer Theory advocates for child pornography and pedophilia.[6] The "normalization" of pedophilia is underway in our society with the use of terms like "minor-attracted person." We should exercise zero tolerance for such evil.

We must also defund all institutions that propagate Queer Theory, like Planned Parenthood, the United Nations, and the World Health Organization, and prohibit them from setting foot on public school property.

#4. Ban Puberty Blockers, Cross-Sex Hormones, and Transgender Surgeries for Children

We must ban transgender surgeries for children and prohibit the prescription and distribution of puberty-blocking pharmaceuticals and cross-sex hormones to minors. Until then any organization that prescribes puberty blockers or cross-sex hormones for children or performs transgender surgeries on minors should be prohibited from receiving or using a cent of federal funding (such as Medicaid and Medicare reimbursements). To protect children, we must also amend our state constitutions and pass state legislation with explicit acknowledgment of the inherent right of parents to be the primary guardians and educators of their children.

#5. Fight Back against Public Schools

Get your children out of public schools. A public school classroom is a pit of snakes waiting to devour your child's mind and body. Critical Race Theory. Queer Theory. Comprehensive sexuality education. Diversity, equity, and inclusion. Revisionist history. Anti-white, anti-capitalism, anti-family, anti-American, anti-Christian propaganda. Rescue your child before it's too late. Notify other parents, school boards, and the media of the Marxist curriculum in your children's classroom.

We must prohibit "social-emotional learning" and "teaching for social justice" in public schools. It's just another name for Paulo Freire's "critical consciousness," which is Marxism. It's also quack psychology; it is used to manipulate our children's minds.

If you can, run for an elected position on your local school board, where you will have power over curricula, budgets, administrators, teachers, and the ideology taught to children in the public school system. We need good men and women to clean house in government-run schools across the country. Check out the 1776 Project PAC to see if you're a good candidate for the school board,[7] or find your local Moms for Liberty chapter to learn what you can do (even if you're not on the school board) to enact reform in your local public schools.[8] We must reclaim the institution of public schooling from the Marxists who captured it.

Fight for school choice. School choice improves academic outcomes for students by allowing parents to choose which schools best fit their children (and escape low-caliber schools in their zip code).[9] It puts parents back in charge of educational choices for their children. It forces schools that are indoctrinating youth with Marxist ideology to respond to parental concerns and adjust their curriculum or risk losing students—*and* the funding that comes with the students.

Demand that your elected representatives support school choice. School choice is critical to restoring schools to serve as a bulwark against evil rather than an entity that propagates it.[10]

We must also ban the American School Counselor Association (ASCA) from public schools. Via programs like RAMP (Recognized ASCA Model Program) and a retooled MTSS (Multi-Tiered Systems of Support) program, school counselors are circumventing laws that prohibit teachers and school administrators from talking to children about gender identity and sex. Visit CourageIsAHabit.org to learn more about how to prohibit school counselors from speaking to your children.[11]

#6. Take Back Colleges and Universities

There are three ways to take back universities from the left. First, governors in red states can assert their rightful control of state universities and abolish DEI programs and terminate Marxist faculty. Florida's Republican governor Ron DeSantis, with the help of Manhattan Institute senior fellow Christopher Rufo, is taking the lead on this at the

New College of Florida.[12] Second, the United States Congress can also pass laws to tax university endowments. Third, Congress can prohibit universities that accept federally subsidized student loans and research grants from participating in Critical Race Theory, Queer Theory, DEI, and Marxist indoctrination.

#7. Homeschool Your Children (or Grandchildren)

Public schools are dangerous. Often, private schools are just as bad. But homeschooled students achieve higher academic success, are better "socialized," and avoid the Marxist ideology that awaits children in the public school system. Join the Homeschool Legal Defense Association (HSLDA.org) to learn more about how to get involved in the fight for parental rights and how to get started homeschooling your children.[13]

#8. Ban ESG (Environmental, Social, and Governance) Metrics and DEI (Diversity, Equity, and Inclusion)

The Heartland Institute's Jack McPherrin has laid out specific policy solutions designed to blunt the impact of ESG metrics and eventually eliminate the permeation of ESG in our society.[14] At all levels of government, including the state, federal, and international levels, ESG scores must be combated at every opportunity. Three primary solutions currently exist at the state level. The first bars pension funds from making investments based on politics—such as mitigating "climate change" and advancing social justice causes—rather than on financial return. The second makes it illegal for states to execute contracts with ESG's powerful backers that boycott vital industries like fossil fuel extraction. Much progress has been made on these two fronts; for instance, West Virginia state treasurer Riley Moore barred the state from entering into contracts with BlackRock, Goldman Sachs, JPMorgan Chase, Morgan

Stanley, and Wells Fargo; and any financial institution entering into a state contract cannot boycott energy companies for the duration of that contract.[15] Texas comptroller Glenn Hegar has done the same thing, barring state entities from various dealings with BlackRock, BNP Paribas, Credit Suisse, HSBC, UBS, and many others.[16]

While these first two strategies are laudable, it is more important to strike ESG at its basic principles, which encourage discrimination against any entity deemed unworthy of loans, investments, or insurance policies based on ideological or political grounds. Florida governor DeSantis has championed this approach, and indications are that nearly a score of states are currently pursuing regulatory actions against financial institutions that discriminate against people, businesses, or institutions on meritless ideological or political grounds.[17] This would represent the strongest state-level step to protect traditional American liberties and freedoms against the dictates of ESG metrics.

At the federal level, action must be taken as well. First, Congress must overturn the Biden administration's Department of Labor Rule allowing federal pension funds to consider ESG factors. Second, Congress must direct the Office of the Comptroller of the Currency to remove the pause on the Trump-era regulation that prohibited financial institutions from engaging in discriminatory practices. Third, Congress must also direct the U.S. Securities and Exchange Commission (SEC) to revoke proposed rules surrounding ESG and climate initiatives and stress that the SEC only focus upon protecting investors and upholding fair, orderly, and efficient markets, as is the SEC's primary mandate.

Moreover, the *S* in ESG is almost entirely focused on promoting DEI (diversity, equity, and inclusion). We must ban DEI from the public school system, in K–12 schools and public universities, as well as in private universities that accept federal funds, whether federally subsidized student loads or federal research grants. Likewise, we must prohibit private companies that embrace DEI from doing business with the federal or state governments. We must reject Klaus Schwab's "stakeholder capitalism" in all its forms.

#9. Abolish the Administrative State

We will never drain the swamp, vanquish the deep state, or assert ordered liberty in our nation if we allow unelected, unaccountable partisan bureaucrats to rule us. The administrative state is unconstitutional. We must abolish it. There are three ways this can be accomplished. First, the legislative branch can reclaim its legislative authority. Congress must cease passing bills with vague language that defers "clarification" and rulemaking to the executive branch. Second, the judicial branch can enforce the principle of nondelegation so that the legislative branch doesn't give away its legislative authority. Third, the chief executive can reorganize executive agencies so that "civil servants" can be fired, and conduct stringent employee and institutional reviews upon every cabinet-level department, federal agency, and regulatory body under the federal government's purview, eliminating unnecessary or partisan bureaucrats, or entire executive departments or agencies such as the Department of Education and the Environmental Protection Agency, among many others.

Moreover, Congress must investigate the corruption in the Centers for Disease Control and Prevention (CDC), the Food and Drug Administration (FDA), the National Institutes of Health (NIH), and the institutions they regulate and fund: Big Pharma, Big Food, and Big Science. Likewise, the Department of Justice has ample evidence to launch criminal investigations.

Technocracy is not just "rule by the experts," it's a stepping stone, as we've seen, from capitalism to communism. Don't automatically trust the experts, whether it's the American Academy of Pediatrics, the teachers' unions, the CDC, or anyone else who claims to have a right to control your behavior through "science-based" evidence. Be skeptical, question everything, and think and act independently.

#10. Take Back Your States

I want to see more morality and "original justice" in state laws across the United States. As John Adams said, "Our Constitution was made only for a moral and religious People. It is wholly inadequate to the government of any other."[18] If politicians in our own party refuse to acknowledge the reality of the political enemy we're facing, and instead continue to compromise with Marxists, vote them out. Put God back in public life; He is the only true bulwark against the evil we face. The Pledge of Allegiance. The National Anthem. Prayer in school, on sports fields, and during public events. How can we expect our nation to embrace our constitutionally enshrined heritage of natural law if we don't marinate our culture in the reality of our Creator?

#11. Go to Church

The spiritual enemy we face exploits our vulnerability because of our sin. The eternal state of souls is on the line. As I write this, I sit here reflecting on Jesus Christ, our Lord and Savior. What could be more important than Him? How can we seek Him if we don't know Him? How can we lead others to Him if the evil one muddies our eyes and binds our bodies and souls with communism? Get your family to church.

And pick up your Bible. Listen to the *Bible in a Year* podcast with Father Mike Schmitz.[19] Then listen to the *Catechism in a Year* podcast with Father Mike Schmitz.[20] Read *A Biblical Walk through the Mass: Understanding What We Say and Do in the Liturgy*, by Edward Sri,[21] and *Jesus and the Jewish Roots of the Eucharist*, by Brant Pitre.[22] Get on your knees and pray. Beg God for forgiveness. Let the Holy Spirit teach you how to love like Christ loves you and seek the One who created you in His image and likeness, and your whole family too.

We must cultivate a generation of young men to fill the Church with strong Christian warriors and spiritual leaders. The Catholic Church played a pivotal role in defeating global communism at the end of the twentieth century, and it must play a pivotal role in defeating the Marxism of today, but now the Church is suffering a priest shortage of crisis proportions. Many dioceses in the United States have been labeled missionary outposts and must be staffed by foreign priests. That should be an alarm bell for all of us. Parents, parishes, and the greater Catholic community must work together to combat secularism and foster Christianity within our young American men and women, or we will be lost.

Shepherding our children's souls back into the embrace of their Creator is a monumental priority. Policy-oriented solutions are important. This is even more so. And it begins with us—individually and with our families. Go to Church!

#12. HIDE YOUR CHILDREN

If we don't acknowledge the reality of the enemy we're facing, ideologically and spiritually, we won't fight well against it and we won't win. I want to win because I love the United States of America, one nation under God, indivisible, with liberty and justice for all. I know you do too.

Our children are the last pillar of civil society the Marxists must destroy before the whole cultural bulwark crumbles and Marxism is unleashed on our nation and the world. Marxists and their unwitting allies have wormed their way into every aspect of our lives. They now stand poised to strike their daggers into the hearts of our sons and daughters if we do not shelter them from the evil breathing down their necks.

Give your children shelter from the evil of the world that seeks to destroy their minds, bodies, and souls. Protect their eyes, their minds, their bodies, and their hearts. Protect their innocence.

We must expect escalation from our adversaries. The monumental victories we've secured in the past two years increase the stakes for the Marxists. Now is their decisive moment. This is their last chance. Because of our victories, because we *acknowledge the reality of the political enemy we face*, their time to impose Marxism on our nation is either now or never. They are pulling out all the stops.

But so are we. This is it. This is the battle. Take heart and let's charge for victory together, for our nation, our families, and our children.

Resources for the Fight

The Declaration of Independence

In Congress, July 4, 1776

The unanimous Declaration of the thirteen united States of America, When in the Course of human events, it becomes necessary for one people to dissolve the political bands which have connected them with another, and to assume among the powers of the earth, the separate and equal station to which the Laws of Nature and of Nature's God entitle them, a decent respect to the opinions of mankind requires that they should declare the causes which impel them to the separation.

We hold these truths to be self-evident, that all men are created equal, that they are endowed by their Creator with certain unalienable Rights, that among these are Life, Liberty and the pursuit of Happiness.—That to secure these rights, Governments are instituted among Men, deriving their just powers from the consent of the governed, —That whenever any Form of Government becomes destructive of these ends, it is the Right of the People to alter or to abolish it, and to institute new Government, laying its foundation on such principles and organizing its powers in such form, as to them shall seem most likely to effect their Safety and Happiness. Prudence, indeed, will dictate that Governments long established should not be changed for light and transient causes; and accordingly all experience hath shewn, that mankind are more disposed to suffer, while evils are sufferable, than to right themselves by abolishing the forms to which they are accustomed. But when a long train of abuses and usurpations, pursuing invariably the same Object evinces a design to reduce them under absolute Despotism, it is their right, it is their duty, to throw off such Government, and to provide new Guards for their future security.—Such has been the patient sufferance of these Colonies; and such is now the necessity which constrains them to alter their former Systems of Government. The history of the present King of Great Britain is a history of repeated injuries and usurpations, all having in direct object the establishment of an absolute Tyranny over these States. To prove this, let Facts be submitted to a candid world.

He has refused his Assent to Laws, the most wholesome and necessary for the public good.

He has forbidden his Governors to pass Laws of immediate and pressing importance, unless suspended in their operation till his Assent should be obtained; and when so suspended, he has utterly neglected to attend to them.

He has refused to pass other Laws for the accommodation of large districts of people, unless those people would relinquish the right of Representation in the Legislature, a right inestimable to them and formidable to tyrants only.

He has called together legislative bodies at places unusual, uncomfortable, and distant from the depository of their public Records, for the sole purpose of fatiguing them into compliance with his measures.

He has dissolved Representative Houses repeatedly, for opposing with manly firmness his invasions on the rights of the people.

He has refused for a long time, after such dissolutions, to cause others to be elected; whereby the Legislative powers, incapable of Annihilation, have returned to the People at large for their exercise; the State remaining in the mean time exposed to all the dangers of invasion from without, and convulsions within.

He has endeavoured to prevent the population of these States; for that purpose obstructing the Laws for Naturalization of Foreigners; refusing to pass others to encourage their migrations hither, and raising the conditions of new Appropriations of Lands.

He has obstructed the Administration of Justice, by refusing his Assent to Laws for establishing Judiciary powers.

He has made Judges dependent on his Will alone, for the tenure of their offices, and the amount and payment of their salaries.

He has erected a multitude of New Offices, and sent hither swarms of Officers to harrass our people, and eat out their substance.

He has kept among us, in times of peace, Standing Armies without the Consent of our legislatures.

He has affected to render the Military independent of and superior to the Civil power.

He has combined with others to subject us to a jurisdiction foreign to our constitution, and unacknowledged by our laws; giving his Assent to their Acts of pretended Legislation:

For Quartering large bodies of armed troops among us:

For protecting them, by a mock Trial, from punishment for any Murders which they should commit on the Inhabitants of these States:

For cutting off our Trade with all parts of the world:

For imposing Taxes on us without our Consent:

For depriving us in many cases, of the benefits of Trial by Jury:

For transporting us beyond Seas to be tried for pretended offences:

For abolishing the free System of English Laws in a neighbouring Province, establishing therein an Arbitrary government, and enlarging its Boundaries so as to render it at once an example and fit instrument for introducing the same absolute rule into these Colonies:

For taking away our Charters, abolishing our most valuable Laws, and altering fundamentally the Forms of our Governments:

For suspending our own Legislatures, and declaring themselves invested with power to legislate for us in all cases whatsoever.

He has abdicated Government here, by declaring us out of his Protection and waging War against us.

He has plundered our seas, ravaged our Coasts, burnt our towns, and destroyed the lives of our people.

He is at this time transporting large Armies of foreign Mercenaries to compleat the works of death, desolation and tyranny, already begun with circumstances of Cruelty & perfidy scarcely paralleled in the most barbarous ages, and totally unworthy the Head of a civilized nation.

He has constrained our fellow Citizens taken Captive on the high Seas to bear Arms against their Country, to become the executioners of their friends and Brethren, or to fall themselves by their Hands.

He has excited domestic insurrections amongst us, and has endeavoured to bring on the inhabitants of our frontiers, the merciless Indian Savages, whose known rule of warfare, is an undistinguished destruction of all ages, sexes and conditions.

In every stage of these Oppressions We have Petitioned for Redress in the most humble terms: Our repeated Petitions have been answered only by repeated injury. A Prince whose character is thus marked by every act which may define a Tyrant, is unfit to be the ruler of a free people.

Nor have We been wanting in attentions to our Brittish brethren. We have warned them from time to time of attempts by their legislature to extend an unwarrantable jurisdiction over us. We have reminded them of the circumstances of our emigration and settlement here. We have appealed to their native justice and magnanimity, and we have conjured them by the ties of our common kindred to disavow these usurpations, which, would inevitably interrupt our connections and correspondence. They too have been deaf to the voice of justice and of consanguinity. We must, therefore, acquiesce in the necessity, which denounces our Separation, and hold them, as we hold the rest of mankind, Enemies in War, in Peace Friends.

We, therefore, the Representatives of the united States of America, in General Congress, Assembled, appealing to the Supreme Judge of the world for the rectitude of our intentions, do, in the Name, and by Authority of the good People of these Colonies, solemnly publish and declare, That these United Colonies are, and of Right ought to be Free and Independent States; that they are Absolved from all Allegiance to the British Crown, and that all political connection between them and the State of Great Britain, is and ought to be totally dissolved; and that as Free and Independent States, they have full Power to levy War, conclude Peace, contract Alliances, establish Commerce, and to do all other Acts and Things which Independent States may of right do. And for the support of this Declaration, with a firm reliance on the protection of divine Providence, we mutually pledge to each other our Lives, our Fortunes and our sacred Honor.

GEORGIA
Button Gwinnett
Lyman Hall
George Walton

NORTH CAROLINA
William Hooper
Joseph Hewes
John Penn

SOUTH CAROLINA
Edward Rutledge
Thomas Heyward, Jr.
Thomas Lynch, Jr.
Arthur Middleton

MASSACHUSETTS
John Hancock
Samuel Adams
John Adams
Robert Treat Paine
Elbridge Gerry

MARYLAND
Samuel Chase
William Paca
Thomas Stone
Charles Carroll of Carrollton

VIRGINIA
George Wythe
Richard Henry Lee
Thomas Jefferson
Benjamin Harrison
Thomas Nelson, Jr.
Francis Lightfoot Lee
Carter Braxton

PENNSYLVANIA
Robert Morris
Benjamin Rush
Benjamin Franklin
John Morton
George Clymer
James Smith
George Taylor
James Wilson
George Ross

DELAWARE
Caesar Rodney
George Read
Thomas McKean

NEW YORK
William Floyd
Philip Livingston
Francis Lewis
Lewis Morris

NEW JERSEY
Richard Stockton
John Witherspoon
Francis Hopkinson
John Hart
Abraham Clark

NEW HAMPSHIRE
Josiah Bartlett
William Whipple
Matthew Thornton

RHODE ISLAND
Stephen Hopkins
William Ellery

CONNECTICUT
Roger Sherman
Samuel Huntington
William Williams
Oliver Wolcott

The United States Constitution

We the People of the United States, in Order to form a more perfect Union, establish Justice, insure domestic Tranquility, provide for the common defence, promote the general Welfare, and secure
the Blessings of Liberty to ourselves and our Posterity, do ordain and
establish this Constitution for the United States of America.

Article. I.

Section. 1.

All legislative Powers herein granted shall be vested in a Congress
of the United States, which shall consist of a Senate and House of
Representatives.

Section. 2.

The House of Representatives shall be composed of Members chosen every second Year by the People of the several States, and the Electors in each State shall have the Qualifications requisite for Electors of the most numerous Branch of the State Legislature.

No Person shall be a Representative who shall not have attained to the Age of twenty five Years, and been seven Years a Citizen of the United States, and who shall not, when elected, be an Inhabitant of that State in which he shall be chosen.

Representatives and direct Taxes shall be apportioned among the several States which may be included within this Union, according to their respective Numbers, which shall be determined by adding to the whole Number of free Persons, including those bound to Service for a Term of Years, and excluding Indians not taxed, three fifths of all other Persons. The actual Enumeration shall be made within three Years after the first Meeting of the Congress of the United States, and within every subsequent Term of ten Years, in such Manner as they shall by Law direct. The Number of Representatives shall not exceed one for every thirty Thousand, but each State shall have at Least one Representative; and until such enumeration shall be made, the State of New Hampshire shall be entitled to chuse three, Massachusetts eight, Rhode-Island and Providence Plantations one, Connecticut five, New-York six, New Jersey four, Pennsylvania eight, Delaware one, Maryland six, Virginia ten, North Carolina five, South Carolina five, and Georgia three.

When vacancies happen in the Representation from any State, the Executive Authority thereof shall issue Writs of Election to fill such Vacancies.

The House of Representatives shall chuse their Speaker and other Officers; and shall have the sole Power of Impeachment.

Section. 3.

The Senate of the United States shall be composed of two Senators from each State, chosen by the Legislature thereof, for six Years; and each Senator shall have one Vote.

Immediately after they shall be assembled in Consequence of the first Election, they shall be divided as equally as may be into three Classes. The Seats of the Senators of the first Class shall be vacated at the Expiration of the second Year, of the second Class at the Expiration of the fourth Year, and of the third Class at the Expiration of the sixth Year, so that one third may be chosen every second Year; and if Vacancies happen by Resignation, or otherwise, during the Recess of the Legislature of any State, the Executive thereof may make temporary Appointments until the next Meeting of the Legislature, which shall then fill such Vacancies.

No Person shall be a Senator who shall not have attained to the Age of thirty Years, and been nine Years a Citizen of the United States, and who shall not, when elected, be an Inhabitant of that State for which he shall be chosen.

The Vice President of the United States shall be President of the Senate, but shall have no Vote, unless they be equally divided.

The Senate shall chuse their other Officers, and also a President pro tempore, in the Absence of the Vice President, or when he shall exercise the Office of President of the United States.

The Senate shall have the sole Power to try all Impeachments. When sitting for that Purpose, they shall be on Oath or Affirmation. When the President of the United States is tried, the Chief Justice shall preside: And no Person shall be convicted without the Concurrence of two thirds of the Members present.

Judgment in Cases of Impeachment shall not extend further than to removal from Office, and disqualification to hold and enjoy any

Office of honor, Trust or Profit under the United States: but the Party convicted shall nevertheless be liable and subject to Indictment, Trial, Judgment and Punishment, according to Law.

Section. 4.

The Times, Places and Manner of holding Elections for Senators and Representatives, shall be prescribed in each State by the Legislature thereof; but the Congress may at any time by Law make or alter such Regulations, except as to the Places of chusing Senators.

The Congress shall assemble at least once in every Year, and such Meeting shall be on the first Monday in December, unless they shall by Law appoint a different Day.

Section. 5.

Each House shall be the Judge of the Elections, Returns and Qualifications of its own Members, and a Majority of each shall constitute a Quorum to do Business; but a smaller Number may adjourn from day to day, and may be authorized to compel the Attendance of absent Members, in such Manner, and under such Penalties as each House may provide.

Each House may determine the Rules of its Proceedings, punish its Members for disorderly Behaviour, and, with the Concurrence of two thirds, expel a Member.

Each House shall keep a Journal of its Proceedings, and from time to time publish the same, excepting such Parts as may in their Judgment require Secrecy; and the Yeas and Nays of the Members of either House on any question shall, at the Desire of one fifth of those Present, be entered on the Journal.

Neither House, during the Session of Congress, shall, without the Consent of the other, adjourn for more than three days, nor to any other Place than that in which the two Houses shall be sitting.

Section. 6.

The Senators and Representatives shall receive a Compensation for their Services, to be ascertained by Law, and paid out of the Treasury of the United States. They shall in all Cases, except Treason, Felony and Breach of the Peace, be privileged from Arrest during their Attendance at the Session of their respective Houses, and in going to and returning from the same; and for any Speech or Debate in either House, they shall not be questioned in any other Place.

No Senator or Representative shall, during the Time for which he was elected, be appointed to any civil Office under the Authority of the United States, which shall have been created, or the Emoluments whereof shall have been encreased during such time; and no Person holding any Office under the United States, shall be a Member of either House during his Continuance in Office.

Section. 7.

All Bills for raising Revenue shall originate in the House of Representatives; but the Senate may propose or concur with Amendments as on other Bills.

Every Bill which shall have passed the House of Representatives and the Senate, shall, before it become a Law, be presented to the President of the United States; If he approve he shall sign it, but if not he shall return it, with his Objections to that House in which it shall have originated, who shall enter the Objections at large on their Journal, and proceed to reconsider it. If after such Reconsideration two thirds of that House shall agree to pass the Bill, it shall be sent, together with the Objections, to the other House, by which it shall likewise be reconsidered, and if approved by two thirds of that House, it shall become a Law. But in all such Cases the Votes of both Houses shall be determined by yeas and Nays, and the Names of the Persons voting for and against the Bill shall be entered on the Journal of each House respectively. If any Bill shall not be returned by the President within ten Days (Sundays excepted) after it shall have been presented to him, the Same shall be a Law, in like Manner as if he had signed it, unless the Congress by their Adjournment prevent its Return, in which Case it shall not be a Law.

Every Order, Resolution, or Vote to which the Concurrence of the Senate and House of Representatives may be necessary (except on a question of Adjournment) shall be presented to the President of the United States; and before the Same shall take Effect, shall be approved by him, or being disapproved by him, shall be repassed by two thirds of the Senate and House of Representatives, according to the Rules and Limitations prescribed in the Case of a Bill.

Section. 8.

The Congress shall have Power To lay and collect Taxes, Duties, Imposts and Excises, to pay the Debts and provide for the common Defence and general Welfare of the United States; but all Duties, Imposts and Excises shall be uniform throughout the United States;

To borrow Money on the credit of the United States;

To regulate Commerce with foreign Nations, and among the several States, and with the Indian Tribes;

To establish an uniform Rule of Naturalization, and uniform Laws on the subject of Bankruptcies throughout the United States;

To coin Money, regulate the Value thereof, and of foreign Coin, and fix the Standard of Weights and Measures;

To provide for the Punishment of counterfeiting the Securities and current Coin of the United States;

To establish Post Offices and post Roads;

To promote the Progress of Science and useful Arts, by securing for limited Times to Authors and Inventors the exclusive Right to their respective Writings and Discoveries;

To constitute Tribunals inferior to the supreme Court;

To define and punish Piracies and Felonies committed on the high Seas, and Offences against the Law of Nations;

To declare War, grant Letters of Marque and Reprisal, and make Rules concerning Captures on Land and Water;

To raise and support Armies, but no Appropriation of Money to that Use shall be for a longer Term than two Years;

To provide and maintain a Navy;

To make Rules for the Government and Regulation of the land and naval Forces;

To provide for calling forth the Militia to execute the Laws of the Union, suppress Insurrections and repel Invasions;

To provide for organizing, arming, and disciplining, the Militia, and for governing such Part of them as may be employed in the Service of the United States, reserving to the States respectively, the Appointment of the Officers, and the Authority of training the Militia according to the discipline prescribed by Congress;

To exercise exclusive Legislation in all Cases whatsoever, over such District (not exceeding ten Miles square) as may, by Cession of particular States, and the Acceptance of Congress, become the Seat of the Government of the United States, and to exercise like Authority over all Places purchased by the Consent of the Legislature of the State in which the Same shall be, for the Erection of Forts, Magazines, Arsenals, dock-Yards, and other needful Buildings;—And

To make all Laws which shall be necessary and proper for carrying into Execution the foregoing Powers, and all other Powers vested by this Constitution in the Government of the United States, or in any Department or Officer thereof.

Section. 9.

The Migration or Importation of such Persons as any of the States now existing shall think proper to admit, shall not be prohibited by the

Congress prior to the Year one thousand eight hundred and eight, but a Tax or duty may be imposed on such Importation, not exceeding ten dollars for each Person.

The Privilege of the Writ of Habeas Corpus shall not be suspended, unless when in Cases of Rebellion or Invasion the public Safety may require it.

No Bill of Attainder or ex post facto Law shall be passed.

No Capitation, or other direct, Tax shall be laid, unless in Proportion to the Census or enumeration herein before directed to be taken.

No Tax or Duty shall be laid on Articles exported from any State.

No Preference shall be given by any Regulation of Commerce or Revenue to the Ports of one State over those of another: nor shall Vessels bound to, or from, one State, be obliged to enter, clear, or pay Duties in another.

No Money shall be drawn from the Treasury, but in Consequence of Appropriations made by Law; and a regular Statement and Account of the Receipts and Expenditures of all public Money shall be published from time to time.

No Title of Nobility shall be granted by the United States: And no Person holding any Office of Profit or Trust under them, shall, without the Consent of the Congress, accept of any present, Emolument, Office, or Title, of any kind whatever, from any King, Prince, or foreign State.

Section. 10.

No State shall enter into any Treaty, Alliance, or Confederation; grant Letters of Marque and Reprisal; coin Money; emit Bills of Credit; make any Thing but gold and silver Coin a Tender in Payment of Debts; pass any Bill of Attainder, ex post facto Law, or Law impairing the Obligation of Contracts, or grant any Title of Nobility.

No State shall, without the Consent of the Congress, lay any Imposts or Duties on Imports or Exports, except what may be absolutely necessary for executing it's inspection Laws: and the net Produce of all Duties and Imposts, laid by any State on Imports or Exports, shall be for the Use of the Treasury of the United States; and all such Laws shall be subject to the Revision and Controul of the Congress.

No State shall, without the Consent of Congress, lay any Duty of Tonnage, keep Troops, or Ships of War in time of Peace, enter into any Agreement or Compact with another State, or with a foreign Power, or engage in War, unless actually invaded, or in such imminent Danger as will not admit of delay.

Article. II.

Section. 1.

The executive Power shall be vested in a President of the United States of America. He shall hold his Office during the Term of four Years, and, together with the Vice President, chosen for the same Term, be elected, as follows

Each State shall appoint, in such Manner as the Legislature thereof may direct, a Number of Electors, equal to the whole Number of Senators and Representatives to which the State may be entitled in the Congress: but no Senator or Representative, or Person holding an Office of Trust or Profit under the United States, shall be appointed an Elector.

The Electors shall meet in their respective States, and vote by Ballot for two Persons, of whom one at least shall not be an Inhabitant of the same State with themselves. And they shall make a List of all the Persons voted for, and of the Number of Votes for each; which List they shall sign and certify, and transmit sealed to the Seat of the Government of the United States, directed to the President of the Senate. The President of the Senate shall, in the Presence of the Senate and House of Representatives, open all the Certificates, and the Votes shall then be counted. The Person having the greatest Number of Votes shall be the President, if such Number be a Majority of the whole Number of Electors appointed; and if there be more than one who have such Majority, and have an equal Number of Votes, then the House of Representatives shall immediately chuse by Ballot one of them for President; and if no Person have a Majority, then from the five highest on the List the said House shall in like Manner chuse the President. But in chusing the President, the Votes shall be taken by States, the Representation from each State having one Vote; A quorum for this Purpose shall consist of a Member or Members from two thirds of the States, and a Majority of all the States shall be necessary to a Choice. In every Case, after the Choice of the President, the Person having the greatest Number of Votes of the Electors shall be the Vice President. But if there should remain two or more who have equal Votes, the Senate shall chuse from them by Ballot the Vice President.

The Congress may determine the Time of chusing the Electors, and the Day on which they shall give their Votes; which Day shall be the same throughout the United States.

No Person except a natural born Citizen, or a Citizen of the United States, at the time of the Adoption of this Constitution, shall be eligible to the Office of President; neither shall any Person be eligible to that Office who shall not have attained to the Age of thirty five Years, and been fourteen Years a Resident within the United States.

In Case of the Removal of the President from Office, or of his Death, Resignation, or Inability to discharge the Powers and Duties of the said Office, the Same shall devolve on the Vice President, and the Congress may by Law provide for the Case of Removal, Death, Resignation or Inability, both of the President and Vice President, declaring what Officer shall then act as President, and such Officer shall act accordingly, until the Disability be removed, or a President shall be elected.

The President shall, at stated Times, receive for his Services, a Compensation, which shall neither be encreased nor diminished during the Period for which he shall have been elected, and he shall not receive within that Period any other Emolument from the United States, or any of them.

Before he enter on the Execution of his Office, he shall take the following Oath or Affirmation:—"I do solemnly swear (or affirm) that I will faithfully execute the Office of President of the United States, and will to the best of my Ability, preserve, protect and defend the Constitution of the United States."

Section. 2.

The President shall be Commander in Chief of the Army and Navy of the United States, and of the Militia of the several States, when called into the actual Service of the United States; he may require the Opinion, in writing, of the principal Officer in each of the executive Departments, upon any Subject relating to the Duties of their respective Offices, and he shall have Power to grant Reprieves and Pardons for Offences against the United States, except in Cases of Impeachment.

He shall have Power, by and with the Advice and Consent of the Senate, to make Treaties, provided two thirds of the Senators present concur; and he shall nominate, and by and with the Advice and Consent of the Senate, shall appoint Ambassadors, other public Ministers and Consuls, Judges of the supreme Court, and all other Officers of the United States, whose Appointments are not herein otherwise provided for, and which shall be established by Law: but the Congress may by Law vest the Appointment of such inferior Officers, as they think proper, in the President alone, in the Courts of Law, or in the Heads of Departments.

The President shall have Power to fill up all Vacancies that may happen during the Recess of the Senate, by granting Commissions which shall expire at the End of their next Session.

Section. 3.

He shall from time to time give to the Congress Information of the State of the Union, and recommend to their Consideration such Measures as he shall judge necessary and expedient; he may, on extraordinary Occasions, convene both Houses, or either of them, and in Case of Disagreement between them, with Respect to the Time of Adjournment, he may adjourn them to such Time as he shall think proper; he shall receive Ambassadors and other public Ministers; he shall take Care that the Laws be faithfully executed, and shall Commission all the Officers of the United States.

Section. 4.

The President, Vice President and all civil Officers of the United States, shall be removed from Office on Impeachment for, and Conviction of, Treason, Bribery, or other high Crimes and Misdemeanors.

Article. III.

Section. 1.

The judicial Power of the United States, shall be vested in one supreme Court, and in such inferior Courts as the Congress may from time to time ordain and establish. The Judges, both of the supreme and inferior Courts, shall hold their Offices during good Behaviour, and shall, at stated Times, receive for their Services, a Compensation, which shall not be diminished during their Continuance in Office.

Section. 2.

The judicial Power shall extend to all Cases, in Law and Equity, arising under this Constitution, the Laws of the United States, and

Treaties made, or which shall be made, under their Authority;— to all Cases affecting Ambassadors, other public Ministers and Consuls;—to all Cases of admiralty and maritime Jurisdiction;— to Controversies to which the United States shall be a Party;—to Controversies between two or more States;— between a State and Citizens of another State,—between Citizens of different States,— between Citizens of the same State claiming Lands under Grants of different States, and between a State, or the Citizens thereof, and foreign States, Citizens or Subjects.

In all Cases affecting Ambassadors, other public Ministers and Consuls, and those in which a State shall be Party, the supreme Court shall have original Jurisdiction. In all the other Cases before mentioned, the supreme Court shall have appellate Jurisdiction, both as to Law and Fact, with such Exceptions, and under such Regulations as the Congress shall make.

The Trial of all Crimes, except in Cases of Impeachment, shall be by Jury; and such Trial shall be held in the State where the said Crimes shall have been committed; but when not committed within any State, the Trial shall be at such Place or Places as the Congress may by Law have directed.

Section. 3.

Treason against the United States, shall consist only in levying War against them, or in adhering to their Enemies, giving them Aid and Comfort. No Person shall be convicted of Treason unless on the Testimony of two Witnesses to the same overt Act, or on Confession in open Court.

The Congress shall have Power to declare the Punishment of Treason, but no Attainder of Treason shall work Corruption of Blood, or Forfeiture except during the Life of the Person attainted.

Article. IV.

Section. 1.

Full Faith and Credit shall be given in each State to the public Acts, Records, and judicial Proceedings of every other State. And the Congress may by general Laws prescribe the Manner in which such Acts, Records and Proceedings shall be proved, and the Effect thereof.

Section. 2.

The Citizens of each State shall be entitled to all Privileges and Immunities of Citizens in the several States.

A Person charged in any State with Treason, Felony, or other Crime, who shall flee from Justice, and be found in another State, shall on Demand of the executive Authority of the State from which he fled, be delivered up, to be removed to the State having Jurisdiction of the Crime.

No Person held to Service or Labour in one State, under the Laws thereof, escaping into another, shall, in Consequence of any Law or Regulation therein, be discharged from such Service or Labour, but shall be delivered up on Claim of the Party to whom such Service or Labour may be due.

Section. 3.

New States may be admitted by the Congress into this Union; but no new State shall be formed or erected within the Jurisdiction of any other State; nor any State be formed by the Junction of two or more States, or Parts of States, without the Consent of the Legislatures of the States concerned as well as of the Congress.

The Congress shall have Power to dispose of and make all needful Rules and Regulations respecting the Territory or other Property belonging to the United States; and nothing in this Constitution shall be so construed as to Prejudice any Claims of the United States, or of any particular State.

Section. 4.

The United States shall guarantee to every State in this Union a Republican Form of Government, and shall protect each of them against Invasion; and on Application of the Legislature, or of the Executive (when the Legislature cannot be convened) against domestic Violence.

Article. V.

The Congress, whenever two thirds of both Houses shall deem it necessary, shall propose Amendments to this Constitution, or, on the Application of the Legislatures of two thirds of the several States, shall call a Convention for proposing Amendments, which, in either Case, shall be valid to all Intents and Purposes, as Part of this Constitution, when ratified by the Legislatures of three fourths of the several States, or by Conventions in three fourths thereof, as the one or the other Mode of Ratification may be proposed by the Congress; Provided that no Amendment which may be made prior to the Year One thousand eight hundred and eight shall in any Manner affect the first and fourth Clauses in the Ninth Section of the first Article; and that no State, without its Consent, shall be deprived of its equal Suffrage in the Senate.

Article. VI.

All Debts contracted and Engagements entered into, before the Adoption of this Constitution, shall be as valid against the United States under this Constitution, as under the Confederation.

This Constitution, and the Laws of the United States which shall be made in Pursuance thereof; and all Treaties made, or which shall be made, under the Authority of the United States, shall be the supreme Law of the Land; and the Judges in every State shall be bound thereby, any Thing in the Constitution or Laws of any State to the Contrary notwithstanding.

The Senators and Representatives before mentioned, and the Members of the several State Legislatures, and all executive and judicial Officers, both of the United States and of the several States, shall be bound by Oath or Affirmation, to support this Constitution; but no religious Test shall ever be required as a Qualification to any Office or public Trust under the United States.

Article. VII.

The Ratification of the Conventions of nine States, shall be sufficient for the Establishment of this Constitution between the States so ratifying the Same.

Attest William Jackson Secretary

done in Convention by the Unanimous Consent of the States present the Seventeenth Day of September in the Year of our Lord one thousand seven hundred and Eighty seven and of the Independance of the United States of America the Twelfth In witness whereof We have hereunto subscribed our Names,

G°. Washington
Presidt and deputy from Virginia

DELAWARE
Geo: Read
Gunning Bedford jun
John Dickinson
Richard Bassett
Jaco: Broom

MARYLAND
James McHenry
Dan of St Thos. Jenifer
Danl. Carroll

VIRGINIA
John Blair
James Madison Jr.

NORTH CAROLINA
Wm. Blount
Richd. Dobbs Spaight
Hu Williamson

SOUTH CAROLINA
J. Rutledge
Charles Cotesworth Pinckney
Charles Pinckney
Pierce Butler

GEORGIA
William Few
Abr Baldwin

NEW HAMPSHIRE
John Langdon
Nicholas Gilman

MASSACHUSETTS
Nathaniel Gorham
Rufus King

CONNECTICUT
Wm. Saml. Johnson
Roger Sherman

NEW YORK
Alexander Hamilton

NEW JERSEY
Wil: Livingston
David Brearley
Wm. Paterson
Jona: Dayton

PENNSYLVANIA
B Franklin
Thomas Mifflin
Robt. Morris
Geo. Clymer
Thos. FitzSimons
Jared Ingersoll
James Wilson
Gouv Morris

Qui Pluribus
Encyclical of Pope Pius IX
On Faith and Religion

To All Patriarchs, Primates, Archbishops, and Bishops.
Venerable Brothers, We Greet You and Give You Our
Apostolic Blessing.

For many years past We strove with you, venerable brothers, to devote Our best powers to Our episcopal office — an office full of labor and worry. We strove to feed those committed to Our care on the mountains of Israel, at its streams and in its richest pastures. Our illustrious Predecessor, Gregory XVI, whose famous actions are recorded in the annals of the Church in letters of gold, will surely be remembered and admired by future generations. Now though, upon his death, by the mysterious plan of divine providence, We have been raised to the supreme Pontificate. We did not purpose this nor expect it; indeed Our reaction is great disquietude and anxiety. For if the burden of the Apostolic ministry is rightly considered to be at all times exceedingly heavy and beset with dangers, it is to be dreaded most particularly in these times which are so critical for the Christian commonwealth.

2. We are well aware of Our weakness. So when We reflect on the most serious duties of the supreme apostolate especially in a period of great instability, We would simply have fallen into great sadness, did We not place all Our hope in God who is Our Saviour. For He never abandons those who hope in Him. Time and again, so as to demonstrate what His power can accomplish, He employs weak instruments to rule His Church; in this way, all men may increasingly realize that it is God Himself who governs and protects the Church with His wonderful providence. We are also greatly supported by the comforting consideration that We have you, venerable brothers, as Our helpers and companions in the work of saving souls. For since you have been called to share a portion of Our care, you strive to fulfill your ministry with attentiveness and zeal, and to fight the good fight.

3. For this reason, as soon as We were placed, despite Our unworthiness, on this high See of the prince of the apostles as the representative of the blessed Peter, and received from the eternal Prince of Pastors Himself the most serious divinely given office of feeding and ruling not only the lambs, that is, the whole Christian people, but also the sheep, that is, the bishops, We surely had no greater wish than to address you all with a deep feeling of love. Therefore, since We have now assumed the supreme pontificate in Our Lateran Basilica, We are sending this letter to you without delay, in accordance with the established practice of Our predecessors. Its purpose is to urge that you keep the night-watches over the flock entrusted to your care with the greatest possible eagerness, wakefulness and effort, and that you raise a protecting wall before the House of Israel; do these as you battle with episcopal strength and steadfastness like good soldiers of Christ Jesus against the hateful enemy of the human race.

4. Each of you has noticed, venerable brothers, that a very bitter and fearsome war against the whole Catholic commonwealth is being stirred up by men bound together in a lawless alliance. These men do not preserve sound doctrine, but turn their hearing from the truth. They eagerly attempt to produce from their darkness all sorts of prodigious beliefs, and then to magnify them with all their strength, and to publish them and spread them among ordinary people. We shudder indeed and suffer bitter pain when We reflect on all their outlandish errors and their many harmful methods, plots and contrivances. These men use these means to spread their hatred for truth and light. They are experienced and skillful in deceit, which they use to set in motion their plans to quench peoples' zeal for piety, justice and virtue, to corrupt morals, to cast all divine and human laws into confusion, and to weaken and even possibly overthrow the Catholic religion and civil society. For you know, venerable brothers, that these bitter enemies of the Christian name, are carried wretchedly along by some blind momentum of their mad impiety; they go so far in their rash imagining as to teach without blushing, openly and publicly, daring and unheard-of doctrines, thereby uttering blasphemies against God.[1] They teach that the most holy mysteries of our religion are fictions of human invention, and that the teaching of the Catholic Church is opposed to the good and the prerogatives of human society. They are not even afraid to deny Christ Himself and God.

5. In order to easily mislead the people into making errors, deceiving particularly the imprudent and the inexperienced, they pretend that they alone know the ways to prosperity. They claim for themselves without hesitation the name of "philosophers." They feel as if philosophy, which is wholly concerned with the search for truth in nature, ought to reject those truths which God Himself, the supreme and merciful creator of nature, has deigned to make plain to men as a special gift. With these truths, mankind can gain true happiness and salvation.

So, by means of an obviously ridiculous and extremely specious kind of argumentation, these enemies never stop invoking the power and excellence of human reason; they raise it up against the most holy faith of Christ, and they blather with great foolhardiness that this faith is opposed to human reason.

6. Without doubt, nothing more insane than such a doctrine, nothing more impious or more opposed to reason itself could be devised. For although faith is above reason, no real disagreement or opposition can ever be found between them; this is because both of them come from the same greatest source of unchanging and eternal truth, God. They give such reciprocal help to each other that true reason shows, maintains and protects the truth of the faith, while faith frees reason from all errors and wondrously enlightens, strengthens and perfects reason with the knowledge of divine matters.

7. It is with no less deceit, venerable brothers, that other enemies of divine revelation, with reckless and sacrilegious effrontery, want to import the doctrine of human progress into the Catholic religion. They extol it with the highest praise, as if religion itself were not of God but the work of men, or a philosophical discovery which can be perfected by human means. The charge which Tertullian justly made against the philosophers of his own time "who brought forward a Stoic and a Platonic and a Dialectical Christianity"[2] can very aptly apply to those men who rave so pitiably. Our holy religion was not invented by human reason, but was most mercifully revealed by God; therefore, one can quite easily understand that religion itself acquires all its power from the authority of God who made the revelation, and that it can never be arrived at or perfected by human reason. In order not to be deceived and go astray in a matter of such great importance, human reason should indeed carefully investigate the fact of divine revelation. Having done this, one would be definitely convinced that God has spoken and therefore would show Him rational obedience, as the Apostle very wisely

teaches.[3] For who can possibly not know that all faith should be given to the words of God and that it is in the fullest agreement with reason itself to accept and strongly support doctrines which it has determined to have been revealed by God, who can neither deceive nor be deceived?

8. But how many wonderful and shining proofs are ready at hand to convince the human reason in the clearest way that the religion of Christ is divine and that "the whole principle of our doctrines has taken root from the Lord of the heavens above";[4] therefore nothing exists more definite, more settled or more holy than our faith, which rests on the strongest foundations. This faith, which teaches for life and points towards salvation, which casts out all vices and is the fruitful mother and nurse of the virtues, has been established by the birth, life, death, resurrection, wisdom, wonders and prophecies of Christ Jesus, its divine author and perfector! Shining forth in all directions with the light of teaching from on high and enriched with the treasures of heavenly wealth, this faith grew famed and notable by the foretellings of so many prophets, the lustre of so many miracles, the steadfastness of so many martyrs, and the glory of so many saints! It made known the saving laws of Christ and, gaining in strength daily even when it was most cruelly persecuted, it made its way over the whole world by land and sea, from the sun's rising to its setting, under the single standard of the Cross! The deceit of idols was cast down and the mist of errors was scattered. By the defeat of all kinds of enemies, this faith enlightened with divine knowledge all peoples, races and nations, no matter how barbarous and savage, or how different in character, morals, laws and ways of life. It brought them under the sweet yoke of Christ Himself by proclaiming peace and good tidings to all men!

9. Now, surely all these events shine with such divine wisdom and power that anyone who considers them will easily understand that the Christian faith is the work of God. Human reason knows clearly from these striking and certain proofs that God is the author of this faith;

therefore it is unable to advance further but should offer all obedience to this faith, casting aside completely every problem and hesitation. Human reason is convinced that it is God who has given everything the faith proposes to men for belief and behavior.

10. This consideration too clarifies the great error of those others as well who boldly venture to explain and interpret the words of God by their own judgment, misusing their reason and holding the opinion that these words are like a human work. God Himself has set up a living authority to establish and teach the true and legitimate meaning of His heavenly revelation. This authority judges infallibly all disputes which concern matters of faith and morals, lest the faithful be swirled around by every wind of doctrine which springs from the evilness of men in encompassing error. And this living infallible authority is active only in that Church which was built by Christ the Lord upon Peter, the head of the entire Church, leader and shepherd, whose faith He promised would never fail. This Church has had an unbroken line of succession from Peter himself; these legitimate pontiffs are the heirs and defenders of the same teaching, rank, office and power. And the Church is where Peter is,[5] and Peter speaks in the Roman Pontiff,[6] living at all times in his successors and making judgment,[7] providing the truth of the faith to those who seek it.[8] The divine words therefore mean what this Roman See of the most blessed Peter holds and has held.

11. For this mother and teacher[9] of all the churches has always preserved entire and unharmed the faith entrusted to it by Christ the Lord. Furthermore, it has taught it to the faithful, showing all men truth and the path of salvation. Since all priesthood originates in this church,[10] the entire substance of the Christian religion resides there also.[11] The leadership of the Apostolic See has always been active,[12] and therefore because of its preeminent authority, the whole Church must agree with it. The faithful who live in every place

constitute the whole Church.[13] Whoever does not gather with this Church scatters.[14]

12. We, therefore, placed inscrutably by God upon this Chair of truth, eagerly call forth in the Lord your outstanding piety, venerable brothers. We urge you to strive carefully and zealously to continually warn and exhort the faithful entrusted to your care to hold to these first principles. Urge them never to allow themselves to be deceived and led into error by men who have become abominable in their pursuits. These men attempt to destroy faith on the pretext of human progress, subjecting it in an impious manner to reason and changing the meaning of the words of God. Such men do not shrink from the greatest insults to God Himself, who cares for the good and the salvation of men by means of His heavenly religion.

13. You already know well, venerable brothers, the other portentous errors and deceits by which the sons of this world try most bitterly to attack the Catholic religion and the divine authority of the Church and its laws. They would even trample underfoot the rights both of the sacred and of the civil power. For this is the goal of the lawless activities against this Roman See in which Christ placed the impregnable foundation of His Church. This is the goal of those secret sects who have come forth from the darkness to destroy and desolate both the sacred and the civil commonwealth. These have been condemned with repeated anathema in the Apostolic letters of the Roman Pontiffs who preceded Us.[15] We now confirm these with the fullness of Our Apostolic power and command that they be most carefully observed.

14. This is the goal too of the crafty Bible Societies which renew the old skill of the heretics and ceaselessly force on people of all kinds, even the uneducated, gifts of the Bible. They issue these in large numbers and at great cost, in vernacular translations, which infringe the holy rules of the Church. The commentaries which are included often contain perverse explanations; so, having rejected divine tradition, the doctrine

of the Fathers and the authority of the Catholic Church, they all interpret the words of the Lord by their own private judgment, thereby
perverting their meaning. As a result, they fall into the greatest errors.
Gregory XVI of happy memory, Our superior predecessor, followed
the lead of his own predecessors in rejecting these societies in his
apostolic letters.[16] It is Our will to condemn them likewise.

15. Also perverse is the shocking theory that it makes no difference
to which religion one belongs, a theory which is greatly at variance
even with reason. By means of this theory, those crafty men remove
all distinction between virtue and vice, truth and error, honorable and
vile action. They pretend that men can gain eternal salvation by the
practice of any religion, as if there could ever be any sharing between
justice and iniquity, any collaboration between light and darkness, or
any agreement between Christ and Belial.

16. The sacred celibacy of clerics has also been the victim of conspiracy. Indeed, some churchmen have wretchedly forgotten their
own rank and let themselves be converted by the charms and snares
of pleasure. This is the aim too of the prevalent but wrong method of
teaching, especially in the philosophical disciplines, a method which
deceives and corrupts incautious youth in a wretched manner and
gives it as drink the poison of the serpent in the goblet of Babylon. To
this goal also tends the unspeakable doctrine of Communism, as it
is called, a doctrine most opposed to the very natural law. For if this
doctrine were accepted, the complete destruction of everyone's laws,
government, property, and even of human society itself would follow.

17. To this end also tend the most dark designs of men in the
clothing of sheep, while inwardly ravening wolves. They humbly recommend themselves by means of a feigned and deceitful appearance of
a purer piety, a stricter virtue and discipline; after taking their captives
gently, they mildly bind them, and then kill them in secret. They make
men fly in terror from all practice of religion, and they cut down and

dismember the sheep of the Lord. To this end, finally—to omit other dangers which are too well known to you—tends the widespread disgusting infection from books and pamphlets which teach the lessons of sinning. These works, well-written and filled with deceit and cunning, are scattered at immense cost through every region for the destruction of the Christian people. They spread pestilential doctrines everywhere and deprave the minds especially of the imprudent, occasioning great losses for religion.

18. As a result of this filthy medley of errors which creeps in from every side, and as the result of the unbridled license to think, speak and write, We see the following: morals deteriorated, Christ's most holy religion despised, the majesty of divine worship rejected, the power of this Apostolic See plundered, the authority of the Church attacked and reduced to base slavery, the rights of bishops trampled on, the sanctity of marriage infringed, the rule of every government violently shaken and many other losses for both the Christian and the civil commonwealth. Venerable brothers, We are compelled to weep and share in your lament that this is the case.

19. Therefore, in this great crisis for religion, because We are greatly concerned for the salvation of all the Lord's flock and in fulfillment of the duty of Our Apostolic ministry, We shall certainly leave no measure untried in Our vigorous effort to secure the good of the whole Christian family. Indeed, We especially call forth in the Lord your own illustrious piety, virtue and prudence, venerable brothers. With these and relying on heavenly aid, you may fearlessly defend the cause of God and His holy Church as befits your station and the office for which you are marked. You must fight energetically, since you know very well what great wounds the undefiled Spouse of Christ Jesus has suffered, and how vigorous is the destructive attack of Her enemies. You must also care for and defend the Catholic faith with episcopal strength and see that the flock entrusted to you stands to the end firm and unmoved in

the faith. For unless one preserves the faith entire and uninjured, he will without doubt perish forever.[17]

20. So, in accordance with your pastoral care, work assiduously to protect and preserve this faith. Never cease to instruct all men in it, to encourage the wavering, to convince dissenters, to strengthen the weak in faith by never tolerating and letting pass anything which could in the slightest degree defile the purity of this faith. With the same great strength of mind, foster in all men their unity with the Catholic Church, outside of which there is no salvation; also foster their obedience towards this See of Peter on which rests the entire structure of our most holy religion. See to it with similar firmness that the most holy laws of the Church are observed, for it is by these laws that virtue, religion and piety particularly thrive and flourish.

21. "It is an act of great piety to expose the concealments of the impious and to defeat there the devil himself, whose slaves they are. [18] Therefore We entreat you to use every means of revealing to your faithful people the many kinds of plot, pretense, error, deceit and contrivance which our enemies use. This will turn them carefully away from infectious books. Also exhort them unceasingly to flee from the sects and societies of the impious as from the presence of a serpent, earnestly avoiding everything which is at variance with the wholeness of faith, religion and morality. Therefore, never stop preaching the Gospel, so that the Christian people may grow in the knowledge of God by being daily better versed in the most holy precepts of the Christian law; as a result, they may turn from evil, do good, and walk in the ways of the Lord. You know that you are acting as deputies for Christ, who is meek and humble, and who came not to call the just but sinners. This is the example that we should follow. When you find someone disregarding the commandments and wandering from the path of truth and justice, rebuke them in the spirit of mildness and meekness with paternal warnings; accuse, entreat and reprove them with all kindness,

patience and doctrine. "Often benevolence towards those who are to be corrected achieves more than severity, exhortation more than threats, and love more than power."[19]

22. Strive to instruct the faithful to follow after love and search for peace, diligently pursuing the works of love and peace so that they may love one another with reciprocal charity. They should abolish all disagreements, enmities, rivalries and animosities, thus achieving compatibility. Take pains to impress on the Christian people a due obedience and subjection to rulers and governments. Do this by teaching, in accordance with the warning of the Apostle,[20] that all authority comes from God. Whoever resists authority resists the ordering made by God Himself, consequently achieving his own condemnation; disobeying authority is always sinful except when an order is given which is opposed to the laws of God and the Church.

23. However, priests are the best examples of piety and God's worship,"[21] and people tend generally to be of the same quality as their priests. Therefore devote the greatest care and zeal to making the clergy resplendent for the earnestness of their morals, the integrity, holiness and wisdom of their lives. Let the ecclesiastical training be zealously preserved in compliance with the sacred canons, and whenever it has been neglected, let it be restored to its former splendor. Therefore, as you are well aware, you must take the utmost care, as the Apostle commands, not to impose hands on anyone in haste. Consecrate with holy orders and promote to the performance of the sacred mysteries only those who have been carefully examined and who are virtuous and wise. They can consequently benefit and ornament your dioceses.

24. These are men who avoid everything which is forbidden to clerics, devoting their time instead to reading, exhorting and teaching, "an example to the faithful in word, manner of life, in charity, in faith, in chastity."[22] They win the highest respect from all men, and fashion, summon forth and inspire the people with the Christian way of life.

"For it would certainly be better," as Benedict XIV, Our Predecessor of undying memory very wisely advises, "to have fewer ministers if they be upright, suitable and useful, than many who are likely to accomplish nothing at all for the building up of the body of Christ, which is the Church."[23] You must examine with greater diligence the morals and the knowledge of men who are entrusted with the care and guidance of souls, that they may be eager to continuously feed and assist the people entrusted to them by the administration of the sacraments, the preaching of God's word and the example of good works. They should be zealous in molding them to the whole plan and pattern of a religious way of life, and in leading them on to the path of salvation.

25. When ministers are ignorant or neglectful of their duty, then the morals of the people also immediately decline, Christian discipline grows slack, the practice of religion is dislodged and cast aside, and every vice and corruption is easily introduced into the Church. The word of God, which was uttered for the salvation of souls, is living, efficacious and more piercing than a two-edged sword.[24] So that it may not prove to be unfruitful through the fault of its ministers, never cease, venerable brothers, from encouraging the preachers of this divine word to carry out most religiously the ministry of the Gospel. This should not be carried out by the persuasive words of human wisdom, nor by the profane seductive guise of empty and ambitious eloquence, but rather as a demonstration of the spirit and power.

26. Consequently, by presenting the word of truth properly and by preaching not themselves but Christ crucified, they should clearly proclaim in their preaching the tenets and precepts of our most holy religion in accordance with the teaching of the Catholic Church and the Fathers. They should explain precisely the particular duties of individuals, frighten them from vice, and inspire them with a love of piety. In this way the faithful will avoid all vices and pursue virtues, and so, will be able to escape eternal punishment and gain heavenly glory.

27. In your pastoral care, continuously urge all ecclesiastics to think seriously of their holy ministry. Urge them to carefully fulfill their duties, to greatly love the beauty of God's house, to urgently pray and entreat with deep piety, and to say the canonical hours of the breviary as the Church commands. By these means they will be able both to pray efficaciously for God's help in fulfilling the heavy demands of their duty, and to graciously reconcile God and the Christian people.

28. You know that suitable ministers can only come from clergy who are very well trained, and that the proper training greatly influences the whole future life of clerics. Therefore, continually strive to ensure that young clerics are properly molded even from their earliest years. They should be molded not only in piety and real virtue, but also in literature and the stricter disciplines, especially the sacred ones. So your greatest desire should be, in obedience to the prescript of the fathers at Trent,[25] to set up skillfully and energetically, seminaries if they do not yet exist. If necessary expand those already established, supplying them with the best directors and teachers. Watch continuously and zealously that the young clerics in them are educated in a holy and religious manner, in the fear of the Lord and in ecclesiastical discipline. See that they are carefully and thoroughly improved, especially by the sacred sciences, according to Catholic doctrine, far from all danger of any error. They should also be improved by the traditions of the Church and the writings of the holy Fathers, as well as by sacred ceremonies and rites. Thus you will have energetic, industrious workers endowed with an ecclesiastical spirit, properly prepared by their studies, who in time will be able to tend the Lord's field carefully and fight strenuously in the Lord's battles.

29. Furthermore, you realize that spiritual exercises contribute greatly to the preservation of the dignity and holiness of ecclesiastical orders. Therefore do not neglect to promote this work of salvation and to advise and exhort all clergy to often retreat to a

suitable place for making these exercises. Laying aside external cares and being free to meditate zealously on eternal divine matters, they will be able to wipe away stains caused by the dust of the world and renew their ecclesiastical spirit. And stripping off the old man and his deeds, they will put on the new man who was created in justice and holiness.

30. Do not regret that We have spoken at length on the education and training of the clergy. For you are very well aware many men are weary of the difference, instability and changing nature of their errors, and therefore want to profess our most holy religion. These men, with God's good help, will more easily embrace and practice the teaching, precepts and way of life of this religion if they see that the clergy surpass all others in their piety, integrity and wisdom, and in the noble example they give of all the virtues.

31. We recognize your many worthy attributes: your burning charity towards God and men, your exalted love of the Church, your almost angelic virtues, your episcopal bravery, and your prudence. Being inspired to do His holy will, you are all followers in the footsteps of the Apostles. As bishops, you are the deputies, and thus the imitators of Christ. In your harmonious pursuits you have become a sincere model for your flock, and you enlighten your clergy and faithful people with the splendor of your sanctity. In your compassionate mercy you seek out and overtake with your love the straying and perishing sheep, as the shepherd in the Gospel did. You place them paternally on your shoulders and lead them back to the fold. At no time do you spare either cares or plans or toils in religiously fulfilling your pastoral duties and defending all Our beloved sheep who, redeemed by Christ, have been entrusted to your care from the rage, assault and snares of ravening wolves. You keep them away from poisonous pasture land and drive them on to safe ground, and in all possible ways you lead them by deed, word and example to the harbor of eternal salvation.

32. Therefore, to assure the greater glory of God and the Church, venerable brothers, join together with all eagerness, care and wakefulness to repulse error and to root out vice. When this is accomplished, faith, religion, piety and virtue will increase daily. Then all the faithful, as sons of light, casting aside the works of darkness, may walk worthily, pleasing God in all things and being fruitful in every good work. And in the very great straits, difficulties and dangers which must beset your serious ministry as bishops, especially in these times, do not ever be terrified; rather, be comforted by the strength of the Lord "who looks down on us who carry out his work, approves those who are willing, aids those who do battle, and crowns those who conquer."[26]

33. Nothing is more pleasing to Us than to assist you, whom We love, with affection, advice, and exertion. We devote Ourselves wholeheartedly together with you to protect and spread the glory of God and the Catholic faith; We also endeavor to save souls for whom We are ready to sacrifice life itself, should it be necessary. Come to Us as often as you feel the need of the aid, help and protection of Our authority and that of this See.

34. We hope that Our political leaders will keep in mind, in accordance with their piety and religion, that "the kingly power has been conferred on them not only for ruling the world but especially for the protection of the Church."[27] Sometimes We "act both for the sake of their rule and safety that they may possess their provinces by peaceful right."[28] We hope that with their aid and authority they will support the objects, plans and pursuits which we have in common, and that they will also defend the liberty and safety of the Church, so that "the right hand of Christ may also defend their rule."[29]

35. We hope that all these matters may turn out well and happily. Let us together entreat God in urgent and unceasing prayers, to make up for Our weakness by an abundance of every heavenly grace, to overwhelm with His all-powerful strength those who attack us, and

to increase everywhere faith, piety, devotion and peace. Then when all enemies and errors have been overcome, His holy Church may enjoy the tranquillity it so greatly desires. Then too there may be one fold and one shepherd.

36. That the Lord may more readily respond to Us, let us call as intercessor Her who is always with Him, the most holy Virgin Mary, Immaculate Mother of God. She is the most sweet mother of us all; she is our mediatrix, advocate, firmest hope, and greatest source of confidence. Furthermore, her patronage with God is strongest and most efficacious. Let us invoke too the prince of the Apostles to whom Christ Himself gave the keys of the kingdom of heaven, and whom He made the rock of His Church, against which the gates of hell will never prevail; let us also invoke his fellow-apostle Paul, and all the heavenly saints who are already crowned and hold the palm of victory. We ask that they implore for all Christians the abundance of divine favor which they desire.

37. Finally, as an augury of all the heavenly gifts and as witness of Our great charity towards you, receive the Apostolic Blessing which from deep in Our heart We most lovingly impart to yourselves, venerable brothers, and to all clerics and the faithful laity who are entrusted to your care.

Given in Rome at St. Mary Major's on the 9th of November 1846 in the first year of Our Pontificate.

POPE BI. PIUS IX

Quod Apostolici Muneris
Encyclical of Pope Leo XIII
On Socialism

To the Patriarchs, Primates, Archbishops, and
Bishops of the Catholic World in Grace and
Communion with the Apostolic See.

At the very beginning of Our pontificate, as the nature of Our apostolic office demanded, we hastened to point out in an encyclical letter addressed to you, venerable brethren, the deadly plague that is creeping into the very fibres of human society and leading it on to the verge of destruction; at the same time We pointed out also the most effectual remedies by which society might be restored and might escape from the very serious dangers which threaten it. But the evils which We then deplored have so rapidly increased that We are again compelled to address you, as though we heard the voice of the prophet ringing in Our ears: "Cry, cease not, lift up thy voice like a trumpet."[1] You understand, venerable brethren, that We speak of that sect of men who, under various and almost barbarous names, are called socialists, communists, or nihilists, and who, spread over all the world, and bound together by the closest ties in a wicked confederacy, no longer seek the shelter of secret meetings, but, openly and boldly marching forth in the light of day, strive to bring to a head what they have long been planning—the overthrow of all civil society whatsoever.

Surely these are they who, as the sacred Scriptures testify, "Defile the flesh, despise dominion and blaspheme majesty."[2] They leave nothing untouched or whole which by both human and divine laws has been wisely decreed for the health and beauty of life. They refuse obedience to the higher powers, to whom, according to the admonition of the Apostle, every soul ought to be subject, and who derive the right of governing from God; and they proclaim the absolute equality of all men in rights and duties. They debase the natural union of man and woman, which is held sacred even among barbarous peoples; and its bond, by which the family is chiefly held together, they weaken, or even deliver up to lust. Lured, in fine, by the greed of present goods, which is "the root of all evils, which some coveting have erred from the faith,"[3] they assail the right of property sanctioned by natural law; and by a scheme of horrible wickedness, while they seem desirous of caring for the needs and satisfying the desires of all men, they strive to seize and hold in common whatever has been acquired either by title of lawful inheritance, or by labor of brain and hands, or by thrift in one's mode of life. These are the startling theories they utter in their meetings, set forth in their pamphlets, and scatter abroad in a cloud of journals and tracts. Wherefore, the revered majesty and power of kings has won such fierce hatred from their seditious people that disloyal traitors, impatient of all restraint, have more than once within a short period raised their arms in impious attempt against the lives of their own sovereigns.

2. But the boldness of these bad men, which day by day more and more threatens civil society with destruction, and strikes the souls of

all with anxiety and fear, finds its cause and origin in those poisonous doctrines which, spread abroad in former times among the people, like evil seed bore in due time such fatal fruit. For you know, venerable brethren, that that most deadly war which from the sixteenth century down has been waged by innovators against the Catholic faith, and which has grown in intensity up to today, had for its object to subvert all revelation, and overthrow the supernatural order, that thus the way might be opened for the discoveries, or rather the hallucinations, of reason alone. This kind of error, which falsely usurps to itself the name of reason, as it lures and whets the natural appetite that is in man of excelling, and gives loose rein to unlawful desires of every kind, has easily penetrated not only the minds of a great multitude of men but to a wide extent civil society, also. Hence, by a new species of impiety, unheard of even among the heathen nations, states have been constituted without any count at all of God or of the order established by him; it has been given out that public authority neither derives its principles, nor its majesty, nor its power of governing from God, but rather from the multitude, which, thinking itself absolved from all divine sanction, bows only to such laws as it shall have made at its own will. The supernatural truths of faith having been assailed and cast out as though hostile to reason, the very Author and Redeemer of the human race has been slowly and little by little banished from the universities, the lyceums and gymnasia—in a word, from every public institution. In fine, the rewards and punishments of a future and eternal life having been handed over to oblivion, the ardent desire of happiness has been limited to the bounds of the present. Such doctrines as these having been scattered far and wide, so great a license of thought and action having sprung up on all sides, it is no matter for surprise that men of the lowest class, weary of their wretched home or workshop, are eager to attack the homes and fortunes of the rich; it is no matter for surprise that already there exists no sense of security either in public or private life, and that the human race should have advanced to the very verge of final dissolution.

3. But the supreme pastors of the Church, on whom the duty falls of guarding the Lord's flock from the snares of the enemy, have striven in time to ward off the danger and provide for the safety of the faithful. For, as soon as the secret societies began to be formed, in whose bosom the seeds of the errors which we have already mentioned were even then being nourished, the Roman Pontiffs Clement XII and Benedict XIV did not fail to unmask the evil counsels of the sects, and to warn the faithful of the whole globe against the ruin which would be wrought. Later on again, when a licentious sort of liberty was attributed to man by a set of men who gloried in the name of philosophers,[4] and a new right, as they call it, against the natural and divine law began to be framed and sanctioned, Pope Pius VI, of happy memory, at once exposed in public documents the guile and falsehood of their doctrines, and at the same time foretold with apostolic foresight the ruin into which the people so miserably deceived would be dragged. But, as no adequate precaution was taken to prevent their evil teachings from leading the people more and more astray, and lest they should be allowed to escape in the public statutes of States, Popes Pius VII and Leo XII condemned by anathema the secret sects,[5] and again warned society of the danger which threatened them. Finally, all have witnessed with what solemn words and great firmness and constancy of soul our glorious predecessor, Pius IX, of happy memory, both in his allocutions and in his encyclical letters addressed to the bishops of all the world, fought now against the wicked attempts of the sects, now openly by name against the pest of socialism, which was already making headway.

4. But it is to be lamented that those to whom has been committed the guardianship of the public weal, deceived by the wiles of wicked men and terrified by their threats, have looked upon the Church with a suspicious and even hostile eye, not perceiving that the attempts of the

sects would be vain if the doctrine of the Catholic Church and the authority of the Roman Pontiffs had always survived, with the honor that belongs to them, among princes and peoples. For, "the church of the living God, which is the pillar and ground of truth,"[6] hands down those doctrines and precepts whose special object is the safety and peace of society and the uprooting of the evil growth of socialism.

5. For, indeed, although the socialists, stealing the very Gospel itself with a view to deceive more easily the unwary, have been accustomed to distort it so as to suit their own purposes, nevertheless so great is the difference between their depraved teachings and the most pure doctrine of Christ that none greater could exist: "for what participation hath justice with injustice or what fellowship hath light with darkness?"[7] Their habit, as we have intimated, is always to maintain that nature has made all men equal, and that, therefore, neither honor nor respect is due to majesty, nor obedience to laws, unless, perhaps, to those sanctioned by their own good pleasure. But, on the contrary, in accordance with the teachings of the Gospel, the equality of men consists in this: that all, having inherited the same nature, are called to the same most high dignity of the sons of God, and that, as one and the same end is set before all, each one is to be judged by the same law and will receive punishment or reward according to his deserts. The inequality of rights and of power proceeds from the very Author of nature, "from whom all paternity in heaven and earth is named."[8] But the minds of princes and their subjects are, according to Catholic doctrine and precepts, bound up one with the other in such a manner, by mutual duties and rights, that the thirst for power is restrained and the rational ground of obedience made easy, firm, and noble.

6. Assuredly, the Church wisely inculcates the apostolic precept on the mass of men: "There is no power but from God; and those that are, are ordained of God. Therefore he that resisteth the power resisteth the ordinance of God. And they that resist purchase to themselves

damnation." And again she admonishes those "subject by necessity" to be so "not only for wrath but also for conscience' sake," and to render "to all men their dues; tribute to whom tribute is due, custom to whom custom, fear to whom fear, honor to whom honor."[9] For, He who created and governs all things has, in His wise providence, appointed that the things which are lowest should attain their ends by those which are intermediate, and these again by the highest. Thus, as even in the kingdom of heaven He hath willed that the choirs of angels be distinct and some subject to others, and also in the Church has instituted various orders and a diversity of offices, so that all are not apostles or doctors or pastors,[10] so also has He appointed that there should be various orders in civil society, differing in dignity, rights, and power, whereby the State, like the Church, should be one body, consisting of many members, some nobler than others, but all necessary to each other and solicitous for the common good.

7. But that rulers may use the power conceded to them to save and not to destroy, the Church of Christ seasonably warns even princes that the sentence of the Supreme Judge overhangs them, and, adopting the words of divine wisdom, calls upon all in the name of God: "Give ear, you that rule the people, and that please yourselves in multitudes of nations; for power is given you by the Lord, and strength by the Most High, who will examine your works, and search out your thoughts. . . . For a most severe judgment shall be for them that bear rule. . . . For God will not except any man's person, neither will he stand in awe of any man's greatness, for he hath made the little and the great; and he hath equally care of all. But a greater punishment is ready for the more mighty."[11] And if at any time it happen that the power of the State is rashly and tyrannically wielded by princes, the teaching of the Catholic church does not allow an insurrection on private authority against them, lest public order be only the more disturbed, and lest society take greater hurt therefrom. And when affairs come to such a

pass that there is no other hope of safety, she teaches that relief may
be hastened by the merits of Christian patience and by earnest prayers
to God. But, if the will of legislators and princes shall have sanctioned
or commanded anything repugnant to the divine or natural law, the
dignity and duty of the Christian name, as well as the judgment of the
Apostle, urge that "God is to be obeyed rather than man."[12]

8. Even family life itself, which is the cornerstone of all society and
government, necessarily feels and experiences the salutary power of
the Church, which redounds to the right ordering and preservation of
every State and kingdom. For you know, venerable brethren, that the
foundation of this society rests first of all in the indissoluble union of
man and wife according to the necessity of natural law, and is com-
pleted in the mutual rights and duties of parents and children, masters
and servants. You know also that the doctrines of socialism strive
almost completely to dissolve this union; since, that stability which
is imparted to it by religious wedlock being lost, it follows that the
power of the father over his own children, and the duties of the children
toward their parents, must be greatly weakened. But the Church, on
the contrary, teaches that "marriage, honorable in all,"[13] which God
himself instituted in the very beginning of the world, and made indissoluble for the propagation and preservation of the human species, has
become still more binding and more holy through Christ, who raised
it to the dignity of a sacrament, and chose to use it as the figure of His
own union with the Church.

Wherefore, as the Apostle has it,[14] as Christ is the head of the
Church, so is the man the head of the woman; and as the Church is
subject to Christ, who embraces her with a most chaste and undying
love, so also should wives be subject to their husbands, and be loved
by them in turn with a faithful and constant affection. In like manner
does the Church temper the use of parental and domestic authority,
that it may tend to hold children and servants to their duty, without

going beyond bounds. For, according to Catholic teaching, the authority of our heavenly Father and Lord is imparted to parents and masters, whose authority, therefore, not only takes its origin and force from Him, but also borrows its nature and character. Hence, the Apostle exhorts children to "obey their parents in the Lord, and honor their father and mother, which is the first commandment with promise";[15] and he admonishes parents: "And you, fathers, provoke not your children to anger, but bring them up in the discipline and correction of the Lord."[16] Again, the apostle enjoins the divine precept on servants and masters, exhorting the former to be "obedient to their lords according to the flesh of Christ . . . with a good will serving, as to the Lord"; and the latter, to "forbear threatenings, knowing that the Lord of all is in heaven, and there is no respect of persons with God."[17] If only all these matters were faithfully observed according to the divine will by all on whom they are enjoined, most assuredly every family would be a figure of the heavenly home, and the wonderful blessings there begotten would not confine themselves to the households alone, but would scatter their riches abroad through the nations."

9. But Catholic wisdom, sustained by the precepts of natural and divine law, provides with especial care for public and private tranquility in its doctrines and teachings regarding the duty of government and the distribution of the goods which are necessary for life and use. For, while the socialists would destroy the "right" of property, alleging it to be a human invention altogether opposed to the inborn equality of man, and, claiming a community of goods, argue that poverty should not be peaceably endured, and that the property and privileges of the rich may be rightly invaded, the Church, with much greater wisdom and good sense, recognizes the inequality among men, who are born with different powers of body and mind, inequality in actual possession, also, and holds that the right of property and of ownership, which springs from nature itself, must not be touched and stands inviolate.

For she knows that stealing and robbery were forbidden in so special a manner by God, the Author and Defender of right, that He would not allow man even to desire what belonged to another, and that thieves and despoilers, no less than adulterers and idolaters, are shut out from the Kingdom of Heaven. But not the less on this account does our holy Mother not neglect the care of the poor or omit to provide for their necessities; but, rather, drawing them to her with a mother's embrace, and knowing that they bear the person of Christ Himself, who regards the smallest gift to the poor as a benefit conferred on Himself, holds them in great honor. She does all she can to help them; she provides homes and hospitals where they may be received, nourished, and cared for all the world over and watches over these. She is constantly pressing on the rich that most grave precept to give what remains to the poor; and she holds over their heads the divine sentence that unless they succor the needy they will be repaid by eternal torments. In fine, she does all she can to relieve and comfort the poor, either by holding up to them the example of Christ, "who being rich became poor for our sake,[18] or by reminding them of his own words, wherein he pronounced the poor blessed and bade them hope for the reward of eternal bliss. But who does not see that this is the best method of arranging the old struggle between the rich and poor? For, as the very evidence of facts and events shows, if this method is rejected or disregarded, one of two things must occur: either the greater portion of the human race will fall back into the vile condition of slavery which so long prevailed among the pagan nations, or human society must continue to be disturbed by constant eruptions, to be disgraced by rapine and strife, as we have had sad witness even in recent times.

10. These things being so, then, venerable brethren, as at the beginning of Our pontificate We, on whom the guidance of the whole Church now lies, pointed out a place of refuge to the peoples and the princes tossed about by the fury of the tempest, so now, moved by the extreme

peril that is on them, We again lift up Our voice, and beseech them again and again for their own safety's sake as well as that of their people to welcome and give ear to the Church which has had such wonderful influence on the public prosperity of kingdoms, and to recognize that political and religious affairs are so closely united that what is taken from the spiritual weakens the loyalty of subjects and the majesty of the government. And since they know that the Church of Christ has such power to ward off the plague of socialism as cannot be found in human laws, in the mandates of magistrates, or in the force of armies, let them restore that Church to the condition and liberty in which she may exert her healing force for the benefit of all society.

11. But you, venerable brethren, who know the origin and the drift of these gathering evils, strive with all your force of soul to implant the Catholic teaching deep in the minds of all. Strive that all may have the habit of clinging to God with filial love and revering His divinity from their tenderest years; that they may respect the majesty of princes and of laws; that they may restrain their passions and stand fast by the order which God has established in civil and domestic society. Moreover, labor hard that the children of the Catholic Church neither join nor favor in any way whatsoever this abominable sect; let them show, on the contrary, by noble deeds and right dealing in all things, how well and happily human society would hold together were each member to shine as an example of right doing and of virtue. In fine, as the recruits of socialism are especially sought among artisans and workmen, who, tired, perhaps, of labor, are more easily allured by the hope of riches and the promise of wealth, it is well to encourage societies of artisans and workmen which, constituted under the guardianship of religion, may tend to make all associates contented with their lot and move them to a quiet and peaceful life.

12. Venerable brethren, may He who is the beginning and end of every good work inspire your and Our endeavors. And, indeed, the very

thought of these days, in which the anniversary of our Lord's birth is solemnly observed, moves us to hope for speedy help. For the new life which Christ at His birth brought to a world already aging and steeped in the very depths of wickedness He bids us also to hope for, and the peace which He then announced by the angels to men He has promised to us also. For the Lord's "hand is not shortened that he cannot save, neither is his ear heavy that he cannot hear."[19] In these most auspicious days, then, venerable brethren, wishing all joy and happiness to you and to the faithful of your churches, We earnestly pray the Giver of all good that again "there may appear unto men the goodness and kindness of God our Saviour,"[20] who brought us out of the power of our most deadly enemy into the most noble dignity of the sons of God. And that We may the sooner and more fully gain our wish, do you, venerable brethren, join with Us in lifting up your fervent prayers to God and beg the intercession of the Blessed and Immaculate Virgin Mary, and of Joseph her spouse, and of the blessed Apostles Peter and Paul, in whose prayers We have the greatest confidence. And in the meanwhile We impart to you, with the inmost affection of the heart, and to your clergy and faithful people, the apostolic benediction as an augury of the divine gifts.

Given at St. Peter's, in Rome, on the twenty-eighth day of December, 1878, in the first year of Our pontificate.

LEO XIII

Quadragesimo Anno
Encyclical of Pope Pius XI
On Reconstruction of the Social Order

To Our Venerable Brethren, the Patriarchs, Primates,
Archbishops, Bishops, and Other Ordinaries
In Peace and Communion with the Apostolic See,
And Likewise to All the Faithful of the Catholic World.
Venerable Brethren and Beloved Children, Health and
Apostolic Benediction.

Forty years have passed since Leo XIII's peerless Encyclical, *On the Condition of Workers*, first saw the light, and the whole Catholic world, filled with grateful recollection, is undertaking to commemorate it with befitting solemnity.

2. Other Encyclicals of Our Predecessor had in a way prepared the path for that outstanding document and proof of pastoral care: namely, those on the family and the Holy Sacrament of Matrimony as the source of human society,[1] on the origin of civil authority[2] and

its proper relations with the Church,[3] on the chief duties of Christian citizens,[4] against the tenets of Socialism,[5] against false teachings on human liberty,[6] and others of the same nature fully expressing the mind of Leo XIII. Yet the Encyclical, *On the Condition of Workers*, compared with the rest had this special distinction that at a time when it was most opportune and actually necessary to do so, it laid down for all mankind the surest rules to solve aright that difficult problem of human relations called "the social question."

3. For toward the close of the nineteenth century, the new kind of economic life that had arisen and the new developments of industry had gone to the point in most countries that human society was clearly becoming divided more and more into two classes. One class, very small in number, was enjoying almost all the advantages which modern inventions so abundantly provided; the other, embracing the huge multitude of working people, oppressed by wretched poverty, was vainly seeking escape from the straits wherein it stood.

4. Quite agreeable, of course, was this state of things to those who thought it in their abundant riches the result of inevitable economic laws and accordingly, as if it were for charity to veil the violation of justice which lawmakers not only tolerated but at times sanctioned, wanted the whole care of supporting the poor committed to charity alone. The workers, on the other hand, crushed by their hard lot, were barely enduring it and were refusing longer to bend their necks beneath so galling a yoke; and some of them, carried away by the heat of evil counsel, were seeking the overturn of everything, while others, whom Christian training restrained from such evil designs, stood firm in the judgment that much in this had to be wholly and speedily changed.

5. The same feeling those many Catholics, both priests and laymen, shared, whom a truly wonderful charity had long spurred on to relieve the unmerited poverty of the non-owning workers, and who could in no way convince themselves that so enormous and unjust an inequality

in the distribution of this world's goods truly conforms to the designs of the all-wise Creator.

6. Those men were without question sincerely seeking an immediate remedy for this lamentable disorganization of States and a secure safeguard against worse dangers. Yet such is the weakness of even the best of human minds that, now rejected as dangerous innovators, now hindered in the good work by their very associates advocating other courses of action, and, uncertain in the face of various opinions, they were at a loss which way to turn.

7. In such a sharp conflict of mind, therefore, while the question at issue was being argued this way and that, nor always with calmness, all eyes as often before turned to the Chair of Peter, to that sacred depository of all truth whence words of salvation pour forth to all the world. And to the feet of Christ's Vicar on earth were flocking in unaccustomed numbers, men well versed in social questions, employers, and workers themselves, begging him with one voice to point out, finally, the safe road to them.

8. The wise Pontiff long weighed all this in his mind before God; he summoned the most experienced and learned to counsel; he pondered the issues carefully and from every angle. At last, admonished "by the consciousness of His Apostolic Office"[7] lest silence on his part might be regarded as failure in his duty[8] he decided, in virtue of the Divine Teaching Office entrusted to him, to address not only the whole Church of Christ but all mankind.

9. Therefore on the fifteenth day of May, 1891, that long awaited voice thundered forth; neither daunted by the arduousness of the problem nor weakened by age but with vigorous energy, it taught the whole human family to strike out in the social question upon new paths.

10. You know, Venerable Brethren and Beloved Children, and understand full well the wonderful teaching which has made the Encyclical, *On the Condition of Workers*, illustrious forever. The

Supreme Pastor in this Letter, grieving that so large a portion of mankind should "live undeservedly in miserable and wretched conditions,"[9] took it upon himself with great courage to defend "the cause of the workers whom the present age had handed over, each alone and defenseless, to the inhumanity of employers and the unbridled greed of competitors."[10] He sought no help from either Liberalism or Socialism, for the one had proved that it was utterly unable to solve the social problem aright, and the other, proposing a remedy far worse than the evil itself, would have plunged human society into great dangers.

11. Since a problem was being treated "for which no satisfactory solution" is found "unless religion and the Church have been called upon to aid,"[11] the Pope, clearly exercising his right and correctly holding that the guardianship of religion and the stewardship over those things that are closely bound up with it had been entrusted especially to him and relying solely upon the unchangeable principles drawn from the treasury of right reason and Divine Revelation, confidently and *as one having authority*,[12] declared and proclaimed "the rights and duties within which the rich and the proletariat—those who furnish material things and those who furnish work—ought to be restricted in relation to each other,"[13] and what the Church, heads of States and the people themselves directly concerned ought to do.

12. The Apostolic voice did not thunder forth in vain. On the contrary, not only did the obedient children of the Church hearken to it with marveling admiration and hail it with the greatest applause, but many also who were wandering far from the truth, from the unity of the faith, and nearly all who since then either in private study or in enacting legislation have concerned themselves with the social and economic question.

13. Feeling themselves vindicated and defended by the Supreme Authority on earth, Christian workers received this Encyclical with special joy. So, too, did all those noble-hearted men who, long solicitous

for the improvement of the condition of the workers, had up to that time encountered almost nothing but indifference from many, and even rankling suspicion, if not open hostility, from some. Rightly, therefore, have all these groups constantly held the Apostolic Encyclical from that time in such high honor that to signify their gratitude they are wont, in various places and in various ways, to commemorate it every year.

14. However, in spite of such great agreement, there were some who were not a little disturbed; and so it happened that the teaching of Leo XIII, so noble and lofty and so utterly new to worldly ears, was held suspect by some, even among Catholics, and to certain ones it even gave offense. For it boldly attacked and overturned the idols of Liberalism, ignored long-standing prejudices, and was in advance of its time beyond all expectation, so that the slow of heart disdained to study this new social philosophy and the timid feared to scale so lofty a height. There were some also who stood, indeed, in awe at its splendor, but regarded it as a kind of imaginary ideal of perfection more desirable then attainable.

15. Venerable Brethren and Beloved Children, as all everywhere and especially Catholic workers who are pouring from all sides into this Holy City, are celebrating with such enthusiasm the solemn commemoration of the fortieth anniversary of the Encyclical *On the Condition of Workers*, We deem it fitting on this occasion to recall the great benefits this Encyclical has brought to the Catholic Church and to all human society; to defend the illustrious Master's doctrine on the social and economic question against certain doubts and to develop it more fully as to some points; and lastly, summoning to court the contemporary economic regime and passing judgment on Socialism, to lay bare the root of the existing social confusion and at the same time point the only way to sound restoration: namely, the Christian reform of morals. All these matters which we undertake to treat will fall under three main headings, and this entire Encyclical will be devoted to their development.

16. To begin with the topic which we have proposed first to discuss, We cannot refrain, following the counsel of St. Ambrose[14] who says that "no duty is more important than that of returning thanks," from offering our fullest gratitude to Almighty God for the immense benefits that have come through Leo's Encyclical to the Church and to human society. If indeed We should wish to review these benefits even cursorily, almost the whole history of the social question during the last forty years would have to be recalled to mind. These benefits can be reduced conveniently, however, to three main points, corresponding to the three kinds of help which Our Predecessor ardently desired for the accomplishment of his great work of restoration.

17. In the first place Leo himself clearly stated what ought to be expected from the Church:[15] "Manifestly it is the Church which draws from the Gospel the teachings through which the struggle can be composed entirely, or, after its bitterness is removed, can certainly become more tempered. It is the Church, again, that strives not only to instruct the mind, but to regulate by her precepts the life and morals of individuals, and that ameliorates the condition of the workers through her numerous and beneficent institutions "

18. The Church did not let these rich fountains lie quiescent in her bosom, but from them drew copiously for the common good of the longed-for peace. Leo himself and his Successors, showing paternal charity and pastoral constancy always, in defense especially of the poor and the weak,[16] proclaimed and urged without ceasing again and again by voice and pen the teaching on the social and economic question which *On the Condition of Workers* presented, and adapted it fittingly to the needs of time and of circumstance. And many bishops have done the same, who in their continual and able interpretation of this same teaching have illustrated it with commentaries and in accordance with the mind and instructions of the Holy See provided for its application to the conditions and institutions of diverse regions.[17]

19. It is not surprising, therefore, that many scholars, both priests and laymen, led especially by the desire that the unchanged and unchangeable teaching of the Church should meet new demands and needs more effectively, have zealously undertaken to develop, with the Church as their guide and teacher, a social and economic science in accord with the conditions of our time.

20. And so, with Leo's Encyclical pointing the way and furnishing the light, a true Catholic social science has arisen, which is daily fostered and enriched by the tireless efforts of those chosen men whom We have termed auxiliaries of the Church. They do not, indeed, allow their science to lie hidden behind learned walls. As the useful and well attended courses instituted in Catholic universities, colleges, and seminaries, the social congresses and "weeks" that are held at frequent intervals with most successful results, the study groups that are promoted, and finally the timely and sound publications that are disseminated everywhere and in every possible way, clearly show, these men bring their science out into the full light and stress of life.

21. Nor is the benefit that has poured forth from Leo's Encyclical confined within these bounds; for the teaching which *On the Condition of Workers* contains has gradually and imperceptibly worked its way into the minds of those outside Catholic unity who do not recognize the authority of the Church. Catholic principles on the social question have as a result, passed little by little into the patrimony of all human society, and We rejoice that the eternal truths which Our Predecessor of glorious memory proclaimed so impressively have been frequently invoked and defended not only in non-Catholic books and journals but in legislative halls also courts of justice.

22. Furthermore, after the terrible war, when the statesmen of the leading nations were attempting to restore peace on the basis of a thorough reform of social conditions, did not they, among the norms agreed upon to regulate in accordance with justice and equity the labor of the

workers, give sanction to many points that so remarkably coincide with Leo's principles and instructions as to seem consciously taken therefrom? The Encyclical *On the Condition of Workers*, without question, has become a memorable document and rightly to it may be applied the words of Isaias: "He shall set up a standard to the nations."[18]

23. Meanwhile, as Leo's teachings were being widely diffused in the minds of men, with learned investigations leading the way, they have come to be put into practice. In the first place, zealous efforts have been made, with active good will, to lift up that class which on account of the modern expansion of industry had increased to enormous numbers but not yet had obtained its rightful place or rank in human society and was, for that reason, all but neglected and despised—the workers, We mean—to whose improvement, to the great advantage of souls, the diocesan and regular clergy, though burdened with other pastoral duties, have under the leadership of the Bishops devoted themselves. This constant work, undertaken to fill the workers' souls with the Christian spirit, helped much also to make them conscious of their true dignity and render them capable, by placing clearly before them the rights and duties of their class, of legitimately and happily advancing and even of becoming leaders of their fellows.

24. From that time on, fuller means of livelihood have been more securely obtained; for not only did works of beneficence and charity begin to multiply at the urging of the Pontiff, but there have also been established everywhere new and continuously expanding organizations in which workers, draftsmen, farmers and employees of every kind, with the counsel of the Church and frequently under the leadership of her priests, give and receive mutual help and support.

25. With regard to civil authority, Leo XIII, boldly breaking through the confines imposed by Liberalism, fearlessly taught that government must not be thought a mere guardian of law and of good order, but rather must put forth every effort so that "through the

entire scheme of laws and institutions . . . both public and individual well-being may develop spontaneously out of the very structure and administration of the State."[19] Just freedom of action must, of course, be left both to individual citizens and to families, yet only on condition that the common good be preserved and wrong to any individual be abolished. The function of the rulers of the State, moreover, is to watch over the community and its parts; but in protecting private individuals in their rights, chief consideration ought to be given to the weak and the poor. "For the nation, as it were, of the rich is guarded by its own defenses and is in less need of governmental protection, whereas the suffering multitude, without the means to protect itself relies especially on the protection of the State. Wherefore, since wageworkers are numbered among the great mass of the needy, the State must include them under its special care and foresight."[20]

26. We, of course, do not deny that even before the Encyclical of Leo, some rulers of peoples have provided for certain of the more urgent needs of the workers and curbed more flagrant acts of injustice inflicted upon them. But after the Apostolic voice had sounded from the Chair of Peter throughout the world, rulers of nations, more fully alive at last to their duty, devoted their minds and attention to the task of promoting a more comprehensive and fruitful social policy.

27. And while the principles of Liberalism were tottering, which had long prevented effective action by those governing the State, the Encyclical *On the Condition of Workers* in truth impelled peoples themselves to promote a social policy on truer grounds and with greater intensity, and so strongly encouraged good Catholics to furnish valuable help to heads of States in this field that they often stood forth as illustrious champions of this new policy even in legislatures. Sacred ministers of the Church, thoroughly imbued with Leo's teaching, have, in fact, often proposed to the votes of the peoples' representatives the

very social legislation that has been enacted in recent years and have resolutely demanded and promoted its enforcement.

28. A new branch of law, wholly unknown to the earlier time, has arisen from this continuous and unwearied labor to protect vigorously the sacred rights of the workers that flow from their dignity as men and as Christians. These laws undertake the protection of life, health, strength, family, homes, workshops, wages and labor hazards, in fine, everything which pertains to the condition of wage workers, with special concern for women and children. Even though these laws do not conform exactly everywhere and in all respects to Leo's recommendations, still it is undeniable that much in them savors of the Encyclical, *On the Condition of Workers*, to which great credit must be given for whatever improvement has been achieved in the workers' condition.

29. Finally, the wise Pontiff showed that "employers and workers themselves can accomplish much in this matter, manifestly through those institutions by the help of which the poor are opportunely assisted and the two classes of society are brought closer to each other."[21] First place among these institutions, he declares, must be assigned to associations that embrace either workers alone or workers and employers together. He goes into considerable detail in explaining and commending these associations and expounds with a truly wonderful wisdom their nature, purpose, timeliness, rights, duties, and regulations.

30. These teachings were issued indeed most opportunely. For at that time in many nations those at the helm of State, plainly imbued with Liberalism, were showing little favor to workers' associations of this type; nay, rather they openly opposed them, and while going out of their way to recognize similar organizations of other classes and show favor to them, they were with criminal injustice denying the natural right to form associations to those who needed it most to defend

themselves from ill treatment at the hands of the powerful. There were even some Catholics who looked askance at the efforts of workers to form associations of this type as if they smacked of a socialistic or revolutionary spirit.

31. The rules, therefore, which Leo XIII issued in virtue of his authority, deserve the greatest praise in that they have been able to break down this hostility and dispel these suspicions; but they have even a higher claim to distinction in that they encouraged Christian workers to found mutual associations according to their various occupations, taught them how to do so, and resolutely confirmed in the path of duty a goodly number of those whom socialist organizations strongly attracted by claiming to be the sole defenders and champions of the lowly and oppressed.

32. With respect to the founding of these societies, the Encyclical *On the Condition of Workers* most fittingly declared that "workers' associations ought to be so constituted and so governed as to furnish the most suitable and most convenient means to attain the object proposed, which consists in this, that the individual members of the association secure, so far as is possible, an increase in the goods of body, of soul, and of property," yet it is clear that "moral and religious perfection ought to be regarded as their principal goal, and that their social organization as such ought above all to be directed completely by this goal."[22] For "when the regulations of associations are founded upon religion, the way is easy toward establishing the mutual relations of the members, so that peaceful living together and prosperity will result."[23]

33. To the founding of these associations the clergy and many of the laity devoted themselves everywhere with truly praiseworthy zeal, eager to bring Leo's program to full realization. Thus associations of this kind have molded truly Christian workers who, in combining harmoniously the diligent practice of their occupation with the salutary precepts of

religion, protect effectively and resolutely their own temporal interests and rights, keeping a due respect for justice and a genuine desire to work together with other classes of society for the Christian renewal of all social life.

34. These counsels and instructions of Leo XIII were put into effect differently in different places according to varied local conditions. In some places one and the same association undertook to attain all the ends laid down by the Pontiff; in others, because circumstances suggested or required it, a division of work developed and separate associations were formed. Of these, some devoted themselves to the defense of the rights and legitimate interests of their members in the labor market; others took over the work of providing mutual economic aid; finally still others gave all their attention to the fulfillment of religious and moral duties and other obligations of like nature.

35. This second method has especially been adopted where either the laws of a country, or certain special economic institutions, or that deplorable dissension of minds and hearts so widespread in contemporary society and an urgent necessity of combating with united purpose and strength the massed ranks of revolutionarists, have prevented Catholics from founding purely Catholic labor unions. Under these conditions, Catholics seem almost forced to join secular labor unions. These unions, however, should always profess justice and equity and give Catholic members full freedom to care for their own conscience and obey the laws of the Church. It is clearly the office of bishops, when they know that these associations are on account of circumstances necessary and are not dangerous to religion, to approve of Catholic workers joining them, keeping before their eyes, however, the principles and precautions laid down by Our Predecessor, Pius X of holy memory. [24] Among these precautions the first and chief is this: Side by side with these unions there should always be associations zealously engaged in imbuing and forming their members in the teaching of religion and

morality so that they in turn may be able to permeate the unions with that good spirit which should direct them in all their activity. As a result, the religious associations will bear good fruit even beyond the circle of their own membership.

36. To the Encyclical of Leo, therefore, must be given this credit, that these associations of workers have so flourished everywhere that while, alas, still surpassed in numbers by socialist and communist organizations, they already embrace a vast multitude of workers and are able, within the confines of each nation as well as in wider assemblies, to maintain vigorously the rights and legitimate demands of Catholic workers and insist also on the salutary Christian principles of society.

37. Leo's learned treatment and vigorous defense of the natural right to form associations began, furthermore, to find ready application to other associations also and not alone to those of the workers. Hence no small part of the credit must, it seems, be given to this same Encyclical of Leo for the fact that among farmers and others of the middle class most useful associations of this kind are seen flourishing to a notable degree and increasing day by day, as well as other institutions of a similar nature in which spiritual development and economic benefit are happily combined.

38. But if this cannot be said of organizations which Our same Predecessor intensely desired established among employers and managers of industry—and We certainly regret that they are so few—the condition is not wholly due to the will of men but to far graver difficulties that hinder associations of this kind which We know well and estimate at their full value. There is, however, strong hope that these obstacles also will be removed soon, and even now We greet with the deepest joy of Our soul, certain by no means insignificant attempts in this direction, the rich fruits of which promise a still richer harvest in the future.[25]

39. All these benefits of Leo's Encyclical, Venerable Brethren and Beloved Children, which We have outlined rather than fully described,

are so numerous and of such import as to show plainly that this immortal document does not exhibit a merely fanciful, even if beautiful, ideal of human society. Rather did our Predecessor draw from the Gospel and, therefore, from an ever-living and life-giving fountain, teachings capable of greatly mitigating, if not immediately terminating that deadly internal struggle which is rending the family of mankind. The rich fruits which the Church of Christ and the whole human race have, by God's favor, reaped therefrom unto salvation prove that some of this good seed, so lavishly sown forty years ago, fell on good ground. On the basis of the long period of experience, it cannot be rash to say that Leo's Encyclical has proved itself the *Magna Charta* upon which all Christian activity in the social field ought to be based, as on a foundation. And those who would seem to hold in little esteem this Papal Encyclical and its commemoration either blaspheme what they know not, or understand nothing of what they are only superficially acquainted with, or if they do understand convict themselves formally of injustice and ingratitude.

40. Yet since in the course of these same years, certain doubts have arisen concerning either the correct meaning of some parts of Leo's Encyclical or conclusions to be deduced therefrom, which doubts in turn have even among Catholics given rise to controversies that are not always peaceful; and since, furthermore, new needs and changed conditions of our age have made necessary a more precise application of Leo's teaching or even certain additions thereto, We most gladly seize this fitting occasion, in accord with Our Apostolic Office through which We are debtors to all,[26] to answer, so far as in Us lies, these doubts and these demands of the present day.

41. Yet before proceeding to explain these matters, that principle which Leo XIII so clearly established must be laid down at the outset here, namely, that there resides in Us the right and duty to pronounce with supreme authority upon social and economic matters.[27]

Certainly the Church was not given the commission to guide men to an only fleeting and perishable happiness but to that which is eternal. Indeed "the Church holds that it is unlawful for her to mix without cause in these temporal concerns"[28]; however, she can in no wise renounce the duty God entrusted to her to interpose her authority, not of course in matters of technique for which she is neither suitably equipped nor endowed by office, but in all things that are connected with the moral law. For as to these, the deposit of truth that God committed to Us and the grave duty of disseminating and interpreting the whole moral law, and of urging it in season and out of season, bring under and subject to Our supreme jurisdiction not only social order but economic activities themselves.

42. Even though economics and moral science employs each its own principles in its own sphere, it is, nevertheless, an error to say that the economic and moral orders are so distinct from and alien to each other that the former depends in no way on the latter. Certainly the laws of economics, as they are termed, being based on the very nature of material things and on the capacities of the human body and mind, determine the limits of what productive human effort cannot, and of what it can attain in the economic field and by what means. Yet it is reason itself that clearly shows, on the basis of the individual and social nature of things and of men, the purpose which God ordained for all economic life.

43. But it is only the moral law which, just as it commands us to seek our supreme and last end in the whole scheme of our activity, so likewise commands us to seek directly in each kind of activity those purposes which we know that nature, or rather God the Author of nature, established for that kind of action, and in orderly relationship to subordinate such immediate purposes to our supreme and last end. If we faithfully observe this law, then it will follow that the particular purposes, both individual and social, that are sought in the economic

field will fall in their proper place in the universal order of purposes, and We, in ascending through them, as it were by steps, shall attain the final end of all things, that is God, to Himself and to us, the supreme and inexhaustible Good.

44. But to come down to particular points, We shall begin with ownership or the right of property. Venerable Brethren and Beloved Children, you know that Our Predecessor of happy memory strongly defended the right of property against the tenets of the Socialists of his time by showing that its abolition would result, not to the advantage of the working class, but to their extreme harm. Yet since there are some who calumniate the Supreme Pontiff, and the Church herself, as if she had taken and were still taking the part of the rich against the non-owning workers—certainly no accusation is more unjust than that—and since Catholics are at variance with one another concerning the true and exact mind of Leo, it has seemed best to vindicate this, that is, the Catholic teaching on this matter from calumnies and safeguard it from false interpretations.

45. First, then, let it be considered as certain and established that neither Leo nor those theologians who have taught under the guidance and authority of the Church have ever denied or questioned the twofold character of ownership, called usually individual or social according as it regards either separate persons or the common good. For they have always unanimously maintained that nature, rather the Creator Himself, has given man the right of private ownership not only that individuals may be able to provide for themselves and their families but also that the goods which the Creator destined for the entire family of mankind may through this institution truly serve this purpose. All this can be achieved in no wise except through the maintenance of a certain and definite order.

46. Accordingly, twin rocks of shipwreck must be carefully avoided. For, as one is wrecked upon, or comes close to, what is known as

"individualism" by denying or minimizing the social and public character of the right of property, so by rejecting or minimizing the private and individual character of this same right, one inevitably runs into "collectivism" or at least closely approaches its tenets. Unless this is kept in mind, one is swept from his course upon the shoals of that moral, juridical, and social modernism which We denounced in the Encyclical issued at the beginning of Our Pontificate.[29] And, in particular, let those realize this who, in their desire for innovation, do not scruple to reproach the Church with infamous calumnies, as if she had allowed to creep into the teachings of her theologians a pagan concept of ownership which must be completely replaced by another that they with amazing ignorance call "Christian."

47. In order to place definite limits on the controversies that have arisen over ownership and its inherent duties there must be first laid down as foundation a principle established by Leo XIII: The right of property is distinct from its use.[30] That justice called commutative commands sacred respect for the division of possessions and forbids invasion of others' rights through the exceeding of the limits of one's own property; but the duty of owners to use their property only in a right way does not come under this type of justice, but under other virtues, obligations of which "cannot be enforced by legal action."[31] Therefore, they are in error who assert that ownership and its right use are limited by the same boundaries; and it is much farther still from the truth to hold that a right to property is destroyed or lost by reason of abuse or non-use.

48. Those, therefore, are doing a work that is truly salutary and worthy of all praise who, while preserving harmony among themselves and the integrity of the traditional teaching of the Church, seek to define the inner nature of these duties and their limits whereby either the right of property itself or its use, that is, the exercise of ownership, is circumscribed by the necessities of social living. On the other hand,

those who seek to restrict the individual character of ownership to such a degree that in fact they destroy it are mistaken and in error.

49. It follows from what We have termed the individual and at the same time social character of ownership, that men must consider in this matter not only their own advantage but also the common good. To define these duties in detail when necessity requires and the natural law has not done so, is the function of those in charge of the State. Therefore, public authority, under the guiding light always of the natural and divine law, can determine more accurately upon consideration of the true requirements of the common good, what is permitted and what is not permitted to owners in the use of their property. Moreover, Leo XIII wisely taught "that God has left the limits of private possessions to be fixed by the industry of men and institutions of peoples."[32] That history proves ownership, like other elements of social life, to be not absolutely unchanging, We once declared as follows: "What divers forms has property had, from that primitive form among rude and savage peoples, which may be observed in some places even in our time, to the form of possession in the patriarchal age; and so further to the various forms under tyranny (We are using the word tyranny in its classical sense); and then through the feudal and monarchial forms down to the various types which are to be found in more recent times."[33] That the State is not permitted to discharge its duty arbitrarily is, however, clear. The natural right itself both of owning goods privately and of passing them on by inheritance ought always to remain intact and inviolate, since this indeed is a right that the State cannot take away: "For man is older than the State,"[34] and also "domestic living together is prior both in thought and in fact to uniting into a polity."[35] Wherefore the wise Pontiff declared that it is grossly unjust for a State to exhaust private wealth through the weight of imposts and taxes. "For since the right of possessing goods privately has been conferred not by man's law, but by nature, public authority cannot abolish it, but can only control its

exercise and bring it into conformity with the common weal."[36] Yet
when the State brings private ownership into harmony with the needs
of the common good, it does not commit a hostile act against private
owners but rather does them a friendly service; for it thereby effectively
prevents the private possession of goods, which the Author of nature in
His most wise providence ordained for the support of human life, from
causing intolerable evils and thus rushing to its own destruction; it does
not destroy private possessions, but safeguards them; and it does not
weaken private property rights, but strengthens them.

50. Furthermore, a person's superfluous income, that is, income
which he does not need to sustain life fittingly and with dignity, is not
left wholly to his own free determination. Rather the Sacred Scriptures
and the Fathers of the Church constantly declare in the most explicit
language that the rich are bound by a very grave precept to practice
almsgiving, beneficence, and munificence.

51. Expending larger incomes so that opportunity for gainful work
may be abundant, provided, however, that this work is applied to producing really useful goods, ought to be considered, as We deduce from
the principles of the Angelic Doctor,[37] an outstanding exemplification
of the virtue of munificence and one particularly suited to the needs
of the times.

52. That ownership is originally acquired both by occupancy of a
thing not owned by any one and by labor, or, as is said, by specification,
the tradition of all ages as well as the teaching of Our Predecessor Leo
clearly testifies. For, whatever some idly say to the contrary, no injury is
done to any person when a thing is occupied that is available to all but
belongs to no one; however, only that labor which a man performs in
his own name and by virtue of which a new form or increase has been
given to a thing grants him title to these fruits.

53. Far different is the nature of work that is hired out to others
and expended on the property of others. To this indeed especially

applies what Leo XIII says is "incontestible," namely, that "the wealth of nations originates from no other source than from the labor of workers."[38] For is it not plain that the enormous volume of goods that makes up human wealth is produced by and issues from the hands of the workers that either toil unaided or have their efficiency marvelously increased by being equipped with tools or machines? Every one knows, too, that no nation has ever risen out of want and poverty to a better and nobler condition save by the enormous and combined toil of all the people, both those who manage work and those who carry out directions. But it is no less evident that, had not God the Creator of all things, in keeping with His goodness, first generously bestowed natural riches and resources—the wealth and forces of nature—such supreme efforts would have been idle and vain, indeed could never even have begun. For what else is work but to use or exercise the energies of mind and body on or through these very things? And in the application of natural resources to human use the law of nature, or rather God's will promulgated by it, demands that right order be observed. This order consists in this: that each thing have its proper owner. Hence it follows that unless a man is expending labor on his own property, the labor of one person and the property of another must be associated, for neither can produce anything without the other. Leo XIII certainly had this in mind when he wrote: "Neither capital can do without labor, nor labor without capital."[39] Wherefore it is wholly false to ascribe to property alone or to labor alone whatever has been obtained through the combined effort of both, and it is wholly unjust for either, denying the efficacy of the other, to arrogate to itself whatever has been produced.

54. Property, that is, "capital," has undoubtedly long been able to appropriate too much to itself. Whatever was produced, whatever returns accrued, capital claimed for itself, hardly leaving to the worker enough to restore and renew his strength. For the doctrine was preached that all accumulation of capital falls by an absolutely insuperable

economic law to the rich, and that by the same law the workers are given over and bound to perpetual want, to the scantiest of livelihoods. It is true, indeed, that things have not always and everywhere corresponded with this sort of teaching of the so-called Manchesterian Liberals; yet it cannot be denied that economic social institutions have moved steadily in that direction. That these false ideas, these erroneous suppositions, have been vigorously assailed, and not by those alone who through them were being deprived of their innate right to obtain better conditions, will surprise no one.

55. And therefore, to the harassed workers there have come "intellectuals," as they are called, setting up in opposition to a fictitious law the equally fictitious moral principle that all products and profits, save only enough to repair and renew capital, belong by very right to the workers. This error, much more specious than that of certain of the Socialists who hold that whatever serves to produce goods ought to be transferred to the State, or, as they say "socialized," is consequently all the more dangerous and the more apt to deceive the unwary. It is an alluring poison which many have eagerly drunk whom open Socialism had not been able to deceive.

56. Unquestionably, so as not to close against themselves the road to justice and peace through these false tenets, both parties ought to have been forewarned by the wise words of Our Predecessor: "However the earth may be apportioned among private owners, it does not cease to serve the common interests of all."[40] This same doctrine We ourselves also taught above in declaring that the division of goods which results from private ownership was established by nature itself in order that created things may serve the needs of mankind in fixed and stable order. Lest one wander from the straight path of truth, this is something that must be continually kept in mind.

57. But not every distribution among human beings of property and wealth is of a character to attain either completely or to a satisfactory

degree of perfection the end which God intends. Therefore, the riches that economic-social developments constantly increase ought to be so distributed among individual persons and classes that the common advantage of all, which Leo XIII had praised, will be safeguarded; in other words, that the common good of all society will be kept inviolate. By this law of social justice, one class is forbidden to exclude the other from sharing in the benefits. Hence the class of the wealthy violates this law no less, when, as if free from care on account of its wealth, it thinks it the right order of things for it to get everything and the worker nothing, than does the non-owning working class when, angered deeply at outraged justice and too ready to assert wrongly the one right it is conscious of, it demands for itself everything as if produced by its own hands, and attacks and seeks to abolish, therefore, all property and returns or incomes, of whatever kind they are or whatever the function they perform in human society, that have not been obtained by labor, and for no other reason save that they are of such a nature. And in this connection We must not pass over the unwarranted and unmerited appeal made by some to the Apostle when he said: "If any man will not work neither let him eat."[41] For the Apostle is passing judgment on those who are unwilling to work, although they can and ought to, and he admonishes us that we ought diligently to use our time and energies of body, and mind and not be a burden to others when we can provide for ourselves. But the Apostle in no wise teaches that labor is the sole title to a living or an income.[42]

58. To each, therefore, must be given his own share of goods, and the distribution of created goods, which, as every discerning person knows, is laboring today under the gravest evils due to the huge disparity between the few exceedingly rich and the unnumbered propertyless, must be effectively called back to and brought into conformity with the norms of the common good, that is, social justice.

59. The redemption of the non-owning workers—this is the goal that Our Predecessor declared must necessarily be sought. And the point

is the more emphatically to be asserted and more insistently repeated because the commands of the Pontiff, salutary as they are, have not infrequently been consigned to oblivion either because they were deliberately suppressed by silence or thought impracticable although they both can and ought to be put into effect. And these commands have not lost their force and wisdom for our time because that "pauperism" which Leo XIII beheld in all its horror is less widespread. Certainly the condition of the workers has been improved and made more equitable especially in the more civilized and wealthy countries where the workers can no longer be considered universally overwhelmed with misery and lacking the necessities of life. But since manufacturing and industry have so rapidly pervaded and occupied countless regions, not only in the countries called new, but also in the realms of the Far East that have been civilized from antiquity, the number of the non-owning working poor has increased enormously and their groans cry to God from the earth. Added to them is the huge army of rural wage workers, pushed to the lowest level of existence and deprived of all hope of ever acquiring "some property in land,"[43] and, therefore, permanently bound to the status of non-owning worker unless suitable and effective remedies are applied.

60. Yet while it is true that the status of non owning worker is to be carefully distinguished from pauperism, nevertheless the immense multitude of the non-owning workers on the one hand and the enormous riches of certain very wealthy men on the other establish an unanswerable argument that the riches which are so abundantly produced in our age of "industrialism," as it is called, are not rightly distributed and equitably made available to the various classes of the people.

61. Therefore, with all our strength and effort we must strive that at least in the future the abundant fruits of production will accrue equitably to those who are rich and will be distributed in ample sufficiency among the workers—not that these may become remiss in work, for

man is born to labor as the bird to fly—but that they may increase their property by thrift, that they may bear, by wise management of this increase in property, the burdens of family life with greater ease and security, and that, emerging from the insecure lot in life in whose uncertainties non-owning workers are cast, they may be able not only to endure the vicissitudes of earthly existence but have also assurance that when their lives are ended they will provide in some measure for those they leave after them.

62. All these things which Our Predecessor has not only suggested but clearly and openly proclaimed, We emphasize with renewed insistence in our present Encyclical; and unless utmost efforts are made without delay to put them into effect, let no one persuade himself that public order, peace, and the tranquillity of human society can be effectively defended against agitators of revolution.

63. As We have already indicated, following in the footsteps of Our Predecessor, it will be impossible to put these principles into practice unless the non-owning workers through industry and thrift advance to the state of possessing some little property. But except from pay for work, from what source can a man who has nothing else but work from which to obtain food and the necessaries of life set anything aside for himself through practicing frugality? Let us, therefore, explaining and developing wherever necessary Leo XIII's teachings and precepts, take up this question of wages and salaries which he called one "of very great importance."[44]

64. First of all, those who declare that a contract of hiring and being hired is unjust of its own nature, and hence a partnership-contract must take its place, are certainly in error and gravely misrepresent Our Predecessor whose Encyclical not only accepts working for wages or salaries but deals at some length with its regulation in accordance with the rules of justice.

65. We consider it more advisable, however, in the present condition of human society that, so far as is possible, the work-contract be somewhat modified by a partnership-contract, as is already being done in various ways and with no small advantage to workers and owners. Workers and other employees thus become sharers in ownership or management or participate in some fashion in the profits received.

66. The just amount of pay, however, must be calculated not on a single basis but on several, as Leo XIII already wisely declared in these words: "To establish a rule of pay in accord with justice, many factors must be taken into account."[45]

67. By this statement he plainly condemned the shallowness of those who think that this most difficult matter is easily solved by the application of a single rule or measure—and one quite false.

68. For they are greatly in error who do not hesitate to spread the principle that labor is worth and must be paid as much as its products are worth, and that consequently the one who hires out his labor has the right to demand all that is produced through his labor. How far this is from the truth is evident from that We have already explained in treating of property and labor.

69. It is obvious that, as in the case of ownership, so in the case of work, especially work hired out to others, there is a social aspect also to be considered in addition to the personal or individual aspect. For man's productive effort cannot yield its fruits unless a truly social and organic body exists, unless a social and juridical order watches over the exercise of work, unless the various occupations, being interdependent, cooperate with and mutually complete one another, and, what is still more important, unless mind, material things, and work combine and form as it were a single whole. Therefore, where the social and individual nature of work is neglected, it will be impossible to evaluate work justly and pay it according to justice.

70. Conclusions of the greatest importance follow from this two-fold character which nature has impressed on human work, and it is in accordance with these that wages ought to be regulated and established.

71. In the first place, the worker must be paid a wage sufficient to support him and his family.[46] That the rest of the family should also contribute to the common support, according to the capacity of each, is certainly right, as can be observed especially in the families of farmers, but also in the families of many craftsmen and small shopkeepers. But to abuse the years of childhood and the limited strength of women is grossly wrong. Mothers, concentrating on household duties, should work primarily in the home or in its immediate vicinity. It is an intolerable abuse, and to be abolished at all cost, for mothers on account of the father's low wage to be forced to engage in gainful occupations outside the home to the neglect of their proper cares and duties, especially the training of children. Every effort must therefore be made that fathers of families receive a wage large enough to meet ordinary family needs adequately. But if this cannot always be done under existing circumstances, social justice demands that changes be introduced as soon as possible whereby such a wage will be assured to every adult workingman. It will not be out of place here to render merited praise to all, who with a wise and useful purpose, have tried and tested various ways of adjusting the pay for work to family burdens in such a way that, as these increase, the former may be raised and indeed, if the contingency arises, there may be enough to meet extraordinary needs.

72. In determining the amount of the wage, the condition of a business and of the one carrying it on must also be taken into account; for it would be unjust to demand excessive wages which a business cannot stand without its ruin and consequent calamity to the workers. If, however, a business makes too little money, because of lack of energy or lack of initiative or because of indifference to technical and economic progress, that must not be regarded a just reason for reducing

the compensation of the workers. But if the business in question is not making enough money to pay the workers an equitable wage because it is being crushed by unjust burdens or forced to sell its product at less than a just price, those who are thus the cause of the injury are guilty of grave wrong, for they deprive workers of their just wage and force them under the pinch of necessity to accept a wage less than fair.

73. Let, then, both workers and employers strive with united strength and counsel to overcome the difficulties and obstacles and let a wise provision on the part of public authority aid them in so salutary a work. If, however, matters come to an extreme crisis, it must be finally considered whether the business can continue or the workers are to be cared for in some other way. In such a situation, certainly most serious, a feeling of close relationship and a Christian concord of minds ought to prevail and function effectively among employers and workers.

74. Lastly, the amount of the pay must be adjusted to the public economic good. We have shown above how much it helps the common good for workers and other employees, by setting aside some part of their income which remains after necessary expenditures, to attain gradually to the possession of a moderate amount of wealth. But another point, scarcely less important, and especially vital in our times, must not be overlooked: namely, that the opportunity to work be provided to those who are able and willing to work. This opportunity depends largely on the wage and salary rate, which can help as long as it is kept within proper limits, but which on the other hand can be an obstacle if it exceeds these limits. For everyone knows that an excessive lowering of wages, or their increase beyond due measure, causes unemployment. This evil, indeed, especially as we see it prolonged and injuring so many during the years of Our Pontificate, has plunged workers into misery and temptations, ruined the prosperity of nations, and put in jeopardy the public order, peace, and tranquillity of the whole world. Hence it is contrary to social justice when, for the sake of personal gain and

without regard for the common good, wages and salaries are excessively lowered or raised; and this same social justice demands that wages and salaries be so managed, through agreement of plans and wills, in so far as can be done, as to offer to the greatest possible number the opportunity of getting work and obtaining suitable means of livelihood.

75. A right proportion among wages and salaries also contributes directly to the same result; and with this is closely connected a right proportion in the prices at which the goods are sold that are produced by the various occupations, such as agriculture, manufacturing, and others. If all these relations are properly maintained, the various occupations will combine and coalesce into, as it were, a single body and like members of the body mutually aid and complete one another. For then only will the social economy be rightly established and attain its purposes when all and each are supplied with all the goods that the wealth and resources of nature, technical achievement, and the social organization of economic life can furnish. And these goods ought indeed to be enough both to meet the demands of necessity and decent comfort and to advance people to that happier and fuller condition of life which, when it is wisely cared for, is not only no hindrance to virtue but helps it greatly.[47]

76. What We have thus far stated regarding an equitable distribution of property and regarding just wages concerns individual persons and only indirectly touches social order, to the restoration of which according to the principles of sound philosophy and to its perfection according to the sublime precepts of the law of the Gospel, Our Predecessor, Leo XIII, devoted all his thought and care.

77. Still, in order that what he so happily initiated may be solidly established, that what remains to be done may be accomplished, and that even more copious and richer benefits may accrue to the family of mankind, two things are especially necessary: reform of institutions and correction of morals.

78. When we speak of the reform of institutions, the State comes chiefly to mind, not as if universal well-being were to be expected from its activity, but because things have come to such a pass through the evil of what we have termed "individualism" that, following upon the overthrow and near extinction of that rich social life which was once highly developed through associations of various kinds, there remain virtually only individuals and the State. This is to the great harm of the State itself; for, with a structure of social governance lost, and with the taking over of all the burdens which the wrecked associations once bore, the State has been overwhelmed and crushed by almost infinite tasks and duties.

79. As history abundantly proves, it is true that on account of changed conditions many things which were done by small associations in former times cannot be done now save by large associations. Still, that most weighty principle, which cannot be set aside or changed, remains fixed and unshaken in social philosophy: Just as it is gravely wrong to take from individuals what they can accomplish by their own initiative and industry and give it to the community, so also it is an injustice and at the same time a grave evil and disturbance of right order to assign to a greater and higher association what lesser and subordinate organizations can do. For every social activity ought of its very nature to furnish help to the members of the body social, and never destroy and absorb them.

80. The supreme authority of the State ought, therefore, to let subordinate groups handle matters and concerns of lesser importance, which would otherwise dissipate its efforts greatly. Thereby the State will more freely, powerfully, and effectively do all those things that belong to it alone because it alone can do them: directing, watching, urging, restraining, as occasion requires and necessity demands. Therefore, those in power should be sure that the more perfectly a graduated order is kept among the various associations, in observance of the principle

of "subsidiary function," the stronger social authority and effectiveness will be the happier and more prosperous the condition of the State.

81. First and foremost, the State and every good citizen ought to look to and strive toward this end: that the conflict between the hostile classes be abolished and harmonious cooperation of the Industries and Professions be encouraged and promoted.

82. The social policy of the State, therefore, must devote itself to the re-establishment of the Industries and Professions. In actual fact, human society now, for the reason that it is founded on classes with divergent aims and hence opposed to one another and therefore inclined to enmity and strife, continues to be in a violent condition and is unstable and uncertain.

83. Labor, as Our Predecessor explained well in his Encyclical,[48] is not a mere commodity. On the contrary, the worker's human dignity in it must be recognized. It therefore cannot be bought and sold like a commodity. Nevertheless, as the situation now stands, hiring and offering for hire in the so-called labor market separate men into two divisions, as into battle lines, and the contest between these divisions turns the labor market itself almost into a battlefield where, face to face, the opposing lines struggle bitterly. Everyone understands that this grave evil which is plunging all human society to destruction must be remedied as soon as possible. But complete cure will not come until this opposition has been abolished and well-ordered members of the social body—Industries and Professions—are constituted in which men may have their place, not according to the position each has in the labor market but according to the respective social functions which each performs. For under nature's guidance it comes to pass that just as those who are joined together by nearness of habitation establish towns, so those who follow the same industry or profession—whether in the economic or other field—form guilds or associations, so that many are wont to consider these self-governing organizations, if not essential, at least natural to civil society.

84. Because order, as St. Thomas well explains,[49] is unity arising from the harmonious arrangement of many objects, a true, genuine social order demands that the various members of a society be united together by some strong bond. This unifying force is present not only in the producing of goods or the rendering of services—in which the employers and employees of an identical Industry or Profession collaborate jointly—but also in that common good, to achieve which all Industries and Professions together ought, each to the best of its ability, to cooperate amicably. And this unity will be the stronger and more effective, the more faithfully individuals and the Industries and Professions themselves strive to do their work and excel in it.

85. It is easily deduced from what has been said that the interests common to the whole Industry or Profession should hold first place in these guilds. The most important among these interests is to promote the cooperation in the highest degree of each industry and profession for the sake of the common good of the country. Concerning matters, however, in which particular points, involving advantage or detriment to employers or workers, may require special care and protection, the two parties, when these cases arise, can deliberate separately or as the situation requires reach a decision separately.

86. The teaching of Leo XIII on the form of political government, namely, that men are free to choose whatever form they please, provided that proper regard is had for the requirements of justice and of the common good, is equally applicable in due proportion, it is hardly necessary to say, to the guilds of the various industries and professions.[50]

87. Moreover, just as inhabitants of a town are wont to found associations with the widest diversity of purposes, which each is quite free to join or not, so those engaged in the same industry or profession will combine with one another into associations equally free for purposes connected in some manner with the pursuit of the calling itself. Since these free associations are clearly and lucidly explained by Our

Predecessor of illustrious memory, We consider it enough to emphasize this one point: People are quite free not only to found such associations, which are a matter of private order and private right, but also in respect to them "freely to adopt the organization and the rules which they judge most appropriate to achieve their purpose."[51] The same freedom must be asserted for founding associations that go beyond the boundaries of individual callings. And may these free organizations, now flourishing and rejoicing in their salutary fruits, set before themselves the task of preparing the way, in conformity with the mind of Christian social teaching, for those larger and more important guilds, Industries and Professions, which We mentioned before, and make every possible effort to bring them to realization.

88. Attention must be given also to another matter that is closely connected with the foregoing. Just as the unity of human society cannot be founded on an opposition of classes, so also the right ordering of economic life cannot be left to a free competition of forces. For from this source, as from a poisoned spring, have originated and spread all the errors of individualist economic teaching. Destroying through forgetfulness or ignorance the social and moral character of economic life, it held that economic life must be considered and treated as altogether free from and independent of public authority, because in the market, i.e., in the free struggle of competitors, it would have a principle of self direction which governs it much more perfectly than would the intervention of any created intellect. But free competition, while justified and certainly useful provided it is kept within certain limits, clearly cannot direct economic life—a truth which the outcome of the application in practice of the tenets of this evil individualistic spirit has more than sufficiently demonstrated. Therefore, it is most necessary that economic life be again subjected to and governed by a true and effective directing principle. This function is one that the economic dictatorship which has recently displaced free competition can still less perform, since it is a

headstrong power and a violent energy that, to benefit people, needs to be strongly curbed and wisely ruled. But it cannot curb and rule itself. Loftier and nobler principles—social justice and social charity—must, therefore, be sought whereby this dictatorship may be governed firmly and fully. Hence, the institutions themselves of peoples and, particularly those of all social life, ought to be penetrated with this justice, and it is most necessary that it be truly effective, that is, establish a juridical and social order which will, as it were, give form and shape to all economic life. Social charity, moreover, ought to be as the soul of this order, an order which public authority ought to be ever ready effectively to protect and defend. It will be able to do this the more easily as it rids itself of those burdens which, as We have stated above, are not properly its own.

89. Furthermore, since the various nations largely depend on one another in economic matters and need one another's help, they should strive with a united purpose and effort to promote by wisely conceived pacts and institutions a prosperous and happy international cooperation in economic life.

90. If the members of the body social are, as was said, reconstituted, and if the directing principle of economic-social life is restored, it will be possible to say in a certain sense even of this body what the Apostle says of the mystical body of Christ: "The whole body (being closely joined and knit together through every joint of the system according to the functioning in due measure of each single part) derives its increase to the building up of itself in love."[52]

91. Recently, as all know, there has been inaugurated a special system of syndicates and corporations of the various callings which in view of the theme of this Encyclical it would seem necessary to describe here briefly and comment upon appropriately.

92. The civil authority itself constitutes the syndicate as a juridical personality in such a manner as to confer on it simultaneously a certain monopoly-privilege, since only such a syndicate, when thus approved,

can maintain the rights (according to the type of syndicate) of workers or employers, and since it alone can arrange for the placement of labor and conclude so-termed labor agreements. Anyone is free to join a syndicate or not, and only within these limits can this kind of syndicate be called free; for syndical dues and special assessments are exacted of absolutely all members of every specified calling or profession, whether they are workers or employers; likewise all are bound by the labor agreements made by the legally recognized syndicate. Nevertheless, it has been officially stated that this legally recognized syndicate does not prevent the existence, without legal status, however, of other associations made up of persons following the same calling.

93. The associations, or corporations, are composed of delegates from the two syndicates (that is, of workers and employers) respectively of the same industry or profession and, as true and proper organs and institutions of the State, they direct the syndicates and coordinate their activities in matters of common interest toward one and the same end.

94. Strikes and lock-outs are forbidden; if the parties cannot settle their dispute, public authority intervenes.

95. Anyone who gives even slight attention to the matter will easily see what are the obvious advantages in the system We have thus summarily described: The various classes work together peacefully, socialist organizations and their activities are repressed, and a special magistracy exercises a governing authority. Yet lest We neglect anything in a matter of such great importance and that all points treated may be properly connected with the more general principles which We mentioned above and with those which We intend shortly to add, We are compelled to say that to Our certain knowledge there are not wanting some who fear that the State, instead of confining itself as it ought to the furnishing of necessary and adequate assistance, is substituting itself for free activity; that the new syndical and corporative order savors too much of an involved and political system of administration; and that (in spite of

those more general advantages mentioned above, which are of course fully admitted) it rather serves particular political ends than leads to the reconstruction and promotion of a better social order.

96. To achieve this latter lofty aim, and in particular to promote the common good truly and permanently, We hold it is first and above everything wholly necessary that God bless it and, secondly, that all men of good will work with united effort toward that end. We are further convinced, as a necessary consequence, that this end will be attained the more certainly the larger the number of those ready to contribute toward it their technical, occupational, and social knowledge and experience; and also, what is more important, the greater the contribution made thereto of Catholic principles and their application, not indeed by Catholic Action (which excludes strictly syndical or political activities from its scope) but by those sons of Ours whom Catholic Action imbues with Catholic principles and trains for carrying on an apostolate under the leadership and teaching guidance of the Church—of that Church which in this field also that We have described, as in every other field where moral questions are involved and discussed, can never forget or neglect through indifference its divinely imposed mandate to be vigilant and to teach.

97. What We have taught about the reconstruction and perfection of social order can surely in no wise be brought to realization without reform of morality, the very record of history clearly shows. For there was a social order once which, although indeed not perfect or in all respects ideal, nevertheless, met in a certain measure the requirements of right reason, considering the conditions and needs of the time. If that order has long since perished, that surely did not happen because the order could not have accommodated itself to changed conditions and needs by development and by a certain expansion, but rather because men, hardened by too much love of self, refused to open the order to the increasing masses as they should have done, or because, deceived by

allurements of a false freedom and other errors, they became impatient of every authority and sought to reject every form of control.

98. There remains to Us, after again calling to judgment the economic system now in force and its most bitter accuser, Socialism, and passing explicit and just sentence upon them, to search out more thoroughly the root of these many evils and to point out that the first and most necessary remedy is a reform of morals.

99. Important indeed have the changes been which both the economic system and Socialism have undergone since Leo XIII's time.

100. That, in the first place, the whole aspect of economic life is vastly altered, is plain to all. You know, Venerable Brethren and Beloved Children, that the Encyclical of Our Predecessor of happy memory had in view chiefly that economic system, wherein, generally, some provide capital while others provide labor for a joint economic activity. And in a happy phrase he described it thus: "Neither capital can do without labor, nor labor without capital."[53]

101. With all his energy Leo XIII sought to adjust this economic system according to the norms of right order; hence, it is evident that this system is not to be condemned in itself. And surely it is not of its own nature vicious. But it does violate right order when capital hires workers, that is, the non-owning working class, with a view to and under such terms that it directs business and even the whole economic system according to its own will and advantage, scorning the human dignity of the workers, the social character of economic activity and social justice itself, and the common good.

102. Even today this is not, it is true, the only economic system in force everywhere; for there is another system also, which still embraces a huge mass of humanity, significant in numbers and importance, as for example, agriculture wherein the greater portion of mankind honorably and honestly procures its livelihood. This group, too, is being crushed with hardships and with difficulties, to which

Our Predecessor devotes attention in several places in his Encyclical and which We Ourselves have touched upon more than once in Our present Letter.

103. But, with the diffusion of modern industry throughout the whole world, the "capitalist" economic regime has spread everywhere to such a degree, particularly since the publication of Leo XIII's Encyclical, that it has invaded and pervaded the economic and social life of even those outside its orbit and is unquestionably impressing on it its advantages, disadvantages and vices, and, in a sense, is giving it its own shape and form.

104. Accordingly, when directing Our special attention to the changes which the capitalist economic system has undergone since Leo's time, We have in mind the good not only of those who dwell in regions given over to "capital" and industry, but of all mankind.

105. In the first place, it is obvious that not only is wealth concentrated in our times but an immense power and despotic economic dictatorship is consolidated in the hands of a few, who often are not owners but only the trustees and managing directors of invested funds which they administer according to their own arbitrary will and pleasure.

106. This dictatorship is being most forcibly exercised by those who, since they hold the money and completely control it, control credit also and rule the lending of money. Hence they regulate the flow, so to speak, of the life-blood whereby the entire economic system lives, and have so firmly in their grasp the soul, as it were, of economic life that no one can breathe against their will.

107. This concentration of power and might, the characteristic mark, as it were, of contemporary economic life, is the fruit that the unlimited freedom of struggle among competitors has of its own nature produced, and which lets only the strongest survive; and this is often the same as saying, those who fight the most violently, those who give least heed to their conscience.

108. This accumulation of might and of power generates in turn three kinds of conflict. First, there is the struggle for economic supremacy itself; then there is the bitter fight to gain supremacy over the State in order to use in economic struggles its resources and authority; finally there is conflict between States themselves, not only because countries employ their power and shape their policies to promote every economic advantage of their citizens, but also because they seek to decide political controversies that arise among nations through the use of their economic supremacy and strength.

109. The ultimate consequences of the individualist spirit in economic life are those which you yourselves, Venerable Brethren and Beloved Children, see and deplore: Free competition has destroyed itself; economic dictatorship has supplanted the free market; unbridled ambition for power has likewise succeeded greed for gain; all economic life has become tragically hard, inexorable, and cruel. To these are to be added the grave evils that have resulted from an intermingling and shameful confusion of the functions and duties of public authority with those of the economic sphere—such as, one of the worst, the virtual degradation of the majesty of the State, which although it ought to sit on high like a queen and supreme arbitress, free from all partiality and intent upon the one common good and justice, is become a slave, surrendered and delivered to the passions and greed of men. And as to international relations, two different streams have issued from the one fountain-head: On the one hand, economic nationalism or even economic imperialism; on the other, a no less deadly and accursed internationalism of finance or international imperialism whose country is where profit is.

110. In the second part of this Encyclical where We have presented Our teaching, We have described the remedies for these great evils so explicitly that We consider it sufficient at this point to recall them briefly. Since the present system of economy is founded chiefly upon

ownership and labor, the principles of right reason, that is, of Christian social philosophy, must be kept in mind regarding ownership and labor and their association together, and must be put into actual practice. First, so as to avoid the reefs of individualism and collectivism, the twofold character, that is individual and social, both of capital or ownership and of work or labor must be given due and rightful weight. Relations of one to the other must be made to conform to the laws of strictest justice—commutative justice, as it is called—with the support, however, of Christian charity. Free competition, kept within definite and due limits, and still more economic dictatorship, must be effectively brought under public authority in these matters which pertain to the latter's function. The public institutions themselves, of peoples, moreover, ought to make all human society conform to the needs of the common good; that is, to the norm of social justice. If this is done, that most important division of social life, namely, economic activity, cannot fail likewise to return to right and sound order.

111. Socialism, against which Our Predecessor, Leo XIII, had especially to inveigh, has since his time changed no less profoundly than the form of economic life. For Socialism, which could then be termed almost a single system and which maintained definite teachings reduced into one body of doctrine, has since then split chiefly into two sections, often opposing each other and even bitterly hostile, without either one however abandoning a position fundamentally contrary to Christian truth that was characteristic of Socialism.

112. One section of Socialism has undergone almost the same change that the capitalistic economic system, as We have explained above, has undergone. It has sunk into Communism. Communism teaches and seeks two objectives: Unrelenting class warfare and absolute extermination of private ownership. Not secretly or by hidden methods does it do this, but publicly, openly, and by employing every and all means, even the most violent. To achieve these objectives there

is nothing which it does not dare, nothing for which it has respect or reverence; and when it has come to power, it is incredible and portent-like in its cruelty and inhumanity. The horrible slaughter and destruction through which it has laid waste vast regions of eastern Europe and Asia are the evidence; how much an enemy and how openly hostile it is to Holy Church and to God Himself is, alas, too well proved by facts and fully known to all. Although We, therefore, deem it superfluous to warn upright and faithful children of the Church regarding the impious and iniquitous character of Communism, yet We cannot without deep sorrow contemplate the heedlessness of those who apparently make light of these impending dangers, and with sluggish inertia allow the widespread propagation of doctrine which seeks by violence and slaughter to destroy society altogether. All the more gravely to be condemned is the folly of those who neglect to remove or change the conditions that inflame the minds of peoples, and pave the way for the overthrow and destruction of society.

113. The other section, which has kept the name Socialism, is surely more moderate. It not only professes the rejection of violence but modifies and tempers to some degree, if it does not reject entirely, the class struggle and the abolition of private ownership. One might say that, terrified by its own principles and by the conclusions drawn therefrom by Communism, Socialism inclines toward and in a certain measure approaches the truths which Christian tradition has always held sacred; for it cannot be denied that its demands at times come very near those that Christian reformers of society justly insist upon.

114. For if the class struggle abstains from enmities and mutual hatred, it gradually changes into an honest discussion of differences founded on a desire for justice, and if this is not that blessed social peace which we all seek, it can and ought to be the point of departure from which to move forward to the mutual cooperation of the Industries and Professions. So also the war declared on private ownership, more and

more abated, is being so restricted that now, finally, not the possession itself of the means of production is attacked but rather a kind of sovereignty over society which ownership has, contrary to all right, seized and usurped. For such sovereignty belongs in reality not to owners but to the public authority. If the foregoing happens, it can come even to the point that imperceptibly these ideas of the more moderate socialism will no longer differ from the desires and demands of those who are striving to remold human society on the basis of Christian principles. For certain kinds of property, it is rightly contended, ought to be reserved to the State since they carry with them a dominating power so great that cannot without danger to the general welfare be entrusted to private individuals.

115. Such just demands and desire have nothing in them now which is inconsistent with Christian truth, and much less are they special to Socialism. Those who work solely toward such ends have, therefore, no reason to become socialists.

116. Yet let no one think that all the socialist groups or factions that are not communist have, without exception, recovered their senses to this extent either in fact or in name. For the most part they do not reject the class struggle or the abolition of ownership, but only in some degree modify them. Now if these false principles are modified and to some extent erased from the program, the question arises, or rather is raised without warrant by some, whether the principles of Christian truth cannot perhaps be also modified to some degree and be tempered so as to meet Socialism half-way and, as it were, by a middle course, come to agreement with it. There are some allured by the foolish hope that socialists in this way will be drawn to us. A vain hope! Those who want to be apostles among socialists ought to profess Christian truth whole and entire, openly and sincerely, and not connive at error in any way. If they truly wish to be heralds of the Gospel, let them above all strive to show to socialists that socialist claims, so far as they are just, are far

more strongly supported by the principles of Christian faith and much more effectively promoted through the power of Christian charity.

117. But what if Socialism has really been so tempered and modified as to the class struggle and private ownership that there is in it no longer anything to be censured on these points? Has it thereby renounced its contradictory nature to the Christian religion? This is the question that holds many minds in suspense. And numerous are the Catholics who, although they clearly understand that Christian principles can never be abandoned or diminished seem to turn their eyes to the Holy See and earnestly beseech Us to decide whether this form of Socialism has so far recovered from false doctrines that it can be accepted without the sacrifice of any Christian principle and in a certain sense be baptized. That We, in keeping with Our fatherly solicitude, may answer their petitions, We make this pronouncement: Whether considered as a doctrine, or an historical fact, or a movement, Socialism, if it remains truly Socialism, even after it has yielded to truth and justice on the points which we have mentioned, cannot be reconciled with the teachings of the Catholic Church because its concept of society itself is utterly foreign to Christian truth.

118. For, according to Christian teaching, man, endowed with a social nature, is placed on this earth so that by leading a life in society and under an authority ordained of God[54] he may fully cultivate and develop all his faculties unto the praise and glory of his Creator; and that by faithfully fulfilling the duties of his craft or other calling he may obtain for himself temporal and at the same time eternal happiness. Socialism, on the other hand, wholly ignoring and indifferent to this sublime end of both man and society, affirms that human association has been instituted for the sake of material advantage alone.

119. Because of the fact that goods are produced more efficiently by a suitable division of labor than by the scattered efforts of individuals, socialists infer that economic activity, only the material ends

of which enter into their thinking, ought of necessity to be carried on socially. Because of this necessity, they hold that men are obliged, with respect to the producing of goods, to surrender and subject themselves entirely to society. Indeed, possession of the greatest possible supply of things that serve the advantages of this life is considered of such great importance that the higher goods of man, liberty not excepted, must take a secondary place and even be sacrificed to the demands of the most efficient production of goods. This damage to human dignity, undergone in the "socialized" process of production, will be easily offset, they say, by the abundance of socially produced goods which will pour out in profusion to individuals to be used freely at their pleasure for comforts and cultural development. Society, therefore, as Socialism conceives it, can on the one hand neither exist nor be thought of without an obviously excessive use of force; on the other hand, it fosters a liberty no less false, since there is no place in it for true social authority, which rests not on temporal and material advantages but descends from God alone, the Creator and last end of all things.[55]

120. If Socialism, like all errors, contains some truth (which, moreover, the Supreme Pontiffs have never denied), it is based nevertheless on a theory of human society peculiar to itself and irreconcilable with true Christianity. Religious socialism, Christian socialism, are contradictory terms; no one can be at the same time a good Catholic and a true socialist.

121. All these admonitions which have been renewed and confirmed by Our solemn authority must likewise be applied to a certain new kind of socialist activity, hitherto little known but now carried on among many socialist groups. It devotes itself above all to the training of the mind and character. Under the guise of affection it tries in particular to attract children of tender age and win them to itself, although it also embraces the whole population in its scope in order finally to

produce true socialists who would shape human society to the tenets of Socialism.

122. Since in Our Encyclical, *The Christian Education of Youth*,[56] We have fully taught the principles that Christian education insists on and the ends it pursues, the contradiction between these principles and ends and the activities and aims of this socialism that is pervading morality and culture is so clear and evident that no demonstration is required here. But they seem to ignore or underestimate the grave dangers that it carries with it who think it of no importance courageously and zealously to resist them according to the gravity of the situation. It belongs to Our Pastoral Office to warn these persons of the grave and imminent evil: let all remember that Liberalism is the father of this Socialism that is pervading morality and culture and that Bolshevism will be its heir.

123. Accordingly, Venerable Brethren, you can well understand with what great sorrow We observe that not a few of Our sons, in certain regions especially, although We cannot be convinced that they have given up the true faith and right will, have deserted the camp of the Church and gone over to the ranks of Socialism, some to glory openly in the name of socialist and to profess socialist doctrines, others through thoughtlessness or even, almost against their wills to join associations which are socialist by profession or in fact.

124. In the anxiety of Our paternal solicitude, We give Ourselves to reflection and try to discover how it could happen that they should go so far astray and We seem to hear what many of them answer and plead in excuse: The Church and those proclaiming attachment to the Church favor the rich, neglect the workers and have no concern for them; therefore, to look after themselves they had to join the ranks of socialism.

125. It is certainly most lamentable, Venerable Brethren, that there have been, nay, that even now there are men who, although professing

to be Catholics, are almost completely unmindful of that sublime law of justice and charity that binds us not only to render to everyone what is his but to succor brothers in need as Christ the Lord Himself,[57] and—what is worse—out of greed for gain do not scruple to exploit the workers. Even more, there are men who abuse religion itself, and under its name try to hide their unjust exactions in order to protect themselves from the manifestly just demands of the workers. The conduct of such We shall never cease to censure gravely. For they are the reason why the Church could, even though undeservedly, have the appearance of and be charged with taking the part of the rich and with being quite unmoved by the necessities and hardships of those who have been deprived, as it were, of their natural inheritance. The whole history of the Church plainly demonstrates that such appearances are unfounded and such charges unjust. The Encyclical itself, whose anniversary we are celebrating, is clearest proof that it is the height of injustice to hurl these calumnies and reproaches at the Church and her teaching.

126. Although pained by the injustice and downcast in fatherly sorrow, it is so far from Our thought to repulse or to disown children who have been miserably deceived and have strayed so far from the truth and salvation that We cannot but invite them with all possible solicitude to return to the maternal bosom of the Church. May they lend ready ears to Our voice, may they return whence they have left, to the home that is truly their Father's, and may they stand firm there where their own place is, in the ranks of those who, zealously following the admonitions which Leo promulgated and We have solemnly repeated, are striving to restore society according to the mind of the Church on the firmly established basis of social justice and social charity. And let them be convinced that nowhere, even on earth, can they find full happiness save with Him who, being rich, became poor for our sakes that through His poverty we might become rich,[58] Who was poor and in labors from His youth, Who invited to Himself all that labor and are

heavily burdened that He might refresh them fully in the love of His heart,[59] and Who, lastly, without any respect for persons will require more of them to whom more has been given[60] and "will render to everyone according to his conduct."[61]

127. Yet, if we look into the matter more carefully and more thoroughly, we shall clearly perceive that, preceding this ardently desired social restoration, there must be a renewal of the Christian spirit, from which so many immersed in economic life have, far and wide, unhappily fallen away, lest all our efforts be wasted and our house be builded not on a rock but on shifting sand.[62]

128. And so, Venerable Brethren and Beloved Sons, having surveyed the present economic system, We have found it laboring under the gravest of evils. We have also summoned Communism and Socialism again to judgment and have found all their forms, even the most modified, to wander far from the precepts of the Gospel.

129. "Wherefore," to use the words of Our Predecessor, "if human society is to be healed, only a return to Christian life and institutions will heal it."[63] For this alone can provide effective remedy for that excessive care for passing things that is the origin of all vices; and this alone can draw away men's eyes, fascinated by and wholly fixed on the changing things of the world, and raise them toward Heaven. Who would deny that human society is in most urgent need of this cure now?

130. Minds of all, it is true, are affected almost solely by temporal upheavals, disasters, and calamities. But if we examine things critically with Christian eyes, as we should, what are all these compared with the loss of souls? Yet it is not rash by any means to say that the whole scheme of social and economic life is now such as to put in the way of vast numbers of mankind most serious obstacles which prevent them from caring for the one thing necessary; namely, their eternal salvation.

131. We, made Shepherd and Protector by the Prince of Shepherds, Who Redeemed them by His Blood, of a truly innumerable flock,

cannot hold back Our tears when contemplating this greatest of their dangers. Nay rather, fully mindful of Our pastoral office and with paternal solicitude, We are continually meditating on how We can help them; and We have summoned to Our aid the untiring zeal of others who are concerned on grounds of justice or charity. For what will it profit men to become expert in more wisely using their wealth, even to gaining the whole world, if thereby they suffer the loss of their souls?[64] What will it profit to teach them sound principles of economic life if in unbridled and sordid greed they let themselves be swept away by their passion for property, so that "hearing the commandments of the Lord they do all things contrary."[65]

132. The root and font of this defection in economic and social life from the Christian law, and of the consequent apostasy of great numbers of workers from the Catholic faith, are the disordered passions of the soul, the sad result of original sin which has so destroyed the wonderful harmony of man's faculties that, easily led astray by his evil desires, he is strongly incited to prefer the passing goods of this world to the lasting goods of Heaven. Hence arises that unquenchable thirst for riches and temporal goods, which has at all times impelled men to break God's laws and trample upon the rights of their neighbors, but which, on account of the present system of economic life, is laying far more numerous snares for human frailty. Since the instability of economic life, and especially of its structure, exacts of those engaged in it most intense and unceasing effort, some have become so hardened to the stings of conscience as to hold that they are allowed, in any manner whatsoever, to increase their profits and use means, fair or foul, to protect their hard-won wealth against sudden changes of fortune. The easy gains that a market unrestricted by any law opens to everybody attracts large numbers to buying and selling goods, and they, their one aim being to make quick profits with the least expenditure of work, raise or lower prices by their uncontrolled

business dealings so rapidly according to their own caprice and greed that they nullify the wisest forecasts of producers. The laws passed to promote corporate business, while dividing and limiting the risk of business, have given occasion to the most sordid license. For We observe that consciences are little affected by this reduced obligation of accountability; that furthermore, by hiding under the shelter of a joint name, the worst of injustices and frauds are penetrated; and that, too, directors of business companies, forgetful of their trust, betray the rights of those whose savings they have undertaken to administer. Lastly, We must not omit to mention those crafty men who, wholly unconcerned about any honest usefulness of their work, do not scruple to stimulate the baser human desires and, when they are aroused, use them for their own profit.

133. Strict and watchful moral restraint enforced vigorously by governmental authority could have banished these enormous evils and even forestalled them; this restraint, however, has too often been sadly lacking. For since the seeds of a new form of economy were bursting forth just when the principles of rationalism had been implanted and rooted in many minds, there quickly developed a body of economic teaching far removed from the true moral law, and, as a result, completely free rein was given to human passions.

134. Thus it came to pass that many, much more than ever before, were solely concerned with increasing their wealth by any means whatsoever, and that in seeking their own selfish interests before everything else they had no conscience about committing even the gravest of crimes against others. Those first entering upon this broad way that leads to destruction[66] easily found numerous imitators of their iniquity by the example of their manifest success, by their insolent display of wealth, by their ridiculing the conscience of others, who, as they said, were troubled by silly scruples, or lastly by crushing more conscientious competitors.

135. With the rulers of economic life abandoning the right road, it was easy for the rank and file of workers everywhere to rush headlong also into the same chasm; and all the more so, because very many managements treated their workers like mere tools, with no concern at all for their souls, without indeed even the least thought of spiritual things. Truly the mind shudders at the thought of the grave dangers to which the morals of workers (particularly younger workers) and the modesty of girls and women are exposed in modern factories; when we recall how often the present economic scheme, and particularly the shameful housing conditions, create obstacles to the family bond and normal family life; when we remember how many obstacles are put in the way of the proper observance of Sundays and Holy Days; and when we reflect upon the universal weakening of that truly Christian sense through which even rude and unlettered men were wont to value higher things, and upon its substitution by the single preoccupation of getting in any way whatsoever one's daily bread. And thus bodily labor, which Divine Providence decreed to be performed, even after original sin, for the good at once of man's body and soul, is being everywhere changed into an instrument of perversion; for dead matter comes forth from the factory ennobled, while men there are corrupted and degraded.

136. No genuine cure can be furnished for this lamentable ruin of souls, which, so long as it continues, will frustrate all efforts to regenerate society, unless men return openly and sincerely to the teaching of the Gospel, to the precepts of Him Who alone has the words of everlasting life,[67] words which will never pass away, even if Heaven and earth will pass away.[68] All experts in social problems are seeking eagerly a structure so fashioned in accordance with the norms of reason that it can lead economic life back to sound and right order. But this order, which We Ourselves ardently long for and with all Our efforts promote, will be wholly defective and incomplete unless all the activities of men harmoniously unite to imitate and attain, in so far as it

lies within human strength, the marvelous unity of the Divine plan. We mean that perfect order which the Church with great force and power preaches and which right human reason itself demands, that all things be directed to God as the first and supreme end of all created activity, and that all created good under God be considered as mere instruments to be used only in so far as they conduce to the attainment of the supreme end. Nor is it to be thought that gainful occupations are thereby belittled or judged less consonant with human dignity; on the contrary, we are taught to recognize in them with reverence the manifest will of the Divine Creator Who placed man upon the earth to work it and use it in a multitude of ways for his needs. Those who are engaged in producing goods, therefore, are not forbidden to increase their fortune in a just and lawful manner; for it is only fair that he who renders service to the community and makes it richer should also, through the increased wealth of the community, be made richer himself according to his position, provided that all these things be sought with due respect for the laws of God and without impairing the rights of others and that they be employed in accordance with faith and right reason. If these principles are observed by everyone, everywhere, and always, not only the production and acquisition of goods but also the use of wealth, which now is seen to be so often contrary to right order, will be brought back soon within the bounds of equity and just distribution. The sordid love of wealth, which is the shame and great sin of our age, will be opposed in actual fact by the gentle yet effective law of Christian moderation which commands man to seek first the Kingdom of God and His justice, with the assurance that, by virtue of God's kindness and unfailing promise, temporal goods also, in so far as he has need of them, shall be given him besides.[69]

137. But in effecting all this, the law of charity, "which is the bond of perfection,"[70] must always take a leading role. How completely deceived, therefore, are those rash reformers who concern

themselves with the enforcement of justice alone—and this, commutative justice—and in their pride reject the assistance of charity! Admittedly, no vicarious charity can substitute for justice which is due as an obligation and is wrongfully denied. Yet even supposing that everyone should finally receive all that is due him, the widest field for charity will always remain open. For justice alone can, if faithfully observed, remove the causes of social conflict but can never bring about union of minds and hearts. Indeed all the institutions for the establishment of peace and the promotion of mutual help among men, however perfect these may seem, have the principal foundation of their stability in the mutual bond of minds and hearts whereby the members are united with one another. If this bond is lacking, the best of regulations come to naught, as we have learned by too frequent experience. And so, then only will true cooperation be possible for a single common good when the constituent parts of society deeply feel themselves members of one great family and children of the same Heavenly Father; nay, that they are one body in Christ, "but severally members one of another,"[71] so that "if one member suffers anything, all the members suffer with it."[72] For then the rich and others in positions of power will change their former indifference toward their poorer brothers into a solicitous and active love, listen with kindliness to their just demands, and freely forgive their possible mistakes and faults. And the workers, sincerely putting aside every feeling of hatred or envy which the promoters of social conflict so cunningly exploit, will not only accept without rancor the place in human society assigned them by Divine Providence, but rather will hold it in esteem, knowing well that everyone according to his function and duty is toiling usefully and honorably for the common good and is following closely in the footsteps of Him Who, being in the form of God, willed to be a carpenter among men and be known as the son of a carpenter.

138. Therefore, out of this new diffusion throughout the world of the spirit of the Gospel, which is the spirit of Christian moderation and universal charity, We are confident there will come that longed-for and full restoration of human society in Christ, and that "Peace of Christ in the Kingdom of Christ," to accomplish which, from the very beginning of Our Pontificate, We firmly determined and resolved within Our heart to devote all Our care and all Our pastoral solicitude,[73] and toward this same highly important and most necessary end now, you also, Venerable Brethren, who with Us rule the Church of God under the mandate of the Holy Ghost,[74] are earnestly toiling with wholly praiseworthy zeal in all parts of the world, even in the regions of the holy missions to the infidels. Let well-merited acclamations of praise be bestowed upon you and at the same time upon all those, both clergy and laity, who We rejoice to see, are daily participating and valiantly helping in this same great work, Our beloved sons engaged in Catholic Action, who with a singular zeal are undertaking with Us the solution of the social problems in so far as by virtue of her divine institution this is proper to and devolves upon the Church. All these We urge in the Lord, again and again, to spare no labors and let no difficulties conquer them, but rather to become day by day more courageous and more valiant.[75] Arduous indeed is the task which We propose to them, for We know well that on both sides, both among the upper and the lower classes of society, there are many obstacles and barriers to be overcome. Let them not, however, lose heart; to face bitter combats is a mark of Christians, and to endure grave labors to the end is a mark of them who, as good soldiers of Christ,[76] follow Him closely.

139. Relying therefore solely on the all-powerful aid of Him "Who wishes all men to be saved,"[77] let us strive with all our strength to help those unhappy souls who have turned from God and, drawing them away from the temporal cares in which they are too deeply immersed, let us teach them to aspire with confidence to the things that are eternal.

Sometimes this will be achieved much more easily than seems possible at first sight to expect. For if wonderful spiritual forces lie hidden, like sparks beneath ashes, within the secret recesses of even the most abandoned man—certain proof that his soul is naturally Christian—how much the more in the hearts of those many upon many who have been led into error rather through ignorance or environment.

140. Moreover, the ranks of the workers themselves are already giving happy and promising signs of a social reconstruction. To Our soul's great joy, We see in these ranks also the massed companies of young workers, who are receiving the counsel of Divine Grace with willing ears and striving with marvelous zeal to gain their comrades for Christ. No less praise must be accorded to the leaders of workers' organizations who, disregarding their own personal advantage and concerned solely about the good of their fellow members, are striving prudently to harmonize the just demands of their members with the prosperity of their whole occupation and also to promote these demands, and who do not let themselves be deterred from so noble a service by any obstacle or suspicion. Also, as anyone may see, many young men, who by reason of their talent or wealth will soon occupy high places among the leaders of society, are studying social problems with deeper interest, and they arouse the joyful hope that they will dedicate themselves wholly to the restoration of society.

141. The present state of affairs, Venerable Brethren, clearly indicates the way in which We ought to proceed. For We are now confronted, as more than once before in the history of the Church, with a world that in large part has almost fallen back into paganism. That these whole classes of men may be brought back to Christ Whom they have denied, we must recruit and train from among them, themselves, auxiliary soldiers of the Church who know them well and their minds and wishes, and can reach their hearts with a tender brotherly love. The first and immediate apostles to the workers ought to be workers;

the apostles to those who follow industry and trade ought to be from among them themselves.

142. It is chiefly your duty, Venerable Brethren, and of your clergy, to search diligently for these lay apostles both of workers and of employers, to select them with prudence, and to train and instruct them properly. A difficult task, certainly, is thus imposed on priests, and to meet it, all who are growing up as the hope of the Church, must be duly prepared by an intensive study of the social question. Especially is it necessary that those whom you intend to assign in particular to this work should demonstrate that they are men possessed of the keenest sense of justice, who will resist with true manly courage the dishonest demands or the unjust acts of anyone, who will excel in the prudence and judgment which avoids every extreme, and, above all, who will be deeply permeated by the charity of Christ, which alone has the power to subdue firmly but gently the hearts and wills of men to the laws of justice and equity. Upon this road so often tried by happy experience, there is no reason why we should hesitate to go forward with all speed.

143. These Our Beloved Sons who are chosen for so great a work, We earnestly exhort in the Lord to give themselves wholly to the training of the men committed to their care, and in the discharge of this eminently priestly and apostolic duty to make proper use of the resources of Christian education by teaching youth, forming Christian organizations, and founding study groups guided by principles in harmony with the Faith. But above all, let them hold in high esteem and assiduously employ for the good of their disciples that most valuable means of both personal and social restoration which, as We taught in Our Encyclical, *Mens Nostra*,[78] is to be found in the Spiritual Exercises. In that Letter We expressly mentioned and warmly recommended not only the Spiritual Exercises for all the laity, but also the highly beneficial Workers' Retreats. For in that school of the spirit, not only are the best of Christians developed but true apostles also are

trained for every condition of life and are enkindled with the fire of the heart of Christ. From this school they will go forth as did the Apostles from the Upper Room of Jerusalem, strong in faith, endowed with an invincible steadfastness in persecution, burning with zeal, interested solely in spreading everywhere the Kingdom of Christ.

144. Certainly there is the greatest need now of such valiant soldiers of Christ who will work with all their strength to keep the human family safe from the dire ruin into which it would be plunged were the teachings of the Gospel to be flouted, and that order of things permitted to prevail which tramples underfoot no less the laws of nature than those of God. The Church of Christ, built upon an unshakable rock, has nothing to fear for herself, as she knows for a certainty that the gates of hell shall never prevail against her.[79] Rather, she knows full well, through the experience of many centuries, that she is wont to come forth from the most violent storms stronger than ever and adorned with new triumphs. Yet her maternal heart cannot but be moved by the countless evils with which so many thousands would be afflicted during storms of this kind, and above all by the consequent enormous injury to spiritual life which would work eternal ruin to so many souls redeemed by the Blood of Jesus Christ.

145. To ward off such great evils from human society nothing, therefore, is to be left untried; to this end may all our labors turn, to this all our energies, to this our fervent and unremitting prayers to God! For with the assistance of Divine Grace the fate of the human family rests in our hands.

146. Venerable Brethren and Beloved Sons, let us not permit the children of this world to appear wiser in their generation than we who by the Divine Goodness are the children of the light.[80] We find them, indeed, selecting and training with the greatest shrewdness alert and resolute devotees who spread their errors ever wider day by day through all classes of men and in every part of the world. And whenever they

undertake to attack the Church of Christ more violently, We see them put aside their internal quarrels, assembling in fully in harmony in a single battle line with a completely united effort, and work to achieve their common purpose.

147. Surely there is not one that does not know how many and how great are the works that the tireless zeal of Catholics is striving everywhere to carry out, both for social and economic welfare as well as in the fields of education and religion. But this admirable and unremitting activity not infrequently shows less effectiveness because of the dispersion of its energies in too many different directions. Therefore, let all men of good will stand united, all who under the Shepherds of the Church wish to fight this good and peaceful battle of Christ; and under the leadership and teaching guidance of the Church let all strive according to the talent, powers, and position of each to contribute something to the Christian reconstruction of human society which Leo XIII inaugurated through his immortal Encyclical, *On the Condition of Workers*, seeking not themselves and their own interests, but those of Jesus Christ,[81] not trying to press at all costs their own counsels, but ready to sacrifice them, however excellent, if the greater common good should seem to require it, so that in all and above all Christ may reign, Christ may command to Whom be "honor and glory and dominion forever and ever."[82]

148. That this may happily come to pass, to all of you, Venerable Brethren and Beloved Children, who are members of the vast Catholic family entrusted to Us, but with the especial affection of Our heart to workers and to all others engaged in manual occupations, committed to us more urgently by Divine Providence, and to Christian employers and managements, with paternal love We impart the Apostolic Benediction.

Given at Rome, at Saint Peter's, the fifteenth day of May, in the year 1931, the tenth year of Our Pontificate.

PIUS XI

Divini Redemptoris
Encyclical of Pope Pius XI
On Atheistic Communism

To the Patriarchs, Primates,
Archbishops, Bishops, and Other Ordinaries
In Peace and Communion with the Apostolic See.
Venerable Brethren, Health and Apostolic Benediction.

The promise of a Redeemer brightens the first page of the history of mankind, and the confident hope aroused by this promise softened the keen regret for a paradise which had been lost. It was this hope that accompanied the human race on its weary journey, until in the fullness of time the expected Savior came to begin a new universal civilization, the Christian civilization, far superior even to that which up to this time had been laboriously achieved by certain more privileged nations.

2. Nevertheless, the struggle between good and evil remained in the world as a sad legacy of the original fall. Nor has the ancient tempter ever ceased to deceive mankind with false promises. It is on this account that one convulsion following upon another has marked

the passage of the centuries, down to the revolution of our own days. This modern revolution, it may be said, has actually broken out or threatens everywhere, and it exceeds in amplitude and violence anything yet experienced in the preceding persecutions launched against the Church. Entire peoples find themselves in danger of falling back into a barbarism worse than that which oppressed the greater part of the world at the coming of the Redeemer.

3. This all too imminent danger, Venerable Brethren, as you have already surmised, is bolshevistic and atheistic Communism, which aims at upsetting the social order and at undermining the very foundations of Christian civilization.

4. In the face of such a threat, the Catholic Church could not and does not remain silent. This Apostolic See, above all, has not refrained from raising its voice, for it knows that its proper and social mission is to defend truth, justice and all those eternal values which Communism ignores or attacks. Ever since the days when groups of "intellectuals" were formed in an arrogant attempt to free civilization from the bonds of morality and religion, Our Predecessors overtly and explicitly drew the attention of the world to the consequences of the dechristianization of human society. With reference to Communism, Our Venerable Predecessor, Pius IX, of holy memory, as early as 1846 pronounced a solemn condemnation, which he confirmed in the words of the Syllabus directed against "that infamous doctrine of so-called Communism which is absolutely contrary to the natural law itself, and if once adopted would utterly destroy the rights, property and possessions of all men, and even society itself."[1] Later on, another of Our predecessors, the immortal Leo XIII, in his Encyclical *Quod Apostolici Muneris*, defined Communism as "the fatal plague which insinuates itself into the very marrow of human society only to bring about its ruin."[2] With clear intuition he pointed out that the atheistic movements existing among the masses of the Machine Age had their origin

in that school of philosophy which for centuries had sought to divorce science from the life of the Faith and of the Church.

5. During Our Pontificate We too have frequently and with urgent insistence denounced the current trend to atheism which is alarmingly on the increase. In 1924 when Our relief-mission returned from the Soviet Union We condemned Communism in a special Allocution[3] which We addressed to the whole world. In our Encyclicals *Miserentissimus Redemptor*,[4] *Quadragesimo Anno*,[5] *Caritate Christi*,[6] *Acerba Animi*,[7] *Dilectissima Nobis*,[8] We raised a solemn protest against the persecutions unleashed in Russia, in Mexico and now in Spain. Our two Allocutions of last year, the first on the occasion of the opening of the International Catholic Press Exposition, and the second during Our audience to the Spanish refugees, along with Our message of last Christmas, have evoked a world-wide echo which is not yet spent. In fact, the most persistent enemies of the Church, who from Moscow are directing the struggle against Christian civilization, themselves bear witness, by their unceasing attacks in word and act, that even to this hour the Papacy has continued faithfully to protect the sanctuary of the Christian religion, and that it has called public attention to the perils of Communism more frequently and more effectively than any other public authority on earth.

6. To Our great satisfaction, Venerable Brethren, you have, by means of individual and even joint pastoral Letters, accurately transmitted and explained to the Faithful these admonitions. Yet despite Our frequent and paternal warning the peril only grows greater from day to day because of the pressure exerted by clever agitators. Therefore We believe it to be Our duty to raise Our voice once more, in a still more solemn missive, in accord with the tradition of this Apostolic See, the Teacher of Truth, and in accord with the desire of the whole Catholic world, which makes the appearance of such a document but natural. We trust that the echo of Our voice will reach every mind free from

prejudice and every heart sincerely desirous of the good of mankind. We wish this the more because Our words are now receiving sorry confirmation from the spectacle of the bitter fruits of subversive ideas, which We foresaw and foretold, and which are in fact multiplying fearfully in the countries already stricken, or threatening every other country of the world.

7. Hence We wish to expose once more in a brief synthesis the principles of atheistic Communism as they are manifested chiefly in bolshevism. We wish also to indicate its method of action and to contrast with its false principles the clear doctrine of the Church, in order to inculcate anew and with greater insistence the means by which the Christian civilization, the true *civitas humana*, can be saved from the satanic scourge, and not merely saved, but better developed for the well-being of human society.

8. The Communism of today, more emphatically than similar movements in the past, conceals in itself a false messianic idea. A pseudo-ideal of justice, of equality and fraternity in labor impregnates all its doctrine and activity with a deceptive mysticism, which communicates a zealous and contagious enthusiasm to the multitudes entrapped by delusive promises. This is especially true in an age like ours, when unusual misery has resulted from the unequal distribution of the goods of this world. This pseudo-ideal is even boastfully advanced as if it were responsible for a certain economic progress. As a matter of fact, when such progress is at all real, its true causes are quite different, as for instance the intensification of industrialism in countries which were formerly almost without it, the exploitation of immense natural resources, and the use of the most brutal methods to insure the achievement of gigantic projects with a minimum of expense.

9. The doctrine of modern Communism, which is often concealed under the most seductive trappings, is in substance based on the principles of dialectical and historical materialism previously advocated by

Marx, of which the theoricians of bolshevism claim to possess the only genuine interpretation. According to this doctrine there is in the world only one reality, matter, the blind forces of which evolve into plant, animal and man. Even human society is nothing but a phenomenon and form of matter, evolving in the same way. By a law of inexorable necessity and through a perpetual conflict of forces, matter moves towards the final synthesis of a classless society. In such a doctrine, as is evident, there is no room for the idea of God; there is no difference between matter and spirit, between soul and body; there is neither survival of the soul after death nor any hope in a future life. Insisting on the dialectical aspect of their materialism, the Communists claim that the conflict which carries the world towards its final synthesis can be accelerated by man. Hence they endeavor to sharpen the antagonisms which arise between the various classes of society. Thus the class struggle with its consequent violent hate and destruction takes on the aspects of a crusade for the progress of humanity. On the other hand, all other forces whatever, as long as they resist such systematic violence, must be annihilated as hostile to the human race.

10. Communism, moreover, strips man of his liberty, robs human personality of all its dignity, and removes all the moral restraints that check the eruptions of blind impulse. There is no recognition of any right of the individual in his relations to the collectivity; no natural right is accorded to human personality, which is a mere cog-wheel in the Communist system. In man's relations with other individuals, besides, Communists hold the principle of absolute equality, rejecting all hierarchy and divinely-constituted authority, including the authority of parents. What men call authority and subordination is derived from the community as its first and only font. Nor is the individual granted any property rights over material goods or the means of production, for inasmuch as these are the source of further wealth, their possession would give one man power over another. Precisely on this score, all

forms of private property must be eradicated, for they are at the origin of all economic enslavement .

11. Refusing to human life any sacred or spiritual character, such a doctrine logically makes of marriage and the family a purely artificial and civil institution, the outcome of a specific economic system. There exists no matrimonial bond of a juridico-moral nature that is not subject to the whim of the individual or of the collectivity. Naturally, therefore, the notion of an indissoluble marriage-tie is scouted. Communism is particularly characterized by the rejection of any link that binds woman to the family and the home, and her emancipation is proclaimed as a basic principle. She is withdrawn from the family and the care of her children, to be thrust instead into public life and collective production under the same conditions as man. The care of home and children then devolves upon the collectivity. Finally, the right of education is denied to parents, for it is conceived as the exclusive prerogative of the community, in whose name and by whose mandate alone parents may exercise this right.

12. What would be the condition of a human society based on such materialistic tenets? It would be a collectivity with no other hierarchy than that of the economic system. It would have only one mission: the production of material things by means of collective labor, so that the goods of this world might be enjoyed in a paradise where each would "give according to his powers" and would "receive according to his needs." Communism recognizes in the collectivity the right, or rather, unlimited discretion, to draft individuals for the labor of the collectivity with no regard for their personal welfare; so that even violence could be legitimately exercised to dragoon the recalcitrant against their wills. In the Communistic commonwealth morality and law would be nothing but a derivation of the existing economic order, purely earthly in origin and unstable in character. In a word, the Communists claim to inaugurate a new era and a new civilization which is the result of blind evolutionary forces culminating in a humanity without God.

13. When all men have finally acquired the collectivist mentality in this Utopia of a really classless society, the political State, which is now conceived by Communists merely as the instrument by which the proletariat is oppressed by the capitalists, will have lost all reason for its existence and will "wither away." However, until that happy consummation is realized, the State and the powers of the State furnish Communism with the most efficacious and most extensive means for the achievement of its goal.

14. Such, Venerable Brethren, is the new gospel which bolshevistic and atheistic Communism offers the world as the glad tidings of deliverance and salvation! It is a system full of errors and sophisms. It is in opposition both to reason and to Divine Revelation. It subverts the social order, because it means the destruction of its foundations; because it ignores the true origin and purpose of the State; because it denies the rights, dignity and liberty of human personality.

15. How is it possible that such a system, long since rejected scientifically and now proved erroneous by experience, how is it, We ask, that such a system could spread so rapidly in all parts of the world? The explanation lies in the fact that too few have been able to grasp the nature of Communism. The majority instead succumb to its deception, skillfully concealed by the most extravagant promises. By pretending to desire only the betterment of the condition of the working classes, by urging the removal of the very real abuses chargeable to the liberalistic economic order, and by demanding a more equitable distribution of this world's goods (objectives entirely and undoubtedly legitimate), the Communist takes advantage of the present world-wide economic crisis to draw into the sphere of his influence even those sections of the populace which on principle reject all forms of materialism and terrorism. And as every error contains its element of truth, the partial truths to which We have referred are astutely presented according to the needs of time and place, to conceal, when convenient, the repulsive

crudity and inhumanity of Communistic principles and tactics. Thus the Communist ideal wins over many of the better minded members of the community. These in turn become the apostles of the movement among the younger intelligentsia who are still too immature to recognize the intrinsic errors of the system. The preachers of Communism are also proficient in exploiting racial antagonisms and political divisions and oppositions. They take advantage of the lack of orientation characteristic of modern agnostic science in order to burrow into the universities, where they bolster up the principles of their doctrine with pseudo-scientific arguments.

16. If we would explain the blind acceptance of Communism by so many thousands of workmen, we must remember that the way had been already prepared for it by the religious and moral destitution in which wage-earners had been left by liberal economics. Even on Sundays and holy days, labor-shifts were given no time to attend to their essential religious duties. No one thought of building churches within convenient distance of factories, nor of facilitating the work of the priest. On the contrary, laicism was actively and persistently promoted, with the result that we are now reaping the fruits of the errors so often denounced by Our Predecessors and by Ourselves. It can surprise no one that the Communistic fallacy should be spreading in a world already to a large extent de-Christianized.

17. There is another explanation for the rapid diffusion of the Communistic ideas now seeping into every nation, great and small, advanced and backward, so that no corner of the earth is free from them. This explanation is to be found in a propaganda so truly diabolical that the world has perhaps never witnessed its like before. It is directed from one common center. It is shrewdly adapted to the varying conditions of diverse peoples. It has at its disposal great financial resources, gigantic organizations, international congresses, and countless trained workers. It makes use of pamphlets and reviews, of

cinema, theater and radio, of schools and even universities. Little by
little it penetrates into all classes of the people and even reaches the
better-minded groups of the community, with the result that few are
aware of the poison which increasingly pervades their minds and hearts.

18. A third powerful factor in the diffusion of Communism is the
conspiracy of silence on the part of a large section of the non-Catholic
press of the world. We say conspiracy, because it is impossible otherwise to explain how a press usually so eager to exploit even the little
daily incidents of life has been able to remain silent for so long about
the horrors perpetrated in Russia, in Mexico and even in a great part
of Spain; and that it should have relatively so little to say concerning a
world organization as vast as Russian Communism. This silence is due
in part to shortsighted political policy, and is favored by various occult
forces which for a long time have been working for the overthrow of
the Christian Social Order.

19. Meanwhile the sorry effects of this propaganda are before
our eyes. Where Communism has been able to assert its power—and
here We are thinking with special affection of the people of Russia
and Mexico—it has striven by every possible means, as its champions
openly boast, to destroy Christian civilization and the Christian religion by banishing every remembrance of them from the hearts of men,
especially of the young. Bishops and priests were exiled, condemned
to forced labor, shot and done to death in inhuman fashion; laymen
suspected of defending their religion were vexed, persecuted, dragged
off to trial and thrown into prison.

20. Even where the scourge of Communism has not yet had time
enough to exercise to the full its logical effects, as witness Our beloved
Spain, it has, alas, found compensation in the fiercer violence of its
attack. Not only this or that church or isolated monastery was sacked,
but as far as possible every church and every monastery was destroyed.
Every vestige of the Christian religion was eradicated, even though

intimately linked with the rarest monuments of art and science. The fury of Communism has not confined itself to the indiscriminate slaughter of Bishops, of thousands of priests and religious of both sexes; it searches out above all those who have been devoting their lives to the welfare of the working classes and the poor. But the majority of its victims have been laymen of all conditions and classes. Even up to the present moment, masses of them are slain almost daily for no other offense than the fact that they are good Christians or at least opposed to atheistic Communism. And this fearful destruction has been carried out with a hatred and a savage barbarity one would not have believed possible in our age. No man of good sense, nor any statesman conscious of his responsibility can fail to shudder at the thought that what is happening today in Spain may perhaps be repeated tomorrow in other civilized countries.

21. Nor can it be said that these atrocities are a transitory phenomenon, the usual accompaniment of all great revolutions, the isolated excesses common to every war. No, they are the natural fruit of a system which lacks all inner restraint. Some restraint is necessary for man considered either as an individual or in society. Even the barbaric peoples had this inner check in the natural law written by God in the heart of every man. And where this natural law was held in higher esteem, ancient nations rose to a grandeur that still fascinates—more than it should—certain superficial students of human history. But tear the very idea of God from the hearts of men, and they are necessarily urged by their passions to the most atrocious barbarity.

22. This, unfortunately, is what we now behold. For the first time in history we are witnessing a struggle, cold-blooded in purpose and mapped out to the least detail, between man and "all that is called God."[9] Communism is by its nature anti-religious. It considers religion as "the opiate of the people" because the principles of religion

which speak of a life beyond the grave dissuade the proletariat from the dream of a Soviet paradise which is of this world.

23. But the law of nature and its Author cannot be flouted with impunity. Communism has not been able, and will not be able, to achieve its objectives even in the merely economic sphere. It is true that in Russia it has been a contributing factor in rousing men and materials from the inertia of centuries, and in obtaining by all manner of means, often without scruple, some measure of material success. Nevertheless We know from reliable and even very recent testimony that not even there, in spite of slavery imposed on millions of men, has Communism reached its promised goal. After all, even the sphere of economics needs some morality, some moral sense of responsibility, which can find no place in a system so thoroughly materialistic as Communism. Terrorism is the only possible substitute, and it is terrorism that reigns today in Russia, where former comrades in revolution are exterminating each other. Terrorism, having failed despite all to stem the tide of moral corruption, cannot even prevent the dissolution of society itself.

24. In making these observations it is no part of Our intention to condemn *en masse* the peoples of the Soviet Union. For them We cherish the warmest paternal affection. We are well aware that not a few of them groan beneath the yoke imposed on them by men who in very large part are strangers to the real interests of the country. We recognize that many others were deceived by fallacious hopes. We blame only the system, with its authors and abettors who considered Russia the best-prepared field for experimenting with a plan elaborated decades ago, and who from there continue to spread it from one end of the world to the other.

25. We have exposed the errors and the violent, deceptive tactics of bolshevistic and atheistic Communism. It is now time, Venerable Brethren, to contrast with it the true notion, already familiar to you,

of the *civitas humana* or human society, as taught by reason and Revelation through the mouth of the Church, *Magistra Gentium*.

26. Above all other reality there exists one supreme Being: God, the omnipotent Creator of all things, the all-wise and just Judge of all men. This supreme reality, God, is the absolute condemnation of the impudent falsehoods of Communism. In truth, it is not because men believe in God that He exists; rather because He exists do all men whose eyes are not deliberately closed to the truth believe in Him and pray to Him.

27. In the Encyclical on Christian Education[10] We explained the fundamental doctrine concerning man as it may be gathered from reason and Faith. Man has a spiritual and immortal soul. He is a person, marvelously endowed by his Creator with gifts of body and mind. He is a true "microcosm," as the ancients said, a world in miniature, with a value far surpassing that of the vast inanimate cosmos. God alone is his last end, in this life and the next. By sanctifying grace he is raised to the dignity of a son of God, and incorporated into the Kingdom of God in the Mystical Body of Christ. In consequence he has been endowed by God with many and varied prerogatives: the right to life, to bodily integrity, to the necessary means of existence; the right to tend toward his ultimate goal in the path marked out for him by God; the right of association and the right to possess and use property.

28. Just as matrimony and the right to its natural use are of divine origin, so likewise are the constitution and fundamental prerogatives of the family fixed and determined by the Creator. In the Encyclical on Christian Marriage[11] and in Our other Encyclical on Education, cited above, we have treated these topics at considerable length.

29. But God has likewise destined man for civil society according to the dictates of his very nature. In the plan of the Creator, society is a natural means which man can and must use to reach his destined end. Society is for man and not vice versa. This must not be understood in the sense of liberalistic individualism, which subordinates society to

the selfish use of the individual; but only in the sense that by means of an organic union with society and by mutual collaboration the attainment of earthly happiness is placed within the reach of all. In a further sense, it is society which affords the opportunities for the development of all the individual and social gifts bestowed on human nature. These natural gifts have a value surpassing the immediate interests of the moment, for in society they reflect the divine perfection, which would not be true were man to live alone. But on final analysis, even in this latter function, society is made for man, that he may recognize this reflection of God's perfection, and refer it in praise and adoration to the Creator. Only man, the human person, and not society in any form is endowed with reason and a morally free will.

30. Man cannot be exempted from his divinely-imposed obligations toward civil society, and the representatives of authority have the right to coerce him when he refuses without reason to do his duty. Society, on the other hand, cannot defraud man of his God-granted rights, the most important of which We have indicated above. Nor can society systematically void these rights by making their use impossible. It is therefore according to the dictates of reason that ultimately all material things should be ordained to man as a person, that through his mediation they may find their way to the Creator. In this wise we can apply to man, the human person, the words of the Apostle of the Gentiles, who writes to the Corinthians on the Christian economy of salvation: "All things are yours, and you are Christ's, and Christ is God's."[12] While Communism impoverishes human personality by inverting the terms of the relation of man to society, to what lofty heights is man not elevated by reason and Revelation!

31. The directive principles concerning the social-economic order have been expounded in the social Encyclical of Leo XIII on the question of labor.[13] Our own Encyclical on the Reconstruction of the Social Order[14] adapted these principles to present needs. Then,

insisting anew on the age-old doctrine of the Church concerning the individual and social character of private property, We explained clearly the right and dignity of labor, the relations of mutual aid and collaboration which should exist between those who possess capital and those who work, the salary due in strict justice to the worker for himself and for his family.

32. In this same Encyclical of Ours We have shown that the means of saving the world of today from the lamentable ruin into which a moral liberalism has plunged us, are neither the class-struggle nor terror, nor yet the autocratic abuse of State power, but rather the infusion of social justice and the sentiment of Christian love into the social-economic order. We have indicated how a sound prosperity is to be restored according to the true principles of a sane corporative system which respects the proper hierarchic structure of society; and how all the occupational groups should be fused into a harmonious unity inspired by the principle of the common good. And the genuine and chief function of public and civil authority consists precisely in the efficacious furthering of this harmony and coordination of all social forces.

33. In view of this organized common effort towards peaceful living, Catholic doctrine vindicates to the State the dignity and authority of a vigilant and provident defender of those divine and human rights on which the Sacred Scriptures and the Fathers of the Church insist so often. It is not true that all have equal rights in civil society. It is not true that there exists no lawful social hierarchy. Let it suffice to refer to the Encyclicals of Leo XIII already cited, especially to that on State powers,[15] and to the other on the Christian Constitution of States. [16] In these documents the Catholic will find the principles of reason and the Faith clearly explained, and these principles will enable him to defend himself against the errors and perils of a Communistic conception of the State. The enslavement of man despoiled of his rights, the

denial of the transcendental origin of the State and its authority, the horrible abuse of public power in the service of a collectivistic terrorism, are the very contrary of all that corresponds with natural ethics and the will of the Creator. Both man and civil society derive their origin from the Creator, Who has mutually ordained them one to the other. Hence neither can be exempted from their correlative obligations, nor deny or diminish each other's rights. The Creator Himself has regulated this mutual relationship in its fundamental lines, and it is by an unjust usurpation that Communism arrogates to itself the right to enforce, in place of the divine law based on the immutable principles of truth and charity, a partisan political program which derives from the arbitrary human will and is replete with hate.

34. In teaching this enlightening doctrine the Church has no other intention than to realize the glad tidings sung by the Angels above the cave of Bethlehem at the Redeemer's birth: "Glory to God . . . and . . . peace to men . . . ,"[17] true peace and true happiness, even here below as far as is possible, in preparation for the happiness of heaven—but to men of good will. This doctrine is equally removed from all extremes of error and all exaggerations of parties or systems which stem from error. It maintains a constant equilibrium of truth and justice, which it vindicates in theory and applies and promotes in practice, bringing into harmony the rights and duties of all parties. Thus authority is reconciled with liberty, the dignity of the individual with that of the State, the human personality of the subject with the divine delegation of the superior; and in this way a balance is struck between the due dependence and well-ordered love of a man for himself, his family and country, and his love of other families and other peoples, founded on the love of God, the Father of all, their first principle and last end. The Church does not separate a proper regard for temporal welfare from solicitude for the eternal. If she subordinates the former to the latter according to the words of her divine Founder, "Seek ye first the Kingdom of God

and His justice, and all these things shall be added unto you,"[18] she is nevertheless so far from being unconcerned with human affairs, so far from hindering civil progress and material advancement, that she actually fosters and promotes them in the most sensible and efficacious manner. Thus even in the sphere of social-economics, although the Church has never proposed a definite technical system, since this is not her field, she has nevertheless clearly outlined the guiding principles which, while susceptible of varied concrete applications according to the diversified conditions of times and places and peoples, indicate the safe way of securing the happy progress of society.

35. The wisdom and supreme utility of this doctrine are admitted by all who really understand it. With good reason outstanding statesmen have asserted that, after a study of various social systems, they have found nothing sounder than the principles expounded in the Encyclicals *Rerum Novarum* and *Quadragesimo Anno*. In non-Catholic, even in non-Christian countries, men recognize the great value to society of the social doctrine of the Church. Thus, scarcely a month ago, an eminent political figure of the Far East, a non-Christian, did not hesitate to affirm publicly that the Church, with her doctrine of peace and Christian brotherhood, is rendering a signal contribution to the difficult task of establishing and maintaining peace among the nations. Finally, We know from reliable information that flows into this Center of Christendom from all parts of the world, that the Communists themselves, where they are not utterly depraved, recognize the superiority of the social doctrine of the Church, when once explained to them, over the doctrines of their leaders and their teachers. Only those blinded by passion and hatred close their eyes to the light of truth and obstinately struggle against it.

36. But the enemies of the Church, though forced to acknowledge the wisdom of her doctrine, accuse her of having failed to act in conformity with her principles, and from this conclude to the necessity

of seeking other solutions. The utter falseness and injustice of this accusation is shown by the whole history of Christianity. To refer only to a single typical trait, it was Christianity that first affirmed the real and universal brotherhood of all men of whatever race and condition. This doctrine she proclaimed by a method, and with an amplitude and conviction, unknown to preceding centuries; and with it she potently contributed to the abolition of slavery. Not bloody revolution, but the inner force of her teaching made the proud Roman matron see in her slave a sister in Christ. It is Christianity that adores the Son of God, made Man for love of man, and become not only the "Son of a Carpenter" but Himself a "Carpenter."[19] It was Christianity that raised manual labor to its true dignity, whereas it had hitherto been so despised that even the moderate Cicero did not hesitate to sum up the general opinion of his time in words of which any modern sociologist would be ashamed: "All artisans are engaged in sordid trades, for there can be nothing ennobling about a workshop."[20]

37. Faithful to these principles, the Church has given new life to human society. Under her influence arose prodigious charitable organizations, great guilds of artisans and workingmen of every type. These guilds, ridiculed as "medieval" by the liberalism of the last century, are today claiming the admiration of our contemporaries in many countries who are endeavoring to revive them in some modern form. And when other systems hindered her work and raised obstacles to the salutary influence of the Church, she was never done warning them of their error. We need but recall with what constant firmness and energy Our Predecessor, Leo XIII, vindicated for the workingman the right to organize, which the dominant liberalism of the more powerful States relentlessly denied him. Even today the authority of this Church doctrine is greater than it seems; for the influence of ideas in the realm of facts, though invisible and not easily measured, is surely of predominant importance.

38. It may be said in all truth that the Church, like Christ, goes through the centuries doing good to all. There would be today neither Socialism nor Communism if the rulers of the nations had not scorned the teachings and maternal warnings of the Church. On the bases of liberalism and laicism they wished to build other social edifices which, powerful and imposing as they seemed at first, all too soon revealed the weakness of their foundations, and today are crumbling one after another before our eyes, as everything must crumble that is not grounded on the one corner stone which is Christ Jesus.

39. This, Venerable Brethren, is the doctrine of the Church, which alone in the social as in all other fields can offer real light and assure salvation in the face of Communistic ideology. But this doctrine must be consistently reduced to practice in every-day life, according to the admonition of St. James the Apostle: "Be ye doers of the word and not hearers only, deceiving your own selves."[21] The most urgent need of the present day is therefore the energetic and timely application of remedies which will effectively ward off the catastrophe that daily grows more threatening. We cherish the firm hope that the fanaticism with which the sons of darkness work day and night at their materialistic and atheistic propaganda will at least serve the holy purpose of stimulating the sons of light to a like and even greater zeal for the honor of the Divine Majesty.

40. What then must be done, what remedies must be employed to defend Christ and Christian civilization from this pernicious enemy? As a father in the midst of his family, We should like to speak quite intimately of those duties which the great struggle of our day imposes on all the children of the Church; and We would address Our paternal admonition even to those sons who have strayed far from her.

41. As in all the stormy periods of the history of the Church, the fundamental remedy today lies in a sincere renewal of private and public life according to the principles of the Gospel by all those who belong

to the Fold of Christ, that they may be in truth the salt of the earth to preserve human society from total corruption.

42. With heart deeply grateful to the Father of Light, from Whom descends "every best gift and every perfect gift,"[22] We see on all sides consoling signs of this spiritual renewal. We see it not only in so many singularly chosen souls who in these last years have been elevated to the sublime heights of sanctity, and in so many others who with generous hearts are making their way towards the same luminous goal, but also in the new flowering of a deep and practical piety in all classes of society even the most cultured, as We pointed out in Our recent Motu Proprio *In multis solaciis* of October 28 last, on the occasion of the reorganization of the Pontifical Academy of Sciences.[23]

43. Nevertheless We cannot deny that there is still much to be done in the way of spiritual renovation. Even in Catholic countries there are still too many who are Catholics hardly more than in name. There are too many who fulfill more or less faithfully the more essential obligations of the religion they boast of professing, but have no desire of knowing it better, of deepening their inward conviction, and still less of bringing into conformity with the external gloss the inner splendor of a right and unsullied conscience, that recognizes and performs all its duties under the eye of God. We know how much Our Divine Savior detested this empty pharisaic show, He Who wished that all should adore the Father "in spirit and in truth."[24] The Catholic who does not live really and sincerely according to the Faith he professes will not long be master of himself in these days when the winds of strife and persecution blow so fiercely, but will be swept away defenseless in this new deluge which threatens the world. And thus, while he is preparing his own ruin, he is exposing to ridicule the very name of Christian.

44. And here We wish, Venerable Brethren, to insist more particularly on two teachings of Our Lord which have a special bearing on the present condition of the human race: detachment from earthly goods

and the precept of charity. "Blessed are the poor in spirit" were the first words that fell from the lips of the Divine Master in His sermon on the mount.[25] This lesson is more than ever necessary in these days of materialism athirst for the goods and pleasures of this earth. All Christians, rich or poor, must keep their eye fixed on heaven, remembering that "we have not here a lasting city, but we seek one that is to come."[26] The rich should not place their happiness in things of earth nor spend their best efforts in the acquisition of them. Rather, considering themselves only as stewards of their earthly goods, let them be mindful of the account they must render of them to their Lord and Master, and value them as precious means that God has put into their hands for doing good; let them not fail, besides, to distribute of their abundance to the poor, according to the evangelical precept.[27] Otherwise there shall be verified of them and their riches the harsh condemnation of St. James the Apostle: "Go to now, ye rich men; weep and howl in your miseries which shall come upon you. Your riches are corrupted, and your garments are moth-eaten; your gold and silver is cankered; and the rust of them shall be for a testimony against you and shall eat your flesh like fire. You have stored up to yourselves wrath against the last days. . ."[28]

45. But the poor too, in their turn, while engaged, according to the laws of charity and justice, in acquiring the necessities of life and also in bettering their condition, should always remain "poor in spirit,"[29] and hold spiritual goods in higher esteem than earthly property and pleasures. Let them remember that the world will never be able to rid itself of misery, sorrow and tribulation, which are the portion even of those who seem most prosperous. Patience, therefore, is the need of all, that Christian patience which comforts the heart with the divine assurance of eternal happiness. "Be patient, therefore, brethren," we repeat with St. James, "until the coming of the Lord. Behold the husbandman waiteth for the precious fruit of the earth, patiently bearing until he

receive the early and the later rain. Be you therefore also patient and strengthen your hearts, for the coming of the Lord is at hand."[30] Only thus will be fulfilled the consoling promise of the Lord: "Blessed are the poor!" These words are no vain consolation, a promise as empty as those of the Communists. They are the words of life, pregnant with a sovereign reality. They are fully verified here on earth, as well as in eternity. Indeed, how many of the poor, in anticipation of the Kingdom of Heaven already proclaimed their own: "for yours is the Kingdom of Heaven,"[31] find in these words a happiness which so many of the wealthy, uneasy with their riches and ever thirsting for more, look for in vain!

46. Still more important as a remedy for the evil we are considering, or certainly more directly calculated to cure it, is the precept of charity. We have in mind that Christian charity, "patient and kind,"[32] which avoids all semblance of demeaning paternalism, and all ostentation; that charity which from the very beginning of Christianity won to Christ the poorest of the poor, the slaves. And We are grateful to all those members of charitable associations, from the conferences of St. Vincent de Paul to the recent great relief organizations, which are perseveringly practicing the spiritual and corporal works of mercy. The more the working men and the poor realize what the spirit of love animated by the virtue of Christ is doing for them, the more readily will they abandon the false persuasion that Christianity has lost its efficacy and that the Church stands on the side of the exploiters of their labor.

47. But when on the one hand We see thousands of the needy, victims of real misery for various reasons beyond their control, and on the other so many round about them who spend huge sums of money on useless things and frivolous amusement, We cannot fail to remark with sorrow not only that justice is poorly observed, but that the precept of charity also is not sufficiently appreciated, is not a vital thing in daily life. We desire therefore, Venerable Brethren, that this divine precept,

this precious mark of identification left by Christ to His true disciples, be ever more fully explained by pen and word of mouth; this precept which teaches us to see in those who suffer Christ Himself, and would have us love our brothers as Our Divine Savior has loved us, that is, even at the sacrifice of ourselves, and, if need be, of our very life. Let all then frequently meditate on those words of the final sentence, so consoling yet so terrifying, which the Supreme Judge will pronounce on the day of the Last Judgment: "Come, ye blessed of my Father . . . for I was hungry and you gave me to eat; I was thirsty and you gave me to drink . . . Amen, I say to you, as long as you did it to one of these my least brethren you did it to me."[33] And the reverse: "Depart from me, you cursed, into everlasting fire . . . for I was hungry and you gave me not to eat; I was thirsty and you gave me not to drink . . . Amen, I say to you, as long as you did it not to one of these least, neither did you do it to me."[34]

48. To be sure of eternal life, therefore, and to be able to help the poor effectively, it is imperative to return to a more moderate way of life, to renounce the joys, often sinful, which the world today holds out in such abundance; to forget self for love of the neighbor. There is a divine regenerating force in this "new precept" (as Christ called it) of Christian charity.[35] Its faithful observance will pour into the heart an inner peace which the world knows not, and will finally cure the ills which oppress humanity.

49. But charity will never be true charity unless it takes justice into constant account. The Apostle teaches that "he that loveth his neighbor hath fulfilled the law" and he gives the reason: "For, *Thou shalt not commit adultery, Thou shalt not kill, Thou shalt not steal . . .* and if there be any other commandment, it is comprised in this word: *Thou shalt love thy neighbor as thyself.*"[36] According to the Apostle, then, all the commandments, including those which are of strict justice, as those which forbid us to kill or to steal, may be reduced to the single

precept of true charity. From this it follows that a "charity" which deprives the workingman of the salary to which he has a strict title in justice, is not charity at all, but only its empty name and hollow semblance. The wage-earner is not to receive as alms what is his due in justice. And let no one attempt with trifling charitable donations to exempt himself from the great duties imposed by justice. Both justice and charity often dictate obligations touching on the same subject-matter, but under different aspects; and the very dignity of the workingman makes him justly and acutely sensitive to the duties of others in his regard.

50. Therefore We turn again in a special way to you, Christian employers and industrialists, whose problem is often so difficult for the reason that you are saddled with the heavy heritage of an unjust economic regime whose ruinous influence has been felt through many generations. We bid you be mindful of your responsibility. It is unfortunately true that the manner of acting in certain Catholic circles has done much to shake the faith of the working-classes in the religion of Jesus Christ. These groups have refused to understand that Christian charity demands the recognition of certain rights due to the workingman, which the Church has explicitly acknowledged. What is to be thought of the action of those Catholic employers who in one place succeeded in preventing the reading of Our Encyclical *Quadragesimo Anno* in their local churches? Or of those Catholic industrialists who even to this day have shown themselves hostile to a labor movement that We Ourselves recommended? Is it not deplorable that the right of private property defended by the Church should so often have been used as a weapon to defraud the workingman of his just salary and his social rights?

51. In reality, besides commutative justice, there is also social justice with its own set obligations, from which neither employers nor workingmen can escape. Now it is of the very essence of social justice to demand for each individual all that is necessary for the common good. But just

as in the living organism it is impossible to provide for the good of the whole unless each single part and each individual member is given what it needs for the exercise of its proper functions, so it is impossible to care for the social organism and the good of society as a unit unless each single part and each individual member—that is to say, each individual man in the dignity of his human personality—is supplied with all that is necessary for the exercise of his social functions. If social justice be satisfied, the result will be an intense activity in economic life as a whole, pursued in tranquillity and order. This activity will be proof of the health of the social body, just as the health of the human body is recognized in the undisturbed regularity and perfect efficiency of the whole organism.

52. But social justice cannot be said to have been satisfied as long as workingmen are denied a salary that will enable them to secure proper sustenance for themselves and for their families; as long as they are denied the opportunity of acquiring a modest fortune and forestalling the plague of universal pauperism; as long as they cannot make suitable provision through public or private insurance for old age, for periods of illness and unemployment. In a word, to repeat what has been said in Our Encyclical *Quadragesimo Anno*: "Then only will the economic and social order be soundly established and attain its ends, when it offers, to all and to each, all those goods which the wealth and resources of nature, technical science and the corporate organization of social affairs can give. These goods should be sufficient to supply all necessities and reasonable comforts, and to uplift men to that higher standard of life which, provided it be used with prudence, is not only not a hindrance but is of singular help to virtue."[37]

53. It happens all too frequently, however, under the salary system, that individual employers are helpless to ensure justice unless, with a view to its practice, they organize institutions the object of which is to prevent competition incompatible with fair treatment for the workers.

Where this is true, it is the duty of contractors and employers to support and promote such necessary organizations as normal instruments enabling them to fulfill their obligations of justice. But the laborers too must be mindful of their duty to love and deal fairly with their employers, and persuade themselves that there is no better means of safeguarding their own interests.

54. If, therefore, We consider the whole structure of economic life, as We have already pointed out in Our Encyclical *Quadragesimo Anno*, the reign of mutual collaboration between justice and charity in social-economic relations can only be achieved by a body of professional and inter professional organizations, built on solidly Christian foundations, working together to effect, under forms adapted to different places and circumstances, what has been called the Corporation.

55. To give to this social activity a greater efficacy, it is necessary to promote a wider study of social problems in the light of the doctrine of the Church and under the aegis of her constituted authority. If the manner of acting of some Catholics in the social-economic field has left much to be desired, this has often come about because they have not known and pondered sufficiently the teachings of the Sovereign Pontiffs on these questions. Therefore, it is of the utmost importance to foster in all classes of society an intensive program of social education adapted to the varying degrees of intellectual culture. It is necessary with all care and diligence to procure the widest possible diffusion of the teachings of the Church, even among the working-classes. The minds of men must be illuminated with the sure light of Catholic teaching, and their wills must be drawn to follow and apply it as the norm of right living in the conscientious fulfillment of their manifold social duties. Thus they will oppose that incoherence and discontinuity in Christian life which We have many times lamented. For there are some who, while exteriorly faithful to the practice of their religion, yet in the field of labor and industry, in the professions, trade and business,

permit a deplorable cleavage in their conscience, and live a life too little in conformity with the clear principles of justice and Christian charity. Such lives are a scandal to the weak, and to the malicious a pretext to discredit the Church.

56. In this renewal the Catholic Press can play a prominent part. Its foremost duty is to foster in various attractive ways an ever better understanding of social doctrine. It should, too, supply accurate and complete information on the activity of the enemy and the means of resistance which have been found most effective in various quarters. It should offer useful suggestions and warn against the insidious deceits with which Communists endeavor, all too successfully, to attract even men of good faith.

57. On this point We have already insisted in Our Allocution of May 12th of last year, but We believe it to be a duty of special urgency, Venerable Brethren, to call your attention to it once again. In the beginning Communism showed itself for what it was in all its perversity; but very soon it realized that it was thus alienating the people. It has therefore changed its tactics, and strives to entice the multitudes by trickery of various forms, hiding its real designs behind ideas that in themselves are good and attractive. Thus, aware of the universal desire for peace, the leaders of Communism pretend to be the most zealous promoters and propagandists in the movement for world amity. Yet at the same time they stir up a class-warfare which causes rivers of blood to flow, and, realizing that their system offers no internal guarantee of peace, they have recourse to unlimited armaments. Under various names which do not suggest Communism, they establish organizations and periodicals with the sole purpose of carrying their ideas into quarters otherwise inaccessible. They try perfidiously to worm their way even into professedly Catholic and religious organizations. Again, without receding an inch from their subversive principles, they invite Catholics to collaborate with them in the realm of so-called humanitarianism and charity; and at times even make

proposals that are in perfect harmony with the Christian spirit and the doctrine of the Church. Elsewhere they carry their hypocrisy so far as to encourage the belief that Communism, in countries where faith and culture are more strongly entrenched, will assume another and much milder form. It will not interfere with the practice of religion. It will respect liberty of conscience. There are some even who refer to certain changes recently introduced into soviet legislation as a proof that Communism is about to abandon its program of war against God.

58. See to it, Venerable Brethren, that the Faithful do not allow themselves to be deceived! Communism is intrinsically wrong, and no one who would save Christian civilization may collaborate with it in any undertaking whatsoever. Those who permit themselves to be deceived into lending their aid towards the triumph of Communism in their own country, will be the first to fall victims of their error. And the greater the antiquity and grandeur of the Christian civilization in the regions where Communism successfully penetrates, so much more devastating will be the hatred displayed by the godless.

59. But "unless the Lord keep the city, he watcheth in vain that keepeth it."[38] And so, as a final and most efficacious remedy, We recommend, Venerable Brethren, that in your dioceses you use the most practical means to foster and intensify the spirit of prayer joined with Christian penance. When the Apostles asked the Savior why they had been unable to drive the evil spirit from a demoniac, Our Lord answered: "This kind is not cast out but by prayer and fasting."[39] So, too, the evil which today torments humanity can be conquered only by a world-wide crusade of prayer and penance. We ask especially the Contemplative Orders, men and women, to redouble their prayers and sacrifices to obtain from heaven efficacious aid for the Church in the present struggle. Let them implore also the powerful intercession of the Immaculate Virgin who, having crushed the head of the serpent of old, remains the sure protectress and invincible "Help of Christians."

60. To apply the remedies thus briefly indicated to the task of saving the world as We have traced it above, Jesus Christ, our Divine King, has chosen priests as the first-line ministers and messengers of His gospel. Theirs is the duty, assigned to them by a special vocation, under the direction of their Bishops and in filial obedience to the Vicar of Christ on earth, of keeping alight in the world the torch of Faith, and of filling the hearts of the Faithful with that supernatural trust which has aided the Church to fight and win so many other battles in the name of Christ: "This is the victory which overcometh the world, our Faith."[40]

61. To priests in a special way We recommend anew the oft-repeated counsel of Our Predecessor, Leo XIII, to go to the workingman. We make this advice Our own, and faithful to the teachings of Jesus Christ and His Church, We thus complete it: "Go to the workingman, especially where he is poor; and in general, go to the poor." The poor are obviously more exposed than others to the wiles of agitators who, taking advantage of their extreme need, kindle their hearts to envy of the rich and urge them to seize by force what fortune seems to have denied them unjustly. If the priest will not go to the workingman and to the poor, to warn them or to disabuse them of prejudice and false theory, they will become an easy prey for the apostles of Communism.

62. Indisputably much has been done in this direction, especially after the publication of the Encyclicals *Rerum Novarum* and *Quadragesimo Anno*. We are happy to voice Our paternal approval of the zealous pastoral activity manifested by so many Bishops and priests who have with due prudence and caution been planning and applying new methods of apostolate more adapted to modern needs. But for the solution of our present problem, all this effort is still inadequate. When our country is in danger, everything not strictly necessary, everything not bearing directly on the urgent matter of unified defense, takes second place. So we must act in today's crisis. Every other enterprise, however attractive and helpful,

must yield before the vital need of protecting the very foundation of the Faith and of Christian civilization. Let our parish priest, therefore, while providing of course for the normal needs of the Faithful, dedicate the better part of their endeavors and their zeal to winning back the laboring masses to Christ and to His Church. Let them work to infuse the Christian spirit into quarters where it is least at home. The willing response of the masses, and results far exceeding their expectations, will not fail to reward them for their strenuous pioneer labor. This has been and continues to be our experience in Rome and in other capitals, where zealous parish communities are being formed as new churches are built in the suburban districts, and real miracles are being worked in the conversion of people whose hostility to religion has been due solely to the fact that they did not know it.

63. But the most efficacious means of apostolate among the poor and lowly is the priest's example, the practice of all those sacerdotal virtues which We have described in Our Encyclical *Ad Catholici Sacerdotii*.[41] Especially needful, however, for the present situation is the shining example of a life which is humble, poor and disinterested, in imitation of a Divine Master Who could say to the world with divine simplicity: "The foxes have holes and the birds of the air nests, but the Son of Man hath not where to lay His head."[42] A priest who is really poor and disinterested in the Gospel sense may work among his flock marvels recalling a Saint Vincent de Paul, a Cure of Ars, a Cottolengo, a Don Bosco and so many others; while an avaricious and selfish priest, as We have noted in the above mentioned Encyclical, even though he should not plunge with Judas to the abyss of treason, will never be more than empty "sounding brass" and useless "tinkling cymbal."[43] Too often, indeed, he will be a hindrance rather than an instrument of grace in the midst of his people. Furthermore, where a secular priest or religious is obliged by his office to administer temporal property, let him remember that he is not only to observe scrupulously all that charity

and justice prescribe, but that he has a special obligation to conduct himself in very truth as a father of the poor.

64. After this appeal to the clergy, We extend Our paternal invitation to Our beloved sons among the laity who are doing battle in the ranks of Catholic Action. On another occasion[44] We have called this movement so dear to Our heart "a particularly providential assistance" in the work of the Church during these troublous times. Catholic Action is in effect a *social* apostolate also, inasmuch as its object is to spread the Kingdom of Jesus Christ not only among individuals, but also in families and in society. It must, therefore, make it a chief aim to train its members with special care and to prepare them to fight the battles of the Lord. This task of formation, now more urgent and indispensable than ever, which must always precede direct action in the field, will assuredly be served by study-circles, conferences, lecture-courses and the various other activities undertaken with a view to making known the Christian solution of the social problem.

65. The militant leaders of Catholic Action thus properly prepared and armed, will be the first and immediate apostles of their fellow workmen. They will be an invaluable aid to the priest in carrying the torch of truth, and in relieving grave spiritual and material suffering, in many sectors where inveterate anti-clerical prejudice or deplorable religious indifference has proved a constant obstacle to the pastoral activity of God's ministers. In this way they will collaborate, under the direction of especially qualified priests, in that work of spiritual aid to the laboring classes on which We set so much store, because it is the means best calculated to save these, Our beloved children, from the snares of Communism.

66. In addition to this individual apostolate which, however useful and efficacious, often goes unheralded, Catholic Action must organize propaganda on a large scale to disseminate knowledge of the fundamental principles on which, according to the Pontifical documents, a Christian Social Order must build.

67. Ranged with Catholic Action are the groups which We have been happy to call its auxiliary forces. With paternal affection We exhort these valuable organizations also to dedicate themselves to the great mission of which We have been treating, a cause which today transcends all others in vital importance.

68. We are thinking likewise of those associations of workmen, farmers, technicians, doctors, employers, students and others of like character, groups of men and women who live in the same cultural atmosphere and share the same way of life. Precisely these groups and organizations are destined to introduce into society that order which We have envisaged in Our Encyclical *Quadragesimo Anno*, and thus to spread in the vast and various fields of culture and labor the recognition of the Kingdom of Christ.

69. Even where the State, because of changed social and economic conditions, has felt obliged to intervene directly in order to aid and regulate such organizations by special legislative enactments, supposing always the necessary respect for liberty and private initiative, Catholic Action may not urge the circumstance as an excuse for abandoning the field. Its members should contribute prudently and intelligently to the study of the problems of the hour in the light of Catholic doctrine. They should loyally and generously participate in the formation of the new institutions, bringing to them the Christian spirit which is the basic principle of order wherever men work together in fraternal harmony.

70. Here We should like to address a particularly affectionate word to Our Catholic workingmen, young and old. They have been given, perhaps as a reward for their often heroic fidelity in these trying days, a noble and an arduous mission. Under the guidance of their Bishops and priests, they are to bring back to the Church and to God those immense multitudes of their brother-workmen who, because they were not understood or treated with the respect to which they were entitled, in bitterness have strayed far from God. Let Catholic workingmen

show these their wandering brethren by word and example that the Church is a tender Mother to all those who labor and suffer, and that she has never failed, and never will fail, in her sacred maternal duty of protecting her children. If this mission, which must be fulfilled in mines, in factories, in shops, wherever they may be laboring, should at times require great sacrifices, Our workmen will remember that the Savior of the world has given them an example not only of toil but of self immolation.

71. To all Our children, finally, of every social rank and every nation, to every religious and lay organization in the Church, We make another and more urgent appeal for union. Many times Our paternal heart has been saddened by the divergencies—often idle in their causes, always tragic in their consequences—which array in opposing camps the sons of the same Mother Church. Thus it is that the radicals, who are not so very numerous, profiting by this discord are able to make it more acute, and end by pitting Catholics one against the other. In view of the events of the past few months, Our warning must seem superfluous. We repeat it nevertheless once more, for those who have not understood, or perhaps do not desire to understand. Those who make a practice of spreading dissension among Catholics assume a terrible responsibility before God and the Church.

72. But in this battle joined by the powers of darkness against the very idea of Divinity, it is Our fond hope that, besides the host which glories in the name of Christ, all those—and they comprise the overwhelming majority of mankind—who still believe in God and pay Him homage may take a decisive part. We therefore renew the invitation extended to them five years ago in Our Encyclical *Caritate Christi*, invoking their loyal and hearty collaboration "in order to ward off from mankind the great danger that threatens all alike." Since, as We then said, "belief in God is the unshakable foundation of all social order and of all responsibility on earth, it follows that all those who do not

want anarchy and terrorism ought to take energetic steps to prevent
the enemies of religion from attaining the goal they have so brazenly
proclaimed to the world."[45]

73. Such is the positive task, embracing at once theory and practice,
which the Church undertakes in virtue of the mission, confided to her
by Christ, of constructing a Christian society, and, in our own times,
of resisting unto victory the attacks of Communism. It is the duty of
the Christian State to concur actively in this spiritual enterprise of the
Church, aiding her with the means at its command, which although
they be external devices, have nonetheless for their prime object the
good of souls.

74. This means that all diligence should be exercised by States
to prevent within their territories the ravages of an anti-God campaign which shakes society to its very foundations. For there can be
no authority on earth unless the authority of the Divine Majesty be
recognized; no oath will bind which is not sworn in the Name of the
Living God. We repeat what We have said with frequent insistence in
the past, especially in Our Encyclical *Caritate Christi*: "How can any
contract be maintained, and what value can any treaty have, in which
every guarantee of conscience is lacking? And how can there be talk
of guarantees of conscience when all faith in God and all fear of God
have vanished? Take away this basis, and with it all moral law falls, and
there is no remedy left to stop the gradual but inevitable destruction of
peoples, families, the State, civilization itself."[46]

75. It must likewise be the special care of the State to create those
material conditions of life without which an orderly society cannot
exist. The State must take every measure necessary to supply employ-
ment, particularly for the heads of families and for the young. To
achieve this end demanded by the pressing needs of the common welfare, the wealthy classes must be induced to assume those burdens
without which human society cannot be saved nor they themselves

remain secure. However, measures taken by the State with this end in view ought to be of such a nature that they will really affect those who actually possess more than their share of capital resources, and who continue to accumulate them to the grievous detriment of others.

76. The State itself, mindful of its responsibility before God and society, should be a model of prudence and sobriety in the administration of the commonwealth. Today more than ever the acute world crisis demands that those who dispose of immense funds, built up on the sweat and toil of millions, keep constantly and singly in mind the common good. State functionaries and all employees are obliged in conscience to perform their duties faithfully and unselfishly, imitating the brilliant example of distinguished men of the past and of our own day, who with unremitting labor sacrificed their all for the good of their country. In international trade-relations let all means be sedulously employed for the removal of those artificial barriers to economic life which are the effects of distrust and hatred. All must remember that the peoples of the earth form but one family in God.

77. At the same time the State must allow the Church full liberty to fulfill her divine and spiritual mission, and this in itself will be an effectual contribution to the rescue of nations from the dread torment of the present hour. Everywhere today there is an anxious appeal to moral and spiritual forces; and rightly so, for the evil we must combat is at its origin primarily an evil of the spiritual order. From this polluted source the monstrous emanations of the communistic system flow with satanic logic. Now, the Catholic Church is undoubtedly preeminent among the moral and religious forces of today. Therefore the very good of humanity demands that her work be allowed to proceed unhindered.

78. Those who act otherwise, and at the same time fondly pretend to attain their objective with purely political or economic means, are in the grip of a dangerous error. When religion is banished from the

school, from education and from public life, when the representatives of Christianity and its sacred rites are held up to ridicule, are we not really fostering the materialism which is the fertile soil of Communism? Neither force, however well organized it be, nor earthly ideals however lofty or noble, can control a movement whose roots lie in the excessive esteem for the goods of this world.

79. We trust that those rulers of nations, who are at all aware of the extreme danger threatening every people today, may be more and more convinced of their supreme duty not to hinder the Church in the fulfillment of her mission. This is the more imperative since, while this mission has in view man's happiness in heaven, it cannot but promote his true felicity in time.

80. We cannot conclude this Encyclical Letter without addressing some words to those of Our children who are more or less tainted with the Communist plague. We earnestly exhort them to hear the voice of their loving Father. We pray the Lord to enlighten them that they may abandon the slippery path which will precipitate one and all to ruin and catastrophe, and that they recognize that Jesus Christ, Our Lord, is their only Savior: "For there is no other name under heaven given to man, whereby we must be saved."[47]

81. To hasten the advent of that "peace of Christ in the kingdom of Christ"[48] so ardently desired by all, We place the vast campaign of the Church against world Communism under the standard of St. Joseph, her mighty Protector. He belongs to the working-class, and he bore the burdens of poverty for himself and the Holy Family, whose tender and vigilant head he was. To him was entrusted the Divine Child when Herod loosed his assassins against Him. In a life of faithful performance of everyday duties, he left an example for all those who must gain their bread by the toil of their hands. He won for himself the title of "The Just," serving thus as a living model of that Christian justice which should reign in social life.

82. With eyes lifted on high, our Faith sees the new heavens and the new earth described by Our first Predecessor, St. Peter.[49] While the promises of the false prophets of this earth melt away in blood and tears, the great apocalyptic prophecy of the Redeemer shines forth in heavenly splendor: "Behold, I make all things new."[50] Venerable Brethren, nothing remains but to raise Our paternal hands to call down upon you, upon your clergy and people, upon the whole Catholic family, the Apostolic Benediction.

Given at Rome, at St. Peter's, on the feast of St. Joseph, patron of the universal Church, on the 19th of March, 1937, the 16th year of our Pontificate.

PIUS XI

Acknowledgments

Thank you to my husband, Dan, and to my daughter, for your love, patience, generosity, support, forgiveness, prayer, and the time you gave me to write this book.

Thank you to my mom and dad, Steve and Kathy, for giving me and my sisters and brother shelter from the evil of the world while you raised us to know and love God and country.

Thank you to my mom, Kathy, and to my in-laws, Tom and Jennifer, for dedicating so many hours to playing with your granddaughter so I could write this book.

Thank you to Chad Abbott and my whole team at Soundfront for building a platform to reach millions of people with this message on my show every day.

A special thanks to Jack McPherrin for the critical eye and spectacular suggestions.

And thank you to Regnery for the privilege of writing this book. Thank you to Tom Spence for supporting me, and to Harry Crocker and his team for making this book better.

If you enjoyed it, visit www.lizwheeler.com and share your thoughts with me.

Notes

Introduction: The Threat We're Facing

1. "Tennessee Governor Signs Laws Banning Gender-Affirming Care for Minors and Restricting Drag Shows," CBS News, March 2, 2023, https://www.cbsnews.com/news/tennessee-ban-gender-affirming-care-trans-youth-drag-shows/.

2. Mandalit del Barco, "Some Lawmakers Hope to Crack Down on Drag Shows Watched by Children," NPR, June 16, 2022, https://www.npr.org/2022/06/16/1105544325/drag-shows-children.

3. Lauren Forristal, "Disney+ Reports Its First Subscriber Loss of 2.4M Subscribers, Plans to Lay Off 7K Employees," TechCrunch+, February 8, 2023, https://techcrunch.com/2023/02/08/disney-q1-2023-earnings/.

4. Sharon Bernstein, "Florida Bill Would Ban Gender Studies Majors, Diversity Programs at Universities," Reuters, February 24, 2023, https://www.reuters.com/world/us/florida-bill-would-ban-gender-studies-majors-diversity-programs-universities-2023-02-25/.

5. *Dobbs v. Jackson Women's Health Organization*, 142 S. Ct. 2228 (2022).

6. The White House, "FACT SHEET: Biden-Harris Administration Advances Equality and Visibility for Transgender Americans," news release, March 31, 2022, https://www.whitehouse.gov/briefing-room/statements-releases/2022/03/31/fact-sheet-biden-harris-administration-advances-equality-and-visibility-for-transgender-americans/.

7. Herb Scribner, "Republican Mitt Romney Calls Biden a 'Genuinely Good Man,'" Axios, July 4, 2022, https://www.axios.com/2022/07/04/mitt-romney-biden-trump-atlantic.

8. PBS NewsHour, "Watch Mitt Romney's Full Speech: 'Trump Is a Phony, a Fraud,'" YouTube, March 3, 2016, https://www.youtube.com/watch?v=2iefXdC794I.

9. David French, "Free Speech for Me but Not for Thee," *The Atlantic*, April 11, 2022, https://www.theatlantic.com/ideas/archive/2022/04/republican-dont-say-gay-bill-florida/629516/.

10. Sun Tzu, *The Art of War*, trans. Lionel Giles (London: Luzac & Co., 1910)

Chapter 1: The New Marxists

1. Kar Marx and Friedrich Engels, *Manifesto of the Communist Party*, trans. Samuel Moore (1848; Marx/Engels Internet Archive, 2000), chapter 2, https://www.marxists.org/archive/marx/works/1848/communist-manifesto/ch02.htm.

2. Emily Brooks, "Pete Buttigieg's Father Was a Marxist Professor Who Lauded the Communist Manifesto," *Washington Examiner*, April 2, 2019, https://www.washingtonexaminer.com/news/pete-buttigiegs-father-was-a-marxist-professor-who-lauded-the-communist-manifesto.

3. Demetrio Yocum, "Journal Italian Culture Dedicates Special Issue to Joseph A. Buttigieg," University of Notre Dame: Center for Italian Studies, August 2, 2022, https://italianstudies.nd.edu/news-events/news/journal-italian-culture-dedicates-special-issue-to-joseph-a-buttigieg/.

4. Ellipsis Kiska's. Roger Kiska, "Antonio Gramsci's Long March through History," *Religion & Liberty* 29, no. 3 (2019), https://www.acton.org/religion-liberty/volume-29-number-3/antonio-gramscis-long-march-through-history.

5. Ibid.

6. Mike Gonzalez, "Marxism Underpins Black Lives Matter Agenda," The Heritage Foundation, September 8, 2021, https://www.heritage.org/progressivism/commentary/marxism-underpins-black-lives-matter-agenda.

7. Marx and Engels, *Manifesto of the Communist Party*, chapter 2.

8. Friedrich Engels, *The Origin of the Family, Private Property and the State* (New York: Verso Books, 2021).

9. David T. McLellan et al., "Karl Marx: German Philosopher," *Encyclopedia Britannica*, March 10, 2023, https://www.britannica.com/biography/Karl-Marx.

10. James von Geldern, "Conflict with the Church," Seventeen Moments in Soviet History, n.d., https://soviethistory.msu.edu/1917-2/conflict-with-the-church/.

11. Fulton J. Sheen, *Communism and the Conscience of the West* (Indianapolis: Bobbs-Merrill, 1948).

12. Vladimir Lenin, "The Attitude of the Workers' Party to Religion," *Proletary*, no. 45, May 13, 1909, https://www.marxists.org/archive/lenin/works/1909/may/13.htm.

13. Jennifer Eremeeva, "'Godless Utopia: The Anti-Religious Campaign in Russia,'" *Moscow Times*, October 12, 2019, https://www.themoscowtimes .com/2019/10/12/godless-utopia-the-anti-religious-campaign-in-russia -a67699.

14. "Communist Reign of Terror Killed 200,000 Clergymen," *Orlando Sentinel*, December 2, 1995, https://www.orlandosentinel.com/1995/12/02/communist -reign-of-terror-killed-200000-clergymen/.

15. "Decree on Press," November 9, 1917, http://www.hist.msu.ru/ER/Etext /DEKRET/press.htm.

16. G. K. Chesterton, *What I Saw in America* (London: Hodder and Stoughton, 1922), 12.

17. Ryan Foley, "Over a Quarter of College and High School Students 'Never' Attend Church, New Poll Finds," The Christian Post, April 15, 2021, https:// www.christianpost.com/news/over-one-quarter-of-young-americans-never -attend-church-poll.html.

18. Jeffrey M. Jones, "U.S. Church Membership Falls below Majority for First Time," Gallup, March 9, 2021, https://news.gallup.com/poll/341963/church -membership-falls-below-majority-first-time.aspx.

19. Jennifer Graham, "Perspective: We're Watching 'Post-Christian America' Unfold in Real Time," *Deseret News*, March 21, 2022, https://www.deseret .com/2022/3/21/22989309/perspective-our-new-poll-shows-were-watching -post-christian-america-unfold-in-real-time-faith-church.

20. Pius XI, *Quadragesimo anno* (Rome: Vatican, 1931), https://www.vatican .va/content/pius-xi/en/encyclicals/documents/hf_p-xi_enc_19310515 _quadragesimo-anno.html.

21. Ion Mihai Pacepa and Ronald J. Rychlak, *Disinformation: Former Spy Chief Reveals Secret Strategies for Undermining Freedom, Attacking Religion, and Promoting Terrorism* (Independently published, 2013).

22. Ion Mihai Pacepa, "Moscow's Assault on the Vatican," *National Review*, January 25, 2007, https://www.nationalreview.com/2007/01/moscows -assault-vatican-ion-mihai-pacepa/.

23. Ibid.

24. Iben Thranholm, "Catholic Abuse Crisis Is Likely No Accident, but a Strategy to 'Destroy Church from Within,'" *Corrispondenza Romana*, September 19, 2018, https://www.corrispondenzaromana.it/international- news/catholic-abuse-crisis-is-likely-no-accident-but-a-strategy-to-destroy- church-from-within/.

25. Kevin Symonds, "Rethinking Bella Dodd and Infiltration of the Catholic Priesthood," *Homiletic & Pastoral Review*, December 24, 2021, https:// www.hprweb.com/2021/12/rethinking-bella-dodd-and-infiltration-of-the -catholic-priesthood/.

26. Thranholm, "Catholic Abuse Crisis."

27. Brackets and ellipsis Thranholm's. Ibid.

28. Symonds, "Rethinking Bella Dodd."

29. Ellipses Martin's. David Martin, "The Communist Infiltration of the Catholic Church," *Daily Knight*, April 16, 2021, https://www.knightsrepublic.com /single-post/the-communist-infiltration-of-the-catholic-church.

30. Thranholm, "Catholic Abuse Crisis."

31. Charles M. Mangan, "History of Russia's Consecration to Mary," *Arlington Catholic Herald*, March 25, 2022, https://www.catholicherald.com/article /columns/history-of-russias-consecration-to-mary/.

32. Bracketed ellipses Thranholm's. Thranholm, "Catholic Abuse Crisis."

33. Pius XI, *Quadragesimo anno*.

34. Gregory A. Smith, "Just One-Third of U.S. Catholics Agree with Their Church That Eucharist Is Body, Blood of Christ," Pew Research Center, August 5, 2019, https://www.pewresearch.org/short-reads/2019/08/05/ transubstantiation-eucharist-u-s-catholics/.

35. *Catechism of the Catholic Church*, 2nd ed. (2003), part 2, section 2, chapter 1, article 3.

36. Tara Isabella Burton, "The Prosperity Gospel, Explained: Why Joel Osteen Believes That Prayer Can Make You Rich," *Vox*, September 1, 2017, https:// www.vox.com/identities/2017/9/1/15951874/prosperity-gospel-explained -why-joel-osteen-believes-prayer-can-make-you-rich-trump; "Is Hillsong a Biblically Solid Church?," GotQuestions.org, April 1, 2022, https://www .gotquestions.org/Hillsong-Church.html.

37. Dan Avery, "Evangelical Lutheran Church Elects First Transgender Bishop," NBC News, May 12, 2021, https://www.nbcnews.com/nbc-out/out-news/ evangelical-lutheran-church-elects-first-transgender-bishop-rcna902.

38. "Stances of Faiths on LGBTQ Issues: Episcopal Church," Human Rights Campaign, n.d., https://www.hrc.org/resources/stances-of-faiths-on-lgbt -issues-episcopal-church.

39. Penelope Overton, "Bishop Deeley Calls Proposal to Allow Abortions Late in Pregnancy 'Beyond Troubling,'" *Portland Press Herald*, January 19, 2023, https://www.pressherald.com/2023/01/18/bishop-deeley-calls-gov-mills -proposal-to-allow-abortions-late-in-pregnancy-extreme/.

40. Yuliya Talmazan, "Actor John Cena Apologizes to Chinese Audience after Calling Taiwan a Country," NBC News, May 26, 2021, https://www .nbcnews.com/news/world/actor-john-cena-apologizes-after-taiwan -comment-n1268526.

41. Kenneth Billingsley, "Hollywood's Missing Movies," *Reason*, June 2000, https://reason.com/2000/06/01/hollywoods-missing-movies/.

42. Ibid.

43. Ibid.

44. Ibid.

45. Ibid.

46. Mark Horowitz, "HUAC-a-Mole," *Commentary*, June 2018, https://www
.commentary.org/articles/mark-horowitz/hoac-a-mole-history/.

47. Billingsley, "Hollywood's Missing Movies."

48. Ibid.

49. David Folkenflik, "'The New York Times' Can't Shake the Cloud over a
90-Year-Old Pulitzer Prize," NPR, May 8, 2022, https://www.npr.org/2022
/05/08/1097097620/new-york-times-pulitzer-ukraine-walter-duranty.

50. Thomas G. Del Beccaro, "America's Tradition of Media Bias," *Washington
Times*, October 18, 2016, https://www.washingtontimes.com/news/2016/oct
/18/americas-tradition-of-media-bias/.

51. Ibid.

52. Bruce Thornton, "A Brief History of Media Bias," Hoover Institution, June
12, 2013, https://www.hoover.org/research/brief-history-media-bias.

53. David T. Beito, "FDR's War against the Press," *Reason*, May 2017, https://
reason.com/2017/04/05/roosevelts-war-against-the-pre/.

54. Ibid.

55. Paul Matzko, "The Sordid History of the Fairness Doctrine," Cato Institute,
January 30, 2021, https://www.cato.org/article/sordid-history-fairness
-doctrine.

56. Allum Bokhari, "Woke Reddit Bans the Word 'Groomer' as 'Hate Speech,'"
Breitbart, July 18, 2022, https://www.breitbart.com/tech/2022/07/18/woke
-reddit-bans-the-word-groomer-as-hate-speech/; Claire Goforth, "Twitter
Says It Bans Using 'Groomer' as an Anti-LGBTQ Slur—But Its Enforcement
Is Lacking (Updated)," Daily Dot, July 22, 2022, https://www.dailydot.com
/debug/twitter-ban-groomers-lgbtq-slur/.

57. Libs of TikTok (@libsoftiktok), Twitter, n.d., https://twitter.com/libsoftiktok
?ref_src=twsrc%5Egoogle%7Ctwcamp%5Eserp%7Ctwgr%5Eauthor;
Allum Bokhari, "Twitter Censors Libs of TikTok for Exposing Drag Queen
Child Grooming," Breitbart, June 9, 2022, https://www.breitbart.com/tech
/2022/06/09/twitter-censors-libs-of-tiktok-for-exposing-drag-queen-child
-grooming/.

58. Lindsay Kornick, "WaPo Blames Libs of Tiktok for Exposing Hospital
Providing 'Erroneous Information' on Child Hysterectomies," Fox News,
August 28, 2022, https://www.foxnews.com/media/wapo-blames-libs-tiktok
-exposing-hospital-providing-erroneous-information-child-hysterectomies.

59. Bobby Burack, "YouTube Now Allows Users to Say Masks Didn't Stop COVID Spread," OutKick, August 24, 2022, https://www.outkick.com/youtube-now-allows-users-to-say-masks-didnt-stop-covid-spread/.

60. Jingyi Xiao et al., "Nonpharmaceutical Measures for Pandemic Influenza in Nonhealthcare Settings—Personal Protective and Environmental Measures Centers for Disease Control and Prevention," *Policy Review* 26, no. 5 (2020): 967–75, https://wwwnc.cdc.gov/eid/article/26/5/19-0994_article ; Darragh Roche, "Fauci Said Masks 'Not Really Effective in Keeping Out Virus,' Email Reveals," *Newsweek*, June 2, 2021, https://www.newsweek.com/fauci-said-masks-not-really-effective-keeping-out-virus-email-reveals-1596703.

61. "COVID-19 Medical Misinformation Policy," YouTube Help, 2023, https://support.google.com/youtube/answer/9891785?hl=en.

62. Elise Stefanik (@EliseStefanik), "President Trump's lawsuit against Big Tech . . . ," Twitter, July 16, 2021, 3:36 p.m., https://twitter.com/EliseStefanik/status/1416119590166409221.

63. Alex Berenson (@AlexBerenson), "My first #TwitterFiles report . . ." (thread), Twitter, January 9, 2023, 2:21 p.m., https://twitter.com/AlexBerenson/status/1612529981841629207; Alex Berenson, "From the Twitter Files: Pfizer Board Member Scott Gottlieb Secretly Pressed Twitter to Hide Posts Challenging His Company's Massively Profitable Covid Jabs," Unreported Truths (Substack), January 9, 2023, https://alexberenson.substack.com/p/from-the-twitter-files-pfizer-board.

64. Michael Shellenberger (@shellenberger), "In Twitter Files #6, we saw the FBI relentlessly seek to exercise influence over Twitter . . ." (thread), Twitter, December 19, 2022, 11:11 a.m., https://twitter.com/shellenberger/status/1604872112795045888; Victor Nava, "Ex-CIA Moscow Station Chief Reveals Why He Refused to Sign Hunter Biden's Laptop 'Disinfo' Letter," *New York Post*, April 28, 2023, https://nypost.com/2023/04/28/former-cia-moscow-station-chief-reveals-why-he-refused-to-sign-hunter-biden-laptop-letter/.

65. Clint Cooper, "Cooper: One in Six Biden Voters Would Have Changed Their Minds If They Had Known the Full Story," *Chattanooga Times Free Press*, November 26, 2020, https://www.timesfreepress.com/news/2020/nov/26/cooper-biden-voters/.

66. Jamie Dettmer, "What Russia's Schoolchildren Are Being Taught about Ukraine," *Politico*, August 31, 2022, https://www.politico.eu/article/russia-school-children-teacher-ukraine-history/.

67. Bill Wanlund, "Worth Noting, by Bill Wanlund: The Kids Are Alright," Public Diplomacy Council of America, 2023, https://publicdiplomacy.org/news_manager.php?page=27227.

68. John P. Kaminski and Jill Adair McCaughan, *A Great and Good Man: George Washington in the Eyes of His Contemporaries* (Lanham, Maryland: Rowman & Littlefield, 2007), 116n1.

69. Thomas Jefferson et al., "Report of the Commissioners Appointed to Fix the Site of the University of Virginia," in *The Founders' Constitution*, ed. Philip B. Kurland and Ralph Lerner, vol. 1 (Chicago: University of Chicago Press, 1986), https://press-pubs.uchicago.edu/founders/documents/v1ch18s33.html.

70. Kerry McDonald, "Public Schools Were Designed to Indoctrinate Immigrants," FEE Stories, October 24, 2017, https://fee.org/articles/public-schools-were-designed-to-indoctrinate-immigrants/.

71. Madeline Malisa and Michael Greibrok, "Soros District Attorneys Make Our Cities Unsafe: Are They Also Making Elections Less Secure?," Foundation for Government Accountability, November 16, 2022, https://thefga.org/research/soros-district-attorneys-make-cities-unsafe-elections-less-secure/.

72. J. D. Tuccille, "American Revolution Images Might Reveal You as a 'Violent Extremist,' Says the FBI," *Reason*, August 8, 2022, https://reason.com/2022/08/08/american-revolution-images-might-reveal-you-as-a-violent-extremist-says-the-fbi/.

73. C. J. Ciaramella, "It's (Almost) Always the Feds: How the FBI Fabricates Schemes to Entrap Would-Be Radicals," *Reason*, October 2022, https://reason.com/2022/09/04/its-almost-always-the-feds/.

74. Ben Feuerherd, "Feds ReportedlyRaid Project Veritas–Linked Apartments over Ashley Biden's Diary," *New York Post*, November 5, 2021, https://nypost.com/2021/11/05/feds-raid-project-veritas-linked-apartments-over-ashley-bidens-diary-report/.

75. Noah Manskar, "Riots Following George Floyd's Death May Cost Insurance Companies up to $2B," *New York Post*, September 16, 2020, https://nypost.com/2020/09/16/riots-following-george-floyds-death-could-cost-up-to-2b/; Jemima McEvoy, "14 Days of Protests, 19 Dead," *Forbes*, June 8, 2020, https://www.forbes.com/sites/jemimamcevoy/2020/06/08/14-days-of-protests-19-dead/?sh=29812fd94de4

76. Ben Kesslen, "Clinton Campaign, DNC Fined by FEC for Lying about Steele Dossier Payments," *New York Post*, March 30, 2022, https://nypost.com/2022/03/30/clinton-campaign-dnc-fined-by-fec-for-lying-about-steele-dossier-payments/.

Chapter 2: A Nuclear (Family) Bomb

1. "Love, Marriage, and the Baby Carriage: The Rise in Unwed Childbearing," United States Joint Economic Committee, December 11, 2017, https://www.jec.senate.gov/public/index.cfm/republicans/analysis?ID=E0C3BA6E-840A-4B5E-A5BF-B43FC0BB5331.

2. "U.S. Single Parent Households," My Safe Harbor, n.d., https://post.ca.gov /portals/0/post_docs/publications/Building%20a%20Career%20Pipeline %20Documents/safe_harbor.pdf.

3. "Robert Owen, Critique of Individualism (1825–1826)," H105, American History I, n.d., https://kdhist.sitehost.iu.edu/H105-documents-web/week11 /Owen1826.html.

4. Dan O'Donnell, "The Failed Socialist State in Midwestern American," MacIver Institute, February 26, 2020, https://www.maciverinstitute.com /2020/02/the-failed-socialist-state-in-midwestern-america/.

5. Paul Kengor, *Takedown: From Communists to Progressives, How the Left Has Sabotaged Family and Marriage* (Washington, D.C.: WND Books, 2015), 7.

6. Ibid., 7–8.

7. Christopher Turner, "Wilhelm Reich: The Man Who Invented Free Love," *The Guardian*, July 8, 2011, https://www.theguardian.com/books/2011/jul /08/wilhelm-reich-free-love-orgasmatron.

8. Italics in the original. Ibid.

9. Ibid.

10. Allessandro D'Aloia, "Marxism and Psychoanalysis—Notes on Wilhelm Reich's Life and Works," In Defense of Marxism, July 8, 2005, https://www .marxist.com/marxism-psychoanalysis-wilhelm-reich.htm.

11. Ben Wattenberg, "Betty Friedan and 'The Feminine Mystique,'" *The First Measured Century*, n.d., https://www.pbs.org/fmc/segments/progseg11.htm.

12. Betty Friedan, *The Feminine Mystique*, 50th anniversary ed. (New York: W. W. Norton & Company, 2013).

13. Betsey Stevenson and Justin Wolfers, "The Paradox of Declining Female Happiness," Yale Law, October 16, 2008, https://law.yale.edu/sites/default /files/documents/pdf/Intellectual_Life/Stevenson_Paradox DecliningFemaleHappiness_Dec08.pdf.

14. Friedan, *Feminine Mystique*.

15. David Horowitz, "Betty Friedan's Secret Communist Past," *Salon*, January 18, 1999, https://www.writing.upenn.edu/~afilreis/50s/friedan-per- horowitz.html.

16. Daniel Horowitz, "Rethinking Betty Friedan and the Feminine Mystique: Labor Union Radicalism and Feminism in Cold War America," *American Quarterly* 48, no. 1 (1996): 1–42, https://doi.org/10.1353/aq.1996.0010.

17. Ibid.

18. Ibid.

19. Ibid.
20. Ibid.
21. Ibid.
22. Betty Friedan, *It Changed My Life: Writings on the Women's Movement* (Cambridge, Massachusetts: Harvard University Press, 1998), 4.
23. MSNBC, "Second Gentleman Doug Emhoff Condemns Toxic Masculinity," YouTube, March 4, 2023, https://www.youtube.com/watch?v= 9nK9GGSrTJ4.
24. Rebecca Keegan, "Inside James Cameron's Billion-Dollar Bet on 'Avatar,'" *Hollywood Reporter*, November 30, 2022, https://www.hollywoodreporter .com/feature/james-cameron-interview-avatar-the-way-of-water-franchise -future-1235271483/.
25. *The Mask You Live In*. Directed by Jennifer Siebel Newsom, Produced by Jennifer Siebel Newsom, Jessica Anthony, and Jessica Congdon (The Representation Project, 2015).
26. American Enterprise Institute, "Do Men Need to Check Their Privilege? | FACTUAL FEMINIST," YouTube, November 18, 2015, https://www .youtube.com/watch?v=cRsYwu8uD4I.
27. Christina Hoff Sommers, "The Case against the Paycheck Fairness Act," American Enterprise Institute, May 6, 2012, https://www.aei.org/articles/the -case-against-the-paycheck-fairness-act/.
28. "Why Are Suicides So High amongst Men?," Priory, 2023, https://www .priorygroup.com/blog/why-are-suicides-so-high-amongst-men.
29. "Alcohol and Drug Abuse among for [sic] Young Adults," American Addiction Centers, November 10, 2022, https://americanaddictioncenters .org/rehab-guide/addiction-statistics/young-adults.
30. American Enterprise Institute, "Do Men Need to Check Their Privilege?"
31. Ibid.
32. Ibid.
33. Kimberlé Crenshaw, "Demarginalizing the Intersection of Race and Sex: A Black Feminist Critique of Antidiscrimination Doctrine, Feminist Theory and Antiracist Politics," *University of Chicago Legal Forum* 1989, no. 1 (1989): 139–67.
34. Ibid., 140.
35. A. Martínez, "Ideas That Make Up Critical Race Theory Have Been Around Long before It Got Its Name," NPR, September 13, 2022, https://www.npr .org/2022/09/13/1122621454/ideas-that-make-up-critical-race-theory-have -been-around-long-before-it-got-its-.

36. Mike Gonzalez and Jonathan Butcher, "Purging Whiteness To Purge Capitalism," The Heritage Foundation, May 5, 2021, https://www.heritage.org/progressivism/commentary/purging-whiteness-purge-capitalism.

37. W. Bradford Wilcox, "The Evolution of Divorce," *National Affairs*, Fall 2009, https://www.nationalaffairs.com/publications/detail/the-evolution-of-divorce.

38. Judy Parejko, "No-Fault Divorce: America's Divorce Mill," Catholic Exchange, May 18, 2009, https://catholicexchange.com/no-fault-divorce-americas-divorce-mill/.

39. Wilcox, "Evolution of Divorce."

40. "Marriage and Divorce," Centers for Disease Control and Prevention, February 23, 2023, https://www.cdc.gov/nchs/fastats/marriage-divorce.htm#print.

41. "Communism and LGBT Rights," Wikipedia, March 30, 2023, https://en.wikipedia.org/wiki/Communism_and_LGBT_rights.

42. Kengor, *Takedown*.

43. Jim Downs, "Red-Hot Gay Marriage," ed. Sam Haselby, Aeon, April 19, 2016, https://aeon.co/essays/the-radical-roots-of-gay-liberation-are-being-overlooked.

44. Alexandria Ocasio-Cortez's retweet of RuPaul's Drag Race (@RuPaulsDragRace), "The people who change what people think are artists and drag queens . . . ," Twitter, April 10, 2020, 9:51 p.m., https://twitter.com/AOC/status/1248793851671822336.

45. Downs, "Red-Hot Gay Marriage."

46. Ibid.

47. Friedrich Engels, *The Origin of the Family, Private Property and the State* (New York: Verso Books, 2021).

48. Downs, "Red-Hot Gay Marriage."

49. Ibid.

50. Ibid.

51. George Orwell, *Nineteen Eighty-Four* (New York: HarperCollins, 2013).

Chapter 3: The Race Bait

1. Zach Jewell, "Andrew Klavan Explains the Striking Similarities between Critical Theory and Porn," DailyWire+, August 19, 2022, https://www.dailywire.com/news/andrew-klavan-explains-the-striking-similarities-between-critical-theory-and-porn.

2. Ibid.

3. Ibid.

4. Ibid.

5. Liz Wheeler (@LizWheeler), "Are all white people racist? . . . ," Twitter, July 11, 2021, 1:30 p.m., https://twitter.com/Liz_Wheeler/status /1414275795279831040.

6. Anastasia Higginbotham, *Not My Idea: A Book about Whiteness (Ordinary Terrible Things)* (New York: Dottir Press, 2020); Jeff Hirsh, "D65 'Black Lives Matter' Curriculum Questioned," Evanston Now, March 17, 2021, https://evanstonnow.com/d65-black-lives-matter-curriculum-questioned/.

7. Wheeler, "Are all white people racist?"

8. Barbara Applebaum, *Being White, Being Good: White Complicity, White Moral Responsibility, and Social Justice Pedagogy* (Lanham, Maryland: Lexington Books, 2011), 16.

9. Ibid., 179.

10. Robin DiAngelo, *White Fragility: Why It's So Hard for White People to Talk about Racism* (Boston: Beacon Press, 2018), 149.

11. Christopher Eberhart, "Anti-Racist Author DOUBLES Speaking Fee as America Goes Woke," *Daily Mail*, July 2, 2021, https://www.dailymail.co .uk/news/article-9749517/An-anti-racist-author-Robin-DiAngelo-makes -728K-year-speaking-engagements.html.

12. Martin Jay, "The Creation of the Institut für Sozialforschung and Its First Frankfurt Years," in *The Dialectical Imagination. A History of the Frankfurt School and the Institute of Social Research 1923–1950* (Boston: Little, Brown and Company, 1973).

13. "Red Terror," New World Encyclopedia, December 8, 2022, https://www .newworldencyclopedia.org/entry/Red_Terror.

14. "Theses on Feuerbach," Wikipedia, March 11, 2023, https://en.wikipedia .org/wiki/Theses_on_Feuerbach.

15. Andrew Edgar, "Horkheimer, Max (1895–1973)," in The Routledge Encyclopedia of Modernism, 2016, https://www.rem.routledge.com/articles /horkheimer-max-1895-1973.

16. Ibid.

17. Herbert Marcuse, *One-Dimensional Man* (Boston: Beacon Books, 1964), chapter 10, https://www.marcuse.org/herbert/pubs/64onedim/odm10.html.

18. "Critical Legal Theory," Cornell Law School, n.d., https://www.law.cornell .edu/wex/critical_legal_theory.

19. Jonathan Butcher and Mark Gonzalez, "Critical Race Theory, the New Intolerance, and Its Grip on America," The Heritage Foundation,

December 7, 2020, https://www.heritage.org/civil-rights/report/critical-race-theory-the-new-intolerance-and-its-grip-america.

20. Mike Gonzalez, "The Long Shadow of the Identity Politics 'Constitution,'" The Heritage Foundation, December 18, 2020, https://www.heritage.org/civil-society/commentary/the-long-shadow-the-identity-politics-constitution.

21. "The Vetting: Obama Embraces Racialist Harvard Prof," Breitbart, March 7, 2012, https://www.breitbart.com/clips/2012/03/07/obama%20video%20harvard/.

22. Richard Delgado and Jean Stefancic, *Critical Race Theory: An Introduction* 4th ed. (New York: New York University Press, 2023), 4.

23. Richard Delgado and Jean Stefancic, "Living History Interview with Richard Delgado & Jean Stefancic," *Transnational Law and Contemporary Problems* 19, no. 221, (Winter 2010): 221–30, https://digitalcommons.law.seattleu.edu/cgi/viewcontent.cgi?article=1039&context=faculty.

24. Mike Gonzalez and Jonathan Butcher, "Purging Whiteness to Purge Capitalism," The Heritage Foundation, May 5, 2021, https://www.heritage.org/progressivism/commentary/purging-whiteness-purge-capitalism.

Chapter 4: Hook, Line, and Queer Theory

1. "History of Our Leather Women's Group in San Francisco," The Exiles, May 2, 2021, https://theexiles.org/history-new/.

2. "Gayle Rubin," Leatherpedia, n.d., http://www.leatherpedia.org/gayle-rubin/.

3. Gayle S. Rubin, "Thinking Sex: Notes for a Radical Theory of the Politics of Sexuality," in *Pleasure and Danger: Exploring Female Sexuality* (Boston: Routledge & Kegan Paul, 1984), 149, https://sites.middlebury.edu/sexandsociety/files/2015/01/Rubin-Thinking-Sex.pdf.

4. Ibid., 143–79.

5. Ibid., 143.

6. Ibid., 144.

7. Ibid., 146.

8. Ibid.

9. "Who We Are," NAMBLA, December 22, 2022, https://www.nambla.org/welcome.html.

10. Rubin, "Thinking Sex," 147.

11. Erin Doherty, "The Number of LGBTQ-Identifying Adults Is Soaring," Axios, February 19, 2022, https://www.axios.com/2022/02/17/lgbtq-generation-z-gallup.

12. Abigail Shrier, *Irreversible Damage: The Transgender Craze Seducing Our Daughters* (Washington, D.C.: Regnery Publishing, 2020).

13. Jenny Jarvie, "A Transgender Psychologist Has Helped Hundreds of Teens Transition. But Rising Numbers Have Her Concerned," *Los Angeles Times*, April 12, 2022, https://www.latimes.com/world-nation/story/2022-04-12/a-transgender-psychologist-reckons-with-how-to-support-a-new-generation-of-trans-teens.

14. Chrissy Clark, "Montgomery County Schools Saw 582% Increase in Reported Gender Nonconforming Students over Two Years, Data Shows," Daily Caller, October 11, 2022, https://dailycaller.com/2022/10/11/maryland-schools-spike-reported-gender-confused-trans-montgomery-county/.

15. Ibid.

16. Ibid.; Montgomery County Public Schools, "Intake Form: Supporting Student Gender Identity," Montgomery County Public Schools, October 2022, https://ww2.montgomeryschoolsmd.org/departments/forms/pdf/560-80.pdf.

17. Montgomery County Public Schools, *2019–2020 Guidelines for Student Gender Identity in Montgomery County Public Schools* (Rockville, Maryland: Department of Materials Management for the Office of Student and Family Support and Engagement, 2019), 2, https://web.archive.org/web/20211015012718/https:/www.montgomeryschoolsmd.org/uploadedFiles/students/rights/1243%2019_GenderIdentityGuidelinesForStudents_WithCOVER(1).pdf.

18. Ibid.

19. Montgomery County Public Schools, *2019–2020 Guidelines for Student Gender Identity*.

20. Clark, "Montgomery County Schools Saw 582% Increase."

21. José Díaz-Balart, "Florida Teacher Speaks about Passage of 'Don't Say Gay' Bill," MSNBC, March 29, 2022, https://www.msnbc.com/jose-diaz-balart/watch/florida-teacher-speaks-about-passage-of-don-t-say-gay-bill-136493637562.

22. Alec Schemmel, "State Education Framework Outlines Gender Identity Instruction for Kindergarteners," Fox45 News, April 7, 2022, https://foxbaltimore.com/news/local/state-education-framework-pushes-gender-identity-on-kindergarteners.

23. Ian Miller, "National Teacher's Union Provides 'Safe Space' Badges That Display Graphic Content," OutKick, September 22, 2022, https://www.outkick.com/national-teacher-union-safe-space-badges-graphic-content/.

24. James Lindsay, has discernment (@ConceptualJames), "The belief is that the innocence we encourage in children is part of the systems of power . . ." (thread), Twitter, July 9, 2020. 10:35 p.m., https://twitter.com/ConceptualJames/status/1281416777474416640.

25. Hannah Dyer, "Queer Futurity and Childhood Innocence: Beyond the Injury of Development," *Global Studies of Childhood* 7, no. 3 (2017): 292, https://journals.sagepub.com/doi/full/10.1177/2043610616671056.

26. Victor Zitta, *Georg Lukac's Marxism Alienation, Dialectics, Revolution: A Study in Utopia and Ideology* (Dordrecht, Netherlands: Springer Science+Business Media, 1964), 106.

27. Liz Wheeler, "Who Actually Controls the Democratic Party ft. James Lindsay | Ep. 179," YouTube, July 29, 2022, https://www.youtube.com/watch?v=S5dAExU_kwk.

28. Ibid.

29. Mike Gonzalez, "Marxism Underpins Black Lives Matter Agenda," The Heritage Foundation, September 8, 2021, https://www.heritage.org/progressivism/commentary/marxism-underpins-black-lives-matter-agenda.

30. The Spectator, "Candace Owens on Where the Money Donated to 'Black Lives Matter' Has Actually Gone," YouTube, November 2, 2022, https://www.youtube.com/watch?v=ceSDmcOwW14.

Chapter 5: What the Marxists Want

1. Klaus Schwab, "Now is the Time for a 'Great Reset,'" World Economic Forum, June 3, 2020, https://www.weforum.org/agenda/2020/06/now-is-the-time-for-a-great-reset/.

2. "Military Agency Records RG 226," National Archives, August 15, 2016, https://www.archives.gov/research/holocaust/finding-aid/military/rg-226-3h.html; "Norwegian Industrial Workers Museum World Heritage Site," European Route of Industrial Heritage, n.d., https://www.erih.net/i-want-to-go-there/site/norwegian-industrial-workers-museum-world-heritage-site; Johnny Vedmore, "Schwab Family Values," Unlimited Hangout, February 20, 2021, https://unlimitedhangout.com/2021/02/investigative-reports/schwab-family-values/; "Photo of Nazi Military Officer Falsely

Shared as 'World Economic Forum Founder's Father,'" AFP Fact Check, July 5, 2022, https://factcheck.afp.com/doc.afp.com.32DD2YY.

3. Tom Norton, "Fact Check: Was Davos Founder Klaus Schwab's Father Hitler's 'Confidant'?," *Newsweek*, May 26, 2022, https://www.newsweek.com/fact-check-was-davos-founder-klaus-schwabs-father-hitlers-confidant-1710381.

4. Ibid.

5. Carrolline Quigley, "Klaus Schwab Showing You His Bust of Lenin," YouTube, February 13, 2022, https://web.archive.org/web/20230323145650/https://www.youtube.com/watch?v=EeXjEQW03uY.

6. Klaus Schwab with Peter Vanham, *Stakeholder Capitalism: A Global Economy that Works for Progress, People, and Planet* (Hoboken, New Jersey: John Wiley & Sons, 2021).

7. Schwab, "Now Is the Time for a 'Great Reset.'"

8. Ibid.

9. Ibid.

10. Schwab and Vanham, *Stakeholder Capitalism*.

11. Yingzhi Yang and Brenda Goh, "Jack Ma Loses Title as China's Richest Man after Coming under Beijing's Scrutiny," Reuters, March 2, 2021, https://www.reuters.com/article/us-china-alibaba-jackma/jack-ma-loses-title-as-chinas-richest-man-after-coming-under-beijings-scrutiny-idUSKBN2AU0QL.

12. Sam Peach, "Why Did Alibaba's Jack Ma Disappear for Three Months?," BBC News, March 20, 2021, https://www.bbc.com/news/technology-56448688.

13. Kana Inagaki, Leo Lewis, Ryan McMorrow, and Tom Mitchell, "Alibaba Founder Jack Ma Living in Tokyo since China's Tech Crackdown," *Financial Times*, November 29, 2022, https://www.ft.com/content/2f7c7a10-2df3-4f1b-8d2a-eea0e0548713.

14. Drew Donnelly, "China Social Credit System Explained—What Is It & How Does It Work?," Horizons, April 6, 2023, https://nhglobalpartners.com/china-social-credit-system-explained/.

15. Ibid.; Manya Koetse, "Open Sesame: Social Credit in China as Gate to Punitive Measures and Personal Perks," Whats on Weibo, May 27, 2018, https://www.whatsonweibo.com/open-sesame-social-credit-in-china-as-gate-to-punitive-measures-and-personal-perks/; Katie Canales and Aaron Mok, "China's 'Social Credit' System Ranks Citizens and Punishes them with Throttled Internet Speeds and Flight Bans if Communist Party Deems them Untrustworthy," Insider, November 28, 2022, https://www.businessinsider

.com/china-social-credit-system-punishments-and-rewards-explained-2018
-4; Maya Wang, "China's Chilling 'Social Credit' Blacklist," Human Rights
Watch, December 12, 2017, https://www.hrw.org/news/2017/12/12/chinas
-chilling-social-credit-blacklist.

16. "Social Credit Score," Wikipedia, May 17, 2023, https://en.wikipedia.org
/wiki/Social_Credit_System.

17. Rishi Iyengar, "Shanghai Citizens May Soon Have Their Credit Scores
Lowered for Not Visiting Their Parents," *Time*, April 12, 2016, https://time
.com/4290234/china-shanghai-parents-visit-credit-score-lower/.

18. Adrian Zmudzinski, "Chinese Experts Suggest Using Blockchain Tech in
'Social Credit' System," Cointelegraph, January 22, 2020, https://
cointelegraph.com/news/chinese-experts-suggest-using-blockchain-tech-in
-social-credit-system.

19. Rosie Perper, "Chinese Dog Owners Are Being Assigned a Social Credit Score
to Keep Them in Check—and It Seems to Be Working," Insider, October 26,
2018, https://www.businessinsider.com/china-dog-owners-social
-credit-score-2018-10.

20. Zmudzinski, "Chinese Experts Suggest Using Blockchain Tech."

21. Songpinganq (@songpinganq), "It's this Chinese man's 7th time to donate
his blood to boost his social credit rating in 2022 alone. . . . ," Twitter,
April 16, 2023, 3:40 a.m., https://twitter.com/songpinganq/status
/1647505248074989568.

22. Donnelly, "China Social Credit System Explained"; Simina Mistreanu, "Life
Inside China's Social Credit Laboratory," *Foreign Policy*, April 3, 2018,
https://foreignpolicy.com/2018/04/03/life-inside-chinas-social-credit
-laboratory/; John Feng, "How China's Social Credit System Works,"
Newsweek, December 22, 2022, https://www.newsweek.com/china-social
-credit-system-works-explained-1768726.

23. Orange Wang, "China's Social Credit System Will Not Lead to Citizens
Losing Access to Public Services, Beijing Says," *South China Morning Post*,
July 19, 2019, https://www.scmp.com/economy/china-economy/article
/3019333/chinas-social-credit-system-will-not-lead-citizens-losing.

24. Vincent Brussee, "China's Social Credit System Is Actually Quite Boring,"
Foreign Policy, September 15, 2021, https://foreignpolicy.com/2021/09/15/
china-social-credit-system-authoritarian/.

25. Vincent Chow, "China's Corporate Social Credit: A Comprehensive
Compliance Enforcement System," China Law & Practice, February 23,
2019, https://www.chinalawandpractice.com/2019/09/20/chinas-corporate

-social-credit-a-comprehensive-compliance-enforcement-system/?slreturn=
20230417162710.

26. Jack McPherrin, "ESG: Primary Architects and Implementers," The
Heartland Institute, September 5, 2022, https://heartland.org/publications/
esg-primary-architects-and-implementers/.

27. Jack McPherrin, *Environmental, Social, and Governance (ESG) Scores: A
Threat to Individual Liberty, Free Markets, and the U.S. Economy*
(Arlington Heights, Illinois: The Heartland Institute, 2023), https://heartland
.org/wp-content/uploads/2023/04/2023-ESG-ReportvWeb-2.pdf.

28. Ibid.

29. Ibid., 14–16.

30. Jonathan Walter, *Measuring Stakeholder Capitalism: Towards Common
Metrics and Consistent Reporting of Sustainable Value Creation* (Geneva,
Switzerland: World Economic Forum, 2020), 8.

31. McPherrin, *Environmental, Social, and Governance (ESG) Scores*, 17.

32. McPherrin, *Environmental, Social, and Governance (ESG) Scores*.

33. Walter, *Measuring Stakeholder Capitalism*, 24.

34. "Environmental, Social, and Governance (ESG) Scores," The Heartland
Institute, 2023, https://heartland.org/esg/.

35. Riley Moore "Restricted Financial Institution List," West Virginia State
Treasury, July 28, 2022, https://wvtreasury.com/portals/wvtreasury/content
/legal/memorandum/Restricted-Financial-Institutions-List.pdf.

36. Bradford Betz, "SVB Donated $73m to Black Lives Matter Movement, Social
Justice Causes," *New York Post*, March 15, 2023, https://nypost.com/2023
/03/15/svb-donated-73m-to-black-lives-matter-movement-social-justice
-causes/; Prarthana Prakash, "Silicon Valley Bank Had No Official Chief
Risk Officer for 8 Months While the VC Market Was Spiraling," *Fortune*,
March 10, 2023, https://fortune.com/2023/03/10/silicon-valley-bank-chief
-risk-officer/

37. Vivek Ramaswamy, "SVB Doesn't Deserve a Taxpayer Bailout," *Wall Street
Journal*, March 12, 2023, https://www.wsj.com/articles/silicon-valley-bank
-doesnt-deserve-a-taxpayer-bailout-federal-reserve-fdic-risk-startups-treasury
-interest-rates-ad440fe9.

38. James P. Pinkerton, "Pinkerton: Green, Woke, and Now Broke—How SVB
Became the 2nd Biggest Bank Failure in U.S. History," Breitbart, March 11,
2023, https://www.breitbart.com/economy/2023/03/11/pinkerton-green
-woke-and-now-broke-how-svb-became-the-2nd-biggest-bank-failure-in-u-s
-history/.

39. "Stakeholder Capitalism Metrics Initiative: Over 130 Companies Implement Sustainability Reporting Metrics," World Economic Forum, January 9, 2023, https://www.weforum.org/impact/stakeholder-capitalism-reporting-metrics-davos2023/. See also, "Creating a Global Coalition," World Economic Forum, 2023, https://www.weforum.org/stakeholdercapitalism/our-community.

40. Caroline Downey, "Disney Executive Producer Admits to 'Gay Agenda,' 'Adding Queerness' Wherever She Could," *National Review*, March 29, 2022, https://www.nationalreview.com/news/disney-executive-producer-admits-to-gay-agenda-adding-queerness-wherever-she-could/.

41. "TomboyX Compression Top, Full Coverage Medium Support Top," Target.com, accessed June 7, 2023, https://www.target.com/p/tomboyx-compression-top-full-coverage-medium-support-top-black-xxx-small/-/A-88179387.

42. Kate Gibson, "These Companies Are Paying for Abortion Travel," CBS News, July 2, 2022, https://www.cbsnews.com/news/abortion-travel-companies-paying-benefits-amazon-starbucks-target/; "Environmental, Social and Governance Reports," Bank of America, 2023, https://about.bankofamerica.com/en/making-an-impact/esg-reports; "ESG Resources," Citigroup, 2022, https://www.citigroup.com/global/our-impact/environmental-sustainability/esg-resources; "ESG Reporting," Comcast, 2023, https://www.cmcsa.com/esg-reporting; "Environmental, Social and Governance (ESG) Annual Report," CVS Health, 2023, https://www.cvshealth.com/impact/esg-reports/annual-report.html; "Our Approach to Sustainability," Dick's Sporting Goods, 2023, https://investors.dicks.com/esg/default.aspx; "Sustainability and Other Reporting," Goldman Sachs, 2023, https://www.goldmansachs.com/investor-relations/corporate-governance/sustainability-reporting/; Hewlett Packard, *HP Sustainable Impact Report: 2021* (Palo Alto, California: Hewlett Packard, 2021), https://www8.hp.com/h20195/v2/GetPDF.aspx/c08228880.pdf; "Who We Are: Environmental, Social and Governance," JPMorgan Chase, 2023, https://www.jpmorganchase.com/about/governance/esg; "ESG Strategy: Thriving Together," Kroger, 2022, https://www.thekrogerco.com/esgreport/; "Lyft's 2022 Environmental, Social, and Corporate Governance Report," Lyft, October 5, 2022, https://www.lyft.com/blog/posts/lyfts-2022-esg-report; "Doing Well by Doing Good: Mastercard Corporate Sustainability Report 2021," Mastercard, 2023, https://www.mastercard.com/global/en/vision/corp-responsibility.html; "Environmental Social Governance Resources," Meta, 2022, https://investor.fb.com/esg-resources/default.aspx; "Global

Impact," PayPal, 2023, https://about.pypl.com/values-in-action/reporting
/global-impact-report/default.aspx; Proctor & Gamble, *2021 Citizenship
Report: Summary* (Cincinnati, Ohio: Proctor & Gamble, 2021), https://us
.pg.com/Citizenship_Report_2021.pdf; "FY23 Stakeholder Impact Report,"
Salesforce, 2023, https://stakeholderimpactreport.salesforce.com;
"Committed to Transparency—People, Planet, Coffee," Starbucks, 2023,
https://www.starbucks.com/responsibility/reporting-hub/; Tesla, *Impact
Report: 2021* (Austin, Texas: Tesla, 2021), https://www.tesla.com/ns_videos
/2021-tesla-impact-report.pdf; "ESG Reporting," Uber, 2023, https://www
.uber.com/us/en/community/esg/; "ESG Reporting Center," The Walt Disney
Company, 2022, https://impact.disney.com/esg-reporting/; "ESG Investors,"
Yelp, 2023, https://www.yelp-ir.com/ESG-investors/; "Sustainability Report,"
Zillow Group, 2023, https://www.zillowgroup.com/sustainability/.

43. "Bumble Pledges Net Zero Carbon Footprint by 2025," Bumble, 2023,
https://bumble.com/en-us/the-buzz/bumble-climate-pledge-net-zero-carbon
-footprint-environment; "We Are Committed to Reducing Our Impact on
the Planet," Condé Nast, 2023, https://www.condenast.com/sustainability;
"Sustainability," Estée Lauder, 2023, https://www.elcompanies.com/en/our
-commitments/sustainability; "Highlights from the IKEA Sustainability
Report FY22," IKEA, 2023, https://about.ikea.com/en/sustainability
/sustainability-report-highlights; "2022 Environmental Sustainability
Report," Microsoft, 2023, https://www.microsoft.com/en-us/corporate
-responsibility/sustainability/report.

44. Ellipsis McPherrin's. McPherrin, *Environmental, Social, and Governance
(ESG) Scores*, 11–12.

45. Ibid., 40.

46. "September 2022 Meeting," Clinton Foundation, September 19–20, 2022,
https://www.clintonfoundation.org/clinton-global-initiative-september-2022
-annual-meeting/.

47. "'Universal' Metrics to Allow ESG Performance Comparisons," Environment
Analyst UK, September 29, 2020, https://environment-analyst.com/
uk/105988/universal-metrics-to-allow-esg-performance-comparisons; Klaus
Schwab, "Why We Need the 'Davos Manifesto' for a Better Kind of
Capitalism," World Economic Forum, December 1, 2019, https://
www.weforum.org/agenda/2019/12/why-we-need-the-davos-manifesto-
for-better-kind-of-capitalism/.

48. Shaun Robinson, "St. Albans City Council Removes Controversial Equity
Committee Member," VTDigger, June 13, 2022, https://vtdigger.org/2022

/06/13/st-albans-city-council-removes-controversial-equity-committee-member/.

49. GianCarlo Canaparo and Hans A. von Spakovksy, "It's Illegal, Immoral, and Unconstitutional to Ration COVID-19 Treatments Based on Race," The Heritage Foundation, January 12, 2022, https://www.heritage.org/civil-rights/commentary/its-illegal-immoral-and-unconstitutional-ration-covid-19-treatments-based; Eugene Volokh, "Minnesota Government: 'Deprioritiz[e] Access for Patients' to COVID Drugs, Based Partly on Their Being White," *Reason*, January 3, 2022, https://reason.com/volokh/2022/01/03/minnesota-government-deprioritize-access-for-patients-to-covid-drugs-based-partly-on-their-being-white/.

50. Erick Erickson and Bill Blankschaen, *You Will Be Made to Care: The War on Faith, Family, and Your Freedom to Believe* (Washington, D.C.: Regnery Publishing, 2016).

51. New Discourses, "The Marxist Roots of DEI—Session 1: Equity | James Lindsay," YouTube, March 13, 2023, https://www.youtube.com/watch?v=xbby7yFrIxM.

Chapter 6: The Biggest Corporate Groomer of All

1. Abigail Shivers, "Margaret Sanger: Ambitious Feminist and Racist Eugenicist," University of Chicago, September 21, 2022, https://womanisrational.uchicago.edu/2022/09/21/margaret-sanger-the-duality-of-a-ambitious-feminist-and-racist-eugenicist/.

2. Margaret Sanger, *Margaret Sanger: An Autobiography* (New York: W. W. Norton & Company, 1938; Project Gutenberg, 2018), https://www.gutenberg.org/files/56610/56610-h/56610-h.htm.

3. Hayden Ludwig, "Margaret Sanger: The Birth of Birth Control," Capital Research Center, May 19, 2020, https://capitalresearch.org/article/margaret-sanger-part-1/.

4. Sanger, *Margaret Sanger.*

5. Ibid.

6. Margaret Sanger, *The Pivot of Civilization* (Project Gutenberg, 2013), chapter 4, https://www.gutenberg.org/files/1689/1689-h/1689-h.htm.

7. "Margaret Sanger," Influence Watch, 2023, https://www.influencewatch.org/person/margaret-sanger/#note-64.

8. Ibid.

9. Ibid. American Birth Control League Records, 1917–1934 (MS Am 2063), Houghton Library, Harvard University, https://id.lib.harvard.edu/ead/hou00030/catalog.

10. Planned Parenthood, *Here for a Reason: 2020–2021 Annual Report* (New York: Planned Parenthood, 2021), 27, https://www.plannedparenthood.org/uploads/filer_public/40/8f/408fc2ad-c8c2-48da-ad87-be5cc257d370/211214-ppfa-annualreport-20-21-c3-digital.pdf.

11. Susan W. Enouen, "New Research Shows Planned Parenthood Targets Minority Neighborhoods," *Life Issues* 21, no. 2 (2012), 1, 3, 6, https://www.protectingblacklife.org/pdf/PP-Targets-10-2012.pdf; "Planned Parenthood Targets Minority Neighborhoods: Map Guide," Protecting Black Life, n.d., https://protectingblacklife.org/pp_targets/index.html.

12. "Racially-Motivated Donations: Planned Parenthood Accepts Racially Motivated Donations," Live Action, 2023, https://www.liveaction.org/what-we-do/investigations/racially-motivated-donations/.

13. "Planned Parenthood Is Not a Friend to Women," PA Family, 2014, https://pafamily.org/wp-content/uploads/2014/08/Planned_Parenthood_is_NOT_a_friend_to_women.pdf.

14. Planned Parenthood, *Here for a Reason*, 28, 30.

15. Planned Parenthood of Southeastern Pennsylvania, "Welcome to Planned Parenthood!," Planned Parenthood, n.d., https://www.plannedparenthood.org/uploads/filer_public/db/88/db881467-f6e5-47a3-a6a3-2c7d3ea545e0/gac2.pdf.

16. Ellipsis in the original. "Sanger in the USSR," The Margaret Sanger Papers Project, 1992, https://sanger.hosting.nyu.edu/articles/sanger_in_ussr/.

17. Ryan Bomberger, "Planned Parenthood's Annual Report: Aborting Science, History and Humans," The Christian Post, June 1, 2017, https://www.christianpost.com/news/planned-parenthoods-annual-report-aborting-science-history-humans.html.

18. Paul Kengor, *Takedown: From Communists to Progressives, How the Left has Sabotaged Family and Marriage* (Washington, D.C.: WND Books, 2015), 48.

19. Ibid.; Paul Kengor, *Dupes: How America's Adversaries Have Manipulated Progressives for a Century* (Wilmington, Delaware: ISI Books, 2011), 54.

20. Martin Gardner, "H. G. Wells in Russia: Wells Had a Defective Vision of Lenin's Communist State," Foundation for Economic Education, May 1, 1995, https://fee.org/articles/h-g-wells-in-russia/.

21. Florida Governor's Office, "Governor Ron DeSantis Signs Historic Bill to Protect Parental Rights in Education," news release, March 28, 2022, https://flgov.com/2022/03/28/governor-ron-desantis-signs-historic-bill-to-protect-parental-rights-in-education/.

22. Cathy Young, "Florida's 'Don't Say Gay' Bill Inflames the Culture Wars," Cato Institute, March 30, 2022, https://www.cato.org/commentary/floridas-dont-say-gay-bill-inflames-culture-wars.

23. Parental Rights in Education, House Bill 1557, Florida State Legislature (passed March 28, 2022), https://www.flsenate.gov/Session/Bill/2022/1557/BillText/er/PDF.

24. "Memorandum," Public Opinion Strategies, March 25–28, 2022, https://pos.org/wp-content/uploads/2022/03/POS-National-Poll-Release-Memo.pdf.

25. "Sex Ed & the 'Don't Say Gay' Bill," Planned Parenthood Great Plains Votes," March 26, 2020, https://web.archive.org/web/20220726192956/https:/www.plannedparenthoodaction.org/planned-parenthood-great-plains-votes/blog/sex-ed-amp-the-dont-say-gay-bill.

26. "How Planned Parenthood Teaches Sex Education," Planned Parenthood, 2023, https://www.plannedparenthoodaction.org/issues/sex-education/how-planned-parenthood-teaches-sex-education.

27. Ibid.

28. "Transgender Hormone Therapy," Planned Parenthood, 2023, https://www.plannedparenthood.org/get-care/our-services/transgender-hormone-therapy.

29. "Gender Affirming Hormone Therapy with Informed Consent," Planned Parenthood League of Massachusetts, 2023, https://www.plannedparenthood.org/planned-parenthood-massachusetts/online-health-center/gender-affirming-hormone-therapy.

30. Ibid.

31. "Planned Parenthood Stands for Care," Planned Parenthood, 2023, https://www.plannedparenthood.org.

32. Americans United For Life, *Summary of Known Health-Risks of Abortion: How Abortion Harms Women and Why Concerns for Women's Health Must Be Part of Abortion-Related Policies and Media Debate* (Washington, D.C.: American's United for Life, accessed June 7, 2023), https://aul.org/wp-content/uploads/2019/01/Summary-of-Known-Health-Risks-of-Abortion.pdf.

33. Jack Turban, "The Evidence for Trans Youth Gender-Affirming Medical Care," *Psychology Today*, January 24, 2022, https://www.psychologytoday

.com/us/blog/political-minds/202201/the-evidence-trans-youth-gender
-affirming-medical-care.

34. Leor Sapir, "The Distortions in Jack Turban's Psychology Today Article on 'Gender Affirming Care,'" Reality's Last Stand (Substack), October 7, 2022, https://www.realityslaststand.com/p/the-distortions-in-jack-turbans -psychology.

35. Liz Wheeler, "Researchers LIE about Puberty Blockers ft. Leor Sapir | The Liz Wheeler Show," YouTube, November 13, 2022, https://www.youtube .com/watch?v=t5d4dVdW2rQ.

36. E. Abbruzzese, Stephen B. Levine, and Julia W. Mason, "The Myth of 'Reliable Research' in Pediatric Gender Medicine: A Critical Evaluation of the Dutch Studies—and Research That Has Followed," *Journal of Sex and Marital Therapy* (2023), https://www.tandfonline.com/doi/full/10.1080 /0092623X.2022.2150346?scroll=top&needAccess=true&role=tab&aria -labelledby=full-articl.

37. Abbruzzese, Levine, and Mason, "The Myth of 'Reliable Research' in Pediatric Gender Medicine."

38. Mia Ashton, "Marker of Puberty Blockers Funded Original Study That Led to 'Gender-Affirming Care' for Minors: Dutch Investigative Report," The Post Millennial, January 5, 2023, https://thepostmillennial.com/maker-of -puberty-blockers-funded-original-study-that-led-to-gender-affirming-care -for-minors-dutch-investigative-report?utm_campaign=64466.

39. Jay P. Greene, "Does 'Gender-Affirming Care' for Trans Kids Actually Prevent Suicide? Here's What the Data Say," The Heritage Foundation, June 15, 2022, https://www.heritage.org/gender/commentary/does-gender -affirming-care-trans-kids-actually-prevent-suicide-heres-what-the.

40. Leor Sapir, "Yes, Europe Is Restricting 'Gender-Affirming Care,'" *City Journal*, February 13, 2023, https://www.city-journal.org/article/yes-europe -is-restricting-gender-affirming-care.

41. Richard Rhodes, "Father of the Sexual Revolution," *New York Times*, November 2, 1997, https://www.nytimes.com/1997/11/02/books/father-of -the-sexual-revolution.html.

42. "Diversity of Sexual Orientation," Kinsey Institute, 2023, https:// kinseyinstitute.org/research/publications/historical-report-diversity-of-sexual -orientation.php.

43. "The Kinsey Scale," Kinsey Institute, 2023, https://kinseyinstitute.org /research/publications/kinsey-scale.php.

44. "Diversity of Sexual Orientation."

45. Alan Branch, "Alfred Kinsey: A Brief Summary and Critique," The Ethics & Religious Liberty Commission, May 21, 2014, https://erlc.com/resource-library/articles/alfred-kinsey-a-brief-summary-and-critique/.

46. Jeffery M. Jones, "U.S. LGBT Identification Steady at 7.2%," Gallup, February 22, 2023, https://news.gallup.com/poll/470708/lgbt-identification-steady.aspx.

47. "Alfred Kinsey," Bi.org, 2023, https://bi.org/en/famous/alfred-kinsey.

48. *The Kinsey Syndrome: How One Man Destroyed the Morality of America*, written and directed by Christian J. Pinto (Simi Valley, California: Good Fight Ministries, 2008).

49. Branch, "Alfred Kinsey."

50. Jinit Jain, "Death Anniversary of Alfred Kinsey: 'Father of Sexual Revolution' Who Claimed Babies Have Orgasms, Child Rape Benefits Victims," OpIndia, August 25, 2021, https://www.opindia.com/2021/08/alfred-kinsey-reports-father-of-sexual-revolution-who-said-rape-benefits-children/.

51. Alfred C. Kinsey, Wardell B. Pomeroy, and Clyde E. Martin, *Sexual Behavior in the Human Male* (Bloomington, Indiana: Indiana University Press, 1975).

52. Alfred C. Kinsey, Wardell B. Pomeroy, Clyde E. Martin, and Paul H. Gebhard, *Sexual Behavior in the Human Female* (Bloomington, Indiana: Indiana University Press, 1998), 121–22.

53. Dina Spector, "Why Kinsey's Research Remains Even More Controversial Than the 'Masters of Sex,'" Insider, October 18, 2013, https://www.businessinsider.com/why-alfred-kinsey-was-controversial-2013-10.

54. Sarah D. Goode, "Studies on Adult Sexual Contact with Children," in *Paedophiles in Society: Reflecting on Sexuality, Abuse and Hope* (London: Palgrave Macmillan, 2011).

55. Gayle S. Rubin, "Thinking Sex: Notes for a Radical Theory of the Politics of Sexuality," in *Pleasure and Danger: Exploring Female Sexuality* (Boston: Routledge & Kegan Paul, 1984), 154, https://sites.middlebury.edu/sexandsociety/files/2015/01/Rubin-Thinking-Sex.pdf.

56. "Kinsey: Teaching and Research," American Experience, 2023, https://www.pbs.org/wgbh/americanexperience/features/kinsey-teaching-and-research/.

57. Raquel M. Chanano, "Kinsey's Fraud and Its Consequences for Society," EWTN, n.d., https://www.ewtn.com/catholicism/library/kinseys-fraud-and-its-consequences-for-society-11011.

58. Kinsey Institute, 2023, https://kinseyinstitute.org.

59. "Comprehensive Sexuality Education," World Health Organization, May 18, 2023, https://www.who.int/news-room/questions-and-answers/item /comprehensive-sexuality-education.

60. "The History & Agenda behind CSE," Stop CSE, March 23, 2016, https:// www.comprehensivesexualityeducation.org/history-of-cse/.

61. SIECUS, 2023, https://siecus.org.

62. Miriam Grossman, "A Brief History of Sex Ed: How We Reached Today's Madness," Public Discourse, July 16, 2013, https://www.thepublicdiscourse .com/2013/07/10408/.

63. "Kinsey's Sexual Ideology: A Danger to Public Health," StoptheKinseyInstitute.org, n.d., https://stopthekinseyinstitute.org/more/ public-health/.

64. Grossman, "A Brief History of Sex Ed."

65. First ellipsis mine, latter two ellipses in the original. "Sexes: Attacking the Last Taboo," *Time*, April 14, 1980, https://content.time.com/time/subscriber /article/0,33009,923966-1,00.html.

66. United Nations Educational, Scientific and Cultural Organization, *International Guidelines on Sexuality Education: An Evidence Informed Approach to Effective Sex, Relationships and HIV/STI Education* (Paris: UNESCO, 2009), http://www.comprehensivesexualityeducation.org/wp -content/uploads/int_guidelines_sexuality_education_original.pdf.

Chapter 7: Education Subverted: Critical Pedagogy

1. Paulo Freire, *Pedagogy of the Oppressed*, 30th anniversary ed., trans. Myra Bergman Ramos (New York: Continuum, 2005), 34, https://envs.ucsc.edu /internships/internship-readings/freire-pedagogy-of-the-oppressed.pdf.

2. Peter McLaren, "Paulo Freire's Legacy of Hope and Struggle," *Theology, Culture & Society* 14, no. 4 (1997): 147–53, https://www.chapman.edu /education/_files/freire-legacy.pdf.

3. Freire, *Pedagogy of the Oppressed*, 111.

4. Max Horkheimer, "Traditional and Critical Theory," in *Selected Essays*, trans. Matthew J. O'Connell and others (New York: Continuum, 2002).

5. Freire, *Pedagogy of the Oppressed*, 72.

6. Ibid., 73.

7. Ibid., 48.

8. Ibid., chapter 3.

9. Freire, *Pedagogy of the Oppressed*.

10. Henry A. Giroux, *On Critical Pedagogy*, 2nd ed. (London: Bloomsbury Publishing, 2020).

11. James R. Copland, "How to Regulate Critical Race Theory in Schools: A Primer and Model Legislation," Manhattan Institute, August 26, 2021, https://manhattan.institute/article/how-to-regulate-critical-race-theory-in-schools-a-primer-and-model-legislation#notes; Isaac Gottesman, *The Critical Turn in Education: From Marxist Critique to Poststructuralist Feminism to Critical Theories of Race* (New York: Routledge, 2016), 75–76, quoted in James Lindsay, "Critical Pedagogy," New Discourses, July 7, 2020, https://newdiscourses.com/tftw-critical-pedagogy/.

12. Perpetual Baffour, "Critical Pedagogy: Teaching for Social Justice in Inner-City Classrooms," Honors Theses (Philosophy, Politics, and Economics), no. 24 (2014): 1–42, https://repository.upenn.edu/ppe_honors/24/.

13. Ibid.

14. "Fundamentals of SEL," CASEL, 2023, https://casel.org/fundamentals-of-sel/.

15. Max Eden, "The Trouble with Social Emotional Learning: Four Major Concerns regarding a Burgeoning Education Industry," American Enterprise Institute, April 6, 2022, https://docs.house.gov/meetings/AP/AP07/20220406/114597/HHRG-117-AP07-Wstate-EdenM-20220406.pdf.

16. Ibid.

17. Ibid.

18. James Lindsay, "Social-Emotional Learning (SEL): Social Justice Usage," New Discourses, September 9, 2022, https://newdiscourses.com/tftw-sel/.

19. Ibid.

20. Ibid.

21. Ed Stannard, "Comer Began Movement to Educate Whole Child in 1968," *New Haven Register*, November 26, 2018, https://www.nhregister.com/news/article/Comer-began-movement-to-educate-whole-child-in-13421830.php.

22. Lindsay, "Social-Emotional Learning (SEL)."

23. Ibid.

24. "Linda Darling-Hammond: President and CEO," Learning Policy Institute, 2023, https://learningpolicyinstitute.org/person/linda-darling-hammond.

25. Chrissy Clark, "Biden Education Lead: Chinese Communist Party Has Done 'Magical Work,'" Washington Free Beacon, December 2, 2020, https://freebeacon.com/campus/biden-education-lead-chinese-communist-party-has-done-magical-work/.

26. Ibid.

27. Ibid.

28. Hank Berrien, "Biden Education Transition Leader Praised Communist Chinese Education's 'Magical Work,'" DailyWire+, December 3, 2020, https://www.dailywire.com/news/biden-education-transition-leader-praised -communist-chinese-educations-magical-work.

29. "Our Mission," Nick Woolf, n.d., https://insidesel.com/about/.

30. Joseph A. Durlak, Celene E. Domitrovich, Roger P. Weissberg, and Thomas P. Gullotta, eds., *Handbook of Social and Emotional Learning: Research and Practice* (New York: Guilford Press, 2015),

31. Sam Dillon, "Linda Darling-Hammon," *New York Times*, December 2, 2008, https://www.nytimes.com/2008/12/02/us/politics/02web -darlinghammond.html.

32. Louis Freedberg, "Education Transition Team for Biden Administration Announced, with Linda Darling-Hammond as 'Lead,'" EdSource, November 10, 2020, https://edsource.org/updates/education-transition-team-for-biden -administration-announced-with-linda-darling-hammond-as-lead.

33. Jay Schalin, *The Politicization of University Schools of Education: The Long March through the Education Schools* (Raleigh, North Carolina: James G. Martin Center for Academic Renewal, 2019), https://www.jamesgmartin .center/wp-content/uploads/2019/02/The-Politicization-of-University -Schools-of-Education.pdf.

34. Louis Freedberg, "Linda Darling-Hammond Becomes President of California's State Board of Education," EdSource, March 15, 2019, https:// edsource.org/2019/linda-darling-hammond-sworn-in-as-new-president-of -californias-state-board-of-education/609870.

35. "Fig. 1: CASEL Board of Directors and Officers," CASEL, accessed June 6, 2023, https://casel.org/fig-1-casel-board-of-directors-and-officers/.

36. "Randi Weingarten," Influence Watch, n.d., https://www.influencewatch .org/person/randi-weingarten/.

37. Brittany Bernstein, "Teachers'-Union Head Claims CRT Is Only Taught at Colleges," *National Review*, July 6, 2021, https://www.nationalreview.com /news/teachers-union-head-claims-crt-is-only-taught-at-colleges/.

38. Madeline Will, "Teachers' Unions Vow to Defend Members in Critical Race Theory Fight," *Education Week*, July 6, 2021, https://www.edweek.org /teaching-learning/teachers-unions-vow-to-defend-members-in-critical-race -theory-fight/2021/07.

39. Hannah Grossman, "Nonprofit Partnered with AFT Provides Books with Sex Imagery, Drag Queens and Gender Ideology to K–12 Teachers," Fox

News, September 9, 2022, https://www.foxnews.com/media/org-partnered -with-aft-union-provides-books-with-sex-imagery-drag-queens-and-gender -ideology-to-k-12-teachers.

40. Chris Ayala-Kronos, *The Pronoun Book* (New York: Clarion Books, 2022).

41. Nico Medina, *Who Is RuPaul?* (New York: Penguin Workshop, 2021).

42. Mike Curato, *Flamer* (New York: Henry Holt and Company, 2020).

43. Peter Brown, *Fred Gets Dressed* (Boston: Little, Brown and Company, 2021).

44. Benjamin Alire Sáenz, *Aristotle and Dante Discover the Secrets of the Universe*, 10th anniversary ed. (New York: Simon & Schuster, 2022).

45. Theresa Thorn, *It Feels Good to Be Yourself: A Book about Gender Identity* (New York: Henry Holt and Company, 2019).

46. Jessica Herthel and Jazz Jennings, *I Am Jazz* (New York: Dial Books, 2014).

47. JR Ford and Vanessa Ford, *Calvin* (New York: G. P. Putnam's Sons Books for Young Readers, 2021).

48. Jack Schneider and Jennifer Berkshire, "Parents Claim They Have the Right to Shape Their Kids' School Curriculum. They Don't.," *Washington Post*, October 21, 2021, https://www.washingtonpost.com/outlook/parents-rights -protests-kids/2021/10/21/5cf4920a-31d4-11ec-9241-aad8e48f01ff_story .html.

49. Randi Weingarten (@rweingarten), "Great piece on parents' rights and #publicschools.," Twitter, October 25, 2021, 6:39 p.m., https://twitter.com /rweingarten/status/1452766787343355911?s=12&t=QPBp6R0a_wguEm _wBjKi3g.

50. Randi Weingarten (@rweingarten), "YEs!"@CASELorg: @AFTUnion President @rweingarten in our new report . . . ," Twitter, May 15, 2013, 1:18 p.m., https://twitter.com/rweingarten/status/334719328844910593.

51. Randi Weingarten (@rweingarten), ".@AFTunion educators know social-emotional learning is more important than ever . . . ," Twitter, November 16, 10:30 p.m., https://twitter.com/rweingarten/status/1460812651483652098.

52. Randi Weingarten (@rweingarten), "Only 15% of educators feel comfortable discussing pandemic grief . . . ," Twitter, May 31, 2022, 11:46 p.m., https:// twitter.com/rweingarten/status/1531844600058548225.

53. Randi Weingarten (@rweingarten), "We need to create more social & emotional learning and wrap services around schools . . . ," Twitter, August 18, 2022, 7:53 p.m., https://twitter.com/rweingarten/status /1560414536464797697.

54. Randi Weingarten (@rweingarten), "The importance of social emotional learning," Twitter, October 18, 2021, 3:14 p.m., https://twitter.com /rweingarten/status/1450178596589481985.

55. Randi Weingarten (@rweingarten), "I loved learning about the extensive SEL programs this school has . . . ," Twitter, May 5, 2022, 10:44 p.m., https:// twitter.com/rweingarten/status/1522406975069429760.

56. Randi Weingarten (@rweingarten), "I was blown away by the wellness center. . . . ," Twitter, January 24, 2022, 9:17 p.m., https://twitter.com/rweingarten /status/1485799009805488128.

57. Randi Weingarten (@rweingarten), "Shout out to #NTOY20 finalist @TabathaRosproy . . . ," Twitter, February 25, 2020, 2:56 p.m., https://twitter .com/rweingarten/status/1232393969851461632.

58. *American Educator* 45, no. 2 (Summer 2021), https://www.aft.org/sites /default/files/media/documents/2022/AE-summer2021-web.pdf; Lindsay, "Social-Emotional Learning (SEL)."

59. Kendall Tietz, "World's Largest Library Association Picks Self-Proclaimed Marxist as President," Daily Caller, April 22, 2022, https://dailycaller.com /2022/04/22/randi-weingarten-american-library-association-marxism/.

60. Emily Drabinski (@edrabinski), "I just cannot believe that a Marxist lesbian . . . ," Twitter, April 13, 2022, 7:11 p.m., https://web.archive.org/web /20220421161549/https://twitter.com/edrabinski/status/1514305183 429365767?ref_src=twsrc%5Etfw; Kendall Tietz, "American Library Association Picks Self-Proclaimed Marxist as President," The Daily Signal, April 22, 2022, https://www.dailysignal.com/2022/04/22/american -library-association-picks-self-proclaimed-marxist-as-president/.

61. Ibid.

62. Maia Kobabe, *Gender Queer: A Memoir* (Portland, Oregon: Oni Press, 2019).

63. Ibram X. Kendi, *Antiracist Baby* (New York: Kokila Books, 2020).

64. Christopher F. Rufo, "The Real Story behind Drag Queen Story Hour," *City Journal*, Autumn 2022, https://www.city-journal.org/article/the-real-story -behind-drag-queen-story-hour.

65. Freire, *Pedagogy of the Oppressed*, 34.

Chapter 8: Unsocialized Homeskoolers

1. Elizabeth Bartholet, "Homeschooling: Parent Rights Absolutism vs. Child Rights to Education & Protection," *Arizona Law Review* 62, no. 1 (2020): 1, https://dash.harvard.edu/handle/1/40108859.

2. Ibid., 5–6.

3. Ibid., 6.

4. Ibid.

5. See, for instance, *Pierce v. Society of Sisters*, 268 U.S. 510 (1925), https://supreme.justia.com/cases/federal/us/268/510/; *Wisconsin v. Yoder*, 406 U.S. 205 (1972), https://supreme.justia.com/cases/federal/us/406/205/; *Parham v. J.R.*, 442 U.S. 584, 602 (1979), https://supreme.justia.com/cases/federal/us/442/584/.

6. Brian D. Ray, "Academic Achievement and Demographic Traits of Homeschool Students: A Nationwide Study," Academic Leadership 8, no. 1 (Winter 2010): 1–32, https://www.nheri.org/wp-content/uploads/2018/03/Ray-2010-Academic-Achievement-and-Demographic-Traits-of-Homeschool-Students.pdf.

7. Lisa M. Treleaven, "Quantitative Insights into the Academic Outcomes of Homeschools from the Classic Learning Test," *Home School Researcher* 38, no. 1 (2022): 1–13, https://www.nheri.org/wp-content/uploads/2022/12/HSR381-Treleaven-article-only.pdf.

8. Ying Chen, Christina Hinton, and Tyler J. VanderWeele, "School Types in Adolescence and Subsequent Health and Well-Being in Young Adulthood: An Outcome-Wide Analysis," *PLOS ONE* 16, no. 11 (2021): e0258723, https://journals.plos.org/plosone/article?id=10.1371/journal.pone.0258723.

9. Michael F. Cogan, "Exploring Academic Outcomes of Homeschooled Students," *Journal of College Admission*, Summer 2010, 19–25, https://files.eric.ed.gov/fulltext/EJ893891.pdf.

10. Matt McGregor, "Homeschooling Advocacy Group Reports Significant Increase in Parents Pulling Children out of School," *Epoch Times*, November 25, 2021, https://www.theepochtimes.com/homeschooling-advocacy-group-reports-significant-increase-in-parents-pulling-children-out-of-school_4122144.html.

11. Max Eden, "Harvard vs. the Family," *City Journal*, April 24, 2020, https://www.city-journal.org/article/harvard-vs-the-family.

12. Erin O'Donnell, "The Risks of Homeschooling," *Harvard Magazine*, May–June 2020, https://www.harvardmagazine.com/2020/05/right-now-risks-homeschooling.

13. "Homeschooling Summit: Problems, Politics, and Prospects for Reform—June 18–19, 2020," Harvard Law School: Youth Advocacy & Policy Lab, 2020, https://cap.law.harvard.edu/homeschooling-summit-june-18-19-2020/.

14. The misspelled version of the graphic can be viewed via the Internet Archive's WayBack Machine: https://web.archive.org/web/20200418230937/https://www.harvardmagazine.com/2020/05/right-now-risks-homeschooling.

15. The corrected version can be viewed here: https://www.harvardmagazine.com/2020/05/right-now-risks-homeschooling.

16. Brian D. Ray, "Child Abuse of Public School, Private School, and Homeschool Students: Evidence, Philosophy, and Reason," National Home Education Research Institute, January 23, 2018, https://www.nheri.org/child-abuse-of-public-school-private-school-and-homeschool-students-evidence-philosophy-and-reason/.

17. "'House of Horrors' Parents Get 25 Years to Life in Prison as Siblings Speak Out: 'I'm Taking My Life Back,'" CBS News, April 19, 2019, https://www.cbsnews.com/news/turpin-family-sentencing-david-turpin-louise-turpin-couple-who-held-their-13-children-captive-to-be-sentenced/.

18. O'Donnell, "The Risks of Homeschooling."

19. Corey A. DeAngelis, school choice evangelist (@DeAngelisCorey), "Harvard Law School is officially hosting an anti-homeschooling conference in June. . . .," Twitter, April 20, 2020, 1:16 p.m., https://twitter.com/deangeliscorey/status/1252285110101172224?s=21.

20. Bartholet, "Homeschooling," 6.

21. *Pierce v. Society of Sisters*, 268 U.S. 510 (1925), https://supreme.justia.com/cases/federal/us/268/510/.

22. Ibid., at 535.

23. *Wisconsin v. Yoder*, 406 U.S. 205 (1972), https://supreme.justia.com/cases/federal/us/406/205/.

24. Ibid., at 406.

25. *Parham v. J.R.*, 442 U.S. 584, 602 (1979), https://supreme.justia.com/cases/federal/us/442/584/.

26. Ibid., at 603.

27. Bartholet, "Homeschooling," 57.

28. Ibid., 3–4.

29. Ibid., 4.

30. Brackets in the original. Ibid., 7.

31. O'Donnell, "Risks of Homeschooling."

32. Ibid.

33. Henry T. Edmondson III, *John Dewey & Decline of American Education: How The Patron Saint of Schools Has Corrupted Teaching & Learning* (Wilmington, Delaware: ISI Books, 2006), xiv.

34. John Dewey, *Democracy and Education* (1916; Project Gutenberg, 2015), https://www.gutenberg.org/files/852/852-h/852-h.htm.

35. Ibid.

36. "A Brief History of Public Education: School Choice in America Part II," FreedomWorks, February 13, 2013, https://www.freedomworks.org/a-brief -history-of-public-education-school-choice/.

37. Paul Kengor, *Dupes: How America's Adversaries Have Manipulated Progressives for a Century* (Wilmington, Delaware: ISI Books, 2010), 90.

38. Ibid., 98.

39. Ibid., 94.

40. Ellipsis in the original. Ibid., 95.

41. Ibid., 94.

42. Ibid., 95.

43. Lee Stough, "Social and Emotional Status of Homes Schooled Children and Conventionally Schooled Children in West Virginia" (master's thesis, University of West Virginia, 1992), https://files.eric.ed.gov/fulltext/ED353079 .pdf.

44. Brian D. Ray, "The Social and Emotional Health of Homeschooled Students in the United States: A Population-Based Comparison with Publicly Schooled Students Based on the National Survey of Children's Health, 2007," *Home School Researcher* 31, no. 1 (2015), https://www.nheri.org/home-school -researcher-the-social-and-emotional-health-of-homeschooled-students-in -the-united-states-a-population-based-comparison-with-publicly-schooled -students-based-on-the-national-survey-of-child/.

45. John Wesley Taylor V, "Self-Concept in Home-Schooling Children" (Ph.D. diss., Andrew's University, 1986), 187, https://digitalcommons.andrews.edu /cgi/viewcontent.cgi?article=1725&context=dissertations.

46. Isabel Lyman, "Homeschooling. Back to the Future?," Cato Institute, January 7, 1998, https://files.eric.ed.gov/fulltext/ED415325.pdf.

47. Dewey, *Democracy and Education*.

48. Ibid.

49. Matthew Festenstein, "Dewey's Political Philosophy," *The Stanford Encyclopedia of Philosophy* (Spring 2023 Edition), ed. Edward N. Zalta and Uri Nodelman, https://plato.stanford.edu/Archives/Win2012/entries/dewey -political/.

50. Jim Cork, "John Dewey, Karl Marx, and Democratic Socialism," *Antioch Review* 9, no. 4 (Winter 1949): 435–52, https://www.jstor.org/stable/4609377.

51. John Dewey, *Impressions of Soviet Russia and the Revolutionary World* (New York: New Republic, 1929), 106.

52. Phyllis Sullivan, "John Dewey's Philosophy of Education," *High School Journal* 49, no. 8 (1996): 391–97, https://www.jstor.org/stable/40366240.

53. Bartholet, "Homeschooling," 3.

54. Ibid., 4.

55. Ibid., 1.

56. Ibid., 46.

57. Ellipsis in the original. Ibid., 7.

Chapter 9: "The Experts"

1. Nate Hochman, "Trust the Science?," *National Review,* November 29, 2021, https://www.nationalreview.com/corner/trust-the-science/.

2. Robert B. Carlisle, "The Birth of Technocracy: Science, Society, and Saint-Simonians," *Journal of the History of Ideas* 35, no. 3 (1974): 445–64, https://www.jstor.org/stable/2708793.

3. "Bogdanov, Technocracy and Socialism," *Socialist Standard*, April 2007, https://web.archive.org/web/20110927014144/http:/www.worldsocialism.org/spgb/apr07/page10.html.

4. Ibid.

5. "Technocrat," Scholarly Community Encyclopedia, October 17, 2022, https://encyclopedia.pub/entry/29581.

6. "The Birth of the Technical Alliance," Technocracy Inc., March 31, 2014, https://www.technocracyinc.org/the-birth-of-the-technical-alliance/; "Howard Scott," Scholarly Community Encyclopedia, December 19, 2022, https://encyclopedia.pub/entry/38635.

7. "Howard Scott."

8. "What Is Technocracy?," *The Technocrat* 3, no. 4 (1937), 3, https://archive.org/details/TheTechnocrat-September1937/page/n1/mode/2up.

9. "Police Hold Technocrat Haldeman," *The Leader-Post*, October 8, 1940, https://www.newspapers.com/article/101818960/police-hold-technocrat-haldeman/; John Thornhill, "The March of the Technocrats," *Financial Times*, February 19, 2018, https://www.ft.com/content/df695f10-154d-11e8-9376-4a6390addb44.

10. "Our History," The New School for Social Research, accessed June 7, 2023, https://www.newschool.edu/nssr/history/; Edwin Layton, "Veblen and the Engineers," *American Quarterly* 14, no. 1 (Spring 1962): 66, https://www.jstor.org/stable/2710227?read-now=1&seq=3#page_scan_tab_contents.

11. Layton, "Veblen and the Engineers," 64–72.
12. "The Bill of Rights: A Transcription," National Archives, April 21, 2023, https://www.archives.gov/founding-docs/bill-of-rights-transcript.
13. "The Constitution of the United States: A Transcription," National Archives, February 3, 2023, https://www.archives.gov/founding-docs/constitution-transcript.
14. "The Progressive Era," Bill of Rights Institute, 2023, https://billofrightsinstitute.org/essays/the-progressive-era.
15. Randolph J. May, "Woodrow Wilson's Case against the Constitution," *Washington Times*, May 30, 2018, https://www.washingtontimes.com/news/2018/may/30/woodrow-wilsons-case-against-the-constitution/.
16. Ronald J. Pestritto, "Why the Early Progressives Rejected American Founding Principles," RealClearPublicAffairs, June 8, 2021, https://www.realclearpublicaffairs.com/articles/2021/06/08/why_the_early_progressives_rejected_american_founding_principles_779946.html.
17. "Artl. S1.5.3 Origin of Intelligible Principle Standard," Constitution Annotated, n.d., https://constitution.congress.gov/browse/essay/artI-S1-5-3/ALDE_00001317/%5B'fourteenth',%20'amendment',%20'section',%20'3'%5D.
18. NEA (@NEAToday), "Educators love their students and know better than anyone what they need to learn and to thrive," Twitter, November 12, 2022, 7:32 p.m., https://twitter.com/NEAToday/status/1591587398109929473?lang=en.
19. "Terry McAulliffe's War on Parents" (editorial), *National Review*, October 1, 2021, https://www.nationalreview.com/2021/10/terry-mcauliffes-war-on-parents/.
20. American Academy of Pediatrics, "AAP Policy Statement Urges Support and Care of Transgender and Gender-Diverse Children and Adolescents," news release, September 17, 2018, https://www.aap.org/en/news-room/news-releases/aap/2018/aap-policy-statement-urges-support-and-care-of-transgender-and-gender-diverse-children-and-adolescents/; "In Support of a Rigorous Systematic Review of Evidence and Policy Update for Management of Pediatric Gender Dysphoria," American Academy of Pediatrics, March 31, 2022, https://genspect.org/wp-content/uploads/AAP_Resolution_27_2022.pdf; "Cosleeping and Breastfeeding: The Perfect Combination," (editorial), Mothering, March 17, 2017, https://www.mothering.com/threads/cosleeping-and-breastfeeding-the-perfect-combination.1621219/; Diana Divecha, "Safe Cosleeping Is Better for Babies'

Development Than Sleep Training," Developmental Science, March 31, 2015, https://www.developmentalscience.com/blog/2015/3/31/safe-cosleeping-is-better-for-babies-development; Helen Ball, "Bed-Sharing and Co-Sleeping: Research Overview," Evolutionary Parenting, n.d., https://evolutionaryparenting.com/bed-sharing-and-co-sleeping-research-overview/; "Safe Cosleeping Guidelines: Guidelines to Sleeping Safe with Infants," University of Notre Dame Mother-Baby Behavioral Sleep Laboratory, 2023, https://cosleeping.nd.edu/safe-co-sleeping-guidelines/; "Co-Sleeping," Parent-Infant Research Institute & Infant Clinic, January–March 2008, https://www.piri.org.au/wp-content/uploads/2015/03/newsletterjan-mar08.pdf.

21. "National Vaccine Injury Compensation Program," Health Resources and Services Administration, accessed June 7, 2023, https://www.hrsa.gov/vaccine-compensation.

22. Rob Polansky, Susan Raff, and Evan Sobol, "Bill Proposes Allowing 12-Year-Olds to Get Vaccines without Parental Consent," WFSB 3, January 17, 2023, https://www.wfsb.com/2023/01/17/bill-proposes-allowing-12-year-olds-get-vaccines-without-parental-consent/.

23. Luke Rosiak, "Virginia Dems Introduce Bill Allowing Minors to Consent to Gender Transition, Hide Records from Parents," DailyWire+, January 16, 2023, https://www.dailywire.com/news/virginia-dems-introduce-bill-allowing-minors-to-consent-to-gender-transition-hide-records-from-parents.

Part II: Charting Our Way Back

1. watchdog_jedi, "Encroaching Control—Ronald Reagan," YouTube, March 30, 1961, https://www.youtube.com/watch?v=8gf9Y7UgGi0&t=0s.

Chapter 10: What Is Liberty?

1. Ellipsis mine. Thomas Jefferson to John Trumbull, February 15, 1789, Library of Congress, https://www.loc.gov/exhibits/jefferson/18.html.

2. Ibid.

3. John Locke, *Two Treatises of Government* (London, 1778), 269.

4. Ibid., 396

5. "Declaration of Independence: A Transcription," National Archives, January 31, 2023, https://www.archives.gov/founding-docs/declaration-transcript.

6. David Boaz, "Nation's Libertarian Roots," Cato Institute, February 15, 2015, https://www.cato.org/commentary/nations-libertarian-roots.

7. Locke, *Two Treatises*, 212.

8. Ibid., 195.

9. Ibid., 314–16.
10. "Declaration of Independence."
11. "About the Libertarian Party," Libertarian, 2023, https://www.lp.org/about/.
12. Edmund Burke, "An Appeal from the New to the Old Whigs," in *The Writings and Speeches of Edmund Burke*, ed. P. J. Marshall, Donald C. Bryant, and William B. Todd, vol 4., *Party, Parliament, and the Dividing of the Whigs: 1780–1794* (Oxford, United Kingdom: Oxford University Press, 2015), 394, https://www.oxfordscholarlyeditions.com/display/10.1093/actrade/9780199665198.book.1/actrade-9780199665198-div1-41?r-1=1.000&wm-1=1&t-1=contents-tab&p1-1=1&w1-1=1.000&p2-1=1&w2-1=0.400.
13. Edmund Burke, "Letter to Charles-Jean-François Depont, November 1789," in *Further Reflections on the Revolution in France*, ed. Daniel E. Ritchie (Indianapolis, Indiana: Liberty Fund, Inc., 1992), 7–8.
14. Bruce P. Frohnen, "Burke's Defense of Natural Rights and the Limits of Political Power," Russell Kirk Center, October 18, 2020, https://kirkcenter.org/essays/burkes-defense-of-natural-rights-and-the-limits-of-political-power/.
15. Brian C. Anderson, "Against Perfection," The American Mind, June 8, 2022, https://americanmind.org/features/the-courage-to-see/against-perfection/.
16. Yoram Hazony, *Conservatism: A Rediscovery* (Washington, D.C.: Regnery Gateway, 2022), 34.
17. Liz Wheeler, "Why Are Republicans So Attracted to Libertarianism? ft. Yoram Hazony | Ep. 213," YouTube, October 19, 2022, https://www.youtube.com/watch?v=zIc0FO_FR2w.
18. James Madison, *The Federalist*, no. 51, February 8, 1788, Yale Law School: The Avalon Project, 2008, https://avalon.law.yale.edu/18th_century/fed51.asp.
19. John Adams, "From John Adams to Massachusetts Militia, 11 October 1798," National Archives, n.d., https://founders.archives.gov/documents/Adams/99-02-02-3102.
20. Ibid.
21. George Washington, "State of the Union Address," George Washington's Mount Vernon, January 8, 1790, https://www.mountvernon.org/education/primary-sources/state-of-the-union-address/.
22. Benjamin Wallace-Wells, "David French, Sohrab Ahmari, and the Battle for the Future of Conservatism," *New Yorker*, September 12, 2019, https://www

.newyorker.com/news/the-political-scene/david-french-sohrab-ahmari-and
-the-battle-for-the-future-of-conservatism.

23. William Brangham and Marcia Coyle, "Truth in Advertising or Free Speech
Burden? California Law on 'Crisis Pregnancy Centers' Tested at High Court,"
PBS Newshour, March 20, 2018, https://www.pbs.org/newshour/show/
truth-in-advertising-or-free-speech-burden-california-law-on-crisis-
pregnancy-centers-tested-at-high-court.

24. Brooke Singman, "New California Law Allows Jail Time for Using Wrong
Gender Pronoun, Sponsor Denies That Would Happen," Fox News,
October 9, 2017, https://www.foxnews.com/politics/new-california-law-allows-
jail-time-for-using-wrong-gender-pronoun-sponsor-denies-that-would-
happen.

25. Jacob Geanous, "Ohio Teacher Forced Out for Refusing to Use Students'
Pronouns, Suit Says," *New York Post*, December 17, 2022, https://nypost.
com/2022/12/17/teacher-vivian-geraghty-forced-out-for-refusing-preferred-
pronouns-suit/.

26. "Children of the Immaculate Heart Asks Court to Stop California's
Stonewalling of Teen Rescue Home," Freedom of Conscience Defense Fund,
November 27, 2019, https://fcdflegal.org/children-of-the-
immaculate-heart-asks-court-to-stop-californias-stonewalling-of-teen-
rescue-home/.

27. Thomas Jefferson, "Jefferson's Letter to the Danbury Baptists," Library of
Congress, January 1, 1802, https://www.loc.gov/loc/lcib/9806/danpre.html.

28. "The Constitution of the United States: A Transcription," National Archives,
February 3, 2023, https://www.archives.gov/founding-docs/constitution
-transcript.

Chapter 11: Good versus Evil

1. Pius XI, *Divini redemptoris* (Rome: Vatican, 1937), https://www.vatican.va
/content/pius-xi/en/encyclicals/documents/hf_p-xi_enc_19370319_divini
-redemptoris.html.

2. Herb Scribner, "Republican Mitt Romney Calls Biden a 'Genuinely Good
Man,'" Axios, July 4, 2022, https://www.axios.com/2022/07/04/mitt
-romney-biden-trump-atlantic.

3. Eric Bradner and Catherine Treyz, "Romney Implores: Bring Down Trump,"
CNN Politics, March 3, 2016, https://www.cnn.com/2016/03/03/politics
/mitt-romney-presidential-race-speech/index.html.

4. David French, "Free Speech for Me but Not for Thee," *The Atlantic*, April 11, 2022, https://www.theatlantic.com/ideas/archive/2022/04/republican-dont-say-gay-bill-florida/629516/.

5. Jonah McKeown, "By the Numbers: How the Catholic Church Has Changed during Pope Francis' Pontificate," *Catholic World Report*, March 13, 2023, https://www.catholicworldreport.com/2023/03/13/by-the-numbers-how-the-catholic-church-has-changed-during-pope-francis-pontificate/.

6. Pius IX, *Qui pluribus* (Rome: Vatican, 1846), https://www.papalencyclicals.net/pius09/p9quiplu.htm.

7. Ibid.

8. Ibid.

9. Ibid.

10. Leo XIII, *Quod apostolici muneris* (Rome: Vatican, 1878), https://www.vatican.va/content/leo-xiii/en/encyclicals/documents/hf_l-xiii_enc_28121878_quod-apostolici-muneris.html.

11. Pius XI, *Divini redemptoris*.

12. Ibid.

13. Ibid.

14. Ibid.

15. Russell Kirk, *The Conservative Mind: From Burke to Eliot*, 7th rev. ed. (Washington, D.C.: Regnery Publishing, 2001), 8.

16. "Declaration of Independence: A Transcription," National Archives, January 31, 2023, https://www.archives.gov/founding-docs/declaration-transcript.

17. Charles Grondin, "How Are We the 'Image and Likeness of God'?," Catholic Answers, 2023, https://www.catholic.com/qa/how-are-we-the-image-and-likeness-of-god.

18. Francis Crick, *The Astonishing Hypothesis: The Scientific Search for the Soul* (New York: Touchstone, 1995), 3.

19. Ellipsis in the original. "Catechism of the Catholic Church," Catholic Culture, 2023, https://www.catholicculture.org/culture/library/catechism/index.cfm?recnum=5497.

20. Robert S. Barker, "Natural Law and the United States Constitution," *Review of Metaphysics* 66 (November 2012):

21. Thomas Aquinas, *Summa Theologica* I-II, 91.2, trans. Fathers of the English Dominican Province (Cincinnati: Benziger Bros., 1947), https://www.sacred-texts.com/chr/aquinas/summa/sum229.htm.

22. Ibid., 95.2, https://www.sacred-texts.com/chr/aquinas/summa/sum233.htm.

23. "12-Augustine of Hippo: Summary," Cambridge Core, n.d., https://www
.cambridge.org/core/books/abs/great-christian-jurists-and-legal-collections
-in-the-first-millennium/augustine-of-hippo/12AA3658621EB2FDD92C60
BF16C0617B.

24. "Catechism of the Catholic Church: I. The Natural Moral Law," Vatican,
n.d., https://www.vatican.va/archive/ENG0015/__P6U.HTM.

25. Ibid.

26. Pius IX, *Qui pluribus*.

27. Joseph Hamburger, "Review: *Edmund Burke and the Natural Law* by
Peter J. Stanlis," *Yale Law Journal* 68, no. 4 (1959): 835, https://
openyls.law.yale.edu/bitstream/handle/20.500.13051/14479/46_68Yal
eLJ831_1958_1959_.pdf?sequence=2.

28. Ibid., 833.

29. Bruce P. Frohnen, "Burke's Defense of Natural Rights and the Limits of
Political Power," Russell Kirk Center, October 18, 2020, https://kirkcenter
.org/essays/burkes-defense-of-natural-rights-and-the-limits-of-political
-power/#_edn6.

30. "Edmund Burke on Liberty as 'Social' Not 'Individual' Liberty," Online
Library of Liberty, 2023, https://oll.libertyfund.org/quote/edmund-burke-on
-liberty-as-social-not-individual-liberty-1789.

31. James Madison, *The Federalist*, no. 51, February 8, 1788, Yale Law School:
The Avalon Project, 2008, https://avalon.law.yale.edu/18th_century/fed51
.asp.

Chapter 12: How We Win

1. "Rewatch the 2023 GRAMMYs Premiere Ceremony in Full," Recording
Academy Grammy Awards, 2023, https://www.grammy.com/videos/2023
-grammys-premiere-ceremony-rewatch-full.

2. Luke Rudkowski (@Lukewearechange), "Perfect ad placement by @pfizer,"
Twitter, February 5, 10:55 p.m., https://twitter.com/Lukewearechange/status
/1622443871450894338.

3. W. Bradford Wilcox, Wendy Wang, and Ian Rowe, "Less Poverty, Less
Prison, More College: What Two Parents Mean for Black and White
Children," Institute for Family Studies, June 17, 2021, https://ifstudies.org
/blog/less-poverty-less-prison-more-college-what-two-parents-mean-for
-black-and-white-children; Nicholas Zill, "Growing Up with Mom and Dad:
New Data Confirm the Tide Is Turning," Institute for Family Studies, June

18, 2021, https://ifstudies.org/blog/growing-up-with-mom-and-dad-new
-data-confirm-the-tide-is-turning.

4. Jarrett Stepman, "Florida to Teach Students about Evils of Communism.
Some on the Left Aren't Happy about It," The Daily Signal, May 12, 2022,
https://www.dailysignal.com/2022/05/12/florida-to-teach-students-about
-evils-of-communism-some-on-the-left-arent-happy-about-it.

5. For instance, see Dana Kennedy, "Librarians Go Radical as New Woke
Policies Take Over: Experts," *New York Post*, September 10, 2022, https://
nypost.com/2022/09/10/librarians-go-radical-as-new-woke-policies-take
-over-experts/.

6. Gayle S. Rubin, "Thinking Sex: Notes for a Radical Theory of the Politics
of Sexuality," in *Pleasure and Danger: Exploring Female Sexuality* (Boston:
Routledge & Kegan Paul, 1984), 143–79, https://sites.middlebury.edu
/sexandsociety/files/2015/01/Rubin-Thinking-Sex.pdf

7. 1776 Project PAC, 2021, https://1776projectpac.com.

8. "Find a Chapter near You," Moms for Liberty, 2022, https://www
.momsforliberty.org/chapters/.

9. Greg Forster, *A Win-Win Solution: The Empirical Evidence on School
Choice*, 4th ed. (Indianapolis, Indiana: Friedman Foundation, 2016).

10. "What Is School Choice?," EdChoice, 2023, https://www.edchoice.org
/school-choice/what-is-school-choice/.

11. Courage Is A Habit, 2023, https://courageisahabit.org.

12. Zac Anderson and Steven Walker, "DeSantis Signs Bill Banning Funding for
College Diversity Programs," *Sarasota Herald-Tribune*, May 19, 2023,
https://www.heraldtribune.com/story/news/politics/2023/05/15/florida-gov
-ron-desantis-signs-diversity-equity-inclusion-bill-at-new-college-with-chris
-rufo/70217794007/.

13. HSLDA, 2023, https://hslda.org.

14. Jack McPherrin, *Environmental, Social, and Governance (ESG) Scores: A
Threat to Individual Liberty, Free Markets, and the U.S. Economy*
(Arlington Heights, Illinois: The Heartland Institute, 2023), https://heartland
.org/wp-content/uploads/2023/04/2023-ESG-ReportvWeb-2.pdf.

15. Riley Moore, "Restricted Financial Institution List," West Virginia Treasury,
July 28, 2022, https://wvtreasury.com/portals/wvtreasury/content/legal
/memorandum/Restricted-Financial-Institutions-List.pdf.

16. "Divestment Statute Lists," Comptroller.Texas.gov, 2023, https://comptroller
.texas.gov/purchasing/publications/divestment.php.

17. "Governor Ron DeSantis Leads Alliance of 18 States to Fight against Biden's
ESG Financial Fraud," news release, Ron DeSantis: 46th Governor of Florida,

March 16, 2023, https://www.flgov.com/2023/03/16/governor-ron-desantis
-leads-alliance-of-18-states-to-fight-against-bidens-esg-financial-fraud/.

18. John Adams, "From John Adams to Massachusetts Militia, 11 October
1798," National Archives, https://founders.archives.gov/documents/Adams
/99-02-02-3102.

19. Mike Schmitz, *The Bible in a Year*, podcast, Ascension, https://podcasts.apple
.com/us/podcast/the-bible-in-a-year-with-fr-mike-schmitz/id1539568321.

20. Mike Schmitz, *The Catechism in a Year*, podcast, Ascension, https://podcasts
.apple.com/us/podcast/the-catechism-in-a-year-with-fr-mike-schmitz
/id1648949780.

21. Edward Sri, *A Biblical Walk through the Mass: Understanding What We
Say and Do in the Liturgy*, 2nd ed. (West Chester, Pennsylvania: Ascension
Press, 2011).

22. Brant Pitre, *Jesus and the Jewish Roots of the Eucharist: Unlocking the
Secrets of the Last Supper* (New York: Doubleday, 2011).

Appendix III: *Qui Pluribus*

1. Ap 13.6.
2. Tertullian, de Praescript., chap. 8.
3. Rom 13.1
4. St. John Chrysostom, hom. 1 in Isaiah.
5. St. Ambrose on Ps 40.
6. Council of Chalcedon, Act. 2.
7. Synod of Ephes., Act. 3.
8. St. Peter Chrysologus, epistle to Eutyches.
9. Council of Trent, session 7 on baptism.
10. St. Cyprian, epistle 55 to Pope Cornelius.
11. Synod. Letter of John of Constantinople to Pope Hormisdas and Sozomen,
Hist., III. 8.
12. St. Augustine, epistle 162.
13. St. Irenaeus, Adv. Haer. III, 3.
14. St. Jerome, epistle to Pope Damasus.
15. Clement XII, constitution Providas; Pius VII, constitution Ecclesiam a Jesu
Christo; Leo XII, constitution Ubi graviora.
16. Gregory XVI, encyclical letter Inter praecipuas machinationes.
17. Ex Symbolo Quicumque.
18. St. Leo. sermon 8.4.
19. Council of Trent, session 13, chap. on reform.

20. Rom 12.1-2.
21. Council of Trent, session 22, chap. 1 on reform.
22. Tm 4.12.
23. Benedict XIV, encyclical letter Ubi primum.
24. Heb 4.12.
25. Council of Trent, session 23, chap. 18, on reform.
26. St. Cyprian, epistle 77 to Nemesianus and other martyrs.
27. St. Leo, epistle 156 (123) to Emperor Leo.
28. St. Leo, epistle 43 (34) to Emperor Theodosius.
29. Ibid.

Appendix IV: *Quod Apostolici Muneris*

1. Isa. 58:1.
2. Jude 8.
3. 1 Tim. 6:10.
4. See above, p. 155, note 2.
5. On Freemasonry, *Humanum genus*.
6. 1 Tim. 3:15.
7. 2 Cor. 6:14.
8. Eph. 3:15.
9. Rom. 13a, 7.
10. 1 Cor. 12:28.
11. Wisd. 6:3–4, 8–9.
12. Acts 5:29.
13. Heb. 13:4.
14. Eph. 6:23.
15. Eph. 6:1–2.
16. Eph. 6:4.
17. Eph. 6:5–9.
18. 2 Cor. 8:9.
19. Isa. 59:1.
20. Titus 3:4.

Appendix V: *Quadragesimo Anno*

1. Encyclical, *Arcanum*, Feb. 10, 1880.
2. Encyclical, *Diuturnum*, June 20, 1881.
3. Encyclical, *Immortale Dei*, Nov. 1, 1885.
4. Encyclical, *Sapientiae Christianae*, Jan. 10, 1890.

5. Encyclical, *Quod Apostolici Muneris*, Dec. 28, 1878.
6. Encyclical, *Libertas*, June 20, 1888.
7. Encyclical, *On the Condition of Workers*, May 15, 1891, 3.
8. Encyclical, *On the Condition of Workers*, cf. 24.
9. Encyclical, *On the Condition of Workers*, cf. 15.
10. Encyclical, *On the Condition of Workers*, cf. 6.
11. Encyclical, *On the Condition of Workers*, 24.
12. Cf. Matt. 7:29.
13. Encyclical, *On the Condition of Workers*, 4.
14. St. Ambrose, *De excessu fratris sui Satyri*, 1, 44.
15. Encyclical, *On the Condition of Workers*, 25.
16. Let it be sufficient to mention some of these only: Leo XIII's Apostolic Letter *Praeclara*, June 20, 1894, and Encyclical *Graves de Communi*, Jan. 18, 1901; Pius X's Motu Proprio *De Actione Populari Christiana*, Dec. 8, 1903; Benedict XV's Encyclical *Ad Beatissimi*, Nov. 1, 1914; Pius IX's Encyclical *Ubi Arcano*, Dec. 23, 1922, and Encyclical *Rite Expiatis*, Apr. 30, 1926.
17. Cf. *La Hierarchie catholique et le probleme social depuis l'Encyclique "Rerum Novarum,"* 1891–1931, pp. XVI–335; ed. "Union internationale d'Etudes sociales fondee a Malines, en 1920, sous la presidence du Card. Mercier." Paris, Editions "Spes," 1931.
18. Isa. 11:12.
19. Encyclical, *On the Condition of Workers*, 48.
20. Encyclical, *On the Condition of Workers*, 54.
21. Encyclical, *On the Condition of Workers*, 68.
22. Encyclical, *On the Condition of Workers*, 77.
23. Encyclical, *On the Condition of Workers*, 78.
24. Pius X, Encyclical, *Singulari Quadam*, Sept. 24, 1912.
25. Cf. the Letter of the Sacred Congregation of the Council to the Bishop of Lille, June 5, 1929.
26. Cf. Rom. 1:14.
27. Cf. Encyclical, *On the Condition of Workers*, 24–25.
28. Pius XI, Encyclical, *Ubi Arcano*, Dec. 23, 1922.
29. Encyclical, *Ubi Arcano*, Dec. 23, 1922.
30. Encyclical, *On the Condition of Workers*, 35.
31. Encyclical, *On the Condition of Workers*, 36.
32. Encyclical, *On the Condition of Workers*, 14.
33. Allocation to the Convention of Italian Catholic Action, May 16, 1926.

34. Encyclical, *On the Condition of Workers*, 12.
35. Encyclical, *On the Condition of Workers*, 20.
36. Encyclical, *On the Condition of Workers*, 67.
37. Cf. St. Thomas, *Summa theologica*, II-II, Q. 134.
38. Encyclical, *On the Condition of Workers*, 51.
39. Encyclical, *On the Condition of Workers*, 28.
40. Encyclical, *On the Condition of Workers*, 14.
41. II Thess. 3:10.
42. Cf. II Thess. 3:8-10.
43. Encyclical, *On the Condition of Workers*, 66.
44. Encyclical, *On the Condition of Workers*, 61.
45. Encyclical, *On the Condition of Workers*, 31.
46. Cf. Encyclical, *Casti Connubii*, Dec. 31, 1930.
47. Cf. St. Thomas, *De regimine principum* I, 15; Encyclical, *On the Condition of Workers*, 49–51.
48. Cf. Encyclical, *On the Condition of Workers*, 31, Art. 2.
49. St. Thomas, *Contra Gentiles*, III, 71; cf. *Summa theologica*.
50. Encyclical, *Immortale Dei*, Nov. 1, 1885.
51. Cf Encyclical, *On the Condition of Workers*, 76.
52. Eph. 4:16.
53. Encyclical, *On the Condition of Workers*, 28
54. Cf. Rom. 13:1.
55. Cf. Encyclical, *Diuturnum illud*, June 29, 1881.
56. Encyclical, *Divini illius Magistri*, Dec. 31, 1929.
57. Cf. Jas. 2.
58. II Cor. 8:9.
59. Matt. 11:28.
60. Cf. Luke 12:48.
61. Matt. 16:27.
62. Cf. Matt. 7:24ff.
63. Encyclical, *On the Condition of Workers*, 41.
64. Cf. Matt. 16:26.
65. Cf. Judg. 2:17.
66. Cf. Matt. 7:13.
67. Cf. John 6:69.
68. Cf. Matt. 24:35.
69. Cf. Matt. 6:33.
70. Col. 3:14.

71. Rom. 12:5.
72. I Cor. 12:26.
73. Encyclical, *Ubi Arcano*, Dec. 23, 1922.
74. Cf. Act. 20:28.
75. Cf. Deut. 31:7.
76. Cf. II Tim. 2:3.
77. I Tim. 2:4.
78. Encyclical, *Mens Nostra*, Dec. 20, 1929.
79. Cf. Matt. 16:18.
80. Cf. Luke 16:8.
81. Cf. Phil. 2:21.
82. Apoc. 5:13.

Appendix VI: *Divini Redemptoris*

1. Encycl. *Qui Pluribus*, Nov. 9, 1864 (*Acta Pii* IX, Vol I, p. 13). Cf. *Syllabus*, IV, (A.S.S., vol. III, p. 170).
2. Encycl. *Quod Apostolici Muneris*, Dec. 28, 1928 (*Acta Leonis* XIII, Vol. 1, p. 46).
3. Dec. 18, 1924: A.A.S., Vol. XVI (1924), pp. 494-495.
4. May 8, 1928: A.A.S., Vol. XX (1928), pp. 165-178.
5. May 15, 1931: A.A.S., Vol. XXIII (1931), pp. 177-228.
6. May 3, 1932: A.A.S., Vol. XXIV (1932), pp. 177-194.
7. Sept. 29, 1932: A.A.S., Vol. XXIV (1932), pp. 321-332.
8. June 3, 1933: A.A.S., Vol. XXV (1933), pp. 261-274.
9. Cf. II Thessalonians, II, 4.
10. Encycl. *Divini Illius Magistri*, Dec. 31, 1929 (A.A.S., Vol. XXII, 1930, pp. 47–86).
11. Encycl. *Casti Connubii*, Dec. 31, 1930 (A.A.S., Vol. XXII, 1930, pp. 539–592).
12. I Corinthians, III, 23.
13. Encycl. *Rerum Novarum*, May 15, 1891 (*Acta Leonis* XIII, Vol. IV, pp. 177–209).
14. Encycl. *Quadragesimo Anno*, May 15, 1931 (A.A.S., Vol. XXIII, 1931, pp. 177–228).
15. Encycl. *Diuturnum Illud*, June 20, 1881 (*Acta Leonis* XIII, Vol. I, pp. 210–22).
16. Encycl. *Immortale Dei*, Nov. 1, 1885 (*Acta Leonis* XIII, Vol. II, pp. 146–168).

17. St. Luke, 11, 14.
18. St. Matthew, VI, 33.
19. Cf. St. Matthew, XIII, 55; St. Mark, VI, 3.
20. Cicero, *De Officiis*, Bk. I, c. 42.
21. St. James, I, 22.
22. St. James, I, 17.
23. A.A.S., vol. XXVIII (1936); pp. 421–424.
24. St. John, IV, 23.
25. St. Matthew, V, 3.
26. Hebrews, XIII, 14.
27. St. Luke, XI, 41.
28. St. James, V, 1-3.
29. St. Matthew, V, 3.
30. St. James, V, 7, 8.
31. St. Luke, VI, 20.
32. I Corinthians, XIII, 4.
33. St. Matthew, XXV, 34–40.
34. St. Matthew, XXV, 41–45.
35. St. John, XIII, 34.
36. Romans, XIII, 8, 9.
37. Encycl. *Quadragesimo Anno*, May 15, 1931 (A.A.S., Vol. XXIII, 1931, p. 202).
38. Psalms, CXXVI, 1.
39. St. Matthew, XVII, 20
40. I Epist. St. John, V, 4.
41. Dec. 20, 1935, A.A.S., vol. XXVIII (1936), pp. 5–53.
42. St. Matthew, VIII, 20.
43. I Corinthians, XIII, 1.
44. May 12, 1936.
45. Encycl. *Caritate Christi*, May 3, 1932 (A.A.S., vol. XXIV, p. 184).
46. Encycl. *Caritate Christi*, May 3, 1932 (A.A.S., vol. XXIV, 1932, p. 190).
47. Acts, IV, 12.
48. Encycl. *Ubi Arcano*, Dec. 23, 1922 (A.A.S., Vol. XIV, 1922, p. 691).
49. II Epist. St. Peter, III, 13; cf. Isaias, LXV, 17 and LXVI, 22; Apoc., XXI, 1.
50. Apoc. XXI, 5.

Index

A
abortion, 5, 8, 13, 77, 84, 91, 96,
101–2, 147, 158, 160, 165, 186
Adams, John, 162, 195
addiction, 37, 47–48
administrative state, 138, 141–42,
145–46, 148, 184, 194
Adorno, Theodor, 51
American Academy of Pediatrics, xiv,
138, 148, 194
American Civil Liberties Union, 60
American Federation of Teachers
(AFT), 106, 113–16
American Political Science Association,
144
American School Counselor Association
(ASCA), 191
Anderson, Erica, 63
antiracism, xiii, 38–39, 48, 110, 117
Applebaum, Barbara, 15, 49, 183
Aquinas, Thomas, 178–79
atheism, 7, 26, 91, 129–30, 177
Augustine, 179

B
Barker, Robert, 178
Bartholet, Elizabeth, 119–25, 127–29,
134–35, 184
Bell, Derrick, 15, 54, 183
Berenson, Alex, 22
Biden, Joe, xiii, 21–22, 27–28, 113, 169,
193

BIPOC (black, indigenous, people of
color), 71
birth control, 89–92, 94, 186
Black Lives Matter, 6, 26–27, 72,
82–83, 130, 158
Bogdanov, Alexander, 139–40, 148
Bolsheviks, xv, 7–8, 42–43, 51, 74,
91–92, 130–32, 134–35, 139, 171,
175, 184
Brisbane, Albert, 31, 141
Brock University, 67
Burke, Edmund, 157–64, 166–67, 180,
185
Buttigieg, Joseph, 4
Buttigieg, Pete, 4

C
Calderone, Mary, 101–2
capitalism, xv–xvi, 2–3, 5–6, 31–32,
35, 42, 44, 50, 53, 67, 73, 75–77, 80,
84, 86–87, 116, 130–31, 139–140,
148, 184, 190, 194
Catholic Church, 9–13, 170, 172,
174–75, 177–79, 185, 196
censorship, 16–17, 19–22
Centers for Disease Control and
Prevention (CDC), xii, 138, 148, 194
Chinese Communist Party (CCP), 14,
73–74, 77–80, 112, 183
church, 5, 7–10, 12–13, 28, 38, 42, 160,
166, 175, 182, 185, 195–96
civil rights, 20, 40, 128, 147, 180

civil society, 3, 28, 162, 172–73, 176, 180, 182, 196
civilization, 52, 90, 139, 174
  Western, xiv, 33, 53, 55, 67, 182
Clinton, Bill, 85, 114
Clinton, Hillary, 28, 114
Clinton Global Initiative, 85
Collaborative for Academic, Social, and Emotional Learning (CASEL), 109–13, 117
collectivism, 2, 30–31, 82, 131, 133–35, 141, 173
Columbia University, 52, 140
Comer, James, 111–12
communism, xvi, 1–4, 6–12, 14–16, 30–31, 41, 51, 60, 70, 74–75, 77–80, 87, 92, 105, 111–12, 125, 130–32, 134–35, 139–41, 148–50, 169–75, 178–79, 181–85, 188, 194–96
Communist Manifesto, 2, 43, 171
comprehensive sexuality education (CSE), xv, 101–2, 130, 147, 184, 190
Congress, 31, 43, 60, 138, 142–43, 192–94
consciousness, 5, 46, 52–53, 107–10, 184, 190
conservatism, xi, xiii, 15, 19, 21–22, 26–27, 49, 53, 83, 114, 156, 158–65, 167, 169–70, 175, 178, 180, 185
Constitution, U.S., 17, 40, 45, 50, 54, 127, 142–46, 157, 161–63, 166–67, 178–80, 182, 185, 195
contraception, 89–90, 160
COVID-19, 5, 16, 20–22, 75, 79, 83, 86, 135, 145, 147
Crenshaw, Kimberlé, xiv, 38–40, 54, 182
Crick, Francis, 177
Critical Legal Studies (CLS), 53–55, 183
Critical Legal Theory, 6
Critical Pedagogy, 108–9, 111–12, 119, 184
Critical Race Theory (CRT), ix, xii–xv, 4, 27, 39, 47–50, 52–55, 58–59, 61–62, 69–70, 72, 93, 109–11,

114–115, 120, 124, 130, 133, 145, 147, 165, 174, 183–84, 187–88, 190, 192
Critical Theory, xv, 4, 39, 51–55, 59, 106, 108, 183
cultural hegemony, 2–5, 182, 186

D
Darling-Hammond, Linda, 112–13, 117
Declaration of Independence, 30, 153–55, 161, 176
DEI (diversity, equity, and inclusion), x, xv, 40, 50, 71, 77, 81–87, 130, 183, 191–93
Delgado, Richard, 54, 183
democracy, 3, 21, 119–20, 128–29, 132, 134–35, 145–46, 184
DeSantis, Ron, 93, 191, 193
Dewey, John, xvi, 129–35, 141, 184
DiAngelo, Robin, xv, 49, 183
discrimination, x40–41, 48, 65, 81, 86, 128, 162, 193
Disney, x, xii, xiv, 84, 93
divorce, 8, 41–42, 159–60, 176
Dodd, Bella, 10–12
Downs, Jim, 43–45
Drabinski, Emily, 116–17
drag queens, 43, 117, 163, 180, 189
Dyer, Hannah, 67
dysphoria, 63, 67, 95, 97

E
Eberhart-Bliss, Elicia, 64
Economic and Social Council, United Nations (ECOSOC), 101
Eden, Max, 109–10
Emhoff, Doug, 36
Engels, Friedrich, 1–2, 6, 39, 44–45, 171
entertainment, x, 15, 186
environmental, social, and governance (ESG), 15, 71, 87, 183, 192
environmentalism, 13
equity, 48, 86

Erickson, Erick, 87,
"experts," xiii, xvi, 123, 135–44,
    146–48, 184, 194

F
fascism, 1, 32, 70, 75, 81
Fauci, Anthony, 137–38
Federal Communications Commission
    (FCC), 18–19
feminism, 5, 34–36, 38–39, 41, 53–54,
    60, 92, 182
Feminine Mystique, The, 33–36, 182
femininity, 41, 92, 187
First Amendment, 126–28, 166
Fourier, Charles, 31, 141
Frankfurt School, 1, 39, 50–52, 55,
    106, 183
free love, 32, 68
Freire, Paulo, xv, 103, 105–9, 112–13,
    117, 129–30, 184, 190
French, David, xiii, 163, 169
Friedan, Betty, xiv, 33–36, 41, 182
Fromm, Erich, 51

G
gender, xi, 58–59, 62, 66, 81, 94, 100,
    115,
    affirming care, 20, 62, 64, 94, 97–98,
    binary, 65, 67
    disorder, 95, 97
    dysphoria, 95, 97
    fluidity, 59, 65–66
    ideology, 163, 187, 189
    identity, ix, xii–xiii, xv, 20, 58–59,
        62–66, 69, 72, 93–94, 96, 102,
        115, 148, 183, 186, 188, 191
    nonconforming, 64–66
    roles, 92
    spectrum, 58, 188
    theory, x, 57, 111
    transition, 147–48
Giroux, Henry, 108
Goodnow, Frank, 144–45
governance body composition, 81–82

Gramsci, Antonio, xiv, 1–5, 7–8, 28,
    52, 157, 182, 186
Great Experiment, xvi, 184
Great Reset, 73–77, 80
groomers, x, xii, xv, 20, 51, 58, 62–64,
    66, 68–69, 89, 93, 96, 98–99, 102,
    107, 183–84
Grünberg, Carl, 50

H
Haldeman, Joshua, 141
Hamburger, Joseph, 179–80
Hazony, Yoram, 161–62
Higgins, Michael (father of Margaret
    Sanger), 89
Hill, Marc Lamont, 48–49
Himmelfarb, Gertrude, 162
Hitler, Adolf, 15, 52, 74
Hollywood, 5, 14–15
homeschooling, xii, xvi, 117, 119–24,
    127–28, 132–36, 145, 147, 184, 192
homosexuality, 5, 13, 42–46, 60, 99,
    117, 160, 185
Horkheimer, Max, xv, 50–53, 106, 183
Horowitz, Daniel, 34–36
Horowitz, Mark, 15

I
indoctrination, xii, xv, 23, 26, 62,
    64, 66, 87, 102–3, 105, 130, 171,
    182–84, 188, 192
Institute for Sex Research, 100
Institute for Social Research, 50
intersectionality, xiv, 38–39, 41, 50,
    110, 182, 188
Italian Communist Party, 1

J
Jefferson, Thomas, 23, 25, 153–56,
    161–62, 166
Johns Hopkins University, 144
Johnson, Manning, 11

K
Katz, Jonathan Ned, 45
Kengor, Paul, 31–32, 43, 131
Kinsey, Alfred, xv, 98–102, 184
Kirk, Russell, 175
Klavan, Andrew, 47–48
Knowles, J. Gary, 133

L
Lenin, Vladimir, 7, 23, 74, 92, 105, 108, 139
Leo XIII, 172
LGBTQ, 63–64, 66–69, 71–72, 99, 164, 183, 185–86
    activism, 114
    lobby, xv, 43
LGBTQ+ Caucus of the National Education Association, 66
libertarianism, 156–57, 160–61, 163, 165–67, 176, 185
Lindsay, James, 67, 70, 87, 110–12, 116
Little, Clarence C., 91
Locke, John, 153–57, 160–61, 165–66, 176, 185
Lukács, György, 32, 68, 108

M
Madison, James, 162, 180
Ma, Jack, 77
Marcuse, Herbert, xv, 4, 32, 36, 51–53, 108, 183
marriage, 6, 8, 30–36, 41, 45, 46, 92, 99, 102, 182, 186–87
    gay, 43, 165, 187
    homosexual, 5, 13, 42, 44, 46, 185
    monogamous, 6, 41
    redefinition of, xi, 45
    same-sex, 163
    traditional, xv, 44, 183
Marx, Karl
Marxism, xi, xiii, xv, 2, 4, 6–7, 15, 26, 33, 35–36, 39, 41, 43–46, 49–50, 54, 59, 68, 75, 87, 108, 120, 130,

133, 148, 165, 169–70, 172, 175–76, 179, 182–84, 186, 188, 190, 196–97
masculinity, 36–38, 41, 92, 187
    toxic, 37
McAuliffe, Terry, 147
McLaren, Peter, 108, 117
McPherrin, Jack, 80–81, 85, 192
media, x, 5, 7, 14–19, 22, 28, 93
    mainstream, x, 16, 22, 93, 178, 182, 190
    news, 15–19, 22
    social, x, 21–22, 64, 78, 172
MeToo movement, 5 37
Montgomery County Public Schools, 64–65
Moore, Riley, 82–83, 192
morality, 26, 32–33, 44, 59, 64, 68, 109, 159–67, 175, 183, 185, 195
mothers, xii, 29, 33–34, 36, 41, 61, 92, 96, 186,
Muenzenberg, Willi, 14
Musk, Elon, 20, 141
Mussolini, Benito, 1
mutilation, ix, 62, 70, 96, 164, 180

N
National Education Association, 66, 146
National Home Education Research Institute (NHERI), 121
natural law, 33, 111, 167, 171, 173, 176–81, 185, 195
natural rights, 54, 125, 144, 154–57, 159, 176–77, 182
news media. *See under* media
Newsom, Gavin, 37, 113
Newsom, Jennifer Siebel, 37
nondelegation doctrine, 145, 194
North American Man/Boy Love Association (NAMBLA), 60
Noyes, John Humphrey, 31

O
Obama, Barack, 54, 113

Ocasio-Cortez, Alexandria, 43
ordered liberty, 151, 157, 161–62,
    166–67, 185, 194
original justice, 159, 163–64, 167, 176,
    180, 185, 195
Owen, Robert, 30
Owens, Candace, 72

P
parental rights, xii, xiv, 5, 93, 101–102,
    115, 124–25, 127, 190, 192
patriarchy, 32, 34, 59, 64
pedagogy, 106–12
pedophilia, xii, 6—62, 100, 102, 183,
    189
Phillips, Jack, 13, 87
phrenology, 89–90
Pius IX, 171–72, 179
Pius XI, 9, 12, 169, 172–74
Planned Parenthood, xii, xiv–xv, 58,
    82, 89, 91, 93–96, 98, 101–2, 147,
    184, 189
pornography, 37–38, 42, 47–48, 59–60,
    62, 117, 156–57, 160, 183, 189
privilege, 53, 120, 123
    male, 38, 40–41
    white, 38, 40–41, 49–50, 69, 188
prostitution, 156–57, 160
Protestantism, 9, 13, 25–26, 175
pseudoscience, 90, 98
psychology, xii, 44–45, 63, 96–97,
    110–11, 190
puberty blocking drugs, 63, 95–96, 98,
    198

Q
Queer Theory, xii, xiv–xv, 14, 55,
    57–72, 93, 96, 98, 100, 102, 109,
    111, 114–15, 120, 124, 130, 133,
    145, 147, 158, 165, 174, 183–84,
    188–90, 192

R
racism, ix–x, 5, 39, 40, 48–50, 58, 69,
    86, 89–91, 117, 120, 130, 164

systemic, 40–41, 49, 188
Reagan, Ronald, 15, 19, 42, 149–50
Reich, Wilhelm, xiv, 32–33, 41, 182
religious persecution, x, 12, 40, 86
revisionist history, 40, 50, 190
Roe v. Wade, x, 84
Romney, Mitt, xiii, 169
Roosevelt, Franklin Delano, 18–19,
    141, 145–46
Rubin, Gayle, xv, 57–61, 100, 102, 183
rulemaking, 142, 146, 194
Russia, xvi, 7–8, 12, 16, 22, 28, 42–43,
    51, 92, 130–32, 134–35, 139, 184
    Soviets, xvi, 7–10, 12, 14, 16,
        42–43, 92, 129, 131–32, 171,
        184

S
sadomasochism, 58, 99
Saint-Simon, Henri de, 139, 141
Sanger, Margaret, xv, 89–93, 98, 184
Sapir, Leor, 97
Schlafly, Phyllis, 165
Schwab, Klaus, xv, 73–77, 80, 82,
    84–87, 183, 194
science, x, 5, 7, 21, 24, 89, 98, 107, 120,
    130, 137–40, 144, 146–48, 153,
    178, 194, 195,
Scott, Howard, 140–41
Securities and Exchange Commission
    (SEC), 193
Second Amendment, 145
self-awareness, 109–110
sex essentialism, 58–59
sexism, 39–40
sexual deviancy, 43, 44, 57, 99, 102
Sexuality Information and Education
    Council of the United States
    (SIECUS), 101–102
sexual revolution, xv, 5, 32–33, 36, 41,
    98, 184
shareholder capitalism, 76
Sheen, Fulton J., 10
Shrier, Abigail, 63
Silicon Valley Bank (SVB)
Smyth, William Henry, 140

social awareness, 109, 111
social credit scoring, 78–80, 183,
social-emotional learning (SEL), xii,
    xvi, 108–109, 111–13, 115, 117, 184,
    190
    Transformative. *See* Transformative
    SEL
socialism, 5, 9, 12–13, 30–31, 40,
    43–44, 74–75, 77, 91–92, 129, 134,
    139, 141, 158, 164, 171–72
socialization, 119, 129, 132–35, 145,
    192
social justice, 13, 26, 81, 108–109, 164,
    185, 190, 192
Soros, George, 26
stakeholder capitalism, xv, 75–77, 84,
    86–87, 194
Stonewall riots, the, 43–44
Supreme Court, the, x, 5, 13, 45, 60,
    84, 125–26, 145

T
Technical Alliance, 140
Technocracy, xvi, 136, 138–42,
    146–48, 184, 194
    Technocracy Inc., 140–41
Third Reich, 52, 74
Thornton, Bruce, 17
Tolerance, xv, 69, 86, 128, 163, 165,
    174, 183, 185, 189
Transformative SEL, 109–111, 116,
transgender, xiii, 13, 20, 39, 62–65, 67,
    70, 72, 87, 93–97, 114–15, 148, 160,
    180, 183, 188, 190
    hormone therapy, xii, 91, 94–98,
        102, 190
    ideology, ix, xiii, 5, 20, 57, 62–63,
        96, 130
Trump, Donald, xiii, 16, 21, 27–28,
    169, 193
Turban, Jack, 97–98
Twitter, 20, 22, 64, 93, 115–16, 146

U
United Nations, xv, 85, 101–102, 184,
    189
United Nations Educational, Scientific
    and Cultural Organization
    (UNESCO), 101–102
universal reason, 162
universal rights, 161–62

V
vaccines, xii–xiii, 5, 21, 138, 147–48
Veblen, Thorstein, 139, 141
vilification, xi, 6, 15, 41, 49, 106, 119

W
Washington, George, 23, 162
Webster, Noah, 23
Weil, Felix, 50
Weingarten, Randi, 103, 113–17, 184
Western Civilization, xiv, 9, 12, 33,
    53–55, 59, 67, 73, 182–183
Whitmer, Gretchen, 27
Wilson, Woodrow, 141, 144–145
wokeism, xiv–xv, 80, 83–84, 103,
    105, 108–109, 117, 130, 148, 176,
    183–184
World Economic Forum (WEF), 73–74,
    81–82, 84, 183

Y
Youngkin, Glenn, 147

Z
Zedong, Mao, xv, 70–71, 87, 105, 108,
    183
Zitta, Victor, 68